Instant Pot Duo Crisp Cookbook

800 Recipes For Beginners & Advanced Users

Erin Hardin

Copyright © 2021 by Erin Hardin

All rights reserved worldwide.

ISBN: 979-8761117518

No part of this book may be reproduced or transmitted in any form or by any means, electronic or mechanical, including photocopying, recording or by any information storage and retrieval system, without written permission from the publisher, except for the inclusion of brief quotations in a review.

Warning-Disclaimer

The purpose of this book is to educate and entertain. The author or publisher does not guarantee that anyone following the techniques, suggestions, tips, ideas, or strategies will become successful. The author and publisher shall have neither liability or responsibility to anyone with respect to any loss or damage caused, or alleged to be caused, directly or indirectly by the information contained in this book.

CONTENTS

Introduction 11

Breakfast 13

1. Cheesy Prosciutto Egg Bake 13
2. Crispy Pancetta Hash with Baked Eggs 13
3. Shakshuka with Goat Cheese 13
4. Onion and Cheese Omelet 13
5. Strawberry Bread French Toast 14
6. Raspberry-Cranberry Chia Oatmeal 14
7. Kale-Egg Frittata 14
8. Quick Soft-Boiled Eggs 14
9. Sausage Wrapped Scotch Eggs 15
10. Spicy Deviled Eggs 15
11. French Dip Sandwiches 15
12. Cinnamon Pumpkin Oatmeal 15
13. Savory Custards with Ham & Cheese 16
14. Butternut Squash Cake Oatmeal 16
15. Barbecue Chicken Sandwiches 16
16. Coconut-Berry Oatmeal 16
17. Egg Crumpet Sandwich 17
18. Sausage and Bacon Cheesecake 17
19. Veggie Salmon Balls 17
20. Orange Pepper and Artichoke Frittata 18
21. Plum Breakfast Clafoutis 18
22. Healthy Frittata 18
23. Herbed Homemade Ghee 18
24. Maple Giant Pancake 19
25. Prosciutto, Mozzarella & Egg in a Cup 19
26. Paprika Shirred Eggs 19
27. Chai Latte Steel-Cut Oatmeal 19
28. Cheese & Bacon Grits 20
29. Feta & Poached Egg Tomato Topper 20
30. Morning Minty Chocolate Scones 20
31. Maple-Blueberry Oatmeal 20
32. Berry Scones 21
33. Baked Banana Oats 21
34. Marble Muffins 21
35. Kid's Cinnamon Rolls 21
36. Ham and Cheese Sandwich 22
37. Creamy Zucchini Muffins 22
38. Raspberry and Vanilla Pancake 22
39. Toasted Herb and Garlic Bagel 22
40. Spinach Egg Tart 22
41. Three Meat Cheesy Omelet 23
42. Very Berry Breakfast Puffs 23
43. Crustless Mediterranean Quiche 23
44. Chili Breakfast Sausages 23
45. Almond & Chocolate Bear Claws 24
46. Sweet Bread Pudding with Raisins 24
47. Home-Style Maple-Bacon Donuts 24
48. Cheddar & Turkey Bacon Egg Muffins 24
49. Easy Bagels 25
50. Yummy French Toast Strips 25
51. Pillsbury Danish 25
52. Ham & Cheese Egg Bites 25
53. Garlicky Baby Potatoes 26
54. Morning Bacon Quiche 26
55. Vanilla & Raspberry Puff Pastry 26
56. Hazelnut-Banana Muffins 26
57. Sausage Egg Bake 26
58. Hot Red Poached Eggs 27
59. Feta & Spinach Egg Cups 27
60. Cinnamon Butternut Squash Pie 27
61. Mayo-Chocolate Cake 27

Snacks & Side dishes 28

62. Tangy Cheesy Arancini 28
63. Brazilian Cheese Balls 28
64. Kale-Artichoke Bites 28
65. Hot Chicken Wings 29
66. Hot Buttery Chicken Meatballs 29
67. Cheesy Smashed Sweet Potatoes 29
68. Parmesan Cabbage Side Dish 29
69. BBQ Chicken Drumsticks 30
70. Asparagus Wrapped in Prosciutto with Dip 30
71. Cheese bombs wrapped in Bacon 30
72. Teriyaki Chicken Wings 30
73. Sweet Butter Rolls 31
74. Fried Beef Dumplings 31
75. Wrapped Asparagus in Bacon 31
76. Green Vegan Dip 31
77. Buffalo Chicken Meatballs with Ranch Dip 32
78. Holiday Egg Brulee 32
79. Creamy Tomato & Parsley Dip 32
80. Sweet-Heat Pickled Cucumbers 32
81. Basil Mushroom Stuffed Eggplant Boats 33
82. Scrumptious Honey-Mustard Hot Dogs 33
83. Cauliflower and Cheddar Tater Tots 33
84. Homemade Spinach Hummus 33
85. Melt-in-the-Middle Meatballs 34
86. New York Steak and Minty Cheese 34
87. Bacon & Cheese Dip 34
88. Sweet Paprika Hard-Boiled Eggs 34
89. Air Fried Pin Wheels 34
90. Ajillo Green Beans 35
91. Steamed Kale with Cashew Dressing 35

92. Easy Garbanzo Beans 35
93. Herby Fish Skewers 35
94. Crispy Rosemary Potato Fries 35
95. Crispy Cheesy Straws 36
96. Turkey Scotch Eggs 36
97. Tomato & Mozzarella Bruschetta 36
98. Chicken & Cheese Bake 36
99. Parmesan Lentil Purée 36
100. Bacon & Potato Balls 37
101. Tomato Tofu Bake 37
102. Chessy Kale & Sweet Potato Stew 37
103. Sweet Barley Porridge 37
104. Eggplant Chips with Honey 38
105. Nutty & Zesty Brussels Sprouts with Raisins 38
106. Cumin Baby Carrots 38
107. Garlic and Rosemary Mushrooms 38
108. Parmesan Knots 38
109. Veggie Sautée 39
110. Farmer Muffins 39
111. Rich Sweet Potato Stew 39
112. Coconut Brussels Sprouts 39
113. Mexican Corn in the Cob 39
114. Chinese-Style Veggie Stir-Fry 40
115. Avocados with a Surprise 40
116. Tender Potato Wedges 40
117. Crispy Broccoli 40
118. Golden Butternut Squash 40
119. Cheesy Fingers 41
120. Parmesan Zucchini Fries 41
121. Mozzarella Bread 41
122. French Onion-Green Bean Casserole 41
123. Lemon Nachos 42
124. Buttered Asparagus 42
125. Glazed Baby Carrots 42
126. Petit Corn Dog Bites 42
127. Cheesy Biscuits 42
128. Spiced Cauliflower Tots 43
129. Cheddar Crackers 43
130. Parmesan Spinach Spread 43
131. Roasted Tomato Sauce 43
132. Hot Chicken Dip 44
133. Jalapeño Poppers in Bacon 44
134. Party Pigs in a Blanket 44
135. Ginger Chicken Wings 44
136. Original Pork Egg Rolls 44
137. Hawaiian Rolls 45
138. White Wontons 45
139. Hot Chicken Wings 45
140. Loaded Potato Skins 45

Rice, Grains & Pasta 46

141. Indian-Style Beef with Rice 46
142. Creamed Kale Parmesan Farro 46
143. Simple Brown Rice 46
144. Black Beans Tacos 46
145. Veggie Quinoa Bowls with Pesto 47
146. Shrimp Risotto with Vegetables 47
147. Red Lentil & Spinach Dhal 47
148. Lemony Wild Rice Pilaf 47
149. Parsley-Lime Bulgur Bowl 48
150. Creamy Grana Padano Risotto 48
151. Spinach and Kidney Bean Stew 48
152. Spicy Lentils with Chorizo 48
153. Cheese and Spinach Stuffed Shells 49
154. Tri-Color Quinoa and Pinto Bean Bowl ...49
155. Easy Vegan Sloppy Joes 49
156. Simple Jasmine Rice 49
157. Baked Garbanzo Beans & Pancetta 50
158. Three-Bean Veggie Chili 50
159. Rigatoni with Sausage and Spinach 50
160. Cherry Tomato-Basil Linguine 50
161. Chipotle Mac and Cheese 51
162. Black-Eyed Peas with Kale 51
163. Shrimp Lo Mein 51
164. Pasta Caprese Ricotta-Basil Fusilli 51
165. Beef-Stuffed Pasta Shells 52
166. Pork Spaghetti with Spinach and Tomatoes 52
167. Baked Rigatoni with Beef Tomato Sauce 52
168. Rice Pilaf with Mushrooms 52
169. Turkey Fajita Tortiglioni 53
170. Quinoa with Carrots and Onion 53
171. Chorizo Mac and Cheese 53
172. Indian Yellow Lentils 53
173. Chicken and Chickpea Stew 54
174. South American Black Bean Chili 54
175. Pomodoro Sauce with Rigatoni and Kale 54
176. Spicy Pinto Bean and Corn Stew 54
177. Chili-Garlic Rice Noodles with Tofu 55
178. Chicken Ragù Bolognese 55
179. Italy-Inspired Mac & Cheese 55
180. Pasta alla Bolognese 55
181. Rosemary Trout with Pasta 56
182. Captain´s Seafood Pasta 56
183. Florentine Spaghetti with Chicken 56
184. Chicken Alfredo Fettuccine 56
185. Tuna Pomodoro Pasta 56
186. Wisconsin Mac & Cheese 57
187. White Shrimp Pasta 57
188. Caprese Penne 57
189. Creamy Tuna & Macaroni Casserole 57
190. Favorite Chicken Linguine 57

Vegetarian Recipes 58

- 191. Bok Choy & Zoodle Soup 58
- 192. Roasted Squash & Rice with Crispy Tofu ...58
- 193. Cream of Cauliflower & Butternut Squash ...58
- 194. Tangy Risotto & Roasted Bell Peppers ...59
- 195. Cajun Baked Turnips 59
- 196. Spinach & Butternut Squash Stew ...59
- 197. Mashed Broccoli with Cream Cheese ...60
- 198. Eggplant Lasagna ...60
- 199. Pilau Rice with Veggies ...60
- 200. Pesto Minestrone with Cheesy Bread ...60
- 201. Spinach Pesto Spaghetti Squash ...61
- 202. Pine nuts and Steamed Asparagus ...61
- 203. Rice Stuffed Zucchini Boats ...61
- 204. Zucchini & Quinoa Stuffed Red Peppers ...62
- 205. Creamy Cauliflower & Asparagus Farfalle ...62
- 206. Easy Spanish Rice ...62
- 207. Mushroom Risotto with Swiss Chard ...63
- 208. Sticky Noodles with Tofu & Peanuts ...63
- 209. Crème de la Broc ...63
- 210. Buttered Leafy Greens ...63
- 211. Garganelli with Swiss Cheese and Mushrooms ...64
- 212. Squash Parmesan & Linguine ...64
- 213. Vegetarian Minestrone Soup ...64
- 214. Swiss Cheese & Mushroom Tarts ...65
- 215. Artichoke with Garlic Mayo ...65
- 216. Easy Green Squash Gruyere ...65
- 217. Mushroom Brown Rice Pilaf ...65
- 218. Vegan Carrot Gazpacho ...66
- 219. Chipotle Chili ...66
- 220. Green Cream Soup ...66
- 221. Green Minestrone ...66
- 222. Quick Crispy Kale Chips ...67
- 223. Rice & Olives Stuffed Mushrooms ...67
- 224. Cheesy Stuffed Mushrooms ...67
- 225. Pesto Quinoa Bowls with Veggies ...67
- 226. Asian-Style Tofu Soup ...68
- 227. Aloo Gobi with Cilantro ...68
- 228. Herby-Garlic Potatoes ...68
- 229. Indian Vegan Curry ...68
- 230. Punjabi Palak Paneer ...69
- 231. Green Beans with Feta & Nuts ...69
- 232. Creamy Mashed Potatoes with Spinach ...69
- 233. Potato Filled Bread Rolls ...69
- 234. Thai Vegetable Stew ...70
- 235. Tahini Sweet Potato Mash ...70
- 236. Asparagus with Feta ...70
- 237. Fall Celeriac Pumpkin Soup ...70
- 238. Parsley Mashed Cauliflower ...70
- 239. Carrot & Lentil Chili ...71
- 240. Steamed Artichokes with Lemon Aioli ...71
- 241. Spicy Cauliflower Rice with Peas ...71
- 242. Veggie Skewers ...71
- 243. Morning Burrito Bowls ...72
- 244. Honey-Glazed Acorn Squash ...72
- 245. Red Beans & Rice ...72
- 246. Roasted Vegetable Salad ...72
- 247. Spicy Pepper & Sweet Potato Skewers ...73
- 248. Mashed Parsnips & Cauliflower ...73
- 249. Garlic Veggie Mash with Parmesan ...73
- 250. Avocado Rolls ...73
- 251. Pasta with Roasted Veggies ...74
- 252. Quinoa & Veggie Stuffed Peppers ...74
- 253. Vegetable Tortilla Pizza ...74
- 254. Herby Millet with Cherry Tomatoes ...74
- 255. Three-Cheese Veggie Lasagna ...74
- 256. Green Lasagna Soup ...75
- 257. Paneer Cutlet ...75
- 258. Grilled Tofu Sandwich ...75
- 259. Simple Air Fried Ravioli ...75
- 260. Crispy Nachos ...76
- 261. Poblano & Tomato Stuffed Squash ...76
- 262. Colorful Vegetable Medley ...76
- 263. Paneer Cheese Balls ...76
- 264. Chipotle Vegetarian Chili ...76
- 265. Rosemary Sweet Potato Medallions ...77
- 266. Easy BBQ Tofu ...77
- 267. Quick Crispy Cheese Lings ...77
- 268. Grilled Cheese Sandwiches ...77
- 269. Mexican-Style Taco Filling ...78
- 270. Basil-Kale Pesto Flatbread ...78
- 271. Buttery Spaghetti Squash ...78
- 272. Easy-Peasy Ravioli ...78
- 273. Timeless Black Bean Patties ...78
- 274. Greek Pinwheels ...79
- 275. Eggplant Stacks ...79
- 276. Tex-Mex Lentil Tacos ...79
- 277. Cheese-Stuffed Mushrooms ...79
- 278. Ravioli au Gratin ...80
- 279. Taco Cheese-Bean Enchiladas ...80
- 280. Broccoli & Potato Bake ...80
- 281. Chili Corn Crisps ...80

Poultry Recipes 81

- 282. Lemon Chicken Tenders with Broccoli ...81
- 283. Crispy Chicken Thighs with Carrot Roast ...81
- 284. Chicken with Crunchy Coconut Dumplings ...81
- 285. Chicken Cassoulet with Frijoles ...82
- 286. Garlic Herb Roasted Chicken ...82
- 287. Sweet Sesame Chicken Wings ...82
- 288. BBQ Chicken & Kale Quesadillas ...83
- 289. Mexican Chicken & Wild Rice Bowls ...83
- 290. Chicken with Cilantro Rice ...84
- 291. Black Refried Beans & Chicken Fajitas ...84
- 292. Wine Chicken with Mushrooms & Brussel Sprouts ...84
- 293. Quick Chicken Fried Rice ...85

294. Chicken Potato Pot Pie 85
295. Saucy Shredded Chicken 85
296. Chicken Shawarma Wrap 86
297. Chicken Florentine 86
298. Herby Chicken Breasts 86
299. Herbed Chicken & Biscuit Chili 87
300. Italian Chicken with Herby Dumplings 87
301. Lemon and Paprika Chicken Thighs 87
302. Chicken with Tomato Salsa 88
303. Tandoori Chicken Thighs 88
304. Pesto Chicken with Roasted Pepper Sauce 88
305. Hot Crispy Chicken with Potatoes 89
306. Chicken Meatballs Primavera 89
307. Whole Chicken with Lemon & Onion Stuffing 89
308. Cajun Roasted Chicken with Potato Mash 90
309. Chicken & Green Bean Coconut Curry 90
310. Buffalo Chicken & Navy Bean Chili 90
311. Chicken Noodle Soup with Crispy Bacon 91
312. Coq au Vin 91
313. Honey-Garlic Chicken 91
314. White Wine Chicken 92
315. Chicken Chili with Cannellini Beans 92
316. Spinach & Mushroom Chicken Stew 92
317. Cheesy Buffalo Chicken 93
318. Mediterranean Stuffed Chicken Breasts 93
319. BBQ Chicken Drumettes 93
320. Traditional Chicken Cordon Bleu 94
321. Mexican Green Chili Chicken 94
322. Chicken Caesar Salad with Salted Croutons 94
323. Tandoori Chicken with Cilantro Sauce 95
324. Indian Butter Chicken 95
325. Chicken & Veggie Tacos with Guacamole 96
326. Chicken with Beans & Bacon 96
327. Spicy Salsa Chicken with Feta 96
328. Paprika Buttered Chicken 96
329. Chicken Cacciatore 97
330. Pesto Stuffed Chicken with Green Beans 97
331. Spicy Chicken Wings with Lemon 97
332. Hawaiian-Style Chicken Sliders with Salad 98
333. Sage Chicken Thighs 98
334. Chicken with BBQ Sauce 98
335. Pulled Chicken & Peach Salsa 98
336. Thyme Chicken with Veggies 99
337. Chicken Chickpea Chili 99
338. Chicken in Tikka Masala Sauce 99
339. Sticky Orange Chicken 100
340. Salsa Verde Chicken 100
341. Cajun Chicken with Rice & Peas 100
342. Crumbed Sage Chicken Scallopini 100
343. Asian-Style Chicken 101
344. Chicken Meatballs in Tomato Sauce 101
345. Chicken in Pineapple Gravy 101
346. Za'atar Chicken with Lemony Couscous 101
347. Juicy Orange Chicken 102
348. Creamy Chicken and Quinoa Soup 102
349. Honey-Garlic Chicken & Okra 102
350. Chicken with Prunes 102
351. Herby Chicken with Asparagus Sauce 103
352. Creamy Chicken Pasta with Pesto Sauce 103
353. Cajun Shredded Chicken & Wild Rice 103
354. Chicken & Zucchini Pilaf 104
355. Lettuce Chicken Carnitas Wraps 104
356. Chicken & Sweet Potato Corn Chowder 104
357. Basil & Cheddar Stuffed Chicken 104
358. Hot Chicken Wings 105
359. Sriracha Chicken with Black Beans 105
360. Winter Chicken Thighs with Cabbage 105
361. Saucy Chicken Breasts 105
362. Cordon Bleu Chicken 106
363. Chicken with Tomatoes & Capers 106
364. Chicken Burgers with Avocado 106
365. Shredded Chicken with Lentils & Rice 106
366. Greek-Style Chicken with Potatoes 107
367. Crunchy Chicken Schnitzels 107
368. Chicken Fajitas with Avocado 107
369. Rosemary Lemon Chicken 107
370. Chicken Stroganoff with Fetucini 108
371. Turkey Stuffed Potatoes 108
372. Greek-Style Chicken 108
373. Buttermilk Chicken Thighs 108
374. Tuscany-Style Turkey Soup 109
375. Chicken Tenders with Broccoli & Rice 109
376. Asian Turkey Lettuce Cups 109
377. Honey-Glazed Chicken Kabobs 109
378. Turkey and Brown Rice Salad with Peanuts 110
379. Tom Yum Wings 110
380. Korean-Style Barbecued Satay 110
381. Basil Chicken Thighs with Mushrooms 110
382. Turkey Meatballs with Rigatoni 111
383. Creamy Turkey Enchilada Casserole 111
384. Herby Chicken Thighs 111
385. Sticky Drumsticks 111
386. Sweet Garlicky Chicken Wings 112
387. Spicy Buttered Turkey 112
388. Thyme Turkey Nuggets 112
389. Lemon Turkey Risotto 112
390. Glazed Chicken Thighs 112
391. Spicy Chicken Wings 113
392. Spicy Turkey Casserole 113
393. Greek Turkey Meatballs 113
394. Pulled Chicken 113
395. Mexican Stuffed Bell Peppers 114
396. Pekin-Inspired Chicken Thighs 114
397. Paprika Chicken Breasts 114
398. Party Chicken Legs 114
399. Italian Turkey Polpette 114
400. Louisville-Style Fried Chicken 115
401. BBQ Chicken Enchiladas 115
402. Chicken Nacho Bake 115
403. Sticky Turkey Drumsticks 115
404. Chicken Teriyaki 116
405. German-Inspired Chicken 116

#	Recipe	Page
406.	Teriyaki Chicken Wings	116
407.	Simple Chicken Wings with Yogurt Dip	116
408.	Special Chicken Cordon Bleu	117
409.	Chicken & Broccoli Bake	117
410.	Kiddo Chicken Tenders	117
411.	Buttered Swiss Chard & Chicken	117
412.	School Chicken Popcorns	118
413.	Cheddar Chicken Patties	118
414.	Cheesy Chicken Taquitos	118
415.	Easy Turkey Quinoa	118
416.	Amazing Turkey Burgers	118
417.	Mediterranean Chicken Thighs	119
418.	Ranch Chicken Wings	119
419.	Breaded Chicken Drumsticks	119
420.	Veggie & Chicken Stir-Fry	119
421.	Nevada´s Chicken Thighs	120
422.	Chicken with Apple Sauce	120
423.	Parmesan Broccoli & Chicken Meal	120
424.	Zesty Chicken Thighs	120
425.	Mustardy Shredded Turkey	120
426.	Fast Chicken Breasts	121
427.	Fiery Chicken Sliders	121
428.	Texas-Style Chicken Drumsticks	121
429.	Jamaican Chicken Wings	121

Meat Recipes 122

#	Recipe	Page
430.	Ground Beef Stuffed Empanadas	122
431.	Winter Pot Roast with Biscuits	122
432.	Smoky Horseradish Spare Ribs	122
433.	Steak with Chips	123
434.	Beef & Broccoli Sauce	123
435.	Greek Beef Gyros	123
436.	Thai Roasted Beef	124
437.	Sweet Gingery Beef & Broccoli	124
438.	Honey Short Ribs with Rosemary Potatoes	124
439.	Sticky BBQ Baby Back Ribs	124
440.	Peanut Sauce Beef Satay	125
441.	Classic Carbonnade Flamande	125
442.	Beef Carnitas	126
443.	Beef Congee (Chinese Rice Porridge)	126
444.	Pineapple Appetizer Ribs	126
445.	Beef & Cabbage Stew	126
446.	Short Ribs with Egg Noodles	127
447.	Pot Roast with Broccoli	127
448.	Cheeseburgers in Hoagies	127
449.	Tasty Baby Porcupine Meatballs	128
450.	Beef & Green Bell Pepper Pot	128
451.	Beef Soup with Tortillas	128
452.	Beef & Pepperoncini Peppers	128
453.	Beef and Bell Pepper with Onion Sauce	129
454.	Asian Beef Curry	129
455.	Meatballs with Spaghetti Sauce	129
456.	Beef & Garbanzo Bean Chili	130
457.	Beef & Cheese Stuffed Mushrooms	130
458.	Beef Stew with Beer	130
459.	Cheddar Cheeseburgers	130
460.	Beef Pho with Swiss Chard	131
461.	Spiced Beef Chili	131
462.	Spiced Beef Shapes	131
463.	Meatloaf with Cheesy Mashed Potatoes	132
464.	Beef & Vegetable Stew	132
465.	Beef Roast with Peanut Satay Sauce	132
466.	Beef & Cherry Tagine	132
467.	Caribbean Ropa Vieja	133
468.	Chipotle Beef Brisket	133
469.	Brisket Chili con Carne	133
470.	Short Ribs with Mushrooms & Asparagus Sauce	134
471.	Meatballs with Marinara Sauce	134
472.	Beef Stew with Veggies	134
473.	Beef & Pumpkin Stew	135
474.	Braised Short Ribs with Creamy Sauce	135
475.	Italian-Style Pot Roast	135
476.	BBQ Sticky Baby Back Ribs with	136
477.	Swedish Meatballs with Mashed Cauliflower	136
478.	Hot Pork Carnitas Lettuce Cups	136
479.	Tomatillo & Sweet Potato pork Chili	137
480.	Beer-Braised Short Ribs with Mushrooms	137
481.	Beef & Turnip Chili	137
482.	Sweet-Garlic Pork Tenderloin	138
483.	Crispy Pork Fajitas	138
484.	Ranch Flavored Pork Roast with Gravy	138
485.	Stewed Beef with Portobello Mushrooms	139
486.	Peppercorn Meatloaf	139
487.	Classic Beef Bourguignon	139
488.	Ranch Pork with Mushroom Sauce	139
489.	Mississippi Pot Roast with Potatoes	140
490.	Beef & Bacon Chili	140
491.	Traditional Beef Stroganoff	140
492.	Italian Beef Sandwiches with Pesto	140
493.	Pork Tenderloin with Garlic and Ginger	141
494.	Pork Sandwiches with Slaw	141
495.	BBQ Pork Ribs	141
496.	Cuban-Style Pork	142
497.	Mediterranean Tender Pork Roast	142
498.	Garlicky Braised Pork Neck Bones	142
499.	Sweet & Sour Pork	142
500.	Garlick & Ginger Pork with Coconut Sauce	143
501.	Pork Chops with Broccoli and Gravy	143
502.	Pork Chops with Squash Purée	143
503.	Pork Tenderloin with Sweet Pepper Sauce	144
504.	The Crispiest Roast Pork	144
505.	Pork Carnitas Wraps	144
506.	Savory Pork Loin with Celery Sauce	144
507.	Chunky Pork Meatloaf with Mashed Potatoes	145
508.	Pulled Pork Tacos	145
509.	Italian Sausage with Potato Mash & Gravy	146
510.	Red Pork & Chickpea Stew	146
511.	Char Siew Pork Ribs	146
512.	Baby Back Ribs with BBQ Sauce	146
513.	Spicy Pork Roast with Peanut Sauce	147

514. Jamaican Pulled Pork with Mango Sauce 147
515. Pork Chops with Cremini Mushroom Sauce 147
516. Ragu with Pork & Rigatoni 148
517. Juicy Barbecue Pork Chops 148
518. Sticky Pork Ribs 148
519. Bolognese-Style Pizza 149
520. Apple & Onion Topped Pork Chops 149
521. Honey Barbecue Pork Ribs 149
522. Pork Chops with Plum Sauce 149
523. Philippine-Style Pork Chops 150
524. Teriyaki Pork Noodles 150
525. Italian Sausage with Garlic Mash 150
526. Potato & Ground Pork Chili 150
527. Vietnamese Pork Soup 151
528. Sweet Potato Gratin with Peas & Prosciutto 151
529. Chorizo Stuffed Yellow Bell Peppers 151
530. Sausage with Noodles and Braised Cabbage 152
531. Italian Sausage & Cannellini Stew 152
532. Calzones with Sausage and Mozzarella 152
533. Sausage with Celeriac & Potato Mash 153
534. Beer-Braised Hot Dogs with Peppers 153
535. Sunday Beef Skewers 153
536. Sweet Carrots with Crumbled Bacon 154
537. Holiday Honey-Glazed Ham 154
538. Tasty Ham with Collard Greens 154
539. Crunchy Cashew Lamb Rack 154
540. Holiday Apricot-Lemon Ham 155
541. Winter Minestrone with Pancetta 155
542. Herbed Lamb Chops 155
543. Aromatic Pork Chops 155
544. Lamb Chops & Creamy Potato Mash 156
545. Spicy-Sweet Pork Ribs 156
546. Mustard & Brown Sugar Pork Loin 156
547. BBQ Short Ribs 156
548. Empanadas Argentinas 157
549. Veggie Steak Rolls 157
550. American Cheeseburgers 157
551. Sausage Stuffed Bell Peppers 157
552. Peppery Flank Steak Rolls 158
553. Quick Pork Chops 158
554. Pancetta & Cheese Pinwheels 158
555. Monsieur Burgers 158
556. Buttered Rib Eye Steak 158
557. Mama Polpette 159
558. Italian Meatloaf 159
559. Sirloin Bites with Sriracha Mayo 159
560. Pepperoni Calzones 159

Fish & Seafood 160

561. Herb Salmon with Barley & Haricot Verts 160
562. Lemon Cod Goujons & Rosemary Chips 160
563. Autumn Succotash with Basil-Crusted Fish 160
564. Farfalle Tuna Casserole with Cheese 161
565. Crispy Cod on Lentils 161
566. Traditional Mahi Mahi 161
567. Tuna Salad with Asparagus & Potatoes 162
568. Cajun Salmon with Creamy Grits 162
569. Mediterranean-Style Steamed Cod 162
570. Mackerel en Papillote with Vegetables 163
571. Italian-Style Flounder 163
572. Haddock with Sanfaina 163
573. Paprika & Garlic Salmon 164
574. Spicy Tangy Salmon with Wild Rice 164
575. Salmon with Dill Chutney 164
576. Steamed Sea Bass with Turnips 164
577. Monk Fish with Greens 165
578. Alaskan Cod with Fennel & Beans 165
579. Fish Finger Sandwich 165
580. Pistachio Crusted Salmon 165
581. Smoked Salmon Pilaf with Walnuts 166
582. Parmesan Tilapia 166
583. Tuna Patties 166
584. Cod Cornflakes Nuggets 166
585. Cajun Salmon with Lemon 166
586. Quick & Easy Fried Salmon 167
587. Scottish Seafood Curry 167
588. White Wine Black Mussels 167
589. Mushroom & Shrimp Egg Wrappers 168
590. Sausage & Shrimp Paella 168
591. Spaghetti with Arugula & Scallops 168
592. Crabmeat with Broccoli Risotto 169
593. Creamy Crab Soup 169
594. Prawn Toast 169
595. Seafood Gumbo 170
596. Trout with Tomato Sauce & Spinach 170
597. Potato Chowder with Peppery Prawns 170
598. Mussel Chowder with Oyster Crackers 171
599. White Wine Mussels 171
600. Mustardy Halibut 171
601. Parsley Oyster Stew 171
602. Penne all'Arrabbiata with Seafood & Chorizo 172
603. Rosemary Salmon with Spinach 172
604. Simple Coconut Shrimp 172
605. Lemony Sea Bream 172
606. Fish & Chips with Spinach 173
607. Tilapia Taco Bowls 173
608. Elegant Shrimp Burgers 173
609. Paella Señorito 173
610. Cheesy Shrimp Stew 174
611. Chorizo & Shrimp Boil 174
612. Crab Cakes 174
613. Seared Scallops with Butter-Caper Sauce 174
614. Delicious Coconut Shrimp 174
615. Tomato & Alaskan Cod Fillets 175
616. Chipotle Salmon 175
617. Shrimp & Chickpea Stew 175
618. Blaze Salmon Fillets 175
619. Steamed Salmon with Broccoli 175
620. Lisboa-Style Octopus 176

621.	Diavolo Shrimp 176	634.	Dilly Salmon Fillets....................................179
622.	Cape Cod Scallops 176	635.	Oregano Salmon...179
623.	Rustic Fish Nuggets 176	636.	Perfect Tilapia Fillets 179
624.	Dill & Potato-Crusted Cod........................176	637.	Yummy Snow Crab Legs 179
625.	Tomato Pollock Stew 177	638.	Basic Shrimp Creole 180
626.	Citrusy Catfish..177	639.	South Asparagus & Shrimp 180
627.	Spicy Caramelized Tilapia 177	640.	Salmon al Orange......................................180
628.	Collard Green & Seafood Casserole 177	641.	Glazed Salmon Fillets................................180
629.	Cheddar Haddock Stew 178	642.	Maryland Lobster Tails..............................180
630.	Garlicky Catfish with Dilly Oil Dressing ..178	643.	Louisiana-Style Lobster Tails....................181
631.	Maryland´s Crab Legs 178	644.	Crispy Fried Crab Rangoon......................181
632.	Creole Scallops Wrapped in Bacon...........178	645.	Crunchy Fish Fillet Sandwich 181
633.	Old Bay Salmon Cakes 178	646.	Sesame Teriyaki Salmon............................181

Lunch Recipes...182

647.	Chicken Noodle Soup................................182	688.	Creamy Quinoa & Mushroom Pilaf 192
648.	Pickle and Potato Salad with Feta 182	689.	Basic Applesauce with Cinnamon 192
649.	Classic French Onion Soup 182	690.	Sweet Potato & Chicken Soup 192
650.	Minestrone Soup 182	691.	Spicy Bean Soup 192
651.	Homemade Chicken Soup 183	692.	Vegetarian Cream Soup.............................192
652.	Cream of Mushroom & Spinach Soup 183	693.	Creamy Bean Soup....................................193
653.	Vegetable Soup 183	694.	Autumn Soup 193
654.	Broccoli & Potato Soup 184	695.	Mixed Vegetable & Herb Soup 193
655.	Mexican-Style Chicken Soup....................184	696.	Tasty Chicken Soup with Noodles...........193
656.	Spicy Acorn Squash Soup 184	697.	Spinach-Chicken Soup.............................193
657.	Chicken & Farro Soup...............................184	698.	Spanish-Style Lentil Soup 194
658.	Cream of Pumpkin Chipotle Soup 185	699.	Pinto Bean & Turkey Soup.......................194
659.	Tomato Soup with Cheese Croutons 185	700.	Chili Parsnip Soup 194
660.	Quick Chicken Noodle Soup....................185	701.	Veggie & Lentil Chili 194
661.	Vegetarian Black Bean Soup 185	702.	Cheesy Turkey Chili 194
662.	Acorn Squash Soup with Coconut Milk ..186	703.	Tomato Shrimp Stew 195
663.	Hearty Winter Vegetable Soup..................186	704.	Plantain Bean Stew 195
664.	Cauliflower Cheese Soup 186	705.	The Best Turkey Soup 195
665.	Ramen Spicy Soup with Collard Greens...186	706.	Parsley Chickpea Stew...............................195
666.	Sweet Potato & Egg Salad 187	707.	Chili Cheese Dip 196
667.	Ragu Bolognese..187	708.	Sunset Vegetable Stew 196
668.	Butternut Squash Curry............................187	709.	Juicy Chicken Stew 196
669.	Ham & Mozzarella Eggplant Boats 187	710.	Hot Cheddar Chicken Stew 196
670.	Spicy Borscht Soup 188	711.	Salmon Broth 196
671.	Chicken Broth 188	712.	Seafood Stew..197
672.	Red Lentil Soup with Tortilla Topping....188	713.	Winter Veggie Stew 197
673.	Beef Neck Bone Stock...............................188	714.	Green Pea Stew 197
674.	Leek and Potato Soup with Sour Cream ..188	715.	Vegetable Broth 197
675.	Egg Rolls...189	716.	Peppery Chicken Broth 197
676.	Italian Sausage Patties................................189	717.	Filled Portobello Mushrooms...................198
677.	Perfect Chicken Wings Broth 189	718.	Vegetarian Skewers with Pesto 198
678.	Fire-Roasted Tomato and Chorizo Soup ..189	719.	Pasta Primavera...198
679.	Spicy Beef Broth 190	720.	Original Pomodoro Sauce........................198
680.	Two-Bean Zucchini Soup.........................190	721.	Turkey Meatballs with Goat Cheese 199
681.	Cheat Hawaiian Pizza 190	722.	Tomato-Lentil Sauce.................................199
682.	Flavorful Vegetable Stock..........................190	723.	Honey-Apple Sauce...................................199
683.	Warm Bacon & Potato Salad 190	724.	Feta Pizza Dip..199
684.	Homemade Vegetables Soup 191	725.	Cashew Veggie Sauce.................................199
685.	Garlicky Chicken on Green Bed 191	726.	Meatless Nuggets.......................................200
686.	Curry Egg Salad...191	727.	The Ultimate BBQ Sauce.........................200
687.	Mushroom & Chicken Egg Soup 191	728.	Casserole di Pollo......................................200

- 729. Party Broccoli Cheese Sauce ... 200
- 730. Luxury White Sauce ... 200
- 731. Salsa Picante ... 201
- 732. Taco Meatballs ... 201
- 733. Bagel-Seasoned Tuna Steaks ... 201
- 734. Sweet Pretzel Bites ... 201

Desserts ... 202

- 735. Wheat Flour Cinnamon Balls ... 202
- 736. Apple Vanilla Hand Pies ... 202
- 737. White Filling Coconut and Oat Cookies ... 202
- 738. Tasty Créme Brulee ... 202
- 739. Raspberry Cream Tart ... 203
- 740. Dark Chocolate Brownies ... 203
- 741. Raspberry Crumble ... 204
- 742. Almond Banana Dessert ... 204
- 743. Vanilla Hot Lava Cake ... 204
- 744. Mixed Berry Cobbler ... 204
- 745. White Chocolate Chip Cookies ... 205
- 746. New York Cheesecake ... 205
- 747. Simple Vanilla Cheesecake ... 205
- 748. Holiday Cranberry Cheesecake ... 206
- 749. Strawberry & Lemon Ricotta Cheesecake ... 206
- 750. Chocolate Vanilla Swirl Cheesecake ... 206
- 751. Classic Caramel-Walnut Brownies ... 207
- 752. Blueberry Muffins ... 207
- 753. Molten Lava Cake ... 207
- 754. Lemon Cheesecake with Strawberries ... 208
- 755. Berry Vanilla Pudding ... 208
- 756. Air Fried Doughnuts ... 208
- 757. Homemade Apple Cider ... 208
- 758. Pumpkin Cake ... 209
- 759. Cinnamon Apple Crisp ... 209
- 760. Tiramisu Cheesecake ... 209
- 761. Cheat Apple Pie ... 210
- 762. The Most Chocolaty Fudge ... 210
- 763. Milk Dumplings in Sweet Sauce ... 210
- 764. Pineapple Cake ... 210
- 765. Raspberry Cheesecake ... 211
- 766. Chocolate and Banana Squares ... 211
- 767. No Flour Lime Muffins ... 211
- 768. Air Fried Snickerdoodle Poppers ... 211
- 769. Almond and Apple Delight ... 211
- 770. Cinnamon Mulled Red Wine ... 212
- 771. Moon Milk ... 212
- 772. Chocolate Soufflé ... 212
- 773. Pear Wedges ... 212
- 774. Delicious Pecan Stuffed Apples ... 212
- 775. The Best Molten Lava Cakes ... 213
- 776. Glam Donut Bites ... 213
- 777. Brown Sugar & Butter Bars ... 213
- 778. Cherry Pie ... 213
- 779. Gingery Chocolate Pudding ... 214
- 780. Homemade Brownies ... 214
- 781. Amazing Lemon Bars ... 214
- 782. Mini Apple Pies ... 214
- 783. Cinnamon Monkey Bread ... 215
- 784. Vanilla-Almond Shortbread Cookies ... 215
- 785. Irresistible Almond Butter Cookies ... 215
- 786. Festive Snickerdoodles ... 215
- 787. Chocolate Cheesecake ... 216
- 788. Vanilla-Chocolate Chip Cookies ... 216
- 789. Cinnamon Apple Fritters ... 216
- 790. Winter Cookies ... 216
- 791. Tasty Coconut Cake ... 216
- 792. Pink Lady Baked Apples ... 217
- 793. Coconut Muffins ... 217
- 794. Orange Banana Bread ... 217
- 795. Savory Peaches with Chocolate Biscuits ... 217
- 796. Apricots with Honey Sauce ... 218
- 797. Coconut Milk Crème Caramel ... 218
- 798. Homemade Egg Custard ... 218
- 799. Cheesy Pound Cake ... 218
- 800. Poached Peaches ... 218

INTRODUCTION

Hello… and welcome to my book about the Instant Pot Duo Crisp Pressure Cooker. Let me share all my favorite and amazing recipes with you, so that you can make delicious and scrumptious meals for your family and friends. I'll also let you know what the Instant Pot is all about, so you can see how easy it is to use.

Let me start by saying that I love my Instant Pot! This is the one kitchen tool I can't live without. I used to make meals for my family just because I needed to put something on the table. Now I make great and stunning meals because I'm love in again with cooking for my family.

I've perfected the art of using the Instant Pot… and now I'm sharing it all with you in my recipe book. The Instant Pot is more than just a pressure cooker and air fryer combo. It elevates foods in ways you never imagined.

I've created recipes for every meal and occasion… all the way from breakfast to comforting weeknight dinners to elaborate Sunday dinners when you want to impress family and friends. I've got a recipe for you for all cuisines – fried chicken, stews, soups, and casseroles. And then there's those sweets and desserts that make the perfect finish to any meal. All here for you in one collection of my best recipes.

Just use the Instant Pot once, and you'll be hooked. You'll never go back to cooking food in the oven or on the stovetop ever again. Before you get ready to start cooking, let's find out what the Instant Pot is all about.

What is the Instant Pot Duo Crisp Air Fryer?

The buzz about the Instant Pot Duo Crisp is true. It uses cutting-edge technology to let you air fry foods as well as get all the benefits of a pressure cooker…all in one! You're probably wondering how that can be possible - to have two very different kitchen appliances in one. It's easy. The Instant Pot is both because it has two lids.

Having this one amazing appliance means you can get rid of your pressure cooker, instant pot, dehydrator, roasting pan, air fryer, and slow cooker. Just think of all the kitchen space you'll have when you have one appliance, the Instant Pot, doing all the cooking for you.

Let's look at a closer look at all the benefits of owning one.

Benefits of Using the Isntant Pot Pressure Cooker

It's both an Air Fryer and Pressure Cooker at the same time

I can't say it enough. The convenience of having an air fryer and pressure cooker in one appliance makes your life a breeze. And all those added features the Instant Pot has makes it even better. How many times have you tried to get the Instant Pot of the kitchen appliance cupboard, only to have to move the slow cooker and the pressure cooker out of the way? It's happened to me too many times to count! With the Instant Pot, you can retire those other appliances and free up valuable space in your kitchen.

Get rid of other cookbooks

Meal planning is so much easier with this appliance. You don't have to look through three different cookbooks to find the recipe you want to use – Instant Pot, or maybe it's the slow cooker this time? Now you can use just one set of recipes… my own recipes that let you use the Instant Pot for every meal.

Prepare budget-friendly and healthy meals

Eating meat every day can get expensive. When you have the Instant Pot, you can make delicious meals using lentils and beans. I use these ingredients in many of my recipes – and my meals are never dull or boring. The Instant Pot also lets you cook cheaper cuts of meat to perfection. When you pressure cook a beef shank, it comes out tender and juicy, cooked with sealed in moisture that you don't get when you cook it any other way.

Skip the fats and oils

It's all about frying with the Instant Pot – air frying, that is. This means you can enjoy the taste and convenience of fried foods without using all that oil. This is perfect if you're watching what you eat – and trying to eat healthier. Foods are cooked in added liquid or their own juices, staying moist and delicious.

Add a crispy finish to pressure cooked foods

One of the biggest benefits of the Instant Pot Duo Crisp, and one of my personal favorites, is the finishing touches you can add to food before you serve it. When you cook some foods in the pressure cooker, it can be hard to get a nice crispy finish after it's been cooked. Now, with the Instant Pot, once you've pressure-cooked a whole chicken, you can just remove the liquid and turn on the crisping function. The chicken skin is nicely crisped up, making for a great meal that's sure to impress your family.

Instant Pot DUO CRISP Recipes

The recipes in this book are my absolute favorite… and they're a great introduction to the Instant Pot, highlighting just what this amazing kitchen tool can do for you.

Before you start cooking, here's some valuable information for using my recipes:

Brown and sear some food before putting it into the Instant Pot

Follow my recipes… in some of them, I'll have you brown or sear some of the ingredients, particularly meats, before you start the cooking process. This is so that the juices are sealed into the food, making it cook up that much more tender.

Check some foods to avoid over-cooking

Some foods are easy to over-cook, such as baked foods. In my recipes, I'll remind you if you need to check to avoid over-cooking.

Use hot water when pressure cooking

If you add a tablespoon or two of hot water when you're using a pressure cooker, the pressure will build up faster.

The Bake & Broil function is great for finishing off meals

Many of my recipes use the broil setting to finish off foods and give them a nice, lovely crispy topping. Remember to check during the cooking process to see how crisp the food is getting – you don't want to over-crisp!

Adjusting cooking time

If you're using fewer ingredients, then my recipe calls for remembering to adjust the cooking time to a little less. The same goes if you're using more ingredients than my recipe calls for… adjust, so the Instant Pot cooks a little longer. Just be sure to check near the end of cooking time to see if needs to cook longer.

From Slow Cooker to Instant Pot

Foods cooked in a slow cooker for 4 hours on high can be quickly cooked in the Instant Pot for only 25 to 30 minutes! Follow my recipe… I might have you add a bit more liquid than if you were cooking in a slow cooker.

As you can see, the Instant Pot is just what you need in your life. You'll be cooking exceptional meals in no time! I hope you enjoy my favorite recipes… these are the ones I repeatedly make for my family and friends. It's time to choose your first recipe… and get your Instant Pot Duo Crisp cooking great food!

BREAKFAST

1. Cheesy Prosciutto Egg Bake

Servings: 4 | Ready in about: 45 minutes

4 eggs	1 tsp freshly ground black pepper	8 oz prosciutto, chopped
1 cup whole milk	1 cup shredded Monterey Jack cheese	1 cup water
1 tsp salt	1 orange bell pepper, chopped	

Break the eggs into a bowl, pour in the milk, salt, and black pepper and whisk until combined. Stir in the Monterey Jack Cheese. Put the bell pepper and prosciutto in a cake pan. Then, pour over the egg mixture, cover the pan with aluminum foil, and put on the trivet. Put the trivet in your Instant Pot and pour it into the water.

Seal the pressure lid, choose Pressure Cook, and set to High. Set the time to 20 minutes. When done cooking, do a quick pressure release and carefully remove the lid after the pressure has completely escaped. When baking is complete, take the pan out of the pot, and set it on a heatproof surface, and cool for 5 minutes.

2. Crispy Pancetta Hash with Baked Eggs

Servings: 4 | Ready in about: 50 minutes

6 slices pancetta, chopped	2 potatoes, peeled and diced	Salt and black pepper to taste
1 white onion, diced	1 tsp sweet paprika	4 eggs

Choose Sauté on your Instant Pot. Lay the pancetta in the pot and cook, stirring occasionally, for 5 minutes, or until the pancetta is crispy. Stir in the onion, potatoes, sweet paprika, salt, and black pepper. Close the air fry lid. Choose Bake, set the temperature to 350°F, and the time to 25 minutes. Cook until the turnips are soft and golden brown, stirring occasionally. Crack the eggs on top of the hash, close the air fry lid again, and choose Bake and the time to 10 minutes. Cook the eggs and check two or three times until your desired crispiness has been achieved.

3. Shakshuka with Goat Cheese

Servings: 4 | Ready in about: 50 minutes

3 tbsp ghee	2 garlic cloves, chopped	½ tsp red chili flakes
1 small red onion, chopped	Salt and ground black pepper to taste	4 eggs
½ red bell pepper, seeded and chopped	29 oz canned tomatoes with their juice	⅓ cup crumbled goat cheese
1 banana pepper, seeded and minced	½ tsp smoked paprika	2 tbsp fresh cilantro, chopped

Choose Sauté on your Instant Pot. Melt the ghee and sauté the onion, bell pepper, banana pepper, and garlic. Season lightly with salt and cook for 2 minutes until the vegetables are fragrant. Stir in tomatoes, smoked paprika, red chili flakes, and pepper. Seal the pressure lid, choose Pressure Cook on High and adjust the timer to 4 minutes.

When done, perform a quick pressure release. Gently crack the eggs onto the tomato sauce in different areas. Seal the pressure lid again, choose Steam and adjust the cook time to 3 minutes. When ready, carefully open the pressure lid. Sprinkle with the shakshuka with goat cheese and cilantro. Dish into a serving platter and serve.

4. Onion and Cheese Omelet

Servings: 1 | Ready in about: 10 minutes

2 eggs	1 tsp soy sauce	¼ tsp pepper
2 tbsp grated cheddar cheese	½ onion, sliced	1 tbsp olive oil

Whisk the eggs with pepper, onion, and soy sauce in a bowl until combined. Grease a baking tray with olive oil and pour in the eggs. Close the air fry lid and cook for 6 minutes on Air Fry mode at 350°F. Once the timer beeps, top with the grated cheddar cheese. Fold the omelet in half and serve with a green salad.

5. Strawberry Bread French Toast

Servings: 4 | Ready in about: 45 minutes

3 eggs	1 tsp cinnamon powder	¼ cup ricotta cheese
¼ cup milk	6 slices brioche, cubed	2 tbsp firm unsalted butter, sliced
1 tbsp sugar	3 strawberries, sliced, divided	¼ cup chopped almonds
1 tsp vanilla extract	2 tbsp brown sugar, divided	2 tbsp maple syrup

Crack the eggs into a bowl and whisk with the milk, sugar, vanilla, and cinnamon. Grease a baking dish with cooking spray and in a single layer, spread half of the brioche cubes in the pan. Layer half of the strawberries on the bread and dust with 1 tablespoon brown sugar. Spoon and spread the ricotta cheese on top of the strawberries.

Then, make another layer of bread, strawberries, brown sugar, and ricotta cheese. Pour the egg mixture all over the layered ingredients ensuring to give the bread a good coat. Pour 1 cup water into your Instant Pot. Fix the pan on the trivet, and put the trivet with the pan in the pot. Seal the pressure lid, choose Pressure Cook on High.

Set the timer to 20 minutes. Once the timer has read to the end, perform a quick pressure release to let all the pressure out, and carefully open the lid. Top the French toast with the sliced butter, almonds, and maple syrup. Close the air fry lid, choose Bake, and set the temperature to 390°F for 5 minutes. Check the toast's doneness for your desired crispiness, otherwise, cook for a few more minutes. Serve immediately.

6. Raspberry-Cranberry Chia Oatmeal

Servings: 4 | Ready in about: 30 minutes

2 cups old fashioned oatmeal	½ tsp nutmeg powder	½ cup dried cranberries + for garnish
3¾ cups water	1 tbsp cinnamon powder	2 raspberries, sliced
¼ cup plain vinegar	½ tsp vanilla extract	Honey, for topping

Combine the oatmeal, water, vinegar, nutmeg, cinnamon, vanilla, cranberries, and raspberries in your Instant Pot. Seal the pressure lid, hit Pressure Cook on High, and set the timer to 11 minutes. When ready, perform a natural pressure release for 10 minutes, then a quick pressure release to let off any remaining pressure, and carefully open the lid. Stir the oatmeal, drizzle with honey and more dried cranberries, and serve immediately.

7. Kale-Egg Frittata

Servings: 6 | Ready in about: 20 minutes

6 large eggs	½ tsp grated nutmeg	1 ½ cups kale, chopped
2 tbsp heavy cream	Salt and black pepper to taste	¼ cup grated Parmesan cheese

In a bowl, beat eggs, nutmeg, pepper, salt, and cream until smooth. Stir in Parmesan cheese and kale. Apply a cooking spray to a cake pan. Wrap aluminum foil around outside of the pan to cover completely. Place egg mixture into the prepared pan. Add 1 cup water into your Instant Pot and set in a trivet. Gently lay the pan onto the trivet. Seal the pressure lid, choose Pressure Cook on High, and set the timer to 10 minutes. When ready, release the pressure quickly.

8. Quick Soft-Boiled Eggs

Servings: 4 | Ready in about: 15 minutes

4 large eggs	1 cups water	Salt and black pepper to taste

To the pressure cooker pot, add water and place a trivet. Carefully place eggs on it. Seal the pressure lid, choose Pressure Cook on High, and set the timer to 3 minutes. When cooking is complete, do a quick pressure release. Allow cooling completely in an ice bath. Peel the eggs and season with salt and pepper before serving.

9. Sausage Wrapped Scotch Eggs

Servings: 4 | Ready in about: 55 minutes

1 cup water	12 oz Italian sausage patties	2 tbsp melted unsalted butter
4 eggs	1 cup panko bread crumbs	

Pour 1 cup of water into the inner pot. Put a trivet in the pot and carefully place the eggs on top. Seal the pressure lid, choose Pressure Cook on High, and the cook time to 3 minutes. While cooking the eggs, fill half a bowl with cold water and about a cup full of ice cubes to make an ice bath. After cooking, perform a quick pressure release, and carefully open the lid. Pick up the eggs into the ice bath. Allow cooling for 3 to 4 minutes. Peel the eggs.

Pour the water out of the inner pot and return the pot to the base. Fix in a trivet. Place an egg on each sausage patty. Pull the sausage around the egg and seal the edges. In a small bowl, mix the breadcrumbs with the melted butter. One at a time, dredge the sausage-covered eggs in the crumbs, pressing into the breadcrumbs for a thorough coat.

Arrange on a baking dish. Place the eggs on the trivet. Close the air fry lid, choose Air Fry, adjust the temperature to 400°F, and the cook time to 15 minutes. When the timer has ended, the crumbs should be crisp and a deep golden brown color. Remove the eggs and allow cooling for several minutes. Slice the eggs in half and serve.

10. Spicy Deviled Eggs

Servings: 6 | Ready in about: 20 minutes

1 cup water	¼ cup cream cheese	Salt and ground black pepper to taste
10 large eggs	¼ cup mayonnaise	¼ tsp chili powder

Add water to your Instant Pot. Insert the eggs into the steamer basket and place into yhe pot. Seal the pressure lid, choose Pressure Cook on High, and set the timer to 5 minutes. When ready, release the pressure quickly. Drop eggs into an ice bath to cool. Peel eggs and halve them. Transfer yolks to a bowl and use a fork to mash. Stir in cream cheese, and mayonnaise. Season. Ladle yolk mixture into egg whites.

11. French Dip Sandwiches

Servings: 8 | Ready in about: 1 hour 35 minutes

2 ½ lb beef roast	4 garlic cloves, sliced	1 tsp dried oregano
2 tbsp olive oil	½ cup dry red wine	16 slices Fontina cheese
1 onion, chopped	2 cups beef broth stock	8 split hoagie rolls

Warm oil on Sauté in your Instant Pot and brown the beef for 2 to 3 minutes per side; reserve. Add onion and cook for 3 minutes. Mix in garlic and cook for one a minute until soft. Add red wine to deglaze. Mix in broth and take back the juices and beef to your pressure cooker. Over the meat, scatter some oregano. Seal the pressure lid.

Choose Pressure Cook on High, and set the timer to 50 minutes. Release pressure naturally for around 10 minutes. Transfer the beef to a cutting board and slice. Roll the sliced beef and add a topping of onions. Each sandwich should be topped with 2 slices fontina cheese. Place the sandwiches in the pot, close the air fry lid and select Air Fry. Adjust the temperature to 400°F and the time to 3 minutes. Serve.

12. Cinnamon Pumpkin Oatmeal

Servings: 4 | Ready in about: 25 minutes

1 tbsp butter	¼ tsp cinnamon	3 tbsp maple syrup
2 cups steel cut oats	1 cup pumpkin puree	½ cup pumpkin seeds, toasted

Melt butter on Sauté in your Instant Pot. Add in cinnamon, oats, salt, pumpkin puree and 3 cups water. Seal the pressure lid, choose Pressure Cook on High, and set the timer to 10 minutes. When cooking is complete, do a quick release. Open the lid and stir in maple syrup and top with toasted pumpkin seeds to serve.

13. Savory Custards with Ham & Cheese

Servings: 4 | Ready in about: 40 minutes

2 serrano ham slices, halved widthwise	¼ cup half and half	¼ cup grated Emmental cheese
4 large eggs	¼ tsp salt	¼ cup caramelized white onions
1 oz cottage cheese, softened	Ground black pepper to taste	

Preheat your Instant Pot by choosing Sauté and put in the serrano ham. Cook for 3 to 4 minutes or until browned. Remove to a paper towel-lined plate. Next, use a brush to coat the inside of four 1- cup ramekins with the ham fat. Set the cups aside, then, empty and wipe out the inner pot with a paper towel, and return the pot to the base.

Crack the eggs into a bowl and add the cottage cheese, half and half, salt, and several grinds of black pepper. Use a hand mixer to whisk the ingredients until co cheese lumps remain. Stir in the grated emmental cheese and mix again to incorporate the cheese. Lay a piece of ham in the bottom of each custard cup.

Evenly share the onions among the cups as well as the egg mixture. Cover each cup with aluminum foil. Pour 1 cup of water into the inner pot and fix in a trivet. Arrange the ramekins on top. Lock the pressure lid in Seal position. Choose Pressure Cook on High, and set the timer to 7 minutes. After cooking, perform a quick pressure release. Use tongs to remove the custard cups from the pressure cooker. Cool for 1 to 2 minutes before serving.

14. Butternut Squash Cake Oatmeal

Servings: 4 | Ready in about: 35 minutes

3 ½ cups coconut milk	⅓ cup honey	½ tsp fresh orange zest
1 cup steel-cut oats	1 tsp ground cinnamon	¼ tsp ground nutmeg
1 cup shredded Butternut Squash	¾ tsp ground ginger	¼ cup toasted walnuts, chopped
½ cup sultanas	½ tsp salt	½ tsp vanilla extract

In the pressure cooker, mix sultanas, orange zest, ginger, milk, honey, squash, salt, oats, and nutmeg. Seal the pressure lid, choose Pressure Cook on High, and set the timer to 12 minutes. When ready, do a natural pressure release for 10 minutes. Into the oatmeal, stir in the vanilla extract and sugar. Top with walnuts and serve.

15. Barbecue Chicken Sandwiches

Servings: 4 | Ready in about: 45 minutes

4 chicken thighs, boneless and skinless	2 garlic cloves, minced	1 tbsp mayonnaise
2 cups barbecue sauce	2 tbsp minced fresh parsley	1 ½ cups iceberg lettuce, shredded
1 onion, minced	1 tbsp lemon juice	4 burger buns

Season the chicken with salt, and transfer into the inner pot. Add in garlic, onion and barbeque sauce. Coat the chicken by turning in the sauce. Seal the pressure lid, choose Pressure Cook on High, and set the timer to 15 minutes. When ready, do a natural pressure release for 10 minutes. Shred the chicken and mix into the sauce.

Press Sauté and let the mixture to simmer for 15 minutes to thicken the sauce, until desired consistency. In a large bowl, mix the lemon juice, mayonnaise, salt, and parsley. Toss lettuce into the mixture to coat. Separate the chicken in equal parts to match the sandwich buns. Apply lettuce for topping and complete the sandwiches.

16. Coconut-Berry Oatmeal

Servings: 4 | Ready in about: 20 minutes

1 cup steel cut oats	1 cup blueberries, diced
1 cup coconut milk	½ tsp vanilla extract

Place all ingredients into your Instant Pot. Secure the lid, select Pressure Cook, and cook on High for 3 minutes. When ready, allow pressure to release naturally, for 10 minutes. Carefully open the lid and serve warm.

17. Egg Crumpet Sandwich

Servings: 2 | Ready in about: 25 minutes

2 tbsp butter	2 eggs, large	2 tbsp Monterey Jack cheese, grated
2 tbsp chopped bacon	Salt and ground black pepper to taste	2 crumpets, split

Brush two cups with 1 tbsp of butter. Share the bacon into the cups, crack an egg into each one, and prick the egg yolks with a toothpick in different places. Sprinkle the top with salt and black pepper and divide the cheese on top to cover the eggs. Cover the cups with aluminium foil and crimp the sides down.

Pour 1 cup of water into your Instant Pot, fix a trivet at the bottom the pot, and arrange the cups on top. Seal the pressure lid, select Pressure. Adjust the pressure to High, and the cook time to 1 minute. When done cooking, perform a quick pressure release and carefully open the lid. Remove the trivet and cups without taking off the foil.

Empty the water from the inner pot and return the pot to the base. Use tongs to lift the cups into the bottom of the pot and fix a trivet in the upper position of the pot. Cover the air fry lid, choose Broil, and adjust the time to 2 minutes. While heating, spread the remaining butter over the crumpet halves. Open the air fry lid.

Arrange the crumpet halves on the trivet with the buttered-side up, and close the lid. Choose Broil again and adjust the time to 4 minutes. When ready, transfer to a cutting board and remove the cups. Run a butter knife in and around the cups and turn out each egg onto the lower half of each crumpet. Top with the other half and serve.

18. Sausage and Bacon Cheesecake

Servings: 6 | Ready in about: 25 minutes

8 eggs, cracked into a bowl	1 large red bell pepper, chopped	Salt and black pepper to taste
8 oz breakfast sausage, chopped	1 cup chopped green onion	½ cup milk
3 bacon slices, chopped	1 cup grated Cheddar cheese	4 slices bread, cut into ½-inch cubes
1 large green bell pepper, chopped	1 tsp red chili flakes	2 cups water

Add the eggs, sausage chorizo, bacon slices, green and red bell peppers, green onion, chili flakes, cheddar cheese, salt, pepper, and milk to a bowl and use a whisk to beat them together. Grease a bundt pan with cooking spray and pour the egg mixture into it. After, drop the bread slices in the egg mixture all around while using a spoon to push them into the mixture. Open your Instant Pot, pour in water, and fit a trivet at the center of the pot.

Place bundt pan on the trivet and seal the pressure lid. Select Pressure Cook on High for 6 minutes. Once the timer goes off, do a quick pressure release. Run a knife around the egg in the bundt pan, close the air fry lid and cook for another 4 minutes on Bake on 380°F. When ready, place a serving plate on the bundt pan, and then, turn the egg bundt over. Use a knife to cut the egg into slices. Serve with a sauce of your choice.

19. Veggie Salmon Balls

Servings: 4 | Ready in about: 40 minutes

2 (5 oz) packs steamed salmon flakes	1 red bell pepper, seeded and chopped	4 tbsp mayonnaise
1 Red onion, chopped	4 tbsp butter, divided	2 tsp Worcestershire sauce
1 tsp garlic powder	3 eggs, cracked into a bowl	¼ cup chopped parsley
2 tbsp olive oil	1 cup breadcrumbs	3 large potatoes, cut into chips

Turn on your Instant Pot and select Sauté. Heat the oil and add half of the butter. Once it has melted, add the onions and the chopped red bell peppers. Cook for 6 minutes while stirring occasionally. In a mixing bowl, add salmon flakes, sautéed red bell pepper and onion, breadcrumbs, eggs, mayonnaise, Worcestershire sauce, garlic powder, salt, pepper, and parsley. Use a spoon to mix well while breaking the salmon into the tiny pieces.

Mold 4 patties out of the mixture. Add the remaining butter to melt, and when melted, add the patties. Fry for 4 minutes, flipping once. Then, close the air fry lid, select Bake mode and bake for 4 minutes on 390°F. Remove them onto a wire rack to rest. Serve the cakes with a side of lettuce and potato salad with a mild drizzle of vinaigrette.

20. Orange Pepper and Artichoke Frittata

Servings: 4 | Ready in about: 60 minutes

2 tbsp unsalted butter
½ small red onion, chopped
¼ large orange bell pepper, chopped
1 cup chopped artichoke hearts
8 large eggs
Salt and ground black pepper to taste
¼ cup full cream milk
¾ cup shredded Colby cheese, divided
¼ cup grated Pecorino Romano

On your Instant Pot, press Sauté. Melt the butter and sauté the onion, bell pepper, and artichoke hearts for 5 minutes or until the onion and pepper are soft. While the vegetables soften, whisk the eggs with salt and allow sitting for 1 minute. Pour the milk into the eggs and whisk again then stir ½ cup of colby cheese into the mixture.

When the vegetables are cooked, pour the egg mixture into the pot. Gently stir to distribute the vegetables. Cook the eggs, undisturbed, until the edges are set, 7 to 9 minutes. Run a silicone spatula around the edges of the frittata to loosen from the side of the pot. Close the air fry lid. Choose Bake and set to 390°F and the time to 3 minutes.

After 1 minute, open the lid and sprinkle the remaining Colby and the Pecorino Romano cheese over the frittata. Close the lid and cook for 2 minutes. Open the lid by which time the cheese should have melted and the top not browned, but set. Sprinkle the frittata with black pepper, let rest for 2 minutes, and slice into wedges, to serve.

21. Plum Breakfast Clafoutis

Servings: 4 | Ready in about: 60 minutes

2 tsp butter, softened
1 cup plums, chopped
⅔ cup whole milk
⅓ cup half and half
⅓ cup sugar
½ cup flour
2 large eggs
¼ tsp cinnamon
½ tsp vanilla extract
A pinch of salt
2 tbsp confectioners' sugar

Grease four ramekins with the butter and divide the plums into each cup. Pour the milk, half and half, sugar, flour, eggs, cinnamon, vanilla, and salt in a bowl and use a hand mixer to whisk the ingredients on medium speed until the batter is smooth, about 2 minutes. Pour the batter over the plums two-third way up.

Pour 1 cup of water into the inner pot. Fix a trivet at the bottom of the pot and put the ramekins on the trivet. Lay a square of aluminium foil on the ramekins but don't crimp. Put the pressure lid together and lock in Seal position. Choose Pressure Cook on High and set the time to 11 minutes.

When ready, perform a quick pressure release. Use tongs to remove the foil. Close the air fry lid and choose Bake. Adjust the temperature to 400°F and the time to 6 minutes. Press Start to brown the top of the clafoutis. Check after about 4 minutes to ensure the clafoutis are lightly browned. Bake for a few more minutes. Remove the ramekins onto a flat surface. Cool for 5 minutes, and then dust with the confectioners' sugar. Serve warm.

22. Healthy Frittata

Serves: 2 | Total Time: 15 minutes

4 egg whites
½ cup chopped kale
¼ cup chopped tomatoes
½ tsp salt
¼ cup chopped onion

Preheat your Instant Pot Duo Crisp to 320°F. Whisk egg whites in a large bowl until frothy. Add kale, tomato, salt, and onion and stir until combined. Lightly grease a baking dish, then pour in the egg mixture. Place the pan in the air fryer basket and close the lid. Bake for 8 minutes. The center is just set. Serve warm.

23. Herbed Homemade Ghee

Servings: 10 | Ready in about: 17 minutes

8 oz unsalted butter, softened
2 tbsp parsley, minced
1 tbsp fresh chives, chopped
Sea salt to taste

Set your Instant Pot to Sauté. Melt butter and cook for 7-9 minutes as you stir in cycles of 3 minutes until browning. Allow the butter to slightly cool. Use cheesecloth to strain the butter into a sealable container. Add in parsley, chives, and salt and stir thoroughly. Let cool before closing the lid. Keep in the fridge until ready to use.

24. Maple Giant Pancake

Servings: 6 | Ready in about: 30 minutes

3 cups flour	⅓ cup olive oil	1 ½ tsp baking soda
¾ cup sugar	⅓ cup sparkling water	2 tbsp maple syrup
5 eggs	⅓ tsp salt	A dollop of whipped cream to serve

Start by pouring the flour, sugar, eggs, olive oil, sparkling water, salt, and baking soda into a food processor and blend until smooth. Pour the batter into your Instant Pot and let it sit in there for 15 minutes. Close the lid and secure the pressure valve. Select the Pressure Cook on Low pressure for 10 minutes.

Once the timer goes off, quick-release the pressure valve to let out any steam and open the lid. Gently run a spatula around the pancake to let loose any sticking. Once ready, slide the pancake onto a serving plate and drizzle with maple syrup. Top with the whipped cream to serve.

25. Prosciutto, Mozzarella & Egg in a Cup

Servings: 2 | Ready in about: 20 minutes

2 slices bread	2 eggs	2 tbsp grated mozzarella
2 prosciutto slices, chopped	4 tomato slices	2 tbsp mayonnaise

Grease two large ramekins with cooking spray. Place one bread slice in the bottom of each ramekin. Arrange 1 prosciutto slice and 2 tomato slices on top of each bread slice. Divide the mozzarella between the ramekins. Crack the eggs over the mozzarella. Season with salt and pepper. Place in your Instant Pot and set it to 390°F. Close the air fry lid and cook for 10 minutes on Air Fry mode. Top with mayonnaise to serve.

26. Paprika Shirred Eggs

Servings: 2 | Ready in about: 20 minutes

2 tsp butter, for greasing	4 slices of ham	¼ tsp pepper
4 eggs, divided	3 tbsp Parmesan cheese, grated	2 tsp chopped chives
2 tbsp heavy cream	¼ tsp paprika	

Grease a pie pan with the butter. Arrange the ham slices on the bottom of the pan to cover it completely. Use more slices if needed. Whisk one egg along with the heavy cream, salt, and pepper, in a small bowl. Pour the mixture over the ham slices. Crack the other eggs over the ham. Scatter Parmesan cheese over, close the air fry lid and cook for 14 minutes on Air Fry mode at 390°F. Sprinkle with paprika and garnish with chives.

27. Chai Latte Steel-Cut Oatmeal

Servings: 4 | Ready in about: 20 minutes

3 ½ cups milk	1 tsp coffee	¼ tsp ground allspice
½ cup raw peanuts	1 ½ tsp ground ginger	¼ tsp ground cardamom
1 cup steel-cut oats	1 ¼ tsp ground cinnamon	1 tsp vanilla extract
¼ cup agave syrup	½ tsp salt	

Using an immersion blender, puree peanuts and milk to obtain smooth consistency. Transfer into the cooker pot. To the peanuts-milk mixture, add agave syrup, oats, ginger, allspice, cinnamon, salt, cardamom, tea leaves, and cloves to mix well. Seal the pressure lid, choose Pressure Cook on High, and set the timer to 12 minutes. Let pressure to release naturally on completing the cooking cycle. Add vanilla to the oatmeal and stir before serving.

28. Cheese & Bacon Grits

Servings: 4 | Ready in about: 20 minutes

3 slices smoked bacon, diced	1 cup ground Grits	Salt and black pepper to taste
1 ½ cups grated Cheddar cheese	2 tsp butter	½ cup milk

To preheat your Instant Pot, select Sauté. Cook bacon until crispy, about 5 minutes. Set aside. Add the grits, butter, milk, ½ cup water, salt, and pepper to the pot and stir using a spoon. Seal the pressure lid. Choose Pressure Cook and cook for 3 minutes on High. Once the timer has ended, do a quick pressure release.

Add in cheddar cheese and give the pudding a good stir with the same spoon. Close crisping lid, press Bake button and cook for 8 minutes on 370°F. When ready, dish the cheesy grits into serving bowls and spoon over the crisped bacon. Serve right away with toasted bread.

29. Feta & Poached Egg Tomato Topper

Servings: 4 | Ready in about: 10 minutes

4 large eggs	Salt and black pepper to taste	2 tbsp grated Parmesan cheese
4 small slices feta cheese	1 tsp chopped fresh herbs, of your	
2 Heirloom tomatoes, halved crosswise	choice	

Pour 1 cup water into your Instant Pot and fit in a trivet. Grease the ramekins with the cooking spray and crack each egg into them. Season with salt and pepper. Cover the ramekins with aluminum foil. Place the cups on the trivet. Seal the lid. Select Steam mode for 3 minutes on High pressure. Do a quick pressure release.

Remove the ramekins onto a flat surface. On serving plates, share the halved tomatoes and feta and toss the eggs in the ramekin over on each tomato half. Sprinkle with salt and pepper, Parmesan, and garnish with herbs.

30. Morning Minty Chocolate Scones

Serves: 6 | Total Time: 30 minutes

6 tbsp cold butter	½ tsp baking powder	¾ cup buttermilk
2 tbsp melted butter	½ tsp orange zest	½ cup chocolate chips
2 cups flour	1 tsp cocoa powder	
½ cup brown sugar	1 large egg	

Preheat your Instant Pot Duo Crisp to 320°F. Place the cold butter for 10 minutes in the freezer. Combine flour, brown sugar, cocoa powder, orange zest, and baking powder in a large bowl. Take frozen butter from the freezer and grate it into the bowl. Stir to combine. Add the egg and buttermilk and gently stir to form a soft, sticky dough. Fold in chocolate chips.

Lightly flour a flat work surface. Turn the dough out on the surface and knead gently to form a circle. Cut into 8 triangles. Line the air fry basket with parchment paper. Place the scones in the basket and brush each with the melted butter. Close the fry lid and Air Fry for 15 minutes. Scones will be dark gold with crispy edges. A toothpick inserted in the middle will come out clean. Serve and enjoy!

31. Maple-Blueberry Oatmeal

Servings: 4 | Ready in about: 15 minutes

1 cup Blueberries	2 cups rolled oats	2 tbsp flax meal
4 cups water	1 tsp vanilla	1 tbsp maple syrup

Place all ingredients in your Instant Pot, except for the maple syrup. Stir to combine well. Secure the lid, select Pressure Cook, and cook on High for 3 minutes. Once ready, allow pressure to release naturally for 10 minutes. Then, carefully open the lid and transfer to a serving bowl. Top with the maple syrup and serve.

32. Berry Scones

Serves: 6 | Total Time: 30 minutes

2 tbsp melted butter	½ cup sugar	½ cup sour cream
6 tbsp cold butter	1 tsp baking powder	½ cup blackberries
2 cups flour	1 large egg	

Preheat your Instant Pot Duo Crisp to 320°F. Place the cold butter for 10 minutes in the freezer. Combine flour, sugar, and baking powder in a large bowl. Take frozen butter from the freezer and grate it into the bowl. Mix well. Add the egg and sour cream and gently stir to form a soft, sticky dough. Fold in blackberries.

Lightly flour a flat work surface. Turn the dough out on the surface and knead gently to form a circle. Cut into 8 triangles. Line the air fry basket with parchment paper. Place the scones in the basket and brush each with the melted butter. Close the fry lid and Air Fry for 15 minutes. Scones will be dark gold with crispy edges. A toothpick inserted in the middle will come out clean. Serve and enjoy!

33. Baked Banana Oats

Serves: 2 | Total Time: 15 minutes

1 cup quick-cooking oats	1 banana, mashed	½ tsp chia seeds
1 cup oat milk	2 tbsp brown sugar	½ tsp salt
2 tbsp butter, melted	½ tsp vanilla extract	

Preheat your Instant Pot Duo Crisp to 360°F. Lightly grease a baking pan. Add oats to the pan, then oat milk, and butter. Mix banana, brown sugar, chia seeds, vanilla, and salt in a bowl, then transfer to the baking pan over the oats. Stir to combine. Place the pan in the Instant Pot Duo Crisp in the air fry basket and close the fry lid. Bake for 10 minutes. The top will be brown, and the oats are firm to the touch. Serve and enjoy!

34. Marble Muffins

Serves: 6 | Total Time: 20 minutes

1 cup flour	¼ cup butter, melted	½ cup rice milk
½ cup sugar	1 tsp vanilla extract	1 cup blueberries
1 tsp baking powder	1 egg	

Preheat your Instant Pot Duo Crisp to 300°F. Whisk flour, sugar, and baking powder in a large bowl. Next, stir in butter, vanilla extract, egg, and rice milk until well combined. Fold in blueberries. Fill 12 silicone or aluminum muffin cups about halfway full. Place the cups in the air fry basket and close the fry lid. Bake for 15 minutes. Muffins will start browning on the edges, and a toothpick inserted in the middle will come out clean. Serve.

35. Kid's Cinnamon Rolls

Serves: 8 | Total Time: 25 minutes

1 puff pastry sheet	1 tsp vanilla powder	2 tbsp buttermilk
6 tbsp butter, melted	2 tbsp ground cinnamon	
¾ cup sugar	½ cup confectioners' sugar	

Preheat your Instant Pot Duo Crisp to 320°F. Unroll the puff pastry into a large rectangle. In a small bowl, mix granulated sugar, vanilla powder, and cinnamon. Brush the dough with butter, then sprinkle with sugar and cinnamon mixture evenly from edge to edge. Roll the dough into a log, starting with the long side. Rub a little water along the edge to seal the roll. Slice the dough into eight equal pieces.

Line the air fry basket with parchment. Arrange the rounds in the air fry basket and close the fry lid. Bake for 12 minutes. Rolls will be golden and flaky. While the rolls cool for 5 minutes, whisk together the confectioner's sugar and buttermilk in a small bowl. Drizzle glaze over cinnamon rolls. Serve warm and enjoy!

36. Ham and Cheese Sandwich

Servings: 1 | Ready in about: 10 minutes

2 tsp butter
2 slices of bread
2 slices of American cheese
1 slice of ham

Spread one teaspoon of butter on the outside of each of the bread slices. Place one cheese slice on the inside of one bread slice, top with ham slice and another cheese slice. Cover with the second bread slice to create the sandwich.

Place into the air fry basket, close the air fry lid, and cook for 4 minutes on Air Fry at 390°F. Flip the sandwich and cook for 4 minutes. Cut diagonally the sandwich and serve immediately with ketchup or chutney.

37. Creamy Zucchini Muffins

Servings: 4 | Ready in about: 20 minutes

1 ½ cups flour
1 tsp cinnamon
3 eggs
2 tsp baking powder
1 cup milk
2 tbsp butter, melted
1 tbsp yogurt
½ cup shredded zucchini
2 tbsp cream cheese

In a bowl, whisk the eggs along with a pinch of salt, cinnamon, cream cheese, sifted flour, and baking powder. In another bowl, combine all liquid ingredients. Gently mix the dry and liquid mixtures. Stir in zucchini. Line the muffin tins and pour in the batter. Close the air fry lid and cook for 12 minutes on Air Fry mode at 350°F.

Once the timer beeps, check to ensure the muffins are set. If necessary, return them to your Instant Pot, and cook for 2-3 more minutes. Transfer to a cooling rack before serving. Serve with a scraping of butter.

38. Raspberry and Vanilla Pancake

Servings: 4 | Ready in about: 15 minutes

2 cups all-purpose flour
1 cup milk
3 eggs, beaten
1 tsp baking powder
1 cup brown sugar
1 ½ tsp vanilla extract
½ cup frozen raspberries, thawed
2 tbsp maple syrup
A pinch of salt

In a bowl, mix the sifted flour, baking powder, salt, milk, eggs, vanilla extract, sugar, and maple syrup, until smooth. Gently stir in the raspberries. Grease the air fry basket with cooking spray. Drop the batter into the basket. Close the air fry lid and cook for 10 minutes on Air Fry mode at 390°F. Serve the pancake right away.

39. Toasted Herb and Garlic Bagel

Servings: 1 | Ready in about: 6 minutes

2 tbsp butter, softened
1 tsp dried basil
1 tsp dried parsley
1 tsp garlic powder
1 tbsp Parmesan cheese
1 bagel, halved

Place the bagel halves in your Instant Pot, close the air fry lid and cook for 3 minutes on Air Fry mode at 390°F. Combine the butter, Parmesan, garlic, basil, and parsley, in a small bowl. Season with salt and pepper, to taste. Spread the mixture onto the toasted bagel. Return the bagel to the and cook for an additional 3 minutes on Roast mode. Serve with tangy tomato relish on the side.

40. Spinach Egg Tart

Servings: 6 | Ready in about: 35 minutes

½ cup milk
1 ½ cups water
12 eggs
1 tsp dried thyme
¼ cup grated Parmesan cheese
3 large scallions, sliced
1 cup tomato, chopped
½ tsp salt
3 cups baby spinach
4 tomato slices

Pour 1 cup of water into the Instant Pot. In a bowl, whisk the eggs along with the milk, salt, and thyme. Grease a baking dish with cooking spray, and combine the chopped tomatoes and spinach in it. Pour in the eggs' mixture. Sprinkle the scallions over the eggs, and top with the tomato slices.

Then, sprinkle with Parmesan cheese and give it a good stir. Place the dish inside the Instant Pot, and secure the lid. Select Pressure Cook, and cook on High for 20 minutes. Allow the pressure to release naturally for 10 minutes. Carefully open the lid and serve immediately.

41. Three Meat Cheesy Omelet

Servings: 2 | Ready in about: 20 minutes

1 beef sausage, chopped
4 slices prosciutto, chopped
3 oz salami, chopped
1 cup grated mozzarella cheese
4 eggs
1 tbsp chopped onion
1 tbsp ketchup
A pinch of salt

Preheat your Instant Pot to 350°F on Air Fry mode. Whisk the eggs with the ketchup in a bowl. Stir in the onion. Spritz the inside of the air fry basket with a cooking spray. Add and brown the sausage for about 2 minutes. Combine the egg mixture, mozzarella cheese, salami and prosciutto. Pour the egg mixture over the sausage and stir it. Close the air fry lid and cook for 10 minutes. Once the timer beeps, ensure the omelet is just set. Serve.

42. Very Berry Breakfast Puffs

Servings: 3 | Ready in about: 20 minutes

3 pastry dough sheets
2 tbsp mashed strawberries
2 tbsp mashed raspberries
¼ tsp vanilla extract
2 cups cream cheese
1 tbsp honey

Divide the cream cheese between the dough sheets and spread it evenly. In a small bowl, combine the berries, honey, and vanilla. Divide the mixture between the pastry sheets. Pinch the ends of the sheets, to form puff.

You can seal them by brushing some water onto the edges, or even better, use egg wash. Lay the puffs into a lined baking dish. Place the dish into your Instant Pot, close the air fry lid and cook for 15 minutes on Air Fry mode at 390°F. Once the timer beeps, check the puffs to ensure they're puffed and golden. Serve warm.

43. Crustless Mediterranean Quiche

Servings: 2 | Ready in about: 40 minutes

4 eggs
½ cup chopped tomatoes
1 cup crumbled feta cheese
1 tbsp chopped basil
1 tbsp chopped oregano
¼ cup chopped kalamata olives
¼ cup chopped onion
2 tbsp olive oil
½ cup milk

Brush a pie pan with the olive oil. Beat the eggs along with the milk, salt, and pepper. Stir in all of the remaining ingredients. Pour the egg mixture into the pan. Close the air fry lid and cook for 30 minutes on Air Fry mode at 340°F. Leave to cool before serving.

44. Chili Breakfast Sausages

Serves: 6 | Total Time: 15 minutes

2 tsp olive oil
½ tsp chili oil
1 lb ground pork
2 tbsp brown sugar
Salt and black pepper to taste
½ tsp garlic powder
½ tbsp mustard
½ tsp dried fennel
½ tsp red pepper flakes

Preheat your Instant Pot Duo Crisp to 400°F. Combine all of the ingredients in a large bowl. Divide into 8 equal portions and shape into patties. Lightly brush the patties with olive oil and place them in the air fry basket and close the fry lid. Air Fry for 5 minutes, then flip. Cook for another 5 minutes until patties are evenly brown. Serve.

45. Almond & Chocolate Bear Claws

Serves: 4 | Total Time: 15 minutes

1 frozen puff pastry dough sheet	1 tbsp confectioners' sugar	1 tsp amaretto liqueur
1 large egg, beaten	1 tbsp sliced almonds	
½ cup chocolate-hazelnut spread	½ tsp almond extract	

Preheat your Instant Pot Duo Crisp to 320°F. Unfold puff pastry and cut into 4 equal squares. Beat egg with amaretto liqueur and almond extract and brush each pastry with egg. Spread 2 tablespoons of chocolate-hazelnut spread over the pastry square. Fold horizontally to make a rectangle. Cut four slits evenly spaced on the fold about halfway through the pastry. Sprinkle with confectioners' sugar and almonds. Place bear claws into in the air fry basket and close the fry lid. Air Fry for 10 minutes. The pastry will be puffy and golden. Serve warm.

Line the air fry basket with parchment paper. Place the pastries in the basket in the air fry basket and close the fry lid. Bake for 12 minutes. Flip the pastries and cook for another 3 minutes. Pastries will be golden. While the pastries cool for 10 minutes, whisk the confectioner's sugar, milk, orange zest, and vanilla in a small bowl. When the pastries are cool enough, brush with glaze and refrigerate for 5 minutes. Serve and enjoy!

46. Sweet Bread Pudding with Raisins

Servings: 3 | Ready in about: 45 minutes

8 slices of bread	2 eggs	4 tbsp raisins
½ cup buttermilk	½ tsp vanilla extract	2 tbsp chopped hazelnuts
¼ cup honey	2 tbsp butter, softened	Cinnamon for garnish
1 cup milk	¼ cup sugar	

Beat the eggs along with the buttermilk, honey, milk, vanilla, sugar, and butter. Stir in raisins and hazelnuts. Cut the bread into cubes and place it in a bowl. Pour the milk mixture over the bread. Let soak for about 10 minutes. Close the air fry lid and cook the bread pudding for 25 minutes on Roast mode. Leave the dessert to cool for 5 minutes, then invert onto a plate and sprinkle with cinnamon to serve.

47. Home-Style Maple-Bacon Donuts

Serves: 8 | Total Time: 10 minutes

1 (16.3-oz) can refrigerated biscuit dough, separated

1 cup confectioners' sugar	1 tsp maple extract	6 cooked bacon slices, crumbled
¼ cup half and half	¼ tsp ground nutmeg	

Preheat your Instant Pot Duo Crisp to 350°F. Arrange biscuits in the air fryer basket and close the lid. Air Fry for 3 minutes. Flip the biscuits and cook for another 2 minutes or until the biscuits are golden.

While the biscuits are cooling for 5 minutes, whisk confectioners' sugar, nutmeg, half and half, and maple extract in a bowl until smooth. Dip donut tops into glaze when cooled and place on a rack for 5 minutes until set. Garnish with bacon and serve immediately.

48. Cheddar & Turkey Bacon Egg Muffins

Servings: 4 | Ready in about: 15 minutes

4 turkey bacon slices, diced	4 eggs	4 tbsp shredded cheddar cheese
¼ tsp lemon pepper seasoning	1 scallion, chopped and divided	Salt to taste

In a bowl, whisk together the eggs, lemon pepper, and salt. Divide the cheese, scallion, and bacon between 4 muffin cups. Pour the egg mixture over. Pour 1 cup of water into your Instant Pot and arrange the muffin cups on the rack. Secure the lid, select Pressure Cook, and cook for 10 minutes. When it beeps, do a quick pressure release.

49. Easy Bagels

Serves: 4 | Total Time: 20 minutes

1 cup self-rising flour
1 cup Greek yogurt
3 tbsp honey
1 large egg, whisked
1 tsp poppy seeds

Preheat your Instant Pot Duo Crisp to 320°F. Mix flour, yogurt, and honey in a large bowl to form the dough. Lightly flour a work surface and turn the dough out onto the surface. Knead for 3 minutes and form into a ball. Divide the dough into 4 equal sections. Roll each section into a rope, then connect the two ends to make a bagel shape. Brush both sides of the bagel with egg and sprinkle with poppy seeds.

Place the bagel into in the air fry basket and close the fry lid. Air Fry for 5 minutes. Flip the bagels, then cook for another 5 minutes for even browning. Let cool for 5 minutes. Serve and enjoy!

50. Yummy French Toast Strips

Serves: 4 | Total Time: 15 minutes

4 challah bread slices
2 large eggs
¼ cup heavy cream
4 tbsp butter, melted
½ cup sugar
1 tbsp honey
1 ½ tbsp ground cinnamon

Preheat your Instant Pot Duo Crisp to 350°F. Whisk together eggs and heavy cream in a bowl. Cut bread into sticks and dip into egg mixture. Transfer to the air fry basket. Close the fry lid and Air Fry for 5 minutes. Flip the toast and cook for another 3 minutes. Both sides will be golden.

While the French toast is cooking, combine sugar and cinnamon in a bowl. When the toast is made, drizzle the sticks with butter and honey until completely coated. Dip the sticks in the cinnamon-sugar mixture and shake off excess. Serve warm.

51. Pillsbury Danish

Serves: 4 | Total Time: 15 minutes

1 puff pastry dough sheet
1 large egg, beaten
4 oz mascarpone, softened
¼ cup confectioners' sugar
1 tsp vanilla extract
½ tsp lemon juice
½ tsp lemon zest

Preheat your Instant Pot Duo Crisp to 320°F. Unfold puff pastry and cut into 4 equal squares. Fold each pastry by bringing in all four corners toward the center, leaving a 1-inch square. Brush each pastry with the beaten egg.

Combine mascarpone cheese, confectioners' sugar, vanilla, lemon zest and lemon juice in a bowl. Place 2 tablespoons of cream cheese mixture into the center of each pastry. Arrange the danishes in the air fry basket and close the fry lid. Bake for 10 minutes. Danishes will be puffy and golden. Let cool for 5 minutes and serve warm.

52. Ham & Cheese Egg Bites

Serves: 2 | Total Time: 15 minutes

2 eggs
¼ cup goat cheese
¼ cup grated sharp cheddar cheese
Salt and black pepper to taste
6 tbsp diced cooked ham
1 tsp parsley, chopped

Preheat your Instant Pot Duo Crisp to 300°F. Mix the eggs, goat cheese, cheddar cheese, salt, and pepper in a blender. Pulse five times until frothy and combined.

Grease 6 muffin cups. Place 1 tablespoon of ham in the bottom of each cup. Pour equal amounts of egg mixture between the cups. Place the muffin cups in the air fry basket and close the fry lid. Bake for 8-10 minutes. Egg bites will be firm in the center. Remove and cool for 3 minutes. Sprinkle with parsley and serve warm.

53. Garlicky Baby Potatoes

Serves: 4 | Total Time: 30 minutes

1 lb cooked baby potatoes, quartered	½ tsp garlic powder	1 tbsp chopped parsley
2 tbsp olive oil	1 tbsp dried thyme	Salt and black pepper to taste

Preheat your Instant Pot Duo Crisp to 400°F. Drizzle oil over the potatoes, then add garlic powder, salt, thyme, salt, and pepper. Gently stir to coat. Transfer to the air fry basket and close the fry lid. Roast for 4 minutes. Shake the basket, then cook for another 4 minutes. Repeat this process one more time. Potatoes will be golden with crisp edges. Serve warm sprinkled with parsley and enjoy!

54. Morning Bacon Quiche

Serves: 4 | Total Time: 30 minutes

1 refrigerated piecrust	Salt and black pepper to taste	1 tbsp chopped parsley
2 large eggs	½ cup grated mozzarella cheese	
¼ cup buttermilk	2 cooked bacon slices, crumbled	

Preheat your Instant Pot Duo Crisp to 350°F. Lightly spray a pie pan with cooking oil. Place crust in the pan and trim to fit. Whisk eggs, buttermilk, salt, and pepper in a bowl. Mix in mozzarella and bacon. Pour mixture into the crust and place in the air fry basket and close the fry lid. Bake for 18 minutes. Eggs will be firm and golden. A knife in the middle will come out clean. Serve warm sprinkled with parsley.

55. Vanilla & Raspberry Puff Pastry

Serves: 6 | Total Time: 25 minutes

1 refrigerated pie crust	½ cup confectioners' sugar	½ tsp orange zest
1 cup raspberry jam	2 tbsp milk	
1 egg, whisked	½ tsp vanilla extract	

Preheat your Instant Pot Duo Crisp to 320°F. Lightly flour a work surface. Lay out pie crust and cut each crust into 6 rectangles. Combine excess dough and roll out to cut into 4 rectangles. Take 1 pastry rectangle and spread with 2 tablespoons of raspberry jam. Top with another pastry rectangle and seal all four edges by pressing with a fork. Repeat the process with the remaining jam and pastry. Brush the top of pastries with the egg. Vent the top by cutting an X to prevent steam from building up.

56. Hazelnut-Banana Muffins

Serves: 6 | Total Time: 20 minutes

1 ½ cups flour	½ cup butter, melted	2 bananas, mashed
½ cup sugar	1 tsp vanilla extract	½ cup chopped hazelnuts
1 tsp baking powder	1 large egg	

Preheat your Instant Pot Duo Crisp to 300°F. Whisk flour, sugar, and baking powder in a large bowl. Stir in butter, vanilla, egg, and bananas until well combined in a thick batter. Fold in hazelnuts. Divide the batter into 12 silicone muffin cups about half full. Place muffin cups in the air fry basket and close the fry lid. Bake for 15 minutes. Edges will be brown, and a toothpick in the middle comes out clean. Let muffins stand for 5 minutes to cool. Serve.

57. Sausage Egg Bake

Serves: 4 | Total Time: 20 minutes

6 eggs	Salt and black pepper to taste	½ cup grated mozzarella cheese
2 tbsp buttermilk	⅓ lb cooked ground pork sausage	

Preheat your Instant Pot Duo Crisp to 320°F. Whisk eggs, buttermilk, salt, and pepper in a large bowl. Lightly grease a baking pan. Add cooked sausage and arrange in an even layer. Next, pour the egg mixture over the sausage. Top with mozzarella. Place the pan in the air fry basket and close the fry lid. Bake for 15 minutes. The top will be golden, and the center is set. Remove from air fryer and let cool for 5 minutes. Serve warm.

58. Hot Red Poached Eggs

Servings: 4 | Ready in about: 10 minutes

4 eggs	3 tomatoes, chopped	1 tbsp olive oil
½ tsp paprika	1 small red onion, chopped	
1 tsp chili powder	1 tbsp chopped fresh dill	

Pour the 1 cup of water into the Instant Pot and lower the rack. Grease 4 ramekins with the olive oil. Crack the eggs into the ramekins and whisk them slightly.

In a bowl, combine the rest of the ingredients and divide this mixture between the ramekins. Place the ramekins on the rack and secure the lid. Select Pressure Cook and cook for 5 minutes on High. Do a quick release and serve.

59. Feta & Spinach Egg Cups

Servings: 6 | Ready in about: 15 minutes

½ cup shredded mozzarella cheese	1 cup chopped spinach, divided	¼ cup crumbled feta cheese
6 eggs	1 cup water	
Salt and black pepper to taste	1 tomato, chopped	

Pour the water into your Instant Pot. Lower the trivet. Divide the spinach between silicone ramekins. In a bowl, whisk together the eggs, salt and pepper. Stir in the remaining ingredients. Divide that mixture between the ramekins. Place in the Instant Pot. Secure the lid, select Pressure Cook, and cook on High for 8 minutes. Once the timer goes off, do a quick pressure release. Carefully remove the lid and serve immediately.

60. Cinnamon Butternut Squash Pie

Servings: 4 | Ready in about about: 30 minutes

1 lb Butternut Squash, diced	½ cup Milk	1 cup Water
1 Egg	½ tsp Cinnamon	A pinch of Sea Salt
¼ cup Honey	½ tbsp Cornstarch	

Pour the water inside your Instant Pot and add a trivet. Lower the butternut squash onto the trivet. Seal the pressure lid, and cook on Pressure for 4 minutes at High pressure. Whisk all remaining ingredients in a bowl. Do a quick pressure. Drain the squash and add it to the milk mixture. Pour the batter into a greased baking dish. Place in the cooker, and seal the pressure lid. Choose Pressure Cook on High, and set the time to 10 minutes. Do a quick pressure release. Transfer pie to wire rack to cool.

61. Mayo-Chocolate Cake

Serves: 6 | Total Time: 35 minutes

1 cup flour	1 tbsp coconut flakes	1 cup mayonnaise
½ cup sugar	1 tsp baking powder	1 tsp vanilla extract
1 tbsp orange zest	¼ cup cocoa powder	½ cup milk

Preheat your Instant Pot Duo Crisp to 300°F. Mix flour, sugar, baking powder, and cocoa powder in a large bowl. Next, stir in mayonnaise, vanilla, orange zest, and milk until the batter is thick but pourable. Grease a cake pan and pour in the batter. Transfer the pan to the air fryer basket and close the fry lid. Bake for 25 minutes. A toothpick in the middle will come out clean. Serve warm sprinkled with coconut flakes and enjoy!

SNACKS & SIDE DISHES

62. Tangy Cheesy Arancini

Servings: 6 | Ready in about: 105 minutes

½ cup olive oil + 1 tbsp	½ cup apple cider vinegar	Salt and black pepper to taste
1 small white onion, diced	2 cups short-grain rice	2 cups fresh panko bread crumbs
2 garlic cloves, minced	1 ½ cups grated Parmesan	2 large eggs
5 cups chicken stock	1 cup chopped green beans	

Choose Sauté on your Instant Pot. Add 1 tablespoon of oil and the onion, cook the onion until translucent, add the garlic and cook further for 2 minutes or until the garlic starts getting fragrant. Stir in the stock, vinegar, and rice. Seal the pressure lid, choose Pressure Cook on High, and set the time to 7 minutes.

After cooking, perform a natural pressure release for 10 minutes, then a quick pressure release and carefully open the pressure lid. Stir in the Parmesan cheese, green beans, salt, and pepper to mash the rice until a risotto forms. Spoon the mixture into a bowl and set aside to cool completely. Clean the pot.

In a bowl, combine the breadcrumbs and the remaining olive oil. In another bowl, lightly beat the eggs. Form 12 balls out of the risotto or as many as you can get. Dip each into the beaten eggs, and coat in the breadcrumb mixture. Put half of the rice balls in the air fry basket in a single layer. Close the air fry lid, hit Air Fry, set the temperature to 400°F, and set the time to 10 minutes. Leave to cool before serving.

63. Brazilian Cheese Balls

Servings: 4 | Ready in about: 35 minutes

2 cups flour	A pinch of salt	2 cups grated mozzarella cheese
1 cup milk	2 eggs, cracked into a bowl	½ cup olive oil

Select Sauté on your Instant Pot. Add the milk, oil, and salt, and let boil. Add the flour and mix it vigorously with a spoon. Let the mixture cool. Once cooled, use a hand mixer to mix the dough well, and add the eggs and cheese while still mixing. The dough should be thick and sticky.

Use your hands to make 14 balls out of the mixture, and put them in the greased basket. Put the air fry basket the pot and close the air fry lid. Select Air Fry, set the temperature to 380°F and set the timer to 15 minutes. At the 7-minute mark, shake the balls. Serve with lemon aioli, garlic mayo or ketchup.

64. Kale-Artichoke Bites

Servings: 8 | Ready in about: 70 minutes

¼ cup frozen chopped kale	¼ cup goat cheese	½ tsp salt
¼ cup finely chopped artichoke hearts	1 large egg white	½ tsp freshly ground black pepper
¼ cup ricotta cheese	1 tsp dried basil	4 sheets frozen phyllo dough, thawed
2 tbsp grated Parmesan cheese	1 lemon, zested	1 tbsp olive oil

In a bowl, mix kale, artichoke hearts, ricotta cheese, Parmesan, goat cheese, egg white, basil, lemon zest, salt, and pepper. Place a phyllo sheet on a clean flat surface. Brush with olive oil, place a second phyllo sheet on top, and brush with oil. Continue layering to form a pile of 4 oiled sheets. Working from the short side, cut the phyllo sheets into 8 strips. Cut the strips in half to form 16 strips. Spoon 1 tbsp of filling onto 1 short side of every strip.

Fold a corner to cover the filling to make a triangle. Continue repeatedly folding to the end of the strip, creating a triangle-shaped phyllo packet. Repeat the process with the other phyllo bites. Place half of the pastry in the air fry basket in a single layer. Close the lid, choose Air Fry, set the temperature to 350°F, and the timer to 12 minutes. After 6 minutes, open the lid, and flip the bites. Return the basket to the pot and close the lid to continue baking. When ready, take out the bites into a plate. Serve warm.

65. Hot Chicken Wings

Servings: 4 | Ready in about: 60 minutes

½ cup sriracha sauce
2 tbsp butter, melted
1 tbsp lemon juice
2 lb chicken wings, frozen
½ (1-oz) ranch salad mix
½ tsp paprika

Mix ½ cup water, sriracha, butter and lemon juice or vinegar in your Instant Pot. In the air fry basket, put the wings, and then the basket into the pot. Seal the pressure lid, choose Pressure Cook on High, set the timer at 5 minutes. When the timer is done reading, perform a quick pressure release, and carefully open the lid. Pour the paprika and ranch dressing all over the chicken and oil with cooking spray. Cover the air fry lid. Choose Air Fry, set the temperature to 390°F, and the timer to 15 minutes. Choose Start to commence frying. After half the cooking time, open the lid, remove the basket and shake the wings. Oil the chicken again with cooking spray and return the basket to the pot. Close the lid and continue cooking until the wings are crispy.

66. Hot Buttery Chicken Meatballs

Servings: 6 | Ready in about: 90 minutes

1 lb ground chicken
1 green bell pepper, minced
2 celery stalks, minced
¼ cup crumbled queso fresco
¼ cup hot sauce
¼ cup panko bread crumbs
1 egg
2 tbsp melted butter
½ cup water

Choose Sauté on your Instant Pot. In a bowl, evenly combine the chicken, bell pepper, celery, queso fresco, hot sauce, breadcrumbs, and egg. Form meatballs out of the mixture. Then, pour the melted butter into the pot and fry the meatballs in batches until lightly browned on all sides. Remove the meatballs to a plate.

Put the air fry basket in the pot. Pour in the water and put all the meatballs in the basket. Seal the pressure lid, choose Pressure Cook on High, and set the timer to 5 minutes. When done, perform a quick pressure release. Remove the water. Close the air fry lid. Choose Air Fry, set the temperature to 400°F, and set the time to 10 minutes. After 5 minutes, open the lid, lift the basket and shake the meatballs. Return the basket to the pot and close the lid to continue cooking until the meatballs are crispy.

67. Cheesy Smashed Sweet Potatoes

Servings: 4 | Ready in about: 70 minutes

12 oz baby sweet potatoes
1 tsp melted butter
¼ cup shredded Monterey Jack cheese
¼ cup sour cream
2 slices bacon, cooked and crumbled
1 tbsp chopped scallions

Toss the sweet potatoes with the melted butter until evenly coated. Add the sweet potatoes to the air fry basket. Close the air fry lid, choose Air Fry, set the temperature to 350°F. Cook for 30 minutes. After 15 minutes, open the lid, pull out the basket and shake the potatoes. Return the basket to the pot and close the lid to continue cooking.

When ended, check the sweet potatoes for your desired crispiness, which should also be fork tender. Take out the sweet potatoes from the basket and use a large spoon to crush the soft potatoes just to split lightly. Top with the cheese, sour cream, bacon, and scallions, and season with salt.

68. Parmesan Cabbage Side Dish

Servings: 4 | Ready in about: 30 minutes

½ head of cabbage, cut into 4 wedges
4 tbsp butter, melted
2 cup Parmesan cheese
Salt and black pepper to taste
1 tsp smoked paprika

Line the basket with parchment paper. Brush the butter over the cabbage wedges. Season with salt and pepper. Coat the cabbage with the Parmesan cheese. Arrange in the basket and sprinkle with paprika. Close the air fry lid and cook for 15 minutes on Air Fry mode, flip over and cook for an additional 10 minutes at 330°F.

69. BBQ Chicken Drumsticks

Servings: 6 | Ready in about: 30 minutes

3 lb chicken drumsticks	Salt to taste	¼ cup butter, melted
3 tbsp garlic powder	1 cup Barbecue sauce	½ cup water

Season drumsticks with garlic powder and salt. Pour the water in your Instant Pot and fit in a trivet. Arrange the drumsticks on top, seal the pressure lid, and select Pressure Cook for 5 minutes. Once the timer has ended, do a natural pressure release for 10 minutes, and then a quick pressure release to let out any more steam. Remove the drumsticks to a air fry basket and add the butter and half of the barbecue sauce.

Stir the chicken until well coated in the sauce. Insert the air fry basket in your Instant Pot and close the air fry lid. Select Air Fry, set to 380°F, and cook for 10 minutes. Select Start. Once nice and crispy, remove drumsticks to a bowl, and top with the remaining barbecue sauces. Stir and serve the chicken with a cheese dip.

70. Asparagus Wrapped in Prosciutto with Dip

Servings: 6 | Ready in about: 15 minutes

1 lb asparagus, stalks trimmed	10 oz Prosciutto, thinly sliced	Cooking spray

For the Dip:

1 cup canned garbanzo beans	2 medium jalapeños, chopped	1 ½ tbsp olive oil
1 medium onion, diced	1 cup crushed tomatoes	1 tsp paprika
2 cloves of garlic, minced	1 cup vegetable broth	½ tsp chili powder

Add the garbanzo beans, onion, jalapeños, garlic, tomatoes, broth, oil, paprika, chili powder, and salt to your Instant Pot. Seal the pressure lid and select Pressure Cook on High for 8 minutes. Once the timer has ended, do a quick pressure release, and open the pot. Transfer the ingredients to a food processor, and blend until creamy and smooth. Set aside. Wrap each asparagus with a slice of prosciutto from top to bottom.

Grease the air fry basket with cooking spray, and add in the wrapped asparagus. Close the air fry lid, select Air Fry mode at 370°F and set the time to 8 minutes. At the 4-minute mark, turn the bombs. Remove the wrapped asparagus onto a plate and serve with bean dip.

71. Cheese bombs wrapped in Bacon

Servings: 8 | Ready in about: 20 minutes

16 oz Mozzarella, cut into 8 pieces	8 bacon slices, cut in half	3 tbsp butter, melted

Wrap each cheese string with a slice of bacon and secure the ends with toothpicks. Set aside. Grease the air fry basket with the melted butter and add in the bombs. Close the air fry lid, select Air Fry mode, and set the temperature to 370°F and set the time to 10 minutes. At the 5-minute mark, turn the bombs. When ready, remove to a paper-lined plate to drain the excess oil. Serve on a platter with toothpicks and tomato dip.

72. Teriyaki Chicken Wings

Servings: 6 | Ready in about: 30 minutes

1 tbsp honey	1 tsp finely ground black pepper	2 tbsp cornstarch
1 cup teriyaki sauce	2 lb chicken wings	1 tsp sesame seeds

In your Instant Pot, combine honey, teriyaki sauce and black pepper until the honey dissolves completely. Toss in chicken to coat. Seal the pressure lid, choose Pressure Cook on High, and set the timer to 10 minutes. When ready, release the pressure quickly. Transfer chicken wings to a platter. Mix 2 tbsp cold water with the cornstarch. Press Sauté and stir in cornstarch slurry into the sauce and cook for 3 to 5 minutes until thickened. Top the chicken with thickened sauce. Add a garnish of sesame seeds, and serve.

73. Sweet Butter Rolls

Serves: 16 | Total Time: 25 minutes + rising time

4 tbsp butter, melted	1 large egg	3 cups flour
¼ cup sugar	1 tsp vanilla extract	1 tbsp powdered sugar
1 tbsp quick-rise yeast	1 tsp salt	

Pour 2 tablespoons of butter in a large bowl along with sugar, 1 cup of hot water, and yeast. Stir with a spatula until yeast is dissolved. Next, stir in egg, vanilla extract, salt, and 2 ¼ cups flour until just combined and sticky. Cover the bowl and let rise in a warm area for 1 hour. When the dough is ready, sprinkle ¼ cup flour on the dough and transfer to a floured work surface. Knead for 2 minutes, then cut the dough into 16 equal pieces.

Preheat your Instant Pot Duo Crisp to 350°F. Lightly spray a cake pan with cooking oil. Sprinkle flour on each roll and arrange them in the pan. Brush the rest of the butter on the rolls and place the pan in the fry basket and close the fry lid. Air Fry for 10 minutes. Rolls will be fluffy and golden on top. Serve sprinkled with powdered sugar.

74. Fried Beef Dumplings

Servings: 8 | Ready in about: 45 minutes

8 oz ground beef	1 garlic clove, minced	½ tsp salt
½ cup grated cabbage	2 tbsp coconut aminos	½ tsp freshly ground black pepper
1 carrot, grated	½ tbsp melted ghee	20 wonton wrappers
1 large egg, beaten	½ tbsp ginger powder	2 tbsp olive oil

In a large bowl, mix the beef, cabbage, carrot, egg, garlic, coconut aminos, ghee, ginger, salt, and black pepper. Put the wonton wrappers on a clean flat surface and spoon 1 tablespoon of the beef mixture into the middle of each wrapper. Run the edges of the wrapper with a little water. Fold the wrapper to cover the filling into a semi-circle shape and pinch the edges to seal. Brush the dumplings with olive oil.

Lay the dumplings in the preheated basket, choose Air Fry, set the temperature to 400°F, and set the time to 12 minutes. frying. After 6 minutes, open the lid, pull out the basket and shake the dumplings. Return the basket to the pot and close the lid to continue frying until the dumplings are crispy to your desire.

75. Wrapped Asparagus in Bacon

Servings: 6 | Ready in about: 30 minutes

1 lb asparagus spears, trimmed	1 lb bacon, sliced	½ cup Parmesan cheese, grated

Place the bacon slices out on a work surface, top each one with one asparagus spear and half of the cheese. Wrap the bacon around the asparagus. Line the air fry basket with parchment paper. Arrange the wraps into the basket. Scatter over the remaining cheese, season with salt and black pepper, and spray with cooking spray. Close the air fry lid and cook for 8 to 10 minutes on Roast mode at 390°F. If necessary work in batches. Serve hot.

76. Green Vegan Dip

Servings: 4 | Ready in about: 20 minutes

10 oz canned green chiles	¾ cup green bell pepper, chopped	½ tsp sea salt
2 cups broccoli florets	¼ cup raw cashews	¼ tsp chili powder
1 cup water	¼ cup soy sauce	¼ tsp garlic powder

In the cooker, add cashews, broccoli, green bell pepper, and water. Seal the pressure lid, choose Pressure Cook on High, and set the timer to 5 minutes. When ready, release the pressure quickly. Drain water from the pot. Add the liquid from canned green chilies, salt, garlic powder, chili powder, soy sauce, and cumin. Use an immersion blender to blend the mixture until smooth. Set aside. Stir green chilies through the dip. Serve.

SNACKS& SIDE DISHES

77. Buffalo Chicken Meatballs with Ranch Dip

Servings: 4 | Ready in about: 34 minutes

5 tbsp Hot sauce	1 egg, beaten	2 tbsp chopped green onions
2 tbsp Buffalo wing sauce	2 tbsp minced garlic	Green onions for garnish
1 lb ground chicken	2 tbsp olive oil	Salt and black pepper to taste

For the dip

½ cup Roquefort cheese, crumbled	2 tbsp mayonnaise	2 tbsp olive oil
¼ tbsp heavy cream	Juice from ½ lemon	

Mix all salsa ingredients in a bowl until uniform and creamy, and refrigerate. Add the ground chicken, salt, garlic, and two tablespoons of green onions. Mix well with your hands. Rub your hands with some oil and form bite-size balls out of the mixture. Lay onto air fry basket. Spray with cooking spray.

Select Air Fry, set the temperature to 385°F and the time to 14 minutes. At the 7-minute mark, turn the meatballs. Add the hot sauce and butter to a bowl and microwave them until the butter melts. Mix the sauce with a spoon. Pour the hot sauce mixture and a half cup of water over the meatballs. Seal the pressure lid and select Pressure Cook on High for 10 minutes. Once the timer has ended, do a quick pressure release. Dish the meatballs. Garnish with green onions, and serve with Roquefort sauce.

78. Holiday Egg Brulee

Servings: 8 | Ready in about: 12 minutes

8 large eggs	Salt to taste	1 cup water

Pour the water in your Instant Pot and fit in a trivet. Put the eggs on the trivet in a single layer, seal the pressure lid, and select Pressure on High Pressure for 5 minutes. Once the timer has ended, do a quick pressure release, and open the pot. Remove the eggs into the ice bath and peel the eggs. Put the peeled eggs in a plate and slice them in half. Sprinkle a bit of salt on them and then followed by the sugar. Lay onto air fry basket. Select Air Fry mode, set the temperature to 390°F and the time to 3 minutes.

79. Creamy Tomato & Parsley Dip

Servings: 6 | Ready in about: 18 minutes

1 cup chopped tomatoes	¼ cup chopped parsley	½ cup heavy cream
10 oz shredded Parmesan cheese	10 oz cream cheese	1 cup water

Pour the tomatoes, parsley, heavy cream, cream cheese, and water in your Instant Pot. Seal the pressure lid and select Pressure for 3 minutes at High. Once the timer has ended, do a natural pressure release for 10 minutes. Stir the mixture with a spoon while mashing the tomatoes with the back of the spoon. Add the parmesan cheese and Close the air fry lid. Select Bake mode, set the temperature to 370°F and the time to 3 minutes. Dish the dip into a bowl and serve with chips or veggie bites.

80. Sweet-Heat Pickled Cucumbers

Servings: 6 | Ready in about: 5 minutes

1 lb small cucumbers, sliced into rings	1 cup sugar	2 tsp salt
2 cups white vinegar	¼ cup green garlic, minced	1 tsp cumin
1 cup water	2 tbsp Dill Pickle Seasoning	

To your Instant Pot, add sliced cucumber, vinegar and pour water on top. Sprinkle sugar over cucumbers. Add cumin, dill pickle seasoning, and salt. Stir well to dissolve the sugar. Seal the pressure lid, choose Pressure Cook on High, and set the timer to 4 minutes. When ready, release the pressure quickly. Ladle cucumbers into a large storage container and pour cooking liquid over the top. Chill for 1 hour.

81. Basil Mushroom Stuffed Eggplant Boats

Servings: 4 | Ready in about: 50 minutes

4 eggplants	1 ½ cups grated cheddar cheese	1 tbsp olive oil
1 lb mushrooms, chopped.	1 cup diced celery	1 tbsp dried basil
1 ½ cups water	1 onion, diced	Salt and black pepper to taste

Cut the eggplants in half and scoop out the flesh. Save the hollowed out eggplants for later. Pour the water into the pressure cooker. Combine the eggplant filling and the remaining ingredients, except for the cheese. Place the eggplant mixture into the cooking liquid in the Instant Pot.

Secure the lid, press Pressure Cook and cook on High for 5 minutes on High. Release the pressure naturally, for 10 minutes. Divide the filling between the eggplants and arrange them on the rack, drizzle with oil, and sprinkle with salt and pepper. Seal the lid and cook on Pressure Cook for 15 minutes. Once it's completed, perform a quick pressure release. Sprinkle with cheese. Return to the pressure cooker and cook for 5 more minutes on SAUTE mode until the cheese starts to melt. Serve immediately.

82. Scrumptious Honey-Mustard Hot Dogs

Servings: 4 | Ready in about: 22 minutes

20 Hot Dogs, cut into 4 pieces	¼ cup honey	½ cup tomato puree
1 tsp Dijon mustard	¼ cup red wine vinegar	¼ cup water
1½ tsp soy sauce	Salt and black pepper to taste	

Add the tomato puree, red wine vinegar, honey, soy sauce, Dijon mustard, salt, and black pepper in a medium bowl. Mix them with a spoon. Put sausage weenies in the air fry basket, and close the air fry lid. Select Air Fry. Set the temperature to 370°F and the timer to 4 minutes. At the 2-minute mark, turn the sausages. Once ready, open the lid and pour the sweet sauce over the sausage weenies. Seal the pressure lid and select Pressure Cook on High for 3 minutes. Once the timer has ended, do a quick pressure release. Serve and enjoy.

83. Cauliflower and Cheddar Tater Tots

Servings: 10 | Ready in about: 35 minutes

2 lb cauliflower florets, steamed	1 cup breadcrumbs	1 tsp chopped oregano
5 oz cheddar cheese	1 egg, beaten	1 tsp chopped chives
1 onion, diced	1 tsp chopped parsley	1 tsp garlic powder

Mash the cauliflower and place it in a large bowl. Add the onion, parsley, oregano, chives, garlic powder, salt, and pepper, and cheddar cheese. Mix with hands until thoroughly combined. Form 12 balls out of the mixture. Line a baking sheet with wax paper. Dip the tater tots into the egg and then coat with breadcrumbs. Arrange them on the baking sheet, close the air fry lid, and cook in your Instant Pot at 350°F for 15 minutes on Air Fry mode.

84. Homemade Spinach Hummus

Servings: 12 | Ready in about: 1 hour 10 minutes

8 cups water	Salt to taste	2 cups spinach, chopped
2 cups dried chickpeas	½ cup tahini	5 garlic cloves, crushed
5 tbsp grapeseed oil	5 tbsp lemon juice	

In your Instant Pot, mix 2 tbsp oil, water, salt, and chickpeas. Seal the pressure lid, choose Pressure Cook on High, and set the timer to 35 minutes. When ready, release the pressure quickly. In a small bowl, reserve ½ cup of the cooking liquid and drain chickpeas. Mix half the reserved cooking liquid and chickpeas in a food processor. Puree until no large chickpeas remain. Add remaining cooking liquid, spinach, lemon juice, salt, garlic, and tahini. Process hummus for 8 minutes until smooth. Stir in the remaining 3 tbsp of olive oil before serving.

85. Melt-in-the-Middle Meatballs

Servings: 6 | Ready in about: 30 minutes

2 lb ground beef	2 tbsp chopped chives	½ cup Parmesan cheese, grated
1 potato, shredded	½ tsp garlic powder	1 package cooked spaghetti to serve
2 eggs, beaten	Salt and black pepper to taste	2 cups tomato sauce to serve

In a large bowl, combine the potato, salt, pepper, garlic powder, eggs, and chives. Form 12 balls out of the mixture. Spray with cooking spray. Arrange half of the balls onto a lined air fry basket. Close the air fry lid and cook for 14 minutes on Air Fry mode at 330°F. After 7 minutes, turn the meatballs. Repeat with the other half. Serve over cooked spaghetti mixed with tomato sauce, sprinkled with Parmesan cheese.

86. New York Steak and Minty Cheese

Servings: 4 | Ready in about: 15 minutes

2 New York strip steaks	8 oz halloumi cheese	2 tbsp chopped mint
12 kalamata olives	2 tbsp chopped parsley	Juice and zest of 1 lemon

Season the steaks with salt and pepper, and gently brush with olive oil. Place into your Instant Pot, close the air fry lid and cook for 6 minutes (for medium rare) on Air Fry mode at 350°F. When ready, remove to a plate and set aside. Drizzle the cheese with olive oil and place it in the pot. Cook for 4 minutes. Remove to a serving platter and serve with sliced steaks and olives, sprinkled with herbs, and lemon zest and juice.

87. Bacon & Cheese Dip

Servings: 10 | Ready in about: 10 minutes

4 chopped tomatoes	1 ¼ cups cream cheese	1 cup water
1¼ cup shredded Monterey Jack cheese	10 bacon slices, chopped roughly	

On your Instant Pot and select Air Fry. Set the temperature to 370°F and the time to 8 minutes. Add the bacon and close the air fry lid. When ready, add the water, cream cheese, and tomatoes. Do Not Stir. Seal the pressure lid and select Pressure Cook for 5 minutes. Do a quick pressure release. Stir in the cheddar cheese. Serve.

88. Sweet Paprika Hard-Boiled Eggs

Servings: 3 | Ready in about: 25 minutes

6 eggs	Salt and black pepper to taste	1 tsp sweet paprika

To your Instant Pot, add 1 cup water and place a trivet on top. Lay eggs on the trivet. Seal the lid, choose Pressure Cook on High, and set the timer to 5 minutes. Once ready, do a natural release for 10 minutes. Transfer the eggs to ice-cold water to cool completely. When cooled, peel and slice; season. Sprinkle with sweet paprika to serve.

89. Air Fried Pin Wheels

Servings: 6 | Ready in about: 50 minutes

1 sheet puff pastry	1 ½ cups Gruyere cheese, grated
8 ham slices	4 tsp Dijon mustard

Place the pastry on a lightly floured flat surface. Brush the mustard over and arrange the ham slices. Top with cheese. Start at the shorter edge and roll up the pastry. Wrap it in a plastic foil and place in the freezer for about half an hour, until it becomes firm and comfortable to cut. Slice the pastry into 6 rounds. Line the air fry basket with parchment paper, and arrange the pinwheels on top. Close the air fry lid and cook for 10 minutes on Air Fry mode at 390°F. Leave to cool on a wire rack before serving.

90. Ajillo Green Beans

Servings: 4 | Ready in about: 10 minutes

1 pound green beans	3 tbsp olive oil	2 tbsp white wine vinegar
1 cup water	3 garlic cloves, minced	Salt and pepper to taste

Combine the water and green beans in your Instant Pot. Secure the lid, select Pressure Cook, and cook on High for 1 minute on High. Carefully open the lid and transfer to a serving bowl. In a small bowl, whisk together the olive oil, vinegar, garlic, salt, and pepper. Pour mixture over the green beans. Toss to combine.

91. Steamed Kale with Cashew Dressing

Servings: 4 | Ready in about: 10 minutes

1 cup raw cashews	1 ½ cups water	1 tbsp seasoning, any
10 oz kale	½ cup nutritional yeast	2 tsp vinegar

Combine the kale and water in your Instant Pot. Secure the lid, select Pressure Cook, and cook on High for 4 minutes. In a food processor, combine the yeast, cashews, and seasonings. Blend until powder forms. Transfer the kale to a serving platter and drizzle with vinegar. Top with the yeast and cashew mixture, and serve.

92. Easy Garbanzo Beans

Servings: 4 | Ready in about: 60 minutes

2 cups veggie broth	1 cup garbanzo beans, soaked	1 ½ tbsp olive oil
2 cups water	½ tsp black pepper	¾ cup chopped onion
1 tsp oregano	1 tsp cumin	2 garlic cloves, minced

Place all of the ingredients in your Instant Pot. Secure the lid, select Pressure Cook and cook for 45 minutes on High. Once the cooking is complete, allow pressure to release naturally for 10 minutes. Carefully open the lid and transfer the Pressure Cook to a deep bowl. Blend with a hand blender until smooth and serve warm.

93. Herby Fish Skewers

Servings: 4 | Ready in about: 75 minutes

3 tbsp olive oil	1 tsp parsley, chopped	1 lemon, cut in wedges to serve
2 garlic cloves, grated	Salt to taste	1 lb cod loin, boneless, skinless, cubed
1 tsp dill, chopped	1 lemon, juiced and zested	

In a bowl, combine the olive oil, garlic, dill, parsley, salt, and lemon juice. Stir in the cod and place in the fridge to marinate for 1 hour. Thread the cod pieces onto halved skewers. Arrange into the greased air fry basket, close the air fry lid, and cook for 10 minutes at 390°F. Flip them over halfway through cooking. When ready, remove to a serving platter, scatter lemon zest and serve with wedges.

94. Crispy Rosemary Potato Fries

Servings: 4 | Ready in about: 30 minutes

4 russet potatoes, cut into sticks	2 garlic cloves, crushed	Salt and black pepper to taste
2 tbsp butter, melted	1 tsp fresh rosemary, chopped	

Add butter, garlic, salt, and pepper to a bowl. Toss until the sticks are well-coated. Lay the potato sticks into the air fry basket. Close the air fry lid and cook for 15 minutes at 390°F. Shake the potatoes every 5 minutes. Once ready, check to ensure the fries are golden and crispy all over if not, return them to cook for a few minutes. Divide standing up between metal cups lined with nonstick baking paper, and serve sprinkled with rosemary.

95. Crispy Cheesy Straws

Servings: 8 | Ready in about: 45 minutes

2 cups cauliflower florets, steamed	3 ½ oz oats	1 tsp mustard
1 egg	1 red onion, diced	5 oz cheddar cheese

Add the oats to a food processor and process until they resemble breadcrumbs. Place the steamed florets in a cheesecloth and squeeze out the excess liquid. Put the florets in a bowl and add in the rest of the ingredient. Mix to combine the ingredients thoroughly. Take a little bit of the mixture and twist it into a straw. Place in the lined air fry basket. Repeat with the rest of the mixture. Close the air fry lid and cook for 10 minutes on Air Fry mode at 350°F. After 5 minutes, turn them over and cook for an additional 10 minutes.

96. Turkey Scotch Eggs

Servings: 6 | Ready in about: 20 minutes

10 oz ground turkey	½ cup flour	Salt and pepper to taste
4 eggs, soft boiled, peeled	2 garlic cloves, minced	½ cup breadcrumbs
1 white onion, chopped	2 eggs, lightly beaten	1 tsp dried mixed herbs

Mix the ground turkey, onion, garlic, salt, and pepper. Shape into 4 balls. Wrap the turkey mixture around each egg, and ensure the eggs are well covered. Dust each egg ball in flour, then dip in the beaten eggs and finally roll in the crumbs, until coated. Spray with cooking spray. Lay the eggs into the air fry basket. Set the temperature to 390°F, close the air fry lid and cook for 15 minutes. After 8 minutes, turn the eggs. Slice in half and serve warm.

97. Tomato & Mozzarella Bruschetta

Servings: 2 | Ready in about: 15 minutes

1 Italian Ciabatta Sandwich Bread	2 garlic cloves, minced	Salt and pepper to taste
Olive oil to brush	1 cup grated mozzarella cheese	
2 tomatoes, chopped	Basil leaves, chopped	

Cut the bread in half, lengthways, then each piece again in half. Drizzle each bit with olive oil and sprinkle with garlic. Top with the grated cheese, salt, and pepper. Place the bruschetta pieces into the air fry basket, close the air fry lid and cook for 12 minutes on Air Fry mode at 380°F. At 6 minutes, check for doneness. Once your Instant Pot beeps, remove the bruschetta to a serving platter, spoon over the tomatoes and chopped basil to serve.

98. Chicken & Cheese Bake

Servings: 6 | Ready in about: 1 hour 18 minutes

1 lb chicken breast	10 oz Cheddar cheese	10 oz cream cheese
½ cup breadcrumbs	½ cup sour cream	½ cup water

Open your Instant Pot and add the chicken, water, and cream cheese. Seal the pressure lid and select Pressure Cook on High for 10 minutes. Once the timer has ended, do a quick pressure release, and open the pot. Shred the chicken with two forks and add the cheddar cheese. Sprinkle with breadcrumbs, and close the air fry lid. Select Bake set the temperature to 380°F and the timer to 3 minutes. Serve warm with veggie bites.

99. Parmesan Lentil Purée

Servings: 6 | Ready in about: 15 minutes

1 lb lentils, cooked	2 tbsp parmesan cheese, grated	¼ cup red wine
2 tbsp tomato paste	2 tbsp olive oil	¼ tsp salt
2 tomatoes, diced	½ tsp oregano, dried	¼ tsp red pepper flakes

Grease your Instant Pot with oil. Press Sauté and add tomatoes, tomato paste, and half cup of water, salt and oregano and cook for 5 minutes, stirring constantly. Add lentils, wine and another half cup of water. Seal the lid, set the steam release handle and press Pressure Cook. Cook for 3 minutes on High. Once it goes off, perform a quick release. Let cool and sprinkle with Parmesan and red pepper flakes before serving.

100. Bacon & Potato Balls

Serves: 4 | Total Time: 25 minutes

2 cups mashed potatoes
¾ cup sour cream
Salt and black pepper to taste
½ cup grated sharp cheddar cheese
½ cup shredded mozzarella
1 cup shredded mozzarella
3 cooked bacon slices, crumbled
1 cup panko bread crumbs
1 tbsp chopped parsley

Preheat your Instant Pot Duo Crisp to 400°F. Combine mashed potatoes, ½ cup sour cream, salt, pepper, cheddar cheese, mozzarella, and bacon in a large bowl. Scoop 2 tablespoons of the potato mixture and shape it into a total of 12 balls. Divide ¼ cup sour cream by coating each ball in it before rolling them in bread crumbs to coat. Line the air fry basket with parchment paper. Transfer the potato balls into the basket and lightly spray with cooking oil. Close the fry lid and Air Fry for 10 minutes. Potato balls will be just brown. Serve topped with parsley.

101. Tomato Tofu Bake

Servings: 4 | Ready in about: 20 minutes + freezing time

1 block of firm tofu, crumbled
¼ cup vegetable broth
1 tbsp Italian seasoning
1 can diced tomatoes
2 tbsp banana pepper rings, jarred

To crumble the tofu, slice it into ½-inch thick slices. Place the slices on a plate, single layer and cover tightly with a plastic wrap. Freeze for 3 hours or until solid. Then, thaw it in the microwave on the defrost setting for around 5 minutes or until the ice crystals disappear. Rub the tofu in your hands and it will crumble. Place all ingredients into your Instant Pot and stir well. Secure the lid, select Pressure Cook, and cook on High for 4 minutes. When ready, perform a quick pressure release and serve.

102. Chessy Kale & Sweet Potato Stew

Servings: 4 | Ready in about: 15 minutes

1 sweet potato, cubed
8 oz feta cheese, cubed
2 cups chopped kale
½ cup veggie broth, divided
2 tsp tamari
1 tsp ground ginger
1 tsp olive oil
½ tsp cayenne pepper
1 tsp lemon juice

Set your Instant Pot to Sauté and heat the oil. Add in the feta cheese and sauté it for 1 minute. Add tamari and half of the broth. Stir to combine and cook for 2 minutes. Pour in the remaining broth and add the potatoes. Secure the lid, press Pressure Cook, and cook on High for 2 minutes on High. Once it goes off, do a quick pressure release. Stir in the kale, cayenne, ginger and secure the lid again. Select Pressure Cook for another minute. Once completed, perform a quick release. Sprinkle lemon juice before serving.

103. Sweet Barley Porridge

Servings: 4 | Ready in about: 35 minutes

½ cup quinoa, raw
½ cup barley, raw
¼ cup dried cranberries
4 cups water
2 tbsp honey
¼ tsp cinnamon
Pinch of sea salt
¼ tsp cardamom

Combine the water, barley, and quinoa in your Instant Pot. Secure the lid, and select the Pressure Cook. Cook for 10 minutes. Once ready, release the pressure naturally for 10 minutes. Stir in the remaining ingredients. Serve.

104. Eggplant Chips with Honey

Servings: 4 | Ready in about: 20 minutes

2 eggplants	⅓ cup olive oil	1 tsp dry thyme
2 tsp honey	⅓ cup cornstarch	A pinch of salt

Cut the eggplants in slices of ½ -inch each. In a big bowl, mix the cornstarch, ½ cup water , olive oil, and eggplant slices, until evenly coated. Line the air fry basket with baking paper and spray with olive oil. Place the eggplants in the basket, scatter with thyme and cook for 15 minutes on Air Fry mode, shaking every 5 minutes at 390°F. When ready, transfer the eggplants to a serving platter and drizzle with honey. Serve with yogurt dip.

105. Nutty & Zesty Brussels Sprouts with Raisins

Servings: 4 | Ready in about: 45 minutes

14 oz Brussels sprouts, steamed	1 tbsp olive oil	2 oz toasted pine nuts
2 oz raisins	Juice and zest of 1 orange	

Soak the raisins in the orange juice and let sit for about 20 minutes. Drizzle the Brussels sprouts with the olive oil, and place them in the air fry basket. Close the air fry lid and cook for 15 minutes on Air Fry mode at 390°F. Remove to a bowl and top with pine nuts, raisins, and orange zest.

106. Cumin Baby Carrots

Servings: 4 | Ready in about: 25 minutes

1 ¼ lb baby carrots	1 tsp cumin seeds	½ tsp garlic powder
2 tbsp olive oil	½ tsp cumin powder	1 handful cilantro, chopped

Place the baby carrots in a large bowl. Add cumin seeds, cumin, olive oil, salt, garlic powder, and pepper, and stir to coat them well. Put the carrots in the air fry basket, close the air fry lid and cook for 20 minutes on Roast at 390°F. Remove to a platter and sprinkle with chopped cilantro, to serve.

107. Garlic and Rosemary Mushrooms

Servings: 4 | Ready in about: 20 minutes

2 rosemary sprigs	¼ cup melted butter	3 garlic cloves, minced
12 oz button mushrooms	Salt and black pepper to taste	

Wash and pat dry the mushrooms and cut them in half. Place in a large bowl. Add the remaining ingredients to the bowl and toss well to combine. Transfer the mushrooms to the basket of your Instant Pot. Close the air fry lid and cook for 12 minutes on Air Fry mode, shaking once halfway through at 350°F.

108. Parmesan Knots

Serves: 5 | Total Time: 25 minutes

1 cup self-rising flour	1 tsp garlic powder	¼ cup grated Parmesan cheese
1 cup plain Greek yogurt	½ tsp dried oregano	
⅓ cup butter, melted	½ tsp dried parsley flakes	

Combine flour and yogurt in a large bowl and let sit for 5 minutes. Preheat your Instant Pot Duo Crisp to 320°F. Transfer dough to a lightly floured work surface and gently knead for 3 minutes or until the dough is no longer sticky. Stretch dough into a rectangle and cut into strips. Tie each strip into a knot, then brush with butter and season with oregano, parsley flakes, and garlic powder. Place knots in the air fry basket and close the fry lid. Air Fry for 6 minutes. Turn the knots and cook for another 2 minutes. Cool for 2 minutes. Sprinkle with Parmesan.

109. Veggie Sautée

Servings: 4 | Ready in about: 30 minutes

1 cup green peas
1 tomato, chopped
4 tbsp of tomato sauce, canned
2 garlic cloves, crushed

1 onion, sliced
2 carrots, sliced
2 sweet potatoes, chopped
1 celery stalk, chopped

4 cups vegetable stock
2 tbsp olive oil

Add all ingredients in the Instant Pot and seal the lid. Select Pressure Cook and cook for 15 minutes on High. Once it goes off, allow for a natural pressure release for 5 minutes. Carefully open the lid and serve.

110. Farmer Muffins

Serves: 4 | Total Time: 15 minutes

½ cup flour
½ cup cornmeal
¼ cup sugar

½ cup cooked bacon, cubed
½ tsp baking powder
¼ cup butter, melted

½ cup heavy cream
1 large egg

Preheat your Instant Pot Duo Crisp to 350°F. Whisk together flour, cornmeal, sugar, and baking powder in a large bowl. Stir in butter, heavy cream, and egg until well combined. Fill 12 silicone or aluminum muffin cups about halfway. Top with bacon. Place in the air fryer basket and close the lid. Bake for 10 minutes or until golden. Serve.

111. Rich Sweet Potato Stew

Servings: 4 | Ready in about: 40 minutes

3 sweet potatoes, chopped
2 carrots, sliced
4 cups water

5 tbsp olive oil
3 tsp tomato sauce
1 onion, chopped

1 tbsp of celery, chopped
1 tbsp of parsley, chopped
1 chili pepper, sliced

Heat oil on Sauté. Add the onions, carrots, celery, and potatoes. Stir-fry for 2-3 minutes. Add the water, tomato sauce, and the potatoes. Give it a good stir and seal the lid. Set to 25 minutes on Pressure Cook. Once the cooking is complete, perform a quick release. Open the cooker and add the remaining ingredients. Secure the lid and cook on High for 3 more minutes.

112. Coconut Brussels Sprouts

Serves: 4 | Total Time: 20 minutes

1 lb Brussels sprouts, halved
2 tbsp coconut oil, melted

Salt and black pepper to taste
1 tbsp chopped cilantro

Preheat your Instant Pot Duo Crisp to 350°F. Drizzle coconut oil over Brussels sprouts in a large bowl. Season with salt and pepper. Transfer to the air fry basket and close the fry lid. Air Fry for 15 minutes, shaking twice until Brussel sprouts are tender. Serve warm sprinkled with cilantro and enjoy!

113. Mexican Corn in the Cob

Serves: 6 | Total Time: 20 minutes

½ cup sour cream
1 ½ tsp chili powder

1 lime, juiced and zested
¼ tsp salt

6 mini corn cobs
½ cup crumbled queso fresco

Preheat your Instant Pot Duo Crisp to 350°F. Combine sour cream, chili powder, lime zest and juice, and salt in a bowl. Coat each corn cob with the mixture and place them in the air fry basket and close the fry lid. Air Fry for 15 minutes until corn is tender. Top with queso fresco and serve warm.

SNACKS& SIDE DISHES

114. Chinese-Style Veggie Stir-Fry

Servings: 4 | Ready in about: 15 minutes

1 tbsp five spice powder	½ cup almond milk	1 tsp chili powder
2 tbsp olive oil	4 cups cubed eggplant	
1 cup vegetable stock	2 cups torn spinach	

Set your Instant Pot to Sauté and heat the oil. Add the eggplant cubes, and stir-fry for 2 minutes. Pour the almond milk, stock, spinach and the seasonings. Give it a good stir and seal the lid. Select Pressure Cook and cook on High for 4 minutes. Perform a quick pressure release and carefully open the lid. Serve and enjoy!

115. Avocados with a Surprise

Servings: 4 | Ready in about: 30 minutes

2 avocados, halved	3 tbsp organic butter, softened	Salt to taste
4 eggs	1 tbsp oregano, dried	

Brush the halved avocados with butter and place them in the Instant Pot. Crack the eggs in each avocado half. Season with salt and oregano and add 1 cup of water to the stainless steel insert of your Instant Pot. Secure the lid, press Pressure Cook and cook on low pressure for 20 minutes. Once done, perform a quick release and serve.

116. Tender Potato Wedges

Serves: 4 | Total Time: 30 minutes

4 boiled russet potatoes, sliced into wedges

2 tsp seasoned salt	½ cup flour	1 tsp smoked paprika
½ cup whole milk	2 tsp onion powder	

Preheat your Instant Pot Duo Crisp to 400°F. Place the potatoes in a bowl and sprinkle them with seasoned salt. Pour in milk, onion, smoked paprika, and toss to coat. On a large plate, add flour. Dredge each wedge lightly in the flour. Transfer wedges to the air fry basket and lightly spray with cooking oil. Close the fry lid and Air Fry for 10 minutes, then turn the wedges. Cook for another 5 minutes until the wedges are golden. Serve warm.

117. Crispy Broccoli

Serves: 4 | Total Time: 15 minutes

12 oz broccoli florets	1 tsp garlic powder
2 tbsp butter, melted	Salt and black pepper to taste

Preheat your Instant Pot Duo Crisp to 360°F. Drizzle butter over broccoli in a bowl. Season with salt, garlic, and pepper. Transfer broccoli to the air fry basket and close the fry lid. Roast for 8-10 minutes, shaking twice or until broccoli is browning on the edges and the center is tender. Serve warm and enjoy!

118. Golden Butternut Squash

Serves: 8 | Total Time: 25 minutes

1 butternut squash, cubed	½ tsp salt	½ tsp ground cinnamon
2 tbsp butter, melted	1 ½ tbsp honey	¼ tsp ground nutmeg

Preheat your Instant Pot Duo Crisp to 400°F. Toss squash and butter in a large bowl. Add salt, honey, nutmeg, and cinnamon to the squash and toss to coat. Transfer squash to the air fry basket and close the fry lid. Bake for 5 minutes. Shake the basket and cook for another 5 minutes. Shake one more time and cook for 5 more minutes. The edges of the squash will be golden and the center tender. Serve warm and enjoy!

119. Cheesy Fingers

Serves: 4 | Total Time: 15 minutes + chilling time

12 mozzarella string cheese sticks
½ cup flour
½ cup corn starch
4 large eggs, beaten
3 ½ cups panko bread crumbs
2 ½ tsp ground allspice
½ tsp salt

Cut mozzarella in half crosswise and transfer to an airtight freezer zip bag. Freeze for at least one hour. Set up three bowls. In the first bowl, mix the flour and corn starch. In the second bowl, add the eggs. In the third bowl, add bread crumbs, ground allspice, and salt and mix well. Take the mozzarella from the freezer. Dip each stick in flour and shake. Next, dip in the eggs to coat and allow excess to drip. Then dredge the mozzarella in the bread crumbs. Repeat the process with the eggs and bread crumbs to double coat. Transfer the breaded mozzarella to a plate and freeze for at least one hour.

Preheat your Instant Pot Duo Crisp to 400°F. Lightly spray each stick with cooking oil. Place in the air fryer basket in a single layer and close the air fryer lid. Air Fry for 5 minutes. Cool for 5 minutes. Serve warm.

120. Parmesan Zucchini Fries

Serves: 4 | Total Time: 55 minutes

3 zucchini, cut into sticks
2 tsp salt
2 large eggs
1 cup grated Parmesan cheese
1 cup panko bread crumbs
½ tsp dried oregano
½ tsp dried basil
½ tsp garlic powder

Preheat your Instant Pot Duo Crisp to 400°F. Whisk eggs and salt in a bowl. In a zippered storage bag, add Parmesan, bread crumbs, oregano, basil, and garlic. First, dip some of the fries in the egg, then transfer to the bag. Zip and shake to coat. Remove the fries and repeat until all of the fries are coated. Lightly spray fries with cooking oil and transfer to the air fry basket. Close the fry lid and Air Fry for 6 minutes, then turn the fries. Cook for another 6 minutes until the fries are browning and crispy. Serve warm and enjoy!

121. Mozzarella Bread

Serves: 6 | Total Time: 25 minutes

1 cup flour
1 cup Greek yogurt
¼ cup butter softened
1 tbsp minced garlic
1 tsp brown sugar
1 tsp yeast
1 cup grated mozzarella cheese

Mix flour, yogurt, yeast, and brown sugar in a large bowl until it becomes sticky and soft. Let sit for 5 minutes. While it sits, combine butter and garlic in a small bowl. Turn out the dough onto a floured work surface. Knead the dough for about a minute and shape it into a round. Brush dough with garlic butter and top with mozzarella.

Preheat your Instant Pot Duo Crisp to 320°F. Put the dough into the air fryer basket and close the fry lid Bake for 12 minutes. Edges will be golden, and mozzarella is browned and melted. Serve warm and enjoy!

122. French Onion-Green Bean Casserole

Serves: 4 | Total Time: 30 minutes

1 (10-oz) can condensed cream of mushroom soup
¼ cup buttermilk
2 (14.5-oz) cans green beans
1 tbsp lemon juice
1 tsp minced garlic
Salt and black pepper to taste
1 cup packaged French fried onions

Preheat your Instant Pot Duo Crisp to 320°F. Combine green beans, lemon juice, soup, and buttermilk in a 4-quart baking dish. Stir in garlic, salt, and pepper. Spread onions over the top. Place the pan in the air fry basket and close the fry lid. Bake for 20 minutes. The top will be just brown, and the casserole is heated through. Serve.

123. Lemon Nachos

Serves: 4 | Total Time: 10 minutes

8 white corn tortillas	2 tbsp lemon juice	1 tbsp chopped scallions
¼ cup olive oil	½ tsp salt	

Preheat your Instant Pot Duo Crisp to 350°F. Cut the tortilla into 4 equal pieces. Brush lightly with olive oil. Place in a single layer in the air fry basket and close the fry lid. Air Fry for 3 minutes. Shake the basket and cook for another 2 minutes. Remove from basket and sprinkle with lemon juice, scallions, and salt. Serve immediately.

124. Buttered Asparagus

Serves: 4 | Total Time: 20 minutes

1 lb asparagus, trimmed	1 minced garlic glove	Salt and black pepper to taste
¼ cup butter, cubed	½ lemon, zested and juiced	2 tbsp grated Parmesan cheese

Preheat your Instant Pot Duo Crisp to 375°F. On a foil square, place asparagus with butter on top. Season with lemon zest, garlic, salt, and pepper. Drizzle with lemon juice. Fold foil over asparagus and tightly seal edges to form a packet. Place the packet in the air fry basket and close the fry lid. Air Fry for 15 minutes. Asparagus will be tender. Serve warm sprinkled with Parmesan cheese.

125. Glazed Baby Carrots

Serves: 4 | Total Time: 20 minutes

1 lb baby carrots	2 tbsp butter, melted	½ tsp dried thyme
¼ cup honey	¼ tsp garlic powder	Salt and black pepper to taste

Preheat your Instant Pot Duo Crisp to 360°F. Arrange carrots in a baking pan. Combine honey, thyme, butter, and garlic powder in a small bowl. Pour over carrots and stir to coat. Season with salt and pepper. Place the pan in the air fry basket and close the fry lid. Roast for 4 minutes. Stir the carrots and Roast for another 4 minutes. Stir one more time and cook for 4 minutes until carrots are tender. Serve warm and enjoy!

126. Petit Corn Dog Bites

Serves: 6 | Total Time: 40 minutes

½ cup cornmeal	1 large egg	2 tsp baking powder
¾ cup flour	3 tbsp sugar	6 beef hot dogs
½ cup milk	½ tsp salt	1 tsp olive oil

Combine cornmeal, flour, milk, egg, salt, olive oil, sugar, and baking powder. Set aside to thicken for at least 5 minutes. Cut each hot dog in half, and then each piece in half again for 4 pieces per hot dog. Use a skewer or fork to dip the hot dog into the cornmeal. Transfer to a tray and freeze for 10 minutes.

Preheat your Instant Pot Duo Crisp to 375°F. Line the air fry basket with parchment paper. Place the corn dogs in the air fry basket and close the fry lid. Air Fry for 5 minutes. Use tongs to turn the corn dogs and cook for another 5 minutes until golden brown. Serve warm.

127. Cheesy Biscuits

Serves: 10 | Total Time: 15 minutes

2 cups flour	½ tsp garlic powder	¾ cup butter, melted
1 tbsp baking powder	½ tsp mustard powder	1 cup grated cheddar cheese
1 tsp salt	¾ cup buttermilk	

Preheat your Instant Pot Duo Crisp to 400°F. Combine flour, mustard powder, baking powder, salt, garlic powder, buttermilk, and ½ cup of butter in a large bowl. When well combined, stir in cheddar cheese. Divide the dough into 10 equal balls. Transfer the balls to the air fryer basket and close the fry lid. Bake for 10 minutes. Edges will be crispy, and biscuits will be golden. Remove biscuits and brush with the rest of the melted butter. Serve warm.

128. Spiced Cauliflower Tots

Serves: 4 | Total Time: 30 minutes

2 cups riced cauliflower
⅓ cup Italian bread crumbs
¼ cup flour
1 large egg
¾ cup grated sharp cheddar cheese
½ cup hot sauce
2 tbsp crushed blue cheese
Salt and black pepper to taste

Preheat your Instant Pot Duo Crisp to 400°F. Line the basket with parchment paper. Combine all of the ingredients, except for the hot sauce, in a large bowl. Scoop 2 tablespoons of mixture and roll into a tater tot. Repeat with the rest of the mixture. Transfer tots to the air fry basket and lightly spray with cooking oil. Close the fry lid and Air Fry for 6 minutes, then turn the tots. Cook for 6 minutes until tots are golden. Serve topped with hot sauce.

129. Cheddar Crackers

Serves: 4 | Total Time: 30 minutes + chilling time

4 oz sharp cheddar cheese, grated
½ cup flour
2 tbsp butter, cubed
½ tsp salt
1 egg yolk, beaten
1 tsp ground fennel seeds
2 tbsp cold water

Use a hand mixer to combine all of the ingredients to make the dough. Shape into a ball and wrap tightly with plastic wrap. Freeze for 15 minutes.

Preheat your Instant Pot Duo Crisp to 375°F. Remove dough from the freezer. Roll out dough on parchment paper into a rectangle. Use a pizza cutter to cut long horizontal and vertical lines to make into squares. Smear with egg yolk and sprinkle with fennel seeds. Place the crackers in the air fryer basket and close the lid. Air Fry for 10 minutes. Let cool for at least 10 minutes. Serve and enjoy!

130. Parmesan Spinach Spread

Serves: 2 | Total Time: 25 minutes

8 oz cream cheese, softened
½ cup mayonnaise
2 tsp minced garlic
¼ tsp onion powder
1 cup grated Parmesan cheese
1 tbsp grated mozzarella cheese
10 oz chopped spinach

Preheat your Instant Pot Duo Crisp to 320°F. Mix cream cheese cheese, onion powder, mayonnaise, garlic, mozzarella cheese, and Parmesan cheese in a large bowl. Fold in spinach. Transfer to a baking pan and place in the air fryer basket. Close the fry lid and Air Fry for 15 minutes. The dip will be bubbling and golden on top.

131. Roasted Tomato Sauce

Serves: 4 | Total Time: 15 minutes

10 tomatoes, quartered
1 white onion, sliced
2 cloves garlic, peeled
2 tbsp olive oil
1 tsp cumin
¼ cup chopped basil
½ tsp salt

Preheat your Instant Pot Duo Crisp to 340°F. Place tomatoes, onion, cumin, and garlic in a baking pan. Coat with oil and toss. Place the pan in the air fry basket and close the fry lid. Roast for 10 minutes, stirring twice or until vegetables are turning brown and caramelized. Transfer to a food processor along with basil and salt. Pulse five times to break down vegetables to desired chunkiness. Serve immediately.

132. Hot Chicken Dip

Serves: 2 | Total Time: 20 minutes

4 oz cream cheese, softened	½ tsp garlic powder	1 cup grated Monterey jack cheese
1 tbsp green onions	½ cup buffalo sauce	2 cups cooked chicken breasts, grated

Preheat your Instant Pot Duo Crisp to 350°F. Combine cream cheese, garlic powder, buffalo sauce, and ½ cup Monterey jack cheese. Fold in chicken and coat with cheese mixture. Transfer to a baking pan and top with ½ cup Monterey jack and sprinkle with green onions. Place the dish in the air fry basket and close the fry lid. Bake for 10 minutes. The top will be brown, and the edges will be bubbling. Serve.

133. Jalapeño Poppers in Bacon

Serves: 4 | Total Time: 25 minutes

3 oz ricotta cheese, crumbled	¼ tsp garlic powder	6 seeded jalapeños, halved lengthwise
½ cup grated sharp cheddar cheese	¼ tsp thyme powder	12 bacon slices

Preheat your Instant Pot Duo Crisp to 400°F. Put ricotta cheese, cheddar cheese, thyme, and garlic powder in a large microwave-safe vowel. Microwave for 20 seconds. Stir softened cheese to combine and spoon into jalapeno halves. Wrap one bacon slice around each jalapeno half until completely covered. Place the jalapenos in the air fry basket and close the fry lid. Air Fry for 6 minutes. Turn the jalapenos and continue cooking for 6 minutes. Serve.

134. Party Pigs in a Blanket

Serves: 6 | Total Time: 15 minutes

1 (8-oz) can crescent rolls	1 large egg, whisked
8 mini cocktail wieners	1 tbsp poppy seeds

Preheat your Instant Pot Duo Crisp to 350°F. Separate crescent rolls into 8 triangles. Place a cocktail wiener on the widest end of the triangle and roll the crescent over the hot dog to the point. Brush each crescent with egg and sprinkle poppy seeds. Place rolls in the air fry basket and close the fry lid. Air Fry for 5 minutes. Use tongs to turn the rolls and cook for another 5 minutes until crescents are golden and hot dogs are brown. Top with poppy seeds.

135. Ginger Chicken Wings

Serves: 4 | Total Time: 25 minutes

1 lb chicken wings, drums, and flats separated		
Salt and black pepper to taste	¼ cup gochujang sauce	¼ cup mayonnaise
1 tsp chili powder	2 tbsp soy sauce	
3 crushed garlic cloves	1 tsp ground ginger	

Preheat your Instant Pot Duo Crisp to 350°F. Season wings with chili powder, salt, and pepper. Place in the air fry basket and close the fry lid. Air Fry for 7 minutes. Use tongs to turn the wings and Cook for another 8 minutes.

While the wings are cooking, combine gochujang sauce, soy sauce, garlic, ginger and mayonnaise in a bowl. Transfer the wings to the bowl and coat with the sauce. Increase air fryer temperature to 400°F. AIR FRY the wings for 5 minutes until golden. Serve warm and enjoy!

136. Original Pork Egg Rolls

Serves: 4 | Total Time: 30 minutes

2 tbsp olive oil	½ tsp salt	8 egg roll wrappers
½ lb ground pork	2 cups broccoli slaw	
3 tbsp soy sauce tamari	½ tsp ground ginger	

Warm the olive oil in your Instant Pot on Sauté. Cook the ground pork for 10 minutes. Crumble with a spoon until fully cooked. Add 2 tablespoons of tamari and salt. Stir and simmer for 2 minutes. Add broccoli slaw, tamari, and ginger. Stir and cook for 5 minutes until slaw is tender. Remove. Place egg roll wrapper with one corner pointing toward you. Top the wrapper with 3 tablespoons of pork on the corner closest to you. Roll that corner over the filling, then tuck in the left and right corners toward the center. Finish rolling up the wrapper. Continue with the rest of the egg rolls. Preheat your Instant Pot Duo Crisp to 350°F. Place rolls in the air fry basket seam side down. Air Fry for 5 minutes, then uses tongs to turn the egg rolls. Cook for another 5 minutes. Serve warm.

137. Hawaiian Rolls

Serves: 3 | Total Time: 20 minutes

6 Hawaiian sweet rolls
12 deli ham slices
6 mozzarella cheese slices
⅓ cup butter, melted
1 ½ tsp minced garlic

Preheat your Instant Pot Duo Crisp to 350°F. Slice the rolls horizontally about ¾ the way through, leaving the roll connected. Layer 2 slices of deli ham and 2 slices of mozzarella cheese inside the roll and close. Repeat for all of the rolls. Mix butter and garlic in a small bowl, then brush the garlic butter all over the rolls. Place in the air fry basket and close the fry lid. Air Fry for 10 minutes. The roll tops will be golden, and the cheese will be melted.

138. White Wontons

Serves: 4 | Total Time: 20 minutes

5 oz cream cheese, softened
1 tsp garlic powder
¼ tsp onion powder
¼ tsp dry coriander
12 wonton wrappers
¼ cup water

Preheat your Instant Pot Duo Crisp to 375°F. Combine cream cheese, coriander, onion powder, and garlic powder in a bowl until smooth. Place 1 tablespoon of the mixture in the ce nter of a wonton wrapper. Rub water on the edges to help seal the wrapper. Fold into a triangle, then lightly spray with cooking oil. Repeat for all of the wontons. Place in the air fry basket and close the fry lid. Air Fry for 8 minutes, 8 flipping once until golden and crispy. Serve warm.

139. Hot Chicken Wings

Serves: 4 | Total Time: 25 minutes

3 lb chicken wings, flats and drums separated
Salt and black pepper to taste
¼ cup butter, melted
¼ cup Tabasco hot sauce
½ cup ketchup

Preheat your Instant Pot Duo Crisp to 375°F. Season wings with salt and pepper. Place in the air fry basket in a single layer and close the fry lid. Air Fry for 10 minutes, then use tongs to turn the wings. Cook for another 10 minutes until golden and crispy. While the wings are cooking, combine butter and Tabasco hot sauce in a bowl. When the wings are done, transfer them to the bowl and toss with sauce until well coated. Serve with ketchup on the side.

140. Loaded Potato Skins

Serves: 4 | Total Time: 50 minutes

4 russet potatoes
½ cup grated sharp cheddar cheese
Salt and black pepper to taste
2 tsp wholegrain mustard
1 tbsp chives, sliced

Preheat your Instant Pot Duo Crisp to 400°F. Poke holes around the potato using a fork. Place in the air fryer basket and close the lid. Bake for 30 minutes or until tender. Allow potatoes to cool. Slice the potatoes in half lengthwise and carefully scoop out the insides. Leave enough flesh to maintain the skin's stability. Reserve extra potato flesh for another use. Add cheddar cheese, mustard, salt, and pepper to the potato skins, then return to the air fry basket. Cook for 5 minutes to melt the cheese. Allow cooling for 5 minutes, then garnish with chives.

RICE, GRAINS & PASTA

141. Indian-Style Beef with Rice

Servings: 5 | Ready in about: 40 minutes

¼ cup yogurt	1 tbsp garam masala	1 onion, chopped
2 cloves garlic, smashed	1 tbsp fresh ginger, grated	1 (14-oz) can puréed tomatoes
1 tbsp olive oil	1 ½ tsp smoked paprika	½ cup beef broth
1 lime, juiced	1 tsp ground cumin	2 cups basmati rice, rinsed
Salt and black pepper to taste	¼ tsp cayenne pepper	½ cup heavy cream
2 lb beef stew meat, cubed	3 tbsp butter	½ bunch fresh cilantro, chopped

In a bowl, mix garlic, lime juice, olive oil, pepper, salt, and yogurt. Stir in the beef to coat. In a different bowl, thoroughly mix paprika, garam masala, cumin, ginger, and cayenne pepper. Melt butter on Sauté and stir-fry the onion and garlic for 3 minutes until translucent. Sprinkle spice mixture over onion. Cook for about 30 seconds.

To the onion, add the beef-yogurt mixture. Cook for 3 to 4 minutes until the meat is slightly cooked. Mix in broth and puréed tomatoes. Set trivet over beef in the pot. In an oven-proof bowl, mix 2 cups water and rice. Set the bowl onto the trivet. Seal the pressure lid, press Pressure Cook, and set the timer to 10 minutes. When ready, release pressure quickly. Remove the bowl with rice and trivet. Add pepper, salt and heavy cream into beef and stir. Fluff the rice and divide it into serving plates. Apply a topping of beef. Use cilantro to garnish.

142. Creamed Kale Parmesan Farro

Servings: 2 | Ready in about: 35 minutes

1 tbsp butter	2 garlic cloves, smashed	1 cup kale, chopped
1 small onion, diced	2 cups vegetable broth	Juice of ½ lemon, juiced
1 cup pearl barley, rinsed and drained	½ cup grated Parmesan + for topping	Salt and black pepper to taste

Warm butter on Sauté in your Instant Pot. Add in onion and cook for 3 minutes until soft. Stir in garlic and barley, and cook for 1-2 minutes until barley is toasted. Mix in broth. Seal the pressure lid and choose Pressure Cook. Set the timer to 9 minutes. Release pressure naturally for 10 minutes. Add Parmesan cheese into barley mixture and stir until fully melted. Just before serving, add lemon juice and kale into barley mixture. Serve.

143. Simple Brown Rice

Servings: 6 | Ready in about: 30 minutes

1 ½ cups brown rice	2 tsp lemon juice	1 tbsp toasted sunflower seeds
3 cups chicken broth	2 tsp sesame olive oil	

Add broth and brown rice to your Instant Pot. Seal the pressure lid, choose Pressure Cook on High, and set the timer to 15 minutes. When ready, release the pressure quickly. Do not open the lid for an additional 5 minutes. Use a fork to fluff rice. Add lemon juice, sunflower seeds and oil.

144. Black Beans Tacos

Servings: 6 | Ready in about: 1 hour 30 minutes

2 cups black beans, soaked overnight	1 tbsp dried oregano	1 avocado, sliced
1 cup shallots, chopped	1 tsp chili powder	Salt to taste
4 cups water	6 soft Taco tortillas	Fresh Cilantro for garnish

Drain the beans and add to your Instant Pot. Mix in the onion, oregano and chili powder. Pour water. Seal the pressure lid, choose Pressure Cook on High, and set the timer to 60 minutes. Do a quick release, carefully open the lid and Allow cooling for a few minutes. Serve with taco tortillas, avocado slices and cilantro.

145. Veggie Quinoa Bowls with Pesto

Servings: 2 | Ready in about: 30 minutes

1 cup quinoa, rinsed and drained
2 cups vegetable broth
Salt and ground black pepper to taste
1 potato, peeled, cubed
1 head broccoli, cut into small florets
1 bunch baby heirloom carrots, peeled
¼ cabbage, sliced
2 eggs
1 avocado, thinly sliced
¼ cup pesto sauce
Lemon wedges, for serving

In your Instant Pot, mix broth, pepper, quinoa, and salt. Set trivet to the inner pot on top of quinoa and add a steamer basket on the trivet. Mix carrots, potato, eggs, and broccoli in the basket. Sprinkle with pepper and salt. Seal the pressure lid, choose Pressure Cook on High, and set the timer to 1 minute. Quick-release the pressure.

Take away the trivet and steamer basket from pot. Set the eggs in a bowl of ice water. Then peel and halve the eggs. Use a fork to fluff quinoa. Adjust the seasonings. In two bowls, equally divide avocado, quinoa, broccoli, eggs, carrots, potato, and a dollop of pesto. Serve alongside a lemon wedge.

146. Shrimp Risotto with Vegetables

Servings: 4 | Ready in about: 1 hour 15 minutes

1 tbsp avocado oil
1 lb asparagus, roughly chopped
1 cup spinach, chopped
1 ½ cups mushrooms, sliced
1 cup rice, rinsed and drained
1¼ cups chicken broth
¾ cup coconut milk
1 tbsp coconut oil
16 shrimp, cleaned and deveined
Salt and ground black pepper to taste
¾ cup Parmesan cheese, shredded

Warm the oil on Sauté in your Instant Pot. Add spinach, mushrooms and asparagus and cook for 10 minutes until cooked through. Add rice, coconut milk and broth to the pot as you stir. Seal the pressure lid, choose Pressure Cook on High, and set the timer to 40 minutes. Do a quick release, open the lid and put the rice on a serving plate. To the pot, add coconut oil and press Sauté. Add shrimp and cook each side taking 4 minutes until cooked through and turns pink. Set the shrimp over rice and season with pepper and salt. Serve topped with Parmesan.

147. Red Lentil & Spinach Dhal

Servings: 6 | Ready in about: 35 minutes

2 tbsp olive oil
1 red jalapeño, seeded and minced
1 cup spinach, chopped
4 cloves garlic, minced
1 tsp fresh ginger, peeled and grated
1 tbsp cumin seeds
1 tbsp coriander seeds
1 tsp ground turmeric
¼ tsp cayenne pepper
1½ cups red lentils
1 tomato, diced
¼ cup lemon juice
Salt to taste
Fresh Cilantro, chopped for garnish
Greek yogurt for garnish

Heat oil on Sauté in your Instant Pot, add cayenne pepper, jalapeño pepper, ginger, turmeric, cumin, and garlic, and coriander and cook for 2-3 minutes until seeds become fragrant and begin to pop. Pour in 3 cups water, tomato, and lentils into pot and stir. Seal the pressure lid, choose Pressure Cook, and set the timer to 10 minutes. Release pressure naturally for 10 minutes. Stir in spinach until wilted. Add lemon juice and season to taste. Divide between serving bowls. Garnish with yogurt and cilantro and serve.

148. Lemony Wild Rice Pilaf

Servings: 6 | Ready in about: 25 minutes

4 cups vegetable broth
2 cups white wild rice, rinsed
1 tbsp butter
Zest and juice from 1 lemon
½ tsp salt
½ tsp ground black pepper

In your Instant Pot, mix rice, lemon zest, butter, and water. Seal the pressure lid, choose Pressure Cook on High, and set the timer to 3 minutes. When ready, release pressure naturally for 10 minutes. Sprinkle salt, lemon juice, and pepper over the pilaf and use a fork to gently fluff.

RICE, GRAINS & PASTA

149. Parsley-Lime Bulgur Bowl

Servings: 4 | Ready in about: 30 minutes

1 tbsp olive oil	1 cup bulgur wheat	1 handful fresh parsley, chopped
1 small onion, chopped	2 ½ cups vegetable broth	10 black olives to garnish
2 cloves garlic, minced	1 tbsp lime juice, or more to taste	Salt and black pepper to taste

Heat oil on Sauté in your Instant Pot, stir in garlic and onion and cook for 10 to 13 minutes until golden brown. Add in cilantro, bulgur, salt, 1 tbsp lime juice, and vegetable broth. Seal the pressure lid, choose Pressure Cook on High, and set the timer to 1 minute. Once ready, do a quick release. Use a fork to fluff bulgur. Add fresh parsley as you stir. Season with additional lime salt, juice, and pepper if desired. Serve in bowls topped with black olives.

150. Creamy Grana Padano Risotto

Servings: 6 | Ready in about: 25 minutes

1 tbsp olive oil	2 cups Carnaroli rice, rinsed	Salt and white pepper to taste
1 white onion, chopped	¼ cup dry white wine	2 tbsp Grana Padano cheese, grated
1 tbsp butter	4 cups chicken stock	¼ tbsp Grana Padano cheese, flakes

Warm oil on Sauté in your Instant Pot. Stir-fry onion for 3 minutes until soft and translucent. Add in butter and rice and cook for 2 minutes, stirring occasionally. Pour wine into the pot to deglaze, scrape away any browned bits of food from the bottom. Stir in stock, pepper, and salt. Seal the pressure lid, choose Pressure Cook on High, and set the timer to 15 minutes. When ready, release the pressure quickly. Sprinkle with grated Parmesan cheese and stir well. Top with flaked cheese for garnish before serving.

151. Spinach and Kidney Bean Stew

Servings: 4 | Ready in about: 45 minutes

2 tbsp olive oil	1 cup celery, chopped	1 tsp dried rosemary
1 onion, chopped	4 cups vegetable broth	1 bay leaf
2 cloves garlic, minced	1 cup white kidney beans, soaked	1 cup spinach, torn into pieces
2 carrots, peeled and sliced	1 tsp dried thyme	Salt and black pepper to taste

Set your Instant Pot to Sauté. Warm olive oil. Stir in garlic and onion and cook for 3 minutes until tender and fragrant. Mix in celery and carrots and cook for 2 to 3 minutes more until they start to soften. To the pot, add vegetable broth, bay leaf, thyme, rosemary, kidney beans, and salt. Seal the pressure lid, choose Pressure Cook. Set the timer to 30 minutes. Quick release the pressure and add spinach to the beans as you stir and allow sit for 2 to 4 minutes until the spinach wilts. Add pepper and salt for seasoning.

152. Spicy Lentils with Chorizo

Servings: 10 | Ready in about: 50 minutes

2 cups lentils, drained and rinsed	½ cup mustard	2 cups brown sugar
7 oz chorizo, sliced	½ cup cider vinegar	1 tbsp salt
1 onion, diced	3 tbsp Worcestershire sauce	1 tbsp black pepper
2 garlic cloves, crushed	2 tbsp maple syrup	1 tsp chili powder
2 cups tomato sauce	2 tbsp liquid smoke	1 tsp paprika
2 cups vegetable broth	1 tbsp lime juice	¼ tsp cayenne pepper

Set to Sauté your Instant Pot. Add in chorizo and cook for 3 minutes as you stir until crisp. Add garlic and onion and cook for 2 more minutes until translucent. Mix tomato sauce, broth, cider vinegar, liquid smoke, Worcestershire sauce, lime juice, mustard, and maple syrup in a mixing bowl. Pour the mixture into the pot. Add in pepper, chili powder, brown sugar, paprika, salt, and cayenne into the sauce as you stir to mix. Mix in lentils. Seal the pressure lid, choose Pressure Cook, and set the timer to 30 minutes. Release pressure quickly.

153. Cheese and Spinach Stuffed Shells

Servings: 6 | Ready in about: 1 hour

2 cups onion, chopped	12 oz jumbo shell pasta	¾ cup grated Pecorino Romano cheese
1 cup carrot, chopped	1 tbsp olive oil	2 tbsp chopped fresh chives
3 garlic cloves, minced	2 cups ricotta cheese, crumbled	1 tbsp chopped fresh dill
3 ½ tbsp olive oil,	1 ½ cup feta cheese, crumbled	Salt and ground black pepper to taste
1 (28 oz) canned tomatoes, crushed	2 cups spinach, chopped	1 cup shredded cheddar cheese

Warm olive oil on Sauté in your Instant Pot. Add in onion, carrot, and garlic, and cook for 5 minutes until tender. Stir in tomatoes and cook for another 10 minutes. Remove to a bowl and set aside. Wipe the pot with a damp cloth, add pasta and cover with enough water. Seal the pressure lid, choose Pressure Cook on High, and set the timer to 5 minutes. Do a quick pressure and drain the pasta. Lightly grease olive oil to a baking sheet.

In a bowl, combine feta and ricotta cheeses. Add in spinach, Pecorino Romano, dill, and chives and stir. Adjust the seasonings. Fill the shells with the mixture. Spread 4 cups tomato sauce on the baking sheet. Place the stuffed shells over with seam-sides down and sprinkle cheddar cheese atop. Use aluminum foil to the cover the baking dish. Pour 1 cup of water in the pot and insert the trivet. Lower the baking dish onto the trivet. Seal the pressure lid, choose Pressure Cook on High, and set the timer to 15 minutes. Once ready, do a quick release. Take away the foil. Place the stuffed shells to serving plates and top with tomato sauce before serving.

154. Tri-Color Quinoa and Pinto Bean Bowl

Servings: 5 | Ready in about: 30 minutes

1 tsp extra-virgin olive oil	1 tsp ground cumin	1 cup Tri-Color Quinoa, rinsed
1 green bell pepper, diced	½ tsp salt	1 cup red salsa
1 onion, diced	14 oz canned pinto beans, drained	1 cup vegetable broth

Warm oil on Sauté in your Instant Pot. Add red onion and green bell pepper as you stir. Add salt and cumin for seasoning and cook for 7-8 minutes until fragrant. To the vegetable mixture, add quinoa, broth, salsa, and pinto beans. Seal the pressure lid, choose Pressure Cook on High, and set the timer to 12 minutes. When ready, do a quick pressure release. Use a fork to fluff quinoa and divide between serving bowls to serve.

155. Easy Vegan Sloppy Joes

Servings: 6 | Ready in about: 45 minutes

2 cups water	2 cups tomato sauce	1 tsp smoked paprika
1 cup pearl barley, rinsed	2 tbsp brown sugar	1 tsp chili powder
1 cup green onion, chopped	2 tbsp Worcestershire sauce	6 brioche buns
1 clove garlic, minced	1 tsp Dijon mustard	Dill Pickles for garnish

In your Instant Pot, mix Worcestershire sauce, water, onion, garlic, brown sugar, barley, tomato sauce, and spices. Seal the pressure lid, choose Pressure Cook on High, and set the timer to 25 minutes. When ready, release the pressure quickly. Press Sauté and cook until the mixture becomes thick. Transfer the sloppy joe mixture to the brioche buns and add a topping of dill pickles.

156. Simple Jasmine Rice

Servings: 4 | Ready in about: 25 minutes

2 cups jasmine rice	3 ½ cups of water	Salt and black pepper to taste

Stir rice and water together in your Instant Pot. Season with salt to taste. Seal the pressure lid, press Pressure Cook on High, and set the timer to 15 minutes. When ready, release pressure naturally for 10 minutes. Use a fork to fluff rice. Season with black pepper before serving.

157. Baked Garbanzo Beans & Pancetta

Servings: 6 | Ready in about: 50 minutes

3 strips pancetta, cut into strips
1 onion, diced
15 oz canned garbanzo beans
2 cups water
1 cup apple cider
2 garlic cloves, minced
½ cup ketchup
¼ cup sugar
1 tsp ground mustard powder
1 tsp salt
1 tsp ground black pepper
Fresh parsley to garnish

Set your Instant Pot to Sauté. Cook pancetta for 5 minutes until crispy. Add onion and garlic, and cook for 3 minutes until soft. Mix in garbanzo beans, ketchup, sugar, salt, apple cider, mustard powder, water, and pepper. Seal the pressure lid, press Pressure Cook on High, and set the timer to 30 minutes. Once done, release pressure naturally for 10 minutes. Serve in bowls garnished with parsley.

158. Three-Bean Veggie Chili

Servings: 8 | Ready in about: 1 hour

1 tbsp canola oil
1 onion, chopped
3 stalks of celery, chopped
1 green bell pepper, chopped
1 head broccoli, chopped into florets
2 tbsp minced garlic
2 tbsp chili powder
2 tsp ground cumin
4 cups vegetable broth
1 (28 oz) can tomatoes, crushed
½ cup pinto beans, soaked overnight
½ cup black beans, soaked overnight
½ cup cannellini beans, soaked
1 bay leaf
Fresh parsley, chopped for garnish

Warm oil on Sauté in your Instant Pot. Add onion and bell pepper, broccoli, and celery, and cook for about 8 minutes until softened. Mix in cumin, chili powder, and garlic and cook for another 1 minute. Add vegetable broth, tomatoes, black beans, salt, cannellini beans, pinto beans, and bay leaf to the pot. Seal the pressure lid, choose Pressure Cook on High, and set the timer to 25 minutes. When ready, do a quick pressure release. Dispose of the bay leaf. Taste and adjust the seasonings. Sprinkle with fresh parsley and serve.

159. Rigatoni with Sausage and Spinach

Servings: 4 | Ready in about: 45 minutes

1 tbsp butter
½ cup diced red bell pepper
1 onion, chopped
3 cups vegetable broth
¼ cup tomato purée
4 sausage links, sliced
2 tsp chili powder
Salt and ground black pepper to taste
12 oz rigatoni pasta
1 cup baby spinach
½ cup Parmesan cheese

Warm the butter on Sauté in your Instant Pot. Add red bell pepper, onion, and sausage, and cook for 5 minutes. Mix in vegetable broth, chili powder, tomato paste, salt, and pepper to combine. Stir in rigatoni pasta. Seal the pressure lid, choose Pressure Cook on High, and set the timer to 12 minutes. When ready, naturally release pressure for 20 minutes. Stir in spinach and let simmer until wilted. Top with Parmesan cheese and serve.

160. Cherry Tomato-Basil Linguine

Servings: 4 | Ready in about: 22 minutes

2 tbsp olive oil
1 small onion, diced
2 garlic cloves, minced
1 cup cherry tomatoes, halved
1 ½ cups vegetable stock
¼ cup julienned basil leaves
1 tsp salt
½ tsp ground black pepper
¼ tsp red chili flakes
1 lb Linguine noodles, halved
Fresh basil leaves for garnish
½ cup Parmigiano-Reggiano, grated

Warm oil on Sauté in your Instant Pot. Add onion and cook for 2 minutes until soft. Mix in garlic and tomatoes and sauté for 4 minutes. Pour in vegetable stock, salt, basil, red chili flakes, and pepper. Add linguine to the tomato mixture until covered. Seal the pressure lid, choose Pressure Cook on High, and set the timer to 5 minutes. When ready, naturally release the pressure for 5 minutes. Stir the mixture to ensure it is broken down. Divide into plates. Top with basil and Parmigiano-Reggiano cheese and serve.

161. Chipotle Mac and Cheese

Servings: 6 | Ready in about: 15 minutes

12 oz macaroni
1 tsp salt
1 tbsp chipotle chili powder
½ tsp ground black pepper
4 tbsp butter
1½ cup milk
4 cups sharp Cheddar cheese, grated
2 cups Pecorino cheese, grated
Salt and black pepper to taste

To your Instant Pot, add salt, 4 cups cold water and macaroni. Seal the pressure lid, choose Pressure Cook on High, and set the timer to 4 minutes. When ready, release the pressure quickly. Add butter to the pasta and stir until melts. Stir in milk, chipotle chili powder, and black pepper. Pour in Pecorino Romano and Cheddar cheeses and stir until well melted. Add pepper and salt to season. Serve.

162. Black-Eyed Peas with Kale

Servings: 6 | Ready in about: 30 minutes

1 tsp olive oil
1 onion, thinly sliced
2 garlic cloves, minced
1 cup fire-roasted red peppers, diced
½ tsp ground allspice
½ tsp red pepper, crushed
Salt to taste
1 ½ cups black-eyed peas, soaked
1 ½ cups vegetable broth
1 bay leaf
1 (15 oz) can fire roasted tomatoes
2 cups chopped kale

Warm oil on Sauté in your Instant Pot. Add onion and cook for 5 minutes until fragrant. Add garlic and fire roasted red peppers and cook for 1 more minute until softened. To the vegetable mixture, add a seasoning of salt, crushed red pepper, and allspice. Add vegetable broth, bay leaf, and black-eyed peas to the pot. Seal the pressure lid, choose Pressure Cook on High, and set the timer to 5 minutes. When ready, do a quick pressure release. Remove the bay leaf and discard. Mix the peas with kale and tomatoes. Close the air fry lid and cook for 2 minutes on Bake at 380 F. Adjust the seasoning and serve.

163. Shrimp Lo Mein

Servings: 2 | Ready in about: 20 minutes

1 tbsp sesame oil
1 lb shrimp, peeled and deveined
½ cup diced onion
2 cloves garlic, minced
1 cup carrots, cut into strips
1 cup green beans, washed
2 cups vegetable stock
3 tbsp soy sauce
2 tbsp rice wine vinegar
10 oz lo mein egg noodles
½ tsp toasted sesame seeds
Sea salt and ground black pepper to taste

Warm oil on Sauté in your Instant Pot. Stir-fry the shrimp for 5 minutes. Remove to a plate and set aside. Add in garlic and onion and cook for 3 minutes until fragrant. Mix in soy sauce, carrots, vegetable stock, green beans, and rice wine vinegar. Add noodles into the mixture and ensure they are covered. Season with pepper and salt. Seal the pressure lid, choose Pressure Cook on High, and set the timer to 5 minutes. When ready, release the pressure quickly. Plate the lo mein, add the reserved shrimp, sprinkle with sesame seeds, and serve.

164. Pasta Caprese Ricotta-Basil Fusilli

Servings: 3 | Ready in about: 15 minutes

1 tbsp olive oil
1 onion, thinly sliced
6 garlic cloves, minced
1 tsp red pepper flakes
2 ½ cups dried fusilli
1 (15 oz) can tomato sauce
1 cup tomatoes, halved
1 cup water
¼ cup basil leaves
1 tsp salt
1 cup Ricotta cheese, crumbled
2 tbsp chopped fresh basil

Warm the oil on Sauté in your Instant Pot. Add in red pepper flakes, garlic, and onion and cook for 3 minutes. Mix in fusilli, tomatoes, water, tomato sauce, and salt. Seal the pressure lid, choose Pressure Cook, and set the timer to 4 minutes. When ready, release the pressure quickly. Top with the ricotta and chopped basil to serve.

165. Beef-Stuffed Pasta Shells

Servings: 4 | Ready in about: 35 minutes

2 tbsp olive oil
1 lb ground beef
16 oz pasta shells
2 cups water

15 oz tomato sauce
15-oz can black beans, drained
15-oz canned corn, drained
10 oz red enchilada sauce

4 oz diced green chiles
1 cup shredded mozzarella cheese
Salt and ground black pepper to taste
Finely chopped parsley for garnish

Heat oil on Sauté in your Instant Pot. Add ground beef and cook for 7 minutes until it starts to brown. Mix in pasta, tomato sauce, enchilada sauce, black beans, water, corn, and green chiles and stir to coat well. Seal the pressure lid, choose Pressure Cook on High, and set the timer to 10 minutes. When ready, do a quick pressure release. Into the pasta mixture, mix in mozzarella cheese until melted. Garnish with parsley to serve.

166. Pork Spaghetti with Spinach and Tomatoes

Servings: 4 | Ready in about: 35 minutes

2 tbsp olive oil
½ cup onion, chopped
1 garlic clove, minced
1 lb pork sausage meat
2 cups water

1 (14 oz) can diced tomatoes, drained
½ cup sun-dried tomatoes
1 tbsp dried oregano
1 tsp Italian seasoning
1 fresh jalapeño chile, minced

1 tsp salt
8 oz dried spaghetti, halved
1 cup spinach

Warm oil on Sauté in your Instant Pot. Add in onion and garlic and cook for 2 minutes until softened. Stir in sausage meat and cook for 5 minutes. Stir in jalapeño, water, sun-dried tomatoes, Italian seasoning, oregano, diced tomatoes, and salt. Mix spaghetti and press to submerge into the sauce. Seal the pressure lid, choose Pressure Cook on High, and set the timer to 9 minutes. When ready, release the pressure quickly. Stir in spinach, close lid again, and simmer on Keep Warm for 5 minutes until spinach is wilted.

167. Baked Rigatoni with Beef Tomato Sauce

Servings: 4 | Ready in about: 75 minutes

1 tbsp butter
2 lb ground beef
2 (24-oz) cans tomato sauce

1 cup dry red wine
16-oz dry rigatoni
½ tsp garlic powder

1 cup cottage cheese
1 cup shredded mozzarella cheese
½ cup chopped fresh parsley

Choose Sauté your Instant Pot. Melt the butter, add the beef and cook for 5 minutes, or until browned and cooked well. Stir in the tomato sauce, 1 cup water, wine, and rigatoni. Season with the garlic powder and salt. Put the pressure lid together and lock in the Seal position. Choose Pressure Cook and set the time to 2 minutes.

When the timer is done, perform a natural pressure release for 10 minutes, then a quick pressure release and carefully open the lid. Stir in the cottage cheese and evenly sprinkle the top of the pasta with the mozzarella cheese. Close the air fry lid. Choose Broil, and set the time to 3 minutes.. Cook for 3 minutes, or until the cheese has melted, slightly browned, and bubbly. Garnish with the parsley and serve immediately.

168. Rice Pilaf with Mushrooms

Servings: 6 | Ready in about: 35 minutes

1 tbsp olive oil
2 cloves garlic, minced
1 yellow onion, finely chopped

2 cups button mushrooms, sliced
4 cups vegetable stock
2 cups white rice

1 tsp salt
2 sprigs parsley, chopped

Select Sauté in your Instant Pot. Add mushrooms, onion, and garlic, and stir-fry for 5 minutes until tender. Mix in rice, stock, and salt. Seal the pressure lid, choose Pressure Cook on High, and set the timer to 20 minutes. When ready, release pressure naturally for 10 minutes. Use a fork to fluff the rice and add parsley before serving.

169. Turkey Fajita Tortiglioni

Servings: 6 | Ready in about: 35 minutes

2 tsp chili powder	1 tbsp olive oil	1 red bell pepper, sliced diagonally
1 tsp cumin	1 medium red onion, cut into wedges	1 yellow bell pepper, sliced diagonally
1 tsp onion powder	4 garlic cloves, minced	1 green bell pepper, sliced diagonally
1 tsp garlic powder	3 cups chicken broth	1 cup shredded Gouda cheese
½ tsp thyme	1 cup salsa	½ cup sour cream
1 ½ lb turkey breast, cut into strips	16 oz tortiglioni	½ cup chopped parsley

In a bowl, mix chili powder, cumin, garlic powder, onion powder, salt, and oregano. Reserve 1 tsp seasoning. Coat turkey with the remaining seasoning. Warm the oil on Sauté in your Instant Pot. Add in turkey strips and cook for 4 to 5 minutes until browned. Place the turkey in a bowl. Cook the onion and garlic lightly for 1 minute until soft.

In the pot, mix salsa and chicken broth and scrape the bottom of any brown bits. Into the broth mixture, stir in tortiglioni pasta and cover with bell peppers and turkey. Seal the pressure lid, choose Pressure Cook for 5 minutes. When ready, do a quick pressure release. Open the lid and sprinkle with gouda cheese and reserved seasoning and stir well. Divide into plates and top with sour cream. Add parsley for garnishing and serve.

170. Quinoa with Carrots and Onion

Servings: 6 | Ready in about: 15 minutes

1 cup quinoa, rinsed	1 large onion, sliced	Salt to taste
2 carrots, cut into sticks	2 tbsp olive oil	Fresh cilantro, chopped for garnish

Heat oil on Sauté in your Instant Pot. Add in onion and carrots and stir-fry for about 10 minutes until tender and crispy. Remove to a plate. Add 2 cups water , salt and quinoa to the steel pot of the pot. Seal the pressure lid, choose Pressure Cook on High, and set the timer to 1 minute. Once ready, do a quick release. Fluff the cooked quinoa with a fork. Transfer to a serving plate and top with the carrots and onion. Serve scattered with cilantro.

171. Chorizo Mac and Cheese

Servings: 6 | Ready in about: 30 minutes

1 lb macaroni	1 tbsp garlic powder	2 cups milk
3 oz chorizo, chopped	2 tbsp minced garlic	2 cups Cheddar cheese, shredded

Put chorizo in your Instant Pot, select Sauté and stir-fry until crisp, about 5 minutes. Set aside. Wipe the pot with kitchen paper. Add in 3 cups water, macaroni, and salt to taste. Seal lid and cook on for 5 minutes High Pressure. When ready, release the pressure quickly. Stir in cheese and milk until the cheese melts. Divide the mac and cheese between serving bowls. Top with chorizo and serve.

172. Indian Yellow Lentils

Servings: 6 | Ready in about: 30 minutes

1 tbsp ghee	1-inch piece of ginger, peeled, minced	2 tbsp garam masala
2 tsp cumin seeds	Sea salt salt	½ tsp ground turmeric
1 onion, chopped	1 tomato, chopped	½ tsp cayenne pepper
4 garlic cloves, minced	2 cups split yellow lentils, soaked	1 tbsp fresh cilantro, finely chopped

Warm ghee on Sauté in your Instant Pot. Add cumin seeds and cook for 10 seconds until they begin to pop. Stir in onion and cook for 2 to 3 minutes until softened. Mix in ginger and garlic and cook for 1 minute as you stir. Sprinkle with salt. Mix in tomato and cook for 3 to 5 minutes until the mixture breaks down. Stir in turmeric, lentils, garam masala, and cayenne and cover with water. Seal the pressure lid, choose Pressure Cook on High, and set the timer to 8 minutes. When ready, release pressure quickly. Serve in bowls sprinkled with fresh cilantro.

173. Chicken and Chickpea Stew

Servings: 6 | Ready in about: 40 minutes

1 lb boneless, skinless chicken legs	2 jalapeño peppers, minced	2 (14 oz) cans chickpeas, drained
2 tsp ground cumin	3 garlic cloves, crushed	Salt to taste
½ tsp cayenne pepper	2 tsp freshly grated ginger	⅔ cup coconut milk
2 tbsp olive oil	¼ cup chicken stock	¼ cup fresh parsley, chopped
1 onion, minced	1 (24 oz) can crushed tomatoes	2 cups hot cooked basmati rice

Season the chicken with salt, cayenne pepper, and cumin. Set your Instant Pot to Sauté. Warm oil. Add in jalapeño peppers and onion and cook for 5 minutes until soft. Mix in ginger and garlic and cook for 3 minutes until tender. Add ¼ cup chicken stock into the pot to ensure the pan is deglazed, from the pan's bottom scrape any browned bits of food. Mix the onion mixture with chickpeas, tomatoes, and salt. Stir in the chicken to coat in sauce.

Seal the pressure lid, choose Pressure Cook, and set the timer to 20 minutes. When ready, release the pressure quickly. Remove the chicken from the cooker and slice into chunks. Into the remaining sauce, mix in coconut milk. Simmer for 5 minutes on Sauté. Split rice into 6 bowls. Top with chicken, sauce, and cilantro for garnish.

174. South American Black Bean Chili

Servings: 8 | Ready in about: 1 hour 10 minutes

1 tsp olive oil	2 cups black beans, soaked	Salt to taste
1 onion, chopped	1 jalapeño pepper, deseeded and diced	Cotija Cheese, crumbled for garnish
3 cloves garlic, minced	1 tsp dried oregano	Fresh cilantro for garnish
6 cups vegetable broth	1 tsp dried chili flakes	

Warm oil on Sauté in your Instant Pot. Add in garlic and onion and cook for 3 to 4 minutes until fragrant. Add beans, vegetable broth, oregano, chili flakes, salt and jalapeño pepper. Seal the pressure lid, choose Pressure Cook on High, and set the timer to 35 minutes. When ready, quick-release pressure. Divide between serving plates. Apply a topping of cilantro and cotija cheese to serve.

175. Pomodoro Sauce with Rigatoni and Kale

Servings: 6 | Ready in about: 15 minutes

1 lb rigatoni pasta	1 tsp chili flakes	1 handful fresh basil, minced
15 oz canned tomato sauce	2 tsp salt	1 cup kale, chopped
3 garlic cloves, minced	2 tbsp extra-virgin olive oil	¼ cup Parmesan cheese

In your Instant Pot, mix tomato sauce, salt, pasta, chili flakes, and garlic powder. Cover with water. Seal lid and cook for 5 minutes on Low Pressure. When ready, release the pressure quickly. Stir in kale until wilted. Plate the pasta and top with the parmesan and basil. Drizzle olive oil over the pasta.

176. Spicy Pinto Bean and Corn Stew

Servings: 6 | Ready in about: 1 hour 5 minutes

2 tbsp olive oil	1 tbsp ground cumin	14 oz canned tomatoes, chopped
1 onion, chopped	1 tsp red pepper flakes	1 tbsp white wine vinegar
1 red bell pepper, chopped	3 cups vegetable stock	½ cup fresh chives, chopped
1 tbsp dried oregano	2 cups dried pinto beans, soaked	¼ cup fresh corn kernels

Set your Instant Pot to Sauté. Stir in oil, bell pepper, pepper flakes, oregano, onion, and cumin. Cook for 3 minutes until soft. Mix in pinto beans, vegetable stock, and tomatoes. Seal the pressure lid, choose Pressure Cook on High, and set the timer to 30 minutes. Release pressure naturally for 20 minutes. Add in salt and vinegar. Divide in serving plates and top with corn and fresh chives.

177. Chili-Garlic Rice Noodles with Tofu

Servings: 6 | Ready in about: 20 minutes

½ cup soy sauce
2 tbsp brown sugar
2 tbsp rice vinegar

1 tbsp sweet chili sauce
1 tbsp sesame oil
1 tsp fresh minced garlic

20 oz extra firm tofu, cubed
8 oz rice noodles
¼ cup chopped chives, for garnish

Heat the oil on Sauté in your Instant Pot and fry the tofu for 5 minutes until golden brown. Set aside. To the pot, add 2 cups water, garlic, olive oil, vinegar, brown sugar, soy sauce, and chili sauce and mix well until smooth. Stir in rice noodles. Seal the pressure lid, choose Pressure Cook on High, and set the timer to 3 minutes. When ready, release the pressure quickly. Split the noodles between bowls. Top with tofu and fresh chives before serving.

178. Chicken Ragù Bolognese

Servings: 8 | Ready in about: 50 minutes

2 tbsp olive oil
6 oz bacon, cubed
1 onion, minced
1 carrot, minced
1 celery stalk, minced

2 garlic cloves, crushed
¼ cup tomato paste
¼ tsp crushed red pepper flakes
1 ½ lb ground chicken
½ cup white wine

1 cup milk
1 cup chicken broth
Salt to taste
1 lb spaghetti

Warm oil on Sauté in your Instant Pot. Add in bacon and fry for 5 minutes until crispy. Add celery, carrot, garlic and onion and cook for 5 minutes until fragrant. Mix in red pepper flakes and tomato paste and cook for 2 minutes. Break chicken into small pieces and place in the pot. Cook for 10 minutes as you stir until browned. Pour in wine and simmer for 2 minutes. Add in chicken broth and milk.

Seal the pressure lid, choose Pressure Cook on High, and set the timer to 15 minutes. When ready, release the pressure quickly. Add in the spaghetti and stir. Seal the pressure lid again, choose Pressure Cook on High, and set the timer to another 5 minutes. When ready, release the pressure quickly. Check the pasta for doneness. If necessary press Sauté and cook for an additional 2 minutes. Adjust the seasoning and serve right away.

179. Italy-Inspired Mac & Cheese

Servings: 4 | Ready in about: 25 minutes

2 tbsp vegetable oil
1 lb macaroni
2 oz goat cheese, crumbled

4 cups of water
½ cup almond milk
1 tsp oregano, dried

1 tsp sea salt
1 tsp Italian seasoning mix
2 tbsp olive oil

Pour 4 cups of water, and add the macaroni and vegetable oil. Secure the lid and et to Pressure Cook and cook for 3 minutes. Once it goes off, perform a quick pressure release. Carefully open the lid. Drain the macaroni in a large colander and set aside. Press Sauté, and add olive oil, milk, oregano, Italian seasoning mix, and salt. Cook for 6 minutes, stirring constantly. Add the macaroni and stir. Cook for 3 more minutes. Remove from the cooker and top with fresh goat's cheese.

180. Pasta alla Bolognese

Servings: 4 | Ready in about: 15 minutes

1 ½ lb ground beef
12 oz water

24 oz pasta sauce
8 oz pasta

1 tsp Italian seasoning

Set on Sauté. Coat the Instant Pot with cooking spray. Add beef, and cook until browned. Stir in the remaining ingredients. Secure the lid, select Pressure Cook, and cook on High for 5 minutes. When ready, do a quick pressure release. Serve and enjoy!

181. Rosemary Trout with Pasta

Servings: 4 | Ready in about: 30 minutes + marinating time

1 lb squid ink pasta
6 oz trout fillet
1 cup olive oil

juice from 1 lemon
1 tsp fresh rosemary, chopped
1 garlic cloves, crushed and halved

2 tbsp fresh parsley, chopped
Salt to taste

In a large bowl, combine olive oil, lemon juice, 1 garlic clove, rosemary and 1 tsp. of salt. Stir well. Add in the fillets in this mixture and refrigerate for half an hour. Remove the fillets from the fridge and add to the Instant Pot along with 1 cup of water. Secure the lid, set the steam release handle and cook on Pressure Cook for 5 minutes. When ready, do a quick pressure release and add the squid ink pasta, and another cup of water. Seal the lid, and cook on Pressure Cook for 5 minutes. Allow for a natural release for 10 minutes. Sprinkle with parsley and serve.

182. Captain´s Seafood Pasta

Servings: 4 | Ready in about: 15 minutes

1 lb squid ink, cooked
1 lb fresh seafood mix
¼ cup olive oil

3 garlic cloves, crushed
1 tbsp fresh parsley, chopped
1 tbsp fresh rosemary, chopped

½ cup white wine
salt to taste

Grease the bottom of the Instant Pot with 3 tbsp. olive oil. Press Sauté and add garlic. Stir-fry for 2 minutes. Add seafood mix, parsley, rosemary, olive oil, wine, half cup of water and a pinch of salt. Stir well. Secure the lid and set the steam release handle. Press Pressure Cook and set 5 minutes. Perform a quick release and open the lid to add the cooked pasta. Stir and serve.

183. Florentine Spaghetti with Chicken

Servings: 4 | Ready in about: 20 minutes

4 cups chicken broth
4 oz mozzarella cheese, sliced
2 garlic cloves, minced

16 oz Whole-Wheat spaghetti
2 cans mushroom soup
4 cups baby spinach

2 chicken breasts, chopped

Set your Instant Pot to Sauté. Add chicken and broth, and bring it to a boil. Stir in the remaining ingredients. Secure the lid, select Pressure Cook, and cook on High for 4 minutes. Serve immediately.

184. Chicken Alfredo Fettuccine

Servings: 4 | Ready in about: 10 minutes

1 cup shredded chicken, cooked
8 oz Whole-Wheat fettuccine

2 cups water
15 oz Alfredo sauce

Add pasta, chicken, and water in your Instant Pot. Secure the lid, select Pressure Cook, and cook on High for 3 minutes. When ready, release the pressure quickly. Stir in the sauce and serve.

185. Tuna Pomodoro Pasta

Servings: 4 | Ready in about: 20 minutes

30 oz can diced tomatoes
2 garlic cloves, minced

3 tbsp capers
2 cans of tuna, 5 oz each

2 tbsp olive oil
4 cups Whole-Wheat pasta, cooked

Set the Instant Pot to Sauté. Heat the oil, and cook the garlic until fragrant. Stir in the remaining ingredients. Secure the lid, and select Pressure Cook. Cook on high for 1 minute. Release the pressure naturally for 5 minutes.

186. Wisconsin Mac & Cheese

Servings: 4 | Ready in about: 20 minutes

2 cups chicken stock
½ cup milk
1 tbsp organic butter
2 ½ cups elbow macaroni
1 ½ cup shredded pepper jack

Place all of the ingredients into your Instant Pot. Stir to combine. Secure the lid, and select Pressure Cook. Cook at high pressure for 7 minutes. When ready, release the pressure quickly, and serve immediately.

187. White Shrimp Pasta

Servings: 4 | Ready in about: 25 minutes

8 oz bowtie Whole-Wheat pasta
1 onion, chopped
12 oz frozen shrimp
1 tbsp olive oil
½ cup yogurt
1 cup grated Parmesan cheese
2 ½ cups chicken broth
1 garlic clove, minced

Set the Instant Pot to Sauté. Heat the oil. Cook the onion for 3 minutes. Add garlic, and cook for 1 minute. Stir in shrimp, pasta, and broth. Cook for 7 minutes. When ready, release the pressure quickly. Drain the pasta and shrimp, and return them back to the cooker. Stir in parmesan and yogurt, and cook on Sauté for 2 minutes. Serve.

188. Caprese Penne

Servings: 4 | Ready in about: 20 minutes

4 cups Whole-Wheat penne
1 onion, sliced
15 oz tomato sauce
1 cup mozzarella balls
4 handful basil leaves, divided
6 garlic cloves, minced
2 cups water
1 cup halved grape tomatoes
1 tbsp olive oil

Set your Instant Pot to Sauté. Heat the oil, and sauté garlic and onion for 3 minutes. Stir in pasta sauce, half of the basil, tomatoes, pasta, and water. Secure the lid, select Pressure Cook, and cook on High for 4 minutes. When ready, release the pressure naturally for 5 minutes. Add mozzarella and basil, and serve immediately.

189. Creamy Tuna & Macaroni Casserole

Servings: 4 | Ready in about: 30 minutes

2 (10.5) oz cans cream of mushroom soup
1 ½ cups shredded cheddar cheese
4 cups Whole-Wheat macaroni
3 ½ cups water
2 cans tuna
1 cup peas, frozen
Salt and black pepper to taste

Combine everything in your Instant Pot, except for the cheese. Select Pressure Cook, and cook on High for 4 minutes. When ready, do a natural release for 10 minutes. Sprinkle the cheese over, secure the lind and cook for 5 more minutes on Pressure Cook at high pressure. When ready, perform a quick pressure release and serve.

190. Favorite Chicken Linguine

Servings: 4 | Ready in about: 30 minutes

4 chicken breasts, diced
1 box linguine
1 cup water
5 garlic cloves, minced
30 cherry tomatoes, halved
1 tbsp organic butter
½ tsp oregano
1 jar spaghetti sauce

Combine half of the spaghetti sauce, water, pasta, and chicken, in your Instant Pot. Stir in garlic, oregano, and tomatoes. Secure the lid, select Pressure Cook, and cook on High for 20 minutes. Once the cooking is completed, perform a quick pressure release. Open the lid and stir in butter. Top with the remaining sauce.

VEGETARIAN RECIPES

191. Bok Choy & Zoodle Soup

Servings: 6 | Ready in about: 35 minutes

6 oz Shitake mushrooms, stems removed and sliced to a 2-inch thickness
1 lb baby bok choy, stems removed
3 carrots, peeled and sliced diagonally
2 zucchinis, spiralized
2 sweet onion, chopped
2-inch ginger, chopped
2 cloves garlic, peeled
2 tbsp sesame oil
2 tbsp soy sauce
2 tbsp chili paste
Salt to taste
Chopped green onion to garnish
Sesame seeds to garnish

In a food processor, add the chili paste, ginger, onion, and garlic. And process them until they are pureed. Turn on your Instant Pot and select Sauté. Pour in the sesame oil. Once it has heated, add the onion puree and cook for 3 minutes while stirring constantly to prevent burning. Add 6 cups water, mushrooms, soy sauce, and carrots.

Close the lid, secure the pressure valve, and select Pressure Cook on High for 5 minutes. Once the timer has ended, do a quick pressure release and open the lid. Add the zucchini noodles and bok choy, and stir to ensure that they are well submerged in the liquid. Adjust the taste with salt, cover the pot with the air fry lid. Let the vegetables cook for 10 minutes on Broil mode. Use a soup spoon to dish the soup with veggies into soup bowls. Sprinkle with green onions and sesame seeds. Serve as a complete meal.

192. Roasted Squash & Rice with Crispy Tofu

Servings: 4 | Ready in about: 70 minutes

¾ cup water
1 small butternut squash, diced
2 tbsp melted butter, divided
Salt and black pepper to taste
1 tbsp coconut aminos
1 (15-oz) block extra-firm tofu, cubed
2 tsp arrowroot starch
1 cup jasmine rice, cooked

Pour the rice and water into your Instant Pot. Seal the pressure lid, choose Pressure Cook and set the time to 2 minutes. In a bowl, toss the butternut squash with 1 tbsp of melted butter and season with salt and pepper. In another bowl, mix the remaining butter and coconut aminos; toss the tofu in the mixture. Pour the arrowroot starch over the tofu and toss again to combine well.

When done cooking the rice, perform a quick pressure release, and carefully open the pressure lid. Put a trivet in your Instant Pot in the higher position and line with aluminum foil. Arrange the tofu and butternut squash on the trivet. Close the air fry lid. Choose Air Fry, set the temperature to 400°F, and set the time to 20 minutes. After 10 minutes, use tongs to turn the butternut squash and tofu. When done cooking, check for your desired crispiness and serve the tofu and squash with the rice.

193. Cream of Cauliflower & Butternut Squash

Servings: 4 | Ready in about: 32 minutes

2 tsp olive oil
1 large white onion, chopped
4 cloves garlic, minced
1 (2 lb) butternut squash, cubed
2 heads cauliflower, cut in florets
3 cups vegetable broth
3 tsp paprika
Salt and black pepper to taste
1 cup milk, full fat

Topping: Grated Cheddar cheese, crumbled bacon, chopped chives, pumpkin seeds

Select Sauté on your Instant Pot. Heat olive oil, add the white onion and garlic and sauté for 3 minutes. Pour in the butternut squash, cauliflower florets, broth, paprika, pepper, and salt. Stir the ingredients with a spoon. Close the lid, secure the pressure valve, select Pressure Cook on High pressure and adjust the time for 8 minutes.

Once the timer has ended, do a quick pressure release, and open the lid. Stir in the milk and use a stick blender to puree the soup. Adjust the seasoning. Stir in cheese, close the air fry lid and cook for 2 minutes on Broil mode. Dish the soup into serving bowls. Add the remaining toppings to the soup and serve warm.

194. Tangy Risotto & Roasted Bell Peppers

Servings: 4 | Ready in about: 80 minutes

2 tbsp ghee	1 tsp grated lemon zest	1 ½ cups grated Parmesan + for garnish
1 garlic clove, minced	2 cups carnaroli rice	
5 cups vegetable stock	4 mixed bell peppers, cut diagonally	
¼ cup freshly squeezed lemon juice	2 tbsp unsalted butter	

On your Instant Pot, choose Sauté. Melt the ghee and cook the garlic until fragrant, about 1 minute. Then, pour the stock, lemon juice, lemon zest, and rice into your Instant Pot. Sprinkle with 1 teaspoon of salt and stir to combine well. Seal the pressure lid, hit Pressure Cook, set to High, and the timer to 7 minutes. While the rice cooks in a bowl, toss the peppers with the remaining ghee, salt, and black pepper.

When the timer has ended, do a natural pressure release for 10 minutes. Stir the butter into the rice until properly mixed. Then, put a trivet inside the pot in the higher position, which will be over the risotto. Arrange the bell peppers on the trivet. Close the air fry lid. Choose Broil and set the time to 8 minutes. When done cooking, take out the trivet from the pot. Stir the Parmesan cheese into the risotto. To serve, spoon the risotto into serving plates, top with the bell peppers and garnish with extra Parmesan. Serve immediately.

195. Cajun Baked Turnips

Servings: 4 | Ready in about: 85 minutes

4 small turnips, scrubbed clean	1 tsp Cajun seasoning mix	⅓ cup grated Parmesan cheese
¼ cup whipping cream	1½ cups shredded Monterey Jack cheese	
¼ cup sour cream		
½ cup chopped roasted red bell pepper	4 green onions, chopped, divided	

Pour 1 cup of water into your Instant Pot. Put in a trivet and place the turnips on top. Seal the pressure lid, choose Pressure Cook on High, and the cooking time to 10 minutes. After cooking, perform a natural pressure release for 5 minutes. Remove the turnips to a cutting board and allow cooling. Slice off a ½-inch piece from the top and the longer side of each turnip. Scoop the pulp into a bowl, including the flesh from the sliced tops making sure not to rip the skin of the turnip apart. In the bowl with the pulp, add the whipping cream and sour cream and use a potato mash to break the pulp and mix the ingredients until smooth.

Stir in the roasted bell pepper, Cajun seasoning, and Monterey Jack cheese. Fetch out 2 tablespoons of green onions and stir the remaining into the mashed turnips. Fill the turnip skins with the mashed mixture and sprinkle with the Parmesan. Pour the water into the inner pot and return the pot to the base. Put the air fry basket into your Instant Pot. Close the air fry lid, choose Air Fry, adjust the temperature to 375°F, and the time to 2 minutes. When the timer is done, put the turnips in the basket. Close the air fry lid, choose Air Fry, adjust the temperature to 375°F, and the cook time to 15 minutes. Garnish with the reserved onions.

196. Spinach & Butternut Squash Stew

Servings: 6 | Ready in about: 65 minutes

1 tbsp butter	4 cups vegetable broth	½ tsp smoked paprika
1 white onion, diced	1 (15-oz) can sundried tomatoes,	1 tsp coriander powder
4 garlic cloves, minced	2 (15-oz) cans chickpeas, drained	Salt and black pepper to taste
2 lb peeled butternut squash, cubed	1 ½ tsp cumin powder	4 cups baby spinach

Chose Sauté on your Instant Pot. Melt the butter and add in the onion and garlic. Cook, stirring occasionally, for 5 minutes or until soft and fragrant. Add the butternut squash, vegetable broth, tomatoes, chickpeas, cumin, paprika, coriander, salt, and black pepper to the pot. Put the pressure lid together and lock in the Seal position. Choose Pressure Cook on High and set the time to 8 minutes. When the timer is done reading, perform a quick pressure release. Stir in the spinach to wilt, adjust the taste with salt and black pepper, and serve warm.

VEGETARIAN RECIPES

197. Mashed Broccoli with Cream Cheese

Servings: 4 | Ready in about: 12 minutes

3 heads broccoli, chopped
6 oz cream cheese
2 cloves garlic, crushed
2 tbsp butter, unsalted
Salt and black pepper to taste
2 cups water

Turn on your Instant Pot and select Sauté. Drop in the butter; once it melts, add the garlic and cook for 30 seconds while stirring frequently to prevent the garlic from burning. Then, add the broccoli, water, salt, and pepper. Close the lid, secure the pressure valve, and select Pressure Cook on High for 5 minutes.

Once the timer has ended, do a quick pressure release and use a stick blender to mash the ingredients until smooth to your desired consistency and well combined. Stir in Cream cheese. Adjust the taste with salt and pepper. Close the air fry lid and cook for 2 minutes on Broil mode. Serve warm.

198. Eggplant Lasagna

Servings: 4 | Ready in about: 25 minutes

3 large eggplants, sliced in ¼ inches
4 ¼ cups Marinara sauce
1 ½ cups shredded Mozzarella cheese
Cooking spray
Chopped fresh basil to garnish
¼ cup Parmesan cheese, grated

Open the pot and grease it with cooking spray. Arrange the eggplant slices in a single layer on the bottom of the pot and sprinkle some cheese all over it. Arrange another layer of eggplant slices on the cheese, sprinkle this layer with cheese also, and repeat the layering of eggplant and cheese until both ingredients are exhausted.

Lightly spray the eggplant with cooking spray and pour the marinara sauce all over it. Close the lid and pressure valve, and select Pressure Cook on High for 8 minutes. Once the timer has stopped, do a quick pressure release, and open the lid. Sprinkle with Parmesan cheese, close the air fry lid and cook for 10 minutes on Bake at 380°F. With two napkins in hand, gently remove the inner pot. Allow cooling for 10 minutes before serving. Garnish the lasagna with basil and serve warm as a side dish.

199. Pilau Rice with Veggies

Servings: 4 | Ready in about: 30 minutes

3 tbsp olive oil
1 tbsp ginger, minced
1 cup onion, chopped
1 cup green peas
1 cup carrot, chopped
1 cup mushroom, chopped
1 cup broccoli, chopped
1 tbsp chili powder
½ tbsp ground cumin
1 tsp garam masala
½ tsp turmeric powder
1 cup basmati rice, rinsed and drained
2 cups vegetable broth
1 tbsp lemon juice
2 tbsp chopped fresh cilantro

Warm 1 tbsp olive oil on Sauté in your Instant Pot. Add in onion and ginger and cook for 3 minutes until soft. Stir in broccoli, green peas, mushrooms, and carrots. Cook for 1 more minute. Add turmeric powder, chili powder, garam masala, and cumin for seasoning. Cook for 1 minute until soft. Add ¼ cup water into the pot to deglaze. Scrape the bottom to get rid of any browned bits. To the vegetables, add the remaining water and rice. Seal the pressure lid, choose Pressure Cook on High, and set the timer to 1 minute. Release pressure naturally. Use a fork to fluff rice, sprinkle with lemon juice. Divide onto plates and garnish with cilantro.

200. Pesto Minestrone with Cheesy Bread

Servings: 4 | Ready in about: 60 minutes

3 tbsp ghee
1 medium red onion, diced
1 celery stalk, diced
1 large carrot, peeled and diced
1 small yellow squash, diced
1 (14-oz) can chopped tomatoes
1 (27-oz) can cannellini beans, rinsed
3 cups water
1 cup chopped zucchini
1 bay leaf
1 tsp mixed herbs
¼ tsp cayenne pepper
1 Pecorino Romano rind
3 tbsp butter, at room temperature
¼ cup grated Pecorino Romano cheese
1 garlic clove, minced
4 slices white bread
⅓ cup pesto

On your Instant Pot, choose Sauté. Melt the ghee and sauté the onion, celery, and carrot for 3 minutes or until the vegetables start to soften. Stir in the yellow squash, tomatoes, beans, water, zucchini, bay leaf, mixed herbs, cayenne pepper, salt, and Pecorino Romano rind. Seal the pressure lid, choose Pressure Cook on High, and set the time to 4 minutes. In a bowl, mix the butter, shredded cheese, and garlic. Spread the mixture on the bread slices.

After cooking the soup, perform a natural pressure release for 10 minutes. Carefully open the lid. Adjust the taste of the soup with salt and black pepper, and remove the bay leaf. Put a trivet in the upper position of the pot and lay the bread slices on the trivet with the buttered-side up. Close the air fry lid. Choose Broil, adjust the cook time to 5 minutes, and press Start to begin broiling. When the bread is crispy, remove the trivet and set aside. Ladle the soup into bowls and drizzle the pesto over. Serve with the garlic toasts.

201. Spinach Pesto Spaghetti Squash

Servings: 4 | Ready in about: 11 minutes

4 lb spaghetti squash	1 cup water	

For the Pesto

½ cup spinach, chopped	2 garlic cloves, minced	Salt and ground pepper, to taste
2 tbsp walnuts	Zest and juice from ½ lemon	⅓ cup extra virgin olive oil

In a food processor, put all the pesto ingredients and blend until everything is well incorporated. Season to taste and set aside. Put the squash on a flat surface and use a knife to slice in half lengthwise. Scoop out all seeds and discard them. Open your Instant Pot, pour the water into it and fit a trivet at the bottom.

Place the squash halves on the trivet, seal the lid, and select Steam for 5 minutes. Once ready, do a quick pressure release. Remove the squash halves onto a cutting board and use a fork to separate the pulp strands into spaghetti-like pieces. Return to the pot and close the air fry lid. Cook for 2 minutes on Broil. Top with the spinach pesto.

202. Pine nuts and Steamed Asparagus

Servings: 4 | Ready in about: 15 minutes

1 ½ lb asparagus, ends trimmed	1 cup water	½ cup chopped Pine Nuts
Salt and pepper, to taste	1 tbsp butter	1 tbsp olive oil to garnish

Open your Instant Pot, pour the water, and fit in a trivet. Place the asparagus on the trivet, close the air fry lid, select Air Fry, and set the time to 8 minutes at 380°F. At the 4-minute mark, turn the asparagus over. When ready, remove to a plate, sprinkle with salt and pepper, and set aside. Select Sauté on your Instant Pot and melt the butter. Add the pine nuts and cook for 3 minutes until golden. Pour over the asparagus and drizzle olive oil.

203. Rice Stuffed Zucchini Boats

Servings: 4 | Ready in about: 55 minutes

2 small zucchini	½ cup chopped tomatoes	2 tbsp melted butter, divided
½ cup cooked white short-grain rice	½ cup chopped toasted cashew nuts	Salt and black pepper to taste
½ cup canned white beans, drained	½ cup grated Parmesan cheese	

Cut each zucchini in half and then cut in half lengthwise and scoop out the pulp. Chop the pulp roughly and place in a medium bowl. In the bowl, add the rice, beans, tomatoes, cashew nuts, ¼ cup of Parmesan cheese, 1 tablespoon of melted butter, salt, and black pepper. Combine the mixture well but not to break the beans. Spoon the mixed ingredients into the zucchini boats and arrange them on the basket. Close the air fry lid. Choose Air Fry, set the temperature to 400°F, and the time to 15 minutes.

After 15 minutes, sprinkle the zucchini boats with the remaining Parmesan and butter. Close the air fry lid. Choose Broil, set the time to 5 minutes, and choose Start to broil. When done cooking, ensure it is as crisp as you desire; otherwise broil for a few more minutes. Remove the zucchinis and serve.

204. Zucchini & Quinoa Stuffed Red Peppers

Servings: 4 | Ready in about: 40 minutes

4 red bell peppers
2 large tomatoes, chopped
1 small onion, chopped
2 cloves garlic, minced

1 tbsp olive oil
1 cup quinoa, rinsed
2 cups vegetable broth
1 small zucchini, chopped

½ tsp smoked paprika
½ cup chopped mushrooms
Salt and black pepper to taste
1 cup grated Gouda cheese

Select Sauté on your Instant Pot. Heat the olive oil and then add the onion and garlic. Sauté for 3 minutes to soften, stirring occasionally. Include the tomatoes, cook for 3 minutes and then add the quinoa, zucchinis, and mushrooms. Season with paprika, salt, and black pepper and stir with a spoon. Cook for 5-7 minutes.

Use a knife to cut the bell peppers in halves (lengthwise) and remove their seeds and stems. Spoon the quinoa mixture into the bell peppers. Put the peppers in a greased baking dish and pour the broth over. Wipe the pot clean with some paper towels, and pour the 1 cup water into it. After, fit the steamer rack at the bottom of the pot.

Place the baking dish on the rack, cover with aluminum foil, seal the lid, and select Pressure Cook for 15 minutes. Do a quick pressure release. Remove the aluminum foil and sprinkle with the gouda cheese. Close the air fry lid, select Bake and cook for 10 minutes at 375°F. Serve the peppers right away.

205. Creamy Cauliflower & Asparagus Farfalle

Servings: 4 | Ready in about: 60 minutes

1 bunch asparagus, chopped
2 cups cauliflower florets
3 tbsp melted butter, divided
Salt to taste

10 oz farfalle
3 garlic cloves, minced
2 ½ cups vegetable stock
½ cup heavy cream

1 cup cherry tomatoes, halved
¼ cup chopped basil
½ cup grated Parmesan cheese

Put the air fry basket in your Instant Pot. Close the air fry lid, choose Air Fry, adjust the temperature to 375°F, and the time to 2 minutes. Pour the asparagus and cauliflower into a large bowl and drizzle with 1 tablespoon of melted butter. Season with ½ teaspoon of salt and toss. Open the cooker and transfer the vegetables to the basket.

Close the air fry lid, choose Air Fry, adjust the temperature to 375°F, and set the timer to 10 minutes. Press Start to begin roasting. After 5 minutes, carefully open the lid and mix the vegetables. Close the lid and continue cooking. When done roasting, take out the basket, and cover the top with aluminum foil. Set aside.

Place the farfalle into the inner pot and add the remaining butter. Using tongs, toss the farfalle to coat, and add the remaining salt, garlic, and water. Stir to combine. Seal the pressure lid, choose Pressure Cook on High, and the cooking time to 5 minutes. After cooking, do a quick pressure release and carefully open the lid.

Stir the heavy cream and tomatoes into the pasta, tossing well. Choose Sauté. Press Start to simmer the cream until the sauce has your desired consistency. Gently mix in the asparagus and cauliflower. Allow warming to soften the vegetables, then stir in the basil and Parmesan cheese. Dish the creamy farfalle and serve warm.

206. Easy Spanish Rice

Servings: 4 | Ready in about: 50 minutes

3 tbsp ghee
1 small onion, chopped
2 garlic cloves, minced
1 banana pepper, seeded and chopped

1 cup jasmine rice
⅓ cup red salsa
¼ cup stewed tomatoes
½ cup vegetable stock

1 tsp Mexican Seasoning Mix
1 (16-oz) can pinto beans, drained
1 tsp salt
1 tbsp chopped fresh parsley

On your Instant Pot, choose Sauté. Add the ghee to melt and cook the onion, garlic, and banana pepper in the ghee. Cook for 2 minutes or until fragrant. Stir in the rice, salsa, tomato sauce, vegetable stock, Mexican seasoning, pinto beans, and salt. Seal the pressure lid, choose Pressure Cook on High and adjust the cook time to 6 minutes. After cooking, do a natural pressure release for 10 minutes. Stir in the parsley, dish the rice, and serve.

207. Mushroom Risotto with Swiss Chard

Servings: 4 | Ready in about: 60 minutes

3 tbsp ghee, divided	⅓ cup white wine	½ cup sautéed mushrooms
1 small bunch Swiss chard, chopped	2 cups vegetable stock	½ cup caramelized onions
1 cup short-grain rice	½ tsp salt	⅓ cup grated Pecorino Romano cheese

Press Sauté on your Instant Pot. Melt 2 tbsp of ghee and sauté the Swiss chard for 5 minutes until wilted. Set aside. Use a paper towel to wipe out any remaining liquid in the pot and melt the remaining ghee. Stir in rice and cook for 1 minute. Add the wine and cook for 3 minutes with occasional stirring until the wine has evaporated. Add in stock and salt. Stir to combine. Seal the pressure lid, choose Pressure Cook on High, and the time to 8 minutes. When the timer is done reading, perform a quick pressure release. Stir in the mushrooms, swiss chard, and onions and let the risotto heat for 1 minute. Mix in the cheese to melt. Serve immediately.

208. Sticky Noodles with Tofu & Peanuts

Servings: 4 | Ready in about: 20 minutes

1 package tofu, cubed	¼ cup orange juice	1 tbsp sriracha
8 oz egg noodles	1 tbsp fresh ginger, peeled and minced	¼ cup roasted peanuts
2 bell peppers, sliced	2 tbsp vinegar	3 scallions, thinly sliced
¼ cup soy sauce	1 tbsp sesame oil	

In your Instant Pot, mix tofu, bell peppers, orange juice, sesame oil, ginger, egg noodles, soy sauce, vinegar, and sriracha. Cover with enough water. Seal the pressure lid, choose Pressure Cook, and set the timer to 2 minutes. When ready, release the pressure quickly. Apply a topping of scallions and peanuts before serving.

209. Crème de la Broc

Servings: 6 | Ready in about: 25 minutes

1 ½ cups grated yellow and white Cheddar + extra for topping		
3 cups heavy cream	4 tbsp flour	3 cloves garlic, minced
3 cups vegetable broth	4 cups chopped broccoli florets	1 tsp Italian Seasoning
4 tbsp butter	1 medium Red onion, chopped	1 ½ oz cream cheese

Select Sauté on your Instant Pot and melt the butter once the pot is ready. Add the flour and use a spoon to stir until it clumps up. Gradually pour in the heavy cream while stirring until white sauce forms. Fetch out the butter sauce into a bowl and set aside. Add the onions, garlic, broth, broccoli, Italian seasoning, and cream cheese.

Use a wooden spoon to stir the mixture. Seal the lid, and select Pressure Cook on High for 12 minutes. Once the timer has ended, do a quick pressure release. Add in butter sauce and cheddar cheese, salt, and pepper. Close the air fry lid and cook on Broil mode for 3 minutes. Dish the soup, top with extra cheese, and serve.

210. Buttered Leafy Greens

Servings: 4 | Ready in about: 10 minutes

2 lb baby spinach	½ lb Swiss chard	Salt and black pepper to season
1 lb kale leaves	1 tbsp dried basil	½ tbsp butter

Turn on your Instant Pot, add the ½ cup water and fit a trivet at the bottom of the pot. Put the spinach, swiss chard, and kale on the trivet. Close the lid, secure the pressure valve, and select Steam mode on High pressure for 3 minutes. Once the timer has ended, do a quick pressure release and open the lid. Remove the trivet with the wilted greens onto a plate and discard the water from the pot. Select Sauté and add the butter. Add the spinach and kale back to the pot and the dried basil. Season with salt and pepper and stir. Close the air fry lid and cook for 4 minutes on Bake at 380°F. Dish the greens into serving plates and serve as a side dish.

211. Garganelli with Swiss Cheese and Mushrooms

Servings: 4 | Ready in about: 60 minutes

8 oz garganelli	1 ½ tsp arrowroot starch	3 tbsp sour cream
1 (12–fluid oz) can evaporated milk	8 oz Swiss cheese, shredded	1½ cups panko breadcrumbs
1 ½ tsp salt	1 recipe sautéed mushrooms	3 tbsp melted unsalted butter
1 large egg	2 tbsp chopped fresh cilantro	3 tbsp grated Cheddar cheese

Pour the garganelli into the inner pot, add half of the evaporated milk, 1 ¼ cups water, and salt. Seal the pressure lid, choose Pressure Cook on High, and the time to 4 minutes. In a bowl, whisk the remaining milk with the egg. In another bowl, combine the arrowroot starch with the Swiss cheese.

When the pasta has cooked, perform a natural pressure release for 10 minutes. Open the lid. Pour in the milk-egg mixture and a large handful of the starch mixture. Stir to melt the cheese and then add the remaining cheese in 3 or 4 batches while stirring to melt. Mix in the mushrooms, cilantro, and sour cream.

In a bowl, mix the breadcrumbs, melted butter, and cheddar cheese. Then, sprinkle the mixture evenly over the pasta. Close the air fry lid. Choose Broil and adjust the time to 5 minutes. Press Start to begin crisping. When done, the top should be brown and crispy, otherwise broil further for 3 minutes, and serve immediately.

212. Squash Parmesan & Linguine

Servings: 4 | Ready in about: 75 minutes

1 lb linguine	2 eggs	1 (24-oz) tomato sauce
2 tsp salt	1 cup seasoned panko breadcrumbs	2 tbsp olive oil
4 cups water + 2 tbsp	½ cup grated Parmesan + for garnish	1 cup shredded mozzarella cheese
1 cup flour	1 yellow squash, peeled and sliced	Minced fresh cilantro for garnish

Break the spaghetti in half and place in your Instant Pot. Pour 4 cups of water and 1 teaspoon of salt. Seal the pressure lid, choose Pressure Cook on High, and set the time to 2 minutes. In a bowl, combine the flour and the remaining salt evenly. In another bowl, whisk the eggs and 2 tablespoons of water.

In a third bowl, mix the breadcrumbs and Parmesan cheese. Coat each squash slice in the flour. Shake off the excess flour, dip the slice in the egg wash, and then dredge in the breadcrumbs. Place on a plate and set aside. When ready, perform a quick pressure release. Drain the pasta through a colander and transfer to the pot.

Pour all but ¼ cup of the tomato sauce over the linguine. Mix gently. Fix a trivet inside the pot over the linguine. Place the breaded squash on the trivet and lightly brush with oil. Close the air fry lid. Choose Air Fry, set the temperature to 350°F, and set the time to 15 minutes. Press Start to cook.

When done cooking, spread the remaining tomato sauce on top of the squash and sprinkle with the mozzarella cheese. Close the air fry lid again, choose Broil, and set the time to 3 minutes. When ready, spoon the pasta into plates, place the breaded squash to the side, and garnish with fresh cilantro.

213. Vegetarian Minestrone Soup

Servings: 4 | Ready in about: 40 minutes

1 (15.5 oz) can Cannellini beans	2 small Red onions, cut into wedges	1 bay leaf
1 Potato, peeled and diced	1 cup chopped celery	4 cups vegetable broth
1 carrot, peeled and chopped	1 tbsp chopped fresh rosemary	2 tsp olive oil
1 cup chopped butternut squash	8 sage leaves, chopped finely	2 tbsp chopped fresh parsley

Add the potato, carrot, squash, onion, celery, rosemary, sage, bay leaf, vegetable broth, salt, pepper, and olive oil to the pot of your Instant Pot. Close the lid, secure the pressure valve, and select Pressure Cook for 7 minutes. Once done, do a quick pressure release. Add the cannellini beans and stir. Close the air fry lid and cook for 5 minutes on Broil. Garnish with fresh parsley and serve with a side of crusted bread.

214. Swiss Cheese & Mushroom Tarts

Servings: 4 | Ready in about: 75 minutes

2 tbsp melted butter, divided	¼ tsp salt	1 sheet puff pastry, thawed
1 small white onion, sliced	¼ tsp freshly ground black pepper	1 cup shredded Swiss cheese
5 oz oyster mushrooms, sliced	¼ cup dry white wine	1 tbsp thinly sliced fresh green onions

Choose Sauté on your Instant Pot. Add 1 tablespoon of butter, the onion, and mushrooms to the pot. Sauté for 5 minutes or until the vegetables are tender and browned. Season with salt and black pepper. Pour in the white wine, and cook until evaporated, about 2 minutes. Spoon the vegetables into a bowl and set aside. Unwrap the puff pastry and cut into 4 squares. Pierce the dough with a fork and brush both sides with the remaining oil. Share half of the cheese over the puff pastry squares, leaving a ½-inch border around the edges.

Also, share the mushroom mixture over the pastry squares and top with the remaining cheese. Put 1 tart in the air fry basket. Close the air fry lid, choose Air Fry, set the temperature to 400°F, and set the time to 6 minutes. After 6 minutes, check the tart for your preferred brownness. Take the tart out of the basket and transfer to a plate. Repeat the process with the remaining tarts. Garnish with the green onions and serve.

215. Artichoke with Garlic Mayo

Servings: 4 | Ready in about: 20 minutes

2 large artichokes	2 garlic cloves, smashed	Salt and black pepper to taste
2 cups water	½ cup mayonnaise	Juice of 1 lime

Using a serrated knife, trim about 1 inch from the artichokes' top. Into your Instant Pot, add water and set trivet over. Lay the artichokes on the trivet. Seal lid and cook for 14 minutes. When ready, release the pressure quickly. Mix the mayonnaise with garlic and lime juice. Season with salt and pepper. Serve.

216. Easy Green Squash Gruyere

Servings: 4 | Ready in about: 70 minutes

1 large green squash, sliced	1½ cups panko breadcrumbs	2 cups tomato sauce
3 tbsp melted unsalted butter	⅓ cup grated Gruyere cheese	1 cup shredded mozzarella cheese

Season the squash with salt and place it on a wire rack to drain liquid for 10 minutes. In a bowl, combine melted butter, breadcrumbs, and Gruyere cheese. Rinse the squash slices with water and blot dry with paper towels. Arrange the squash in the inner pot in a single layer as much as possible and pour the tomato sauce over the slices. Seal the pressure lid, choose Pressure Cook on High, and the time to 5 minutes.

When the timer has read to the end, perform a quick pressure release. Sprinkle the squash slices with the mozzarella cheese. Close the air fry lid. Choose Bake, adjust the temperature to 375°F, and the cooking time to 2 minutes. Press Start to broil. After, carefully open the lid and sprinkle the squash with the breadcrumb mixture. Close the air fry lid again, choose Bake, adjust the temperature to 375°F, and the cooking time to 8 minutes.

217. Mushroom Brown Rice Pilaf

Servings: 4 | Ready in about: 15 minutes

2 cups brown rice, rinsed	3 tsp olive oil	¼ cup Romano cheese, grated
4 cups vegetable broth	1 cup Portobello mushrooms, sliced	2 sprigs parsley, to garnish

Heat the oil on Sauté in your Instant Pot and stir-fry the mushrooms for 3 minutes until golden. Season with salt, and add rice and broth. Close the lid, secure the pressure valve, and select Pressure Cook on High for 5 minutes. Once the timer has ended, do a quick pressure release and open the lid. Spread the cheese over and close the air fry lid. Select Bake, adjust to 375°F and the timer to 2 minutes. To serve, top with freshly chopped parsley.

218. Vegan Carrot Gazpacho

Servings: 4 | Ready in about: 2 hour 30 minutes

1 lb trimmed carrots	1 cucumber, peeled and chopped	1 red onion, chopped
1 pinch salt	¼ cup extra-virgin olive oil	2 cloves garlic
1 lb tomatoes, chopped	2 tbsp lemon juice	2 tbsp white wine vinegar

To your Instant Pot, add carrots, salt, and water. Seal the pressure lid, choose Pressure Cook on High, and set the timer to 20 minutes. Once ready, do a quick release. Set the beets in a bowl and place in the refrigerator to cool. In a blender, add carrots, cucumber, red onion, pepper, garlic, olive oil, tomatoes, lemon juice, vinegar, and salt. Blend until very smooth. Place gazpacho in a serving bowl, chill while covered for 2 hours.

219. Chipotle Chili

Servings: 4 | Ready in about: 35 minutes

4 celery stalks, chopped	2 tsp smoked paprika	2 cups tomato sauce
2 (15-oz) cans diced tomatoes	2 green bell pepper, diced	1.5 oz dark chocolate, chopped
1 tbsp olive oil	1 tbsp cinnamon powder	1 small chipotle, minced
3 carrots, chopped	1 tbsp cumin powder	1 ½ cups walnuts, chopped + to garnish
2 cloves garlic, minced	1 sweet onion, chopped	Chopped cilantro to garnish

On your Instant Pot and select Sauté. Heat the oil and add the onion, celery, and carrots. Sauté for 4 minutes. Add the garlic, cumin, cinnamon, and paprika. Stir and cook for 2 minutes. Include bell peppers, tomatoes, tomato sauce, chipotle, ½ cup water, and walnuts stir. Seal the lid and select Pressure Cook for 15 minutes.

Once the timer has ended, do a quick pressure release, and open the lid. Pour the chopped chocolate in and stir it until it melts and is well incorporated into the chili. Adjust the taste with salt and pepper. Close the air fry lid and cook for 5 minutes on Broil. Garnish it with the remaining walnuts and cilantro. Serve with some noodles.

220. Green Cream Soup

Servings: 4 | Ready in about: 25 minutes

½ lb kale leaves, chopped	1 onion, chopped	Salt and pepper, to taste
½ lb spinach leaves, chopped	4 cloves garlic, minced	1 ½ tbsp white wine vinegar
½ lb Swiss chard leaves, chopped	4 cups vegetable broth	Chopped Peanuts to garnish
1 tbsp olive oil	1 ¼ cup heavy cream	

Turn on your Instant Pot and select Sauté. Add the olive oil; once it has heated, add the onion and garlic and sauté for 2-3 minutes until soft. Add greens and vegetable broth. Close the lid, secure the pressure valve, and select Pressure Cook on High for 10 minutes. Once the timer has ended, do a quick pressure release. Add the white wine vinegar, salt, and pepper. Use a stick blender to puree the ingredients in the pot. Close the air fry lid and cook for 3 minutes on Broil. Stir in heavy cream. Sprinkle with peanuts and serve.

221. Green Minestrone

Servings: 4 | Ready in about: 30 minutes

2 tbsp olive oil	1 leek, sliced thinly	2 cups vegetable broth
1 head broccoli, cut into florets	1 zucchini, chopped	3 whole black peppercorns
4 celery stalks, sliced thinly	1 cup green beans	2 cups chopped kale

To your Instant Pot, add broccoli, leek, green beans, salt, peppercorns, zucchini, and celery. Mix in vegetable broth, oil, and cover with water. Seal the pressure lid, choose Pressure Cook on High, and set the timer to 4 minutes. Release pressure naturally for 5 minutes, then release the remaining pressure quickly. Add kale into the soup and stir. Set to Keep Warm and cook until tender.

222. Quick Crispy Kale Chips

Servings: 2 | Ready in about: 10 minutes

4 cups kale, stemmed and packed	1 tbsp of yeast flakes	Salt to taste
2 tbsp of olive oil	1 tsp of vegan seasoning	

In a bowl, add the oil, kale, vegan seasoning, and yeast and mix well. Dump the kale in the air fry basket. Set the heat to 370°F, close the air fry lid and fry for a total of 6 minutes on Air Fry mode. Shake it from time to time.

223. Rice & Olives Stuffed Mushrooms

Servings: 4 | Ready in about: 70 minutes

4 Portobello mushrooms, stems and gills removed		
2 tbsp melted butter	¼ cup black olives, pitted and chopped	1 lemon, juiced
½ cup brown rice, cooked	1 green bell pepper, seeded and diced	Salt and black pepper to taste
1 tomato, seed removed and chopped	½ cup feta cheese, crumbled	Minced fresh cilantro for garnish

Brush the mushrooms with the melted butter. Open the air fry lid and arrange the mushrooms open-side up and in a single layer in the air fry basket. Close the air fry lid. Choose Air Fry, set the temperature to 375°F, and the time to 20 minutes. In a bowl, combine the rice, tomato, olives, bell pepper, feta, lemon juice, salt, and pepper.

Open the air fry lid and spoon the rice mixture equally into the 4 mushrooms. Close the lid. Choose Air Fry, set the temperature to 350°F, and set the time to 8 minutes. Press Start to commence cooking. When the mushrooms are ready, remove to a plate, garnish with fresh cilantro and serve immediately.

224. Cheesy Stuffed Mushrooms

Servings: 4 | Ready in about: 40 minutes

¼ cup roasted red bell peppers, chopped		
10 white mushrooms, stems removed	1 small onion, chopped	½ tsp dried oregano
1 red bell pepper, seeded and chopped	¼ cup grated Parmesan cheese	Salt and black pepper to taste
1 green onion, chopped	1 tbsp butter	

Turn on your Instant Pot and select Sauté. Melt the butter and add the roasted and fresh peppers, green onion, onion, oregano, salt, and pepper. Use a spoon to mix and cook for 2 minutes. Spoon the bell pepper mixture into the mushrooms and place the stuffed mushrooms in the pot. Pour in ½ cup water. Seal the lid.

Select Pressure Cook on High for 5 minutes. Once the timer has ended, do a quick pressure release and open the lid. Sprinkle with parmesan cheese and close the air fry lid. Select Bake adjust the temperature to 380°F, and the time to 2 minutes and press Start button. Remove the stuffed mushrooms onto a plate and repeat the cooking process for the remaining mushrooms. Serve hot with a side of steamed green veggies and a sauce.

225. Pesto Quinoa Bowls with Veggies

Servings: 2 | Ready in about: 30 minutes

1 cup quinoa, rinsed	1 cup broccoli florets	1 avocado, thinly sliced
2 cups water	1 carrot, peeled and chopped	¼ cup pesto sauce
Salt and ground black pepper to taste	½ lb Brussels sprouts	Lemon wedges, for serving
1 small beet, peeled and cubed	2 eggs	

In your Instant Pot, mix water, salt, quinoa and pepper. Set a trivet to the pot over quinoa. On the trivet, place eggs, Brussels sprouts, broccoli, beet cubes, carrots, pepper, and salt. Seal the pressure lid, choose Pressure Cook on High, and set the timer to 1 minute. Release pressure naturally for 10 minutes. Remove the trivet from the pot. Set the eggs in a bowl of ice water. Peel and halve the eggs. Use a fork to fluff the quinoa. Separate quinoa, broccoli, avocado, carrots, beet, Brussels sprouts, eggs, and a dollop of pesto into two bowls. Serve alongside a lemon.

226. Asian-Style Tofu Soup

Servings: 4 | Ready in about: 25 minutes

2 tbsp Korean red pepper flakes (gochugaru)
16 oz firm Tofu
7 cloves garlic, minced
1 tbsp sugar
1 tbsp olive oil
2 tbsp ginger paste
¼ cup soy sauce
3 cup sliced bok choy
6 oz dry egg noodles
4 cups vegetable broth
1 cup sliced Shitake mushrooms
½ cup chopped cilantro

Drain the liquid out of the tofu, pat the tofu dry with paper towels, and use a knife to cut them into 1-inch cubes. Turn your Instant Pot on and select Sauté. Pour the oil to heat, add the garlic and ginger, and sauté for 2 minutes. Add the sugar, broth, and soy sauce. Stir and cook for 30 seconds. Include the tofu and bok choy.

Seal the lid and select Pressure Cook on High for 10 minutes. Once the timer has ended, do a quick pressure release and open the lid. Add the zucchini noodles, give it a good stir, and close the air fry lid. Let the soup cook for 4 minutes on Broil mode. Use a soup spoon to fetch the soup into soup bowls, top with cilantro and enjoy.

227. Aloo Gobi with Cilantro

Servings: 4 | Ready in about: 40 minutes

1 tbsp vegetable oil
1 head cauliflower, cut into florets
1 potato, peeled and diced
1 tbsp ghee
2 tsp cumin seeds
1 onion, minced
4 garlic cloves, minced
1 tomato, cored and chopped
1 jalapeño pepper, deseeded and minced
1 tbsp curry paste
1 tsp ground turmeric
½ tsp chili pepper
1 cup water
Salt to taste
A handful of cilantro leaves, chopped

Warm oil on Sauté in your Instant Pot. Add in potato and cauliflower and cook for 8 to 10 minutes until lightly browned. Add salt for seasoning. Set the vegetables to a bowl. Add ghee to the pot. Mix in cumin seeds and cook for 10 seconds until they start to pop. Add onion and garlic and cook for 3 minutes until softened. Add in tomato, curry paste, chili pepper, jalapeño, curry, and turmeric and cook for 5 minutes until the tomato starts to break down. Return potato and cauliflower to the pot. Add water and salt and stir. Seal the pressure lid, choose Pressure Cook, and set the timer to 4 minutes. Release pressure naturally. Top with cilantro and serve.

228. Herby-Garlic Potatoes

Servings: 4 | Ready in about: 30 minutes

1 ½ lb potatoes
3 tbsp butter
3 cloves garlic, thinly sliced
2 tbsp fresh rosemary, chopped
½ tsp fresh thyme, chopped
½ tsp fresh parsley, chopped
¼ tsp ground black pepper
½ cup vegetable broth

Pierce each potato to ensure there are no blowouts when placed under pressure. Melt butter on Sauté in your Instant Pot. Add in potatoes, rosemary, parsley, pepper, thyme, and garlic, and cook for 10 minutes until potatoes are browned. In a bowl, mix miso paste and vegetable stock. Stir into the mixture in the pressure cooker. Seal the pressure lid, choose Pressure Cook on High, and set the timer to 5 minutes. Do pressure quickly.

229. Indian Vegan Curry

Servings: 3 | Ready in about: 25 minutes

1 tbsp butter
1 onion, chopped
2 cloves garlic, minced
1 tsp ginger, grated
1 tsp ground cumin
1 tsp red chili powder
1 tsp salt
½ tsp ground turmeric
1 (15 oz) can chickpeas, drained
1 tomato, diced
⅓ cup water
5 cups collard greens, chopped
½ tsp garam masala
1 tsp lemon juice

Melt butter on Sauté in your Instant Pot. Toss in the onion and cook for 2 minutes until soft. Mix in ginger, cumin powder, turmeric, red chili powder, garlic, and salt and cook for 30 seconds until crispy. Stir in tomatoes. In the pot, mix ⅓ water, tomato and chickpeas. Seal the pressure lid, choose Pressure Cook on High for 4 minutes. When ready, release the pressure quickly. Into the chickpea mixture, stir in lemon juice, collard greens and garam masala until well coated. Cook for 2 to 3 minutes until collard greens wilt. Serve over rice or naan.

230. Punjabi Palak Paneer

Servings: 4 | Ready in about: 20 minutes

¼ cup milk	1 tomato, chopped	1 lb spinach, chopped
2 tbsp butter	1 tsp minced fresh ginger	1 tsp salt, or to taste
1 tsp cumin seeds	1 tsp minced fresh garlic	2 cups paneer, cubed
1 tsp coriander seeds	1 red onion, chopped	1 tsp chili powder

Warm butter on Sauté in your Instant Pot. Add in garlic, cumin seeds, coriander seeds, chili powder, ginger, and garlic and fry for 1 minute until fragrant. Add onion and cook for 2 more minutes until crispy. Add in 1 cup water and spinach. Seal the pressure lid, choose Pressure Cook, and set the timer to 1 minute. When ready, release the pressure quickly. Pulse in a blender to obtain a smooth paste. Mix paneer and tomato with spinach mixture.

231. Green Beans with Feta & Nuts

Servings: 6 | Ready in about: 15 minutes

Juice from 1 lemon	2 lb green beans, trimmed	1 cup feta cheese, crumbled
1½ cups water	1 cup chopped toasted pine nuts	6 tbsp olive oil

Add water to your Instant Pot. Set a trivet over the water. Loosely heap green beans on the trivet. Seal lid and cook on High Pressure for 5 minutes. When the cooking cycle is complete, release pressure quickly. Drop green beans into a salad bowl. Top with olive oil, feta cheese, pepper, and pine nuts.

232. Creamy Mashed Potatoes with Spinach

Servings: 6 | Ready in about: 30 minutes

3 lb potatoes, peeled and quartered	½ cup milk	2 tbsp chopped fresh chives
1½ cups water	⅓ cup butter	2 cups spinach, chopped

In your Instant Pot, mix water, salt and potatoes. Seal the pressure lid, choose Pressure Cook on High, and set the timer to 8 minutes. When ready, release the pressure quickly. Drain potatoes, and reserve the liquid in a bowl. In a large bowl, mash the potatoes. Mix with butter and milk. Season with pepper and salt. With reserved cooking liquid, thin the potatoes to attain the desired consistency. Put the spinach in the remaining potato liquid and stir until wilted. Season with salt and pepper. Drain and serve with potato mash. Garnish with pepper and chives.

233. Potato Filled Bread Rolls

Servings: 4 | Ready in about: 25 minutes

8 slices of bread	2 green chilies, deseeded, chopped	1 tbsp olive oil
5 large potatoes, boiled, mashed	1 medium onion, chopped	2 sprigs curry leaf
½ tsp turmeric	½ tsp mustard seeds	Salt to taste

Combine the olive oil, onion, curry leaves, and mustard seeds in the air fry basket. Cook for 5 minutes. Mix the onion mixture with the mashed potatoes, chilies, turmeric, and some salt. Divide the dough into 8 equal pieces. Trim the sides of the bread, and wet it with some water. Make sure to get rid of the excess water. Take one wet bread slice in your palm and place one of the potato pieces in the center. Roll the bread over the filling, sealing the edges. Place the rolls onto a prepared baking dish, close the air fry lid and cook for 12 minutes on Air Fry at 350°F.

234. Thai Vegetable Stew

Servings: 4 | Ready in about: 30 minutes

1 tbsp coconut oil
1 cup onion, chopped
1 tbsp fresh ginger, minced
2 garlic cloves, minced
3 carrots, peeled and chopped
1 red bell pepper, sliced
1 orange bell pepper, sliced
1 (14 oz) can coconut milk
1 cup bok choy, chopped
½ cup water
2 tbsp red curry paste

Melt coconut oil on Sauté in your Instant Pot. Add in onion and cook for 3 to 4 minutes until soft. Add garlic and ginger and cook for 30 more seconds until soft. Mix in orange bell pepper, red bell pepper and carrots. Cook for 3 to 4 minutes until the peppers become soft and tender. Add curry paste, bok choy, coconut milk, and water and stir well to obtain a consistent color of the sauce. Seal lid and cook for 1 minute on High Pressure. When ready, release the pressure quickly. Serve hot!

235. Tahini Sweet Potato Mash

Servings: 4 | Ready in about: 25 minutes

2 lb sweet potatoes, peeled and cubed
2 tbsp tahini
1 tbsp sugar
¼ tsp ground nutmeg
Chopped fresh chives, for garnish
sea salt to taste

To your Instant Pot, add 1 cup cold water and set a steamer basket into it. Add in sweet potato cubes. Seal the pressure lid, choose Pressure Cook, and set the timer to 8 minutes. When ready, release the pressure quickly. In a bowl, add cooked sweet potatoes and slightly mash. Using a hand mixer, whip in nutmeg, sugar, and tahini until the sweet potatoes attain the consistency you desire. Add salt for seasoning. Top with chives and serve.

236. Asparagus with Feta

Servings: 4 | Ready in about: 15 minutes

1 cup water
1 lb asparagus spears, ends trimmed
1 tbsp olive oil
Salt and black pepper to taste
1 lemon, cut into wedges
1 cup feta cheese, cubed

Into your Instant Pot, add water and set trivet over the water. Place steamer basket on the trivet. Place the asparagus into the steamer basket. Seal the pressure lid, choose Pressure Cook on High, and set the timer to 1 minute. When ready, release the pressure quickly. Add olive oil in a bowl and toss in asparagus until well coated. Season with pepper and salt. Serve alongside feta cheese and lemon wedges.

237. Fall Celeriac Pumpkin Soup

Servings: 4 | Ready in about: 30 minutes

1 celeriac, peeled and cubed
16 oz pumpkin puree
5 stalks celery, chopped
1 white onion, chopped
1 lb green beans, cut in 5 strips each
2 cups vegetable broth
3 cups spinach leaves
1 tbsp chopped basil leaves
¼ tsp dried thyme
⅛ tsp rubbed sage
Salt to taste

Open your Instant Pot and pour in the celeriac, pumpkin puree, celery, onion, green beans, vegetable broth, basil leaves, thyme, sage, and salt. Seal the lid and select Steam for 5 minutes. Once ready, do a quick pressure release. Add in the spinach and stir. Close the air fry lid and cook for 3 minutes on Broil. Serve the soup into bowls.

238. Parsley Mashed Cauliflower

Servings: 4 | Ready in about: 15 minutes

1 head cauliflower
1 tbsp butter
¼ tsp celery salt
¼ cup heavy cream
1 tbsp fresh parsley, finely chopped
⅛ tsp freshly ground black pepper

Into your Instant Pot, add 2 cups water and set trivet on top and lay cauliflower head onto the trivet. Seal the pressure lid, choose Pressure Cook on High, and set the timer to 8 minutes. Release the pressure quickly. Remove the trivet and drain liquid from the pot before returning to the base. Take back the cauliflower to the pot with pepper, heavy cream, salt, and butter. Use an immersion blender to blend until smooth. Top with parsley.

239. Carrot & Lentil Chili

Servings: 4 | Ready in about: 30 minutes

1 tbsp olive oil
1 onion, chopped
1 cup celery, chopped
2 garlic cloves, sliced

1 onion, chopped
3 cups vegetable stock
1 cup dried lentils, rinsed
4 carrots, halved lengthwise

1 tbsp harissa, or more to taste
½ tsp sea salt
A handful of fresh parsley, chopped

Warm olive oil on Sauté in your Instant Pot. Add in onion, garlic, and celery, and cook for 5 minutes until onion is soft. Mix in lentils, carrots, and vegetable stock. Seal the pressure lid, choose Pressure Cook on High, and set the timer to 10 minutes. Release pressure naturally. Mix lentils with salt and harissa and serve topped with parsley.

240. Steamed Artichokes with Lemon Aioli

Servings: 4 | Ready in about: 20 minutes

4 artichokes, trimmed
1 lemon, halved
1 tsp lemon zest

1 tbsp lemon juice
3 cloves garlic, crushed
½ cup mayonnaise

1 cup water
Salt
1 small handful parsley, chopped

On the artichokes cut ends, rub with lemon. Add water into your Instant Pot. Set a trivet over the water. Place the artichokes into the steamer basket with the points upwards. Sprinkle each with salt. Seal lid and cook on High pressure for 10 minutes. When ready, release the pressure quickly. In a bowl, combine mayonnaise, garlic, lemon juice, and lemon zest. Season to taste with salt. Serve with warm steamed artichokes sprinkled with parsley.

241. Spicy Cauliflower Rice with Peas

Servings: 2 | Ready in about: 15 minutes

1 head cauliflower, cut into florets
1 cup water

2 tbsp olive oil
1 tsp chili powder

¼ cup green peas
1 tbsp chopped fresh parsley

Into your Instant Pot, add water. Set a trivet over water. Add cauliflower into the steamer basket. Seal the pressure lid, choose Pressure Cook on High, and set the timer to 1 minute. When ready, release the pressure quickly. Remove the trivet. Drain water from the pot, pat dry, and return to pressure cooker base. Set to Sauté the pot. Warm oil. Add in cauliflower and stir to break into smaller pieces like rice. Stir in chili powder, peas and salt. Place the cauliflower rice into plates and add parsley for garnishing.

242. Veggie Skewers

Servings: 4 | Ready in about: 20 minutes

2 tbsp cornflour
⅔ cup canned beans
⅓ cup grated carrots
2 boiled and mashed potatoes

¼ cup chopped fresh mint leaves
½ tsp garam masala powder
½ cup paneer
1 green chili

1-inch piece of fresh ginger
3 garlic cloves
Salt to taste

Soak 12 skewers until ready to use. Place the beans, carrots, garlic, ginger, chili, paneer, and mint, in a food processor and process until smooth. Transfer to a bowl. Add the mashed potatoes, cornflour, salt, and garam masala powder to the bowl. Mix until fully incorporated. Divide the mixture into 12 equal pieces. Shape each of the pieces around a skewer. Close the air fry lid and cook the skewers for 10 minutes on Air Fry mode at 390°F.

243. Morning Burrito Bowls

Servings: 4 | Ready in about: 30 minutes

2 tbsp olive oil
1 onion
2 garlic cloves, minced
1 tbsp chili powder
2 tsp ground cumin
2 tsp paprika
1 tsp salt
½ tsp black pepper
¼ tsp cayenne pepper
1 cup quinoa, rinsed
1 (14.5 oz) can diced tomatoes
1 (14.5 oz) can black beans, drained
1 ½ cups vegetable stock
1 cup frozen corn kernels
2 tbsp chopped cilantro
1 tbsp roughly chopped fresh coriander
Cheddar cheese, grated for garnish
1 avocado, sliced

Warm oil on Sauté in your Instant Pot. Add in onion and cook for 3 to 5 minutes until fragrant. Add garlic and cook for 2 more minutes until soft and golden brown. Add in chili powder, paprika, cayenne pepper, salt, cumin, and black pepper and cook for 1 minute until spices are soft. Pour quinoa into onion and spice mixture. Stir to coat quinoa completely in spices. Add diced tomatoes, black beans, vegetable stock, and corn. Stir to combine. Seal the pressure lid, choose Pressure Cook for 7 minutes. When ready, release the pressure quickly. Fluff quinoa and season with pepper and salt. Stir in cilantro and top with cheese and avocado slices.

244. Honey-Glazed Acorn Squash

Servings: 4 | Ready in about: 30 minutes

½ cup water
3 tbsp honey, divided
1 lb acorn squash, cut into chunks
2 tbsp butter
1 tbsp dark brown sugar
1 tbsp cinnamon

In a small bowl, mix 1 tbsp honey and water. Pour into your Instant Pot. Add in squash. Seal the and cook on Pressure Cook for 4 minutes. When ready, release the pressure quickly. Transfer the squash to a serving dish. Turn your Instant Pot to Sauté. Mix brown sugar, cinnamon, the remaining 2 tbsp honey and the liquid in the pot Cook as you stir for 4 minutes to obtain a thick consistency and starts to turn caramelized and golden. Spread honey glaze over squash. Add pepper and salt for seasoning.

245. Red Beans & Rice

Servings: 4 | Ready in about: 1 hour

1 cup red beans, rinsed
½ cup rice, rinsed
2 tbsp olive oil
½ tsp cayenne pepper
1 ½ cups vegetable broth
1 onion, diced
1 red bell pepper, diced
1 stalk celery, diced
1 tbsp fresh thyme leaves, or to taste

Into your Instant Pot, add beans and water to cover about 1-inch. Seal the pressure lid, choose Pressure Cook on High, and set the timer to 1 minute. When ready, release the pressure quickly. Drain the beans and set aside. Rinse and pat dry the inner pot. Return inner pot to pressure cooker, add oil to the pot and press Sauté.

Add onion to the oil and cook for 3 minutes until soft. Add celery and pepper and cook for 1 to 2 minutes until fragrant. Add garlic and cook for 30 seconds until soft. Add rice. Transfer the beans back into inner pot and top with broth. Stir black pepper, thyme, cayenne pepper, and salt into the mixture. Seal the pressure lid, choose Pressure Cook on High, and set the timer to 15 minutes. When ready, release pressure quickly. Add more thyme, black pepper and salt as desired.

246. Roasted Vegetable Salad

Servings: 1 | Ready in about: 25 minutes

1 potato, peeled and chopped
¼ onion, sliced
1 carrot, sliced diagonally
½ small beetroot, sliced
1 cup cherry tomatoes
Juice of 1 lemon
A handful of rocket salad
A handful of baby spinach
3 tbsp canned chickpeas
½ tsp cumin
½ tsp turmeric
¼ tsp sea salt
2 tbsp olive oil
Parmesan shavings

Combine the onion, potato, cherry tomatoes, carrot, beetroot, cumin, seas salt, turmeric, and 1 tbsp olive oil in a bowl. Place in your Instant Pot, close the air fry lid and cook for 20 minutes on Air Fry mode at 390°F. Let cool for 2 minutes. Place the rocket, salad, spinach, lemon juice, and 1 tbsp olive oil, into a serving bowl. Mix to combine. Stir in the roasted veggies. Top with chickpeas and Parmesan shavings.

247. Spicy Pepper & Sweet Potato Skewers

Servings: 1 | Ready in about: 20 minutes

1 large sweet potato	1 tsp chili flakes	¼ tsp garlic powder
1 beetroot	¼ tsp black pepper	¼ tsp paprika
1 green bell pepper	½ tsp turmeric	1 tbsp olive oil

Soak 3 to 4 skewers until ready to use. Peel the veggies and cut them into bite-sized chunks. Place the chunks in a bowl along with the remaining ingredients. Mix until fully coated. Thread the veggies in this order: potato, pepper, beetroot. Place in your Instant Pot, close the air fry lid and cook for 15 minutes on Air Fry mode at 350°F. Flip skewers halfway through.

248. Mashed Parsnips & Cauliflower

Servings: 8 | Ready in about: 15 minutes

1 ½ lb parsnips, peeled and cubed	Salt and black pepper to taste	¼ cup grated Parmesan cheese
1 head cauliflower, cut into florets	2 cups water	1 tbsp butter
2 garlic cloves	¼ cup sour cream	2 tbsp minced chives

In your Instant Pot, mix parsnips, garlic, water, salt, cauliflower, and pepper. Seal the pressure lid, choose Pressure Cook, and set the timer to 4 minutes. When ready, release the pressure quickly. Drain parsnips and cauliflower and return to pot. Add Parmesan, butter, and sour cream. Use a potato masher to mash until the desired consistency is attained. Into the mashed parsnip, add 1 tbsp chives. Place on a serving plate and garnish with remaining chives.

249. Garlic Veggie Mash with Parmesan

Servings: 6 | Ready in about: 15 minutes

3 lb Yukon Gold potatoes, chopped	1 cup Parmesan cheese, shredded	1 tsp salt
1 ½ cups cauliflower, cut into florets	¼ cup butter, melted	1 garlic clove, minced
1 carrot, chopped	¼ cup milk	Fresh parsley for garnish

To your Instant Pot, add veggies, salt and cover with enough water. Seal the pressure lid, choose Pressure Cook on High, and set the timer to 10 minutes. When ready, release the pressure quickly. Drain the vegetables and mash them with a potato masher. Add garlic, butter and milk, and whisk until everything is well incorporated. Serve topped with parmesan cheese and chopped parsley.

250. Avocado Rolls

Servings: 5 | Ready in about: 15 minutes | Servings: 5

3 avocados, pitted and peeled	1 tomato, diced	½ tsp salt
10 egg roll wrappers	¼ tsp pepper	

Place all filling ingredients in a bowl. Mash with a fork until somewhat smooth. Divide the feeling between the egg wrappers. Wet your finger and brush along the edges so the wrappers can seal well. Roll and seal the wrappers. Arrange them on the lined air fry basket, and place it into your Instant Pot. Close the air fry lid and cook at 350°F for 5 minutes on Air Fry mode. Serve with chili dipping.

251. Pasta with Roasted Veggies

Servings: 6 | Ready in about: 25 minutes

1 lb penne, cooked
1 zucchini, sliced
1 pepper, sliced
1 acorn squash, sliced
4 oz mushrooms, sliced
½ cup kalamata olives, pitted, halved
¼ cup olive oil
1 tsp Italian seasoning
1 cup grape tomatoes, halved
3 tbsp balsamic vinegar
2 tbsp chopped basil
Salt and pepper, to taste

Combine the pepper, zucchini, squash, mushrooms, and olive oil, in a large bowl. Season with salt and pepper. Close the air fry lid and cook the veggies for 15 minutes on Air Fry mode at 380°F. In a large bowl, combine the penne, roasted vegetables, olives, tomatoes, Italian seasoning, and vinegar. Sprinkle basil and serve.

252. Quinoa & Veggie Stuffed Peppers

Servings: 1 | Ready in about: 16 minutes

¼ cup cooked quinoa
1 bell pepper
½ tbsp diced onion
½ diced tomato, plus one tomato slice
¼ tsp smoked paprika
Salt and pepper, to taste
1 tsp olive oil
¼ tsp dried basil

Core and clean the bell pepper to prepare it for stuffing. Brush the pepper with half of the olive oil on the outside. In a small bowl, combine all of the other ingredients, except the tomato slice and reserved half-teaspoon olive oil. Stuff the pepper with the filling. Top with the tomato slice. Brush the tomato slice with the remaining half-teaspoon of oil and sprinkle with basil. Close the air fry lid and cook for 10 minutes on Air Fry mode at 350°F.

253. Vegetable Tortilla Pizza

Servings: 1 | Ready in about: 15 minutes

1 ½ tbsp tomato paste
¼ cup grated cheddar cheese
¼ cup grated mozzarella cheese
1 tbsp cooked sweet corn
4 zucchini slices
4 eggplant slices
4 red onion Rings
½ green bell pepper, chopped
3 cherry tomatoes, quartered
1 tortilla
¼ tsp basil
¼ tsp oregano

Spread the tomato paste on the tortilla. Arrange the zucchini and eggplant slices first, then green peppers, and onion rings. Lay the cherry tomatoes and sprinkle the sweet corn over. Sprinkle with oregano and basil. Top with cheddar and mozzarella. Place in the pot close the air fry lid and cook for 10 minutes on Air Fry mode at 350°F.

254. Herby Millet with Cherry Tomatoes

Servings: 8 | Ready in about: 1 hour 15 minutes

2 cups millet, rinsed and drained
4 cups vegetable stock
½ sweet onion, chopped
1 cup cherry tomatoes, cut into halves
1 tbsp fresh sage, chopped
1 tsp fresh thyme, chopped
1 tsp fresh parsley, chopped
Salt and ground black pepper to taste

Add millet, onion, and vegetable stock the inner pot of your Instant Pot. Seal the pressure lid, choose Pressure Cook on High, and set the timer to 10 minutes. When ready, release pressure quickly. Fluff the millet with a fork, add in herbs and tomatoes and apply a seasoning of pepper and salt.

255. Three-Cheese Veggie Lasagna

Serves: 4 | Total Time: 50 minutes

1 ¼ cups grated mozzarella cheese
½ cup grated Parmesan cheese
½ cup ricotta cheese
1 cup mushrooms, sliced
Salt and black pepper to taste
2 cups tomato pasta sauce
5 lasagna noodles
1 tbsp chopped oregano

Preheat your Instant Pot Duo Crisp to 360°F. Combine 1 cup of mozzarella cheese, ¼ cup Parmesan, ricotta, salt, and pepper in a large bowl. Lightly spray a round baking pan with cooking oil. Add ½ cup pasta sauce to the bottom of the pan. Arrange ⅓ of the noodles in the pan. You can break them to fit in the pan as needed. Spread ⅓ of the ricotta mixture and mushrooms over the noodles. Repeat the layers two more times until all of the ingredients are used. Top the lasagna with the rest of the Italian-blended cheese. Cover with foil that is long enough to tuck under the bottom of the pan.

Place the pan in the air fry basket and close the fry lid. Bake for 35 minutes. Remove the foil and Bake for another 5 minutes until the top is golden. Remove the pan and top with Parmesan. Allow cool for 5 minutes. Serve sprinkled with oregano, and enjoy!

256. Green Lasagna Soup

Servings: 4 | Ready in about: 30 minutes

1 tsp olive oil	1 cup tomatoes, chopped	2 tsp Italian seasoning
1 cup leeks, chopped	1 carrot, chopped	Salt to taste
2 garlic cloves minced	½ lb broccoli, chopped	2 cups vegetable broth
1 cup tomato paste	¼ cup dried green lentils	3 lasagna noodles

Warm oil on Sauté in your Instant Pot. Add garlic and leeks and cook for 2 minutes until soft. Add tomato paste, carrot, Italian seasoning, broccoli, tomatoes, lentils, and salt. Stir in vegetable broth and lasagna pieces. Seal the pressure lid, choose Pressure Cook on High, and set the timer to 3 minutes. Release pressure naturally for 10 minutes, then release the remaining pressure quickly. Divide soup into serving bowls and serve.

257. Paneer Cutlet

Servings: 1 | Ready in about: 15 minutes

2 cup grated paneer	½ tsp chai masala	½ tsp garlic powder
1 cup grated cheese	1 tsp butter	1 small onion, finely chopped

Mix all ingredients in a bowl. Make cutlets out of the mixture and place them on the greased baking dish. Place the baking dish in your Instant Pot and cook the cutlets on Air Fry for 10 minutes at 350°F.

258. Grilled Tofu Sandwich

Servings: 1 | Ready in about: 20 minutes

2 slices of bread	¼ cup red cabbage, shredded	¼ tsp vinegar
1-inch thick Tofu slice	2 tsp olive oil divided	Salt and pepper, to taste

Place the bread slices and toast for 3 minutes on Roast mode at 350°F. Set aside. Brush the tofu with 1 tsp of oil, and place in the basket of your Instant Pot. Bake for 5 minutes on each side on Roast mode at 350°F. Combine the cabbage, remaining oil, and vinegar, and season with salt and pepper. Place the tofu on top of one bread slice, place the cabbage over, and top with the other bread slice.

259. Simple Air Fried Ravioli

Servings: 6 | Ready in about: 15 minutes

1 package cheese ravioli	¼ cup Parmesan cheese	1 tsp olive oil
2 cup Italian breadcrumbs	1 cup buttermilk	¼ tsp garlic powder

In a bowl, combine the crumbs, Parmesan, garlic powder, and olive oil. Dip the ravioli in the buttermilk and then coat them with the breadcrumb mixture. Line a baking sheet with parchment paper and arrange the ravioli on it. Place in your Instant Pot and cook for 5 minutes on Air Fry at 390°F. Serve the ravioli with marinara jar sauce.

260. Crispy Nachos

Servings: 2 | Ready in about: 20 minutes

1 cup sweet corn
1 cup all-purpose flour
1 tbsp butter
½ tsp chili powder
2-3 tbsp water
Salt to taste

Add a small amount of water to the sweet corn and grind until you obtain an excellent paste. In a bowl, add the flour, the salt, the chili powder, the butter and mix very well. Add the corn and stir well. Start to knead with your palm until you obtain a stiff dough. Dust a little bit of flour and spread the batter with a rolling pin. Make it around ½ inch thick. Cut it in any shape you want and cook in your Instant Pot for 10 minutes on Air Fry mode at 350°F. Serve with guacamole salsa.

261. Poblano & Tomato Stuffed Squash

Servings: 3 | Ready in about: 50 minutes

½ butternut squash
6 grape tomatoes, halved
1 poblano pepper, cut into strips
¼ cup grated mozzarella, optional
2 tsp olive oil divided
Salt and pepper, to taste

Cut trim the ends and cut the squash lengthwise. Scoop the flash out, so you make room for the filling. Brush 1 tsp oil over the squash. Place in your Instant Pot and roast for 30 minutes. Combine the other teaspoon of olive oil with the tomatoes and poblanos. Season with salt and pepper. Place the peppers and tomatoes into the squash. Close the air fry lid and cook for 15 minutes on Air Fry mode at 350°F.

262. Colorful Vegetable Medley

Servings: 4 | Ready in about: 15 minutes

1 small head broccoli, broken into florets
16 asparagus, trimmed
1 head cauliflower, broken into florets
5 oz green beans
2 carrots, cut into ¼-inch rounds
Salt to taste

Into your Instant Pot, add 1 cup water and set trivet on top of water and place steamer basket on top of the trivet. In an even layer, spread green beans, broccoli, cauliflower, asparagus, and carrots in the steamer basket. Seal the pressure lid, choose Pressure Cook on High, and set the timer to 3 minutes on High. When ready, release the pressure quickly. Remove steamer basket from cooker and add salt to vegetables for seasoning. Serve immediately.

263. Paneer Cheese Balls

Servings: 2 | Ready in about: 12 minutes

2 oz paneer cheese
2 tbsp flour
2 medium onions, chopped
1 tbsp corn flour
1 green chili, chopped
A 1-inch ginger piece, chopped
1 tsp red chili powder
a few leaves of coriander, chopped
1 tbsp olive oil

Mix all ingredients, except the oil and the cheese. Take a small part of the mixture, roll it up and slowly press to flatten it. Stuff in 1 cube of cheese and seal the edges. Repeat with the rest of the mixture. Close the air fry lid and fry the balls in your Instant Pot for 12 minutes on Air Fry mode and at 390°F. Serve hot, with ketchup.

264. Chipotle Vegetarian Chili

Servings: 12 | Ready in about: 45 minutes

1 (28 oz) can diced tomatoes
2 cups cashews, chopped
1 cup onion, chopped
1 cup red lentils
1 cup red quinoa
3 chipotle peppers, chopped
3 garlic cloves, minced
2 tbsp chili powder
1 tsp salt
2 cups carrots, chopped
1 (15 oz) can black beans, rinsed
¼ cup fresh parsley, chopped

In your Instant Pot, mix tomatoes, onion, chipotle peppers, chili powder, lentils, walnuts, carrots, quinoa, garlic, and salt. Stir 4 cups water. Seal the pressure lid, choose Pressure Cook on High, and set the timer to 30 minutes. When ready, release the pressure quickly. Into the chili, add black beans. Simmer on Keep Warm until heated through. Add ¼ cup to 1 cup water if you want a thinner consistency. Top with a garnish of parsley.

265. Rosemary Sweet Potato Medallions

Servings: 4 | Ready in about: 25 minutes

1 cup water	1 tsp garlic powder	2 tbsp butter
1 tbsp fresh rosemary	4 sweet potatoes, scrubbed clean	Salt to taste

Into your Instant Pot, add water and place a trivet over the water. Use a fork to prick sweet potatoes all over and set onto the trivet. Seal the pressure lid, choose Pressure Cook on High, and set the timer to 12 minutes. When ready, release the pressure quickly. Transfer sweet potatoes to a cutting board and slice into 1/2-inch medallions and ensure they are peeled. Melt butter on Sauté. Add in the medallions and cook each side for 2 to 3 minutes until browned. Apply salt and garlic powder to season. Serve topped with fresh rosemary.

266. Easy BBQ Tofu

Serves: 4 | Total Time: 25 minutes + marinating time

14 oz extra-firm tofu	1 tsp liquid smoke	½ tsp salt
½ cup barbecue sauce	½ tsp chili garlic sauce	2 tbsp chopped green onions
½ cup brown sugar	1 tsp red pepper flakes	

Preheat your Instant Pot Duo Crisp to 360°F. Cut tofu into 24 equal pieces. Mix the rest of the ingredients, except for the green onions, in a large bowl, then add tofu. Stir until completely coated. Cover and sit on the counter for at least 30 minutes. Lightly spray the air fry basket with cooking oil and add the tofu. Close the fry lid and Air Fry for 5 minutes. Then shakes the basket. Cook for another 5 minutes and shake the basket again. Cook for 5 more minutes until done. Let the tofu cool for 10 minutes. Serve warm sprinkled with green onions and enjoy!

267. Quick Crispy Cheese Lings

Servings: 4 | Ready in about: 15 minutes

4 cups grated cheddar cheese	1 tbsp butter	¼ tsp chili powder
1 cup all-purpose flour	1 tbsp baking powder	¼ tsp salt

Mix the flour and the baking powder. Add the chili powder, salt, butter, cheese and 1-2 tbsp of waterto the mixture. Make a stiff dough. Knead the dough for a while. Sprinkle a tbsp or so of flour on the table. Take a rolling pin and roll the dough into ½ -inch thickness. Cut the dough in any shape you want. Close the air fry lid and fry the cheese lings for 6 minutes at 370° F on Air Fry mode.

268. Grilled Cheese Sandwiches

Serves: 4 | Total Time: 15 minutes

8 sourdough bread slices	½ cup chopped roasted red peppers	4 Havarti cheese slices
4 provolone cheese slices	¼ cup chopped shallots	

Preheat your Instant Pot Duo Crisp to 300°F. Top a slice of bread with a slice of provolone, then add 2 tablespoons of roasted red peppers and 1 tablespoon of shallots. Repeat this process for three more slices of bread. Transfer the loaded bread slices to the air fry basket and Grill for 1 minute. Add 1 slice of Havarti cheese on each slice of bread and top each with a slice of bread. Lightly spray with cooking oil and increase the cooking temperature to 400°F. Cook for 3 minutes, then turn the sandwiches carefully. Cook for another 2 minutes until bread is toasted and cheese is melted. Serve warm and enjoy!

269. Mexican-Style Taco Filling

Serves: 4 | Total Time: 25 minutes

1 cup instant white rice
1 cup salsa
½ cup vegetable broth
1 cup black beans
1 tsp taco seasoning
1 tbsp lime juice
½ cup corn

Preheat your Instant Pot Duo Crisp to 400°F. Combine all ingredients in a 3-quart baking dish. Cover with foil that is long enough to tuck under the bottom of the pan. Close the fry lid and Air Fry for 8 minutes, then stir. Cook for another 7 minutes and stir again. Air Fry for 5 more minutes and serve immediately.

270. Basil-Kale Pesto Flatbread

Serves: 4 | Total Time: 15 minutes

1 cup basil pesto
4 round flatbreads
½ cup chopped kale
8 oz fresh mozzarella cheese, sliced
1 tsp dried coriander
1 tsp red pepper flakes

Preheat your Instant Pot Duo Crisp to 350°F. Spread ¼ cup pesto over each flatbread, then 2 tablespoons kale over the pesto. Top with mozzarella, coriander, and red pepper flakes. Place in the air fry basket and close the fry lid. Bake for 8 minutes. The cheese will be melted and bubbling. Serve warm and enjoy!

271. Buttery Spaghetti Squash

Serves: 4 | Total Time: 50 minutes

1 large spaghetti squash, halved lengthwise and seeded
Salt and black pepper to taste
2 tsp grated Parmesan cheese
1 tsp garlic powder
1 tsp dried parsley
1 tbsp chopped basil
2 tbsp butter, melted

Preheat your Instant Pot Duo Crisp to 350°F. Season squash with salt, pepper, garlic powder, and parsley, then lightly spray with cooking spray. Place the squash skin side down in the air fry basket and close the fry lid. Roast for 30 minutes. Flip the squash skin side up and Roast for another 15 minutes or until fork-tender. Scrape the flesh of the squash to separate strands into a bowl. Toss with butter and sprinkle with Parmesan cheese and basil.

272. Easy-Peasy Ravioli

Serves: 4 | Total Time: 20 minutes

10 oz fresh cheese ravioli
1 cup Italian bread crumbs
2 tbsp grated Parmesan cheese
1 large egg
¼ cup milk
2 tbsp fresh basil
1 cup marinara sauce

Preheat your Instant Pot Duo Crisp to 400°F. Whisk together bread crumbs and Parmesan in a large bowl. Beat egg and milk it in a bowl. Dip ravioli in the egg mixture first, shaking off any drips. Next, press the ravioli into the bread crumb mixture. Lightly spray each side and place in the air fry basket and close the fry lid. Toast for 4 minutes, then use tongs to flip the ravioli. Toast for another 4 minutes until the ravioli is brown and crispy. To serve, warm the marinara sauce and scatter the ravioli with basil. Enjoy!

273. Timeless Black Bean Patties

Serves: 4 | Total Time: 20 minutes

1 (14-oz) can black beans
½ cup diced yellow onions
2 garlic cloves, minced
1 red bell pepper, diced
½ tsp dried coriander
½ tsp ground cumin
½ tsp ground nutmeg
1 large egg
½ cup bread crumbs
Salt and black pepper to taste

Preheat your Instant Pot Duo Crisp to 370°F. Add black beans to a large bowl and pat dry with a paper towel. Mash the beans with a fork until they are mostly broken down. Combine with onions, bell pepper, coriander, garlic, cumin, nutmeg, egg, bread crumbs, salt, and pepper. Divide into 4 portions and shape into patties about ½" thick. Lightly spray both sides with cooking oil, then transfer to the air fry basket. Close the fry lid and Air Fry for 5 minutes. Then flips the patties. Cook for another 5 minutes until the patties are firm and keep their shape.

274. Greek Pinwheels

Serves: 4 | Total Time: 25 minutes

1 puff pastry sheet	10 oz Swiss chard	Salt and dried thyme to taste
3 oz cream cheese, softened	⅓ cup crumbled feta cheese	1 large egg, whisked

Preheat your Instant Pot Duo Crisp to 320°F. Unroll the puff pastry into a flat rectangle. Mix the cream cheese, Swiss chard, and salt in a bowl. Spread the mixture carefully in an even layer on the pastry and leave a ½-inch border around the edges. Top evenly with feta and thyme. Starting with the long side, roll the dough into a log shape, then cut into 12 equal rolls. Brush each roll with egg and transfer to the air fry basket. Close the fry lid and Air Fry for 8 minutes, then flips the rolls. Cook for another 7 minutes. Allow cooling 5 minutes. Serve warm.

275. Eggplant Stacks

Serves: 4 | Total Time: 20 minutes

1 eggplant, sliced	4 fresh mozzarella cheese slices	¼ cup chopped green onions
Salt and black pepper to taste	1 tbsp olive oil	4 tbsp blue cheese salad dressings
4 tomato slices	¼ cup fresh basil, sliced	

Preheat your Instant Pot Duo Crisp to 320°F. Layer eggplant slices in a baking pan. Season with salt and pepper. Next, layer the tomato slices, then the mozzarella slices. Drizzle with oil and place the pan in the air fry basket and close the fry lid. Air Fry for 8 minutes. Eggplant will be tender, and the cheese will be melted. Garnish with basil, blue cheese salad dressing, and green onions before serving.

276. Tex-Mex Lentil Tacos

Serves: 4 | Total Time: 20 minutes

2 (15-oz) cans lentils	8 flour tortillas, warmed	6 radishes, sliced
¼ cup adobo sauce	1 ½ cups chopped avocado	
Salt and black pepper to taste	½ cup chopped cilantro	

Preheat your Instant Pot Duo Crisp to 375°F. Combine lentils, adobo, salt, and pepper in a large bowl. Transfer the lentils to the air fry basket using a slotted spoon. Close the fry lid and Air Fry for 3 minutes. Then shake the basket. Cook for another 3 minutes and shake the basket again. Air Fry for 4 more minutes. To make the taco, top the warm tortilla with ¼ cup lentils and garnish with avocado, radishes, and cilantro. Serve warm and enjoy!

277. Cheese-Stuffed Mushrooms

Serves: 4 | Total Time: 20 minutes

1 tbsp olive oil	¼ cup grated Parmesan cheese	1 tbsp fresh thyme
12 Bella mushroom caps	¼ cup panko bread crumbs	2 tbsp chopped parsley
4 oz cream cheese, softened	1 tsp crushed red pepper flakes	

Preheat your Instant Pot Duo Crisp to 400°F. Mix cream cheese, Parmesan, bread crumbs, thyme, and red pepper flakes in a bowl. Measure about 1 tablespoon of the mixture and stuff it into the mushroom cap. Arrange in a single layer in the air fry basket and close the fry lid. drizzle with olive oil. Bake for 10 minutes or until the cheese is warm and brown. Allow cooling for about 5 minutes. Serve warm sprinkled with parsley and enjoy!

278. Ravioli au Gratin

Serves: 4 | Total Time: 25 minutes

2 cups marinara sauce
2 (10-oz) packages fresh cheese ravioli
12 provolone cheese slices
½ cup Italian bread crumbs
½ cup grated Parmesan cheese
2 tsp dried oregano
2 tbsp chopped green onions
2 tbsp chopped parsley

Preheat your Instant Pot Duo Crisp to 350°F. Spread ⅓ cup marinara on the bottom of a 3-quart pan. Arrange 6 ravioli on top of the sauce, then top with 3 slices of provolone and sprinkle with green onions and oregano. Spread another ⅓ cup of marinara on top of the cheese. Repeat these steps two more times until all of the ingredients are used. Combine bread crumbs and Parmesan in a small bowl, then top the lasagna with it. Cover the pan with enough foil to tuck under the bottom of the pan. Transfer the pan to the air fryer basket and close the fry lid. Bake for 15 minutes. Remove foil and Bake for another 5 minutes to brown the bread crumbs. Top with parsley.

279. Taco Cheese-Bean Enchiladas

Serves: 4 | Total Time: 20 minutes

1 (15-oz) can black beans
1 ½ tbsp taco seasoning
1 cup red enchilada sauce
½ tsp smoked paprika
½ tsp chili powder
½ tsp ground cumin
1 ½ cups grated Mexican-blend cheese
4 flour tortillas

Preheat your Instant Pot Duo Crisp to 320°F. Microwave beans in a large bowl for 1 minute. Divide the beans in half and mash one of the portions of beans. Fold in the whole beans. Stir in taco seasoning, ¼ cup enchilada sauce, smoked paprika, chili powder, cumin, and 1 cup of cheese. Top each tortilla with ¼ cup bean mixture. Fold in the sides and roll the tortilla to close. Place the enchiladas seam side down in a 3-quart baking pan. Top with remaining enchilada sauce and cheese. Transfer the pan to the air fry basket and close the fry lid. Air Fry for 8 minutes. The cheese will be melted, and the sauce will be bubbling. Serve warm and enjoy!

280. Broccoli & Potato Bake

Serves: 4 | Total Time: 40 minutes

4 large russet potatoes
3 tbsp ranch dressing
Salt and black pepper to taste
1 garlic clove, mashed
¼ cup chopped cooked broccoli florets
½ cup grated sharp cheddar cheese
½ cup Parmesan cheese
2 tbsp chopped parsley

Preheat your Instant Pot Duo Crisp to 400°F. Poke several holes in each of the potatoes using a fork. Put the potatoes in the air fry basket and close the fry lid. Bake for 30 minutes. Cool until they are easy to handle.

Slice the potatoes lengthwise and scoop out some of the potato flesh, leaving enough to have the skin keep its shape. Transfer the potato flesh to a large bowl, then add ranch dressing, salt, pepper, garlic, broccoli, Parmesan cheese, and cheddar cheese. Mix well. Spoon the mixture back into the potato skins and transfer the skins to the air fry basket. Bake for another 5 minutes or until the cheese is melted. Serve sprinkled with and parsley.

281. Chili Corn Crisps

Serves: 4 | Total Time: 35 minutes

1 (15.25-oz) can yellow corn
½ cup flour
¾ cup grated pepper jack cheese
1 large egg
¼ tsp ground cumin
½ tsp chili powder
¼ tsp garlic powder
1 tbsp chopped cilantro
Salt and black pepper to taste

Combine all of the ingredients in a large bowl. Measure out portions using a ½-cup scoop. Press into rounds and lightly spray with cooking oil. Freeze for 10 minutes. Preheat your Instant Pot Duo Crisp to 400°F. Transfer fritters to the air fryer basket and close the fry lid Air Fry for 6 minutes. Flip the fritters and cook for another 6 minutes or until brown and firm. Serve warm and enjoy!

POULTRY RECIPES

282. Lemon Chicken Tenders with Broccoli

Servings: 2 | Ready in about: 70 minutes

1 cup basmati rice
1 cup plus 2 tbsp water
1 head broccoli, cut into florets
2 tbsp melted butter, divided
Salt and black pepper to taste
4 boneless, skinless chicken tenders
¼ cup barbecue sauce
¼ cup lemon marmalade
½ tbsp soy sauce
1 tbsp sesame seeds, for garnish
2 tbsp sliced green onions, for garnish

Pour the rice and water into your Instant Pot and stir to combine. Seal the pressure lid, choose Pressure Cook on High, and the timer to 2 minutes. In a bowl, toss the broccoli with 1 tablespoon of melted butter, and season with salt and black pepper. When done cooking, perform a quick pressure release, and carefully open the lid.

Place a trivet inside the pot, which will be over the rice. Then, spray a trivet with cooking spray. Lay the chicken tenders on the trivet and brush with the remaining melted butter. Arrange the broccoli around the chicken. Close the air fry lid. Choose Air Fry, set the temperature to 400°F, and set the time to 10 minutes. Press Start to begin.

In a bowl, mix the barbecue sauce, lemon marmalade, and soy sauce. When done crisping, coat the chicken with the lemon sauce. Turn the chicken over and apply the lemon sauce on the other side. Close the air fry lid, select Broil for 5 minutes. After cooking is complete, check for your desired crispiness and remove the trivet from the pot. Spoon the rice into plates with chicken and broccoli. Top with sesame seeds and green onions and serve.

283. Crispy Chicken Thighs with Carrot Roast

Servings: 4 | Ready in about: 50 minutes

1 ½ cups chicken broth
1 cup basmati rice
4 bone-in, skin-on chicken thighs
2 carrots, chopped
2 tbsp melted butter
2 tsp chicken seasoning
Salt to taste
2 tsp chopped fresh thyme

Pour the chicken broth and rice into your Instant Pot. Then, put in a trivet. Arrange the chicken thighs on the trivet, skin side up, and arrange the carrots around the chicken. Put the pressure lid together and lock in the Seal position. Choose Pressure Cook on High and the time to 2 minutes.

When done, perform a quick pressure release. Brush the carrots and chicken with the melted butter. Season the chicken with the chicken seasoning and salt. Also, season the carrots with the thyme and salt. Close the air fry lid, choose Broil and set the time to 10 minutes. When done cooking, check for your desired crispiness, and turn the pot off. Spoon the rice into serving plates, and serve the chicken and carrots over the rice.

284. Chicken with Crunchy Coconut Dumplings

Servings: 6 | Ready in about: 70 minutes

1 package refrigerated biscuits, at room temperature
1 tbsp ghee
1 white onion, chopped
2 carrots, diced
2 celery stalks, diced
1 lb chicken breasts, cubed
2 cups chicken stock
1 tsp fresh rosemary
½ tsp salt
½ cup heavy cream

Choose Sauté on your Instant Pot. Melt the ghee and sauté the onion until softened, about 3 minutes. Pour the carrots, celery, chicken, and stock into the pot. Season with rosemary and salt. Put the pressure lid together and lock in the Seal position. Choose Pressure Cook on High, and set the time to 2 minutes.

When done cooking, perform a quick pressure release, and carefully open the lid. Stir the heavy cream into the soup. Place a trivet in the higher position inside the pot, over the soup, and arrange the biscuits in a single layer on the trivet. Close the air fry lid. Choose Broil and set the time to 15 minutes. When ready, allow the biscuit and soup to rest for a few minutes and then serve.

285. Chicken Cassoulet with Frijoles

Servings: 4 | Ready in about: 60 minutes

4 small chicken thighs, bone-in skin-on	1 medium carrot, diced	3 cups chicken stock
Salt and black pepper to taste	½ small onion, diced	1 cup panko breadcrumbs
2 pancetta slices, cut into thirds	½ cup dry red wine	
	1 cup Pinto Beans Frijoles, soaked	

Season the chicken on both sides with salt and black pepper and set aside on a wire rack. On your Instant Pot, choose Sauté. Add the pancetta slices in a single layer and cook for 3 to 4 minutes or until browned on one side. Turn and brown the other side. Remove the pancetta to a paper towel-lined plate. Put the chicken thighs in the pot, and fry for 6-7 minutes or until it is golden brown on both sides. Use tongs to pick the chicken into a plate.

Carefully pour out all the fat from the pot, leaving about 1 tablespoon to coat the bottom of the pot. Reserve the remaining fat in a small bowl. Sauté the carrots and onion in the pot for 3 minutes with frequent stirring, until the onion begins to brown. Stir in the wine while scraping off the brown bits at the bottom. Allow boiling until the wine reduces by one-third and stir in the beans and chicken stock.

Seal the pressure lid, choose Pressure Cook on High and the cooking time to 25 minutes. When done cooking, perform a quick pressure release and carefully open the lid. Return the chicken to the pot and cook for 10 minutes. Combine the breadcrumbs with the reserved fat until evenly mixed.

When done cooking, perform a natural pressure release for 5 minutes, then a quick pressure release to let out any remaining steam, and carefully open the lid. Crumble the pancetta over the cassoulet. Spoon the breadcrumbs mixture on top of the beans while avoiding the chicken as much as possible. Close the air fry lid, choose Broil, adjust the time to 7 minutes, and When the cassoulet is ready, allow resting for a few minutes before serving.

286. Garlic Herb Roasted Chicken

Servings: 4 | Ready in about: 70 minutes

1 (3½-lb) whole chicken	2 limes, juiced	2 tbsp Italian herb mix
½ cup white wine	3 tbsp olive oil	1 ½ tbsp ground cumin
Juice of 1 lemon	¼ cup coconut aminos	6 cloves garlic, grated

Remove the neck from inside the chicken's cavity, trim off the excess fat and any remaining feathers. Rinse the chicken thoroughly with water and tie the legs with butcher's twine. Pour the wine and lemon juice into your Instant Pot. Place the chicken in the air fry basket and fix the basket in the higher position of the pot.

Put the pressure lid together and lock in the Seal position. Choose Pressure Cook and set to High. Set the time to 20 minutes. When the timer is done, perform a quick pressure release, and carefully open the pressure lid. In a bowl, combine the lime juice, the olive oil, coconut aminos, Italian herb mix, cumin, garlic and salt.

Mix until thoroughly combined. Brush the mixture over the chicken. Close the air fry lid. Choose Air Fry, set the temperature to 400°F, and set the time to 15 minutes. After about 10 minutes, lift the air fry lid and sprinkle the chicken with the fresh rosemary. Close the air fry lid and continue cooking. Carefully open the lid and transfer the chicken to a plate. Let the chicken rest for 10 minutes before cutting and serving.

287. Sweet Sesame Chicken Wings

Servings: 4 | Ready in about: 65 minutes

24 chicken wings	2 tbsp hot garlic sauce	2 garlic cloves, minced
2 tbsp sesame oil	2 tbsp honey	1 tbsp toasted sesame seeds

Pour 1 cup of water into your Instant Pot and place a trivet in the pot. Place the chicken wings on the trivet. Seal the pressure lid, choose Pressure Cook on High, and the cooking time to 10 minutes. While the wings cook, prepare the glaze. In a large bowl, whisk the sesame oil, hot garlic sauce, honey, and garlic.

After cooking, perform a quick pressure release, and carefully open the lid. Remove the trivet from the pot and empty the water in the pot. Return the pot to the base. Close the air fry lid and choose Air Fry. Adjust the temperature to 375°F and the time to 3 minutes to preheat the inner pot. Toss the wings in the sauce to coat.

Put the wings in the air fry basket, leaving any excess sauce in the bowl. Place the basket in the pot and close the air fry lid. Choose Air Fry and adjust the cooking time to 15 minutes. Press Start to commence crisping. After 8 minutes, open the lid and use tongs to turn the wings. Close the lid to resume browning until the wings are crisp and the glaze set. Before serving, drizzle with any remaining sauce and sprinkle with the sesame seeds.

288. BBQ Chicken & Kale Quesadillas

Servings: 4 | Ready in about: 40 minutes

¼ cup butter, divided
1 (10-to 12-oz) bag fresh baby kale
1 jalapeño pepper, minced
¼ cup minced onion
3 oz cottage cheese, at room temperature
2 tsp Mexican seasoning mix
1 cup shredded cooked chicken
6 oz shredded Cheddar cheese
Cooking spray
4 medium flour tortillas
⅓ cup grated Pecorino Romano cheese

On your Instant Pot, choose Sauté. Melt 1 tbsp butter until foaming. Add the kale and cook for 1 to 2 minutes or until wilted while stirring occasionally. Mix in the jalapeño and onion, continue cooking for 3 minutes, stirring occasionally, until the vegetables have softened and most of the liquid from the kale has evaporated. Mix in the cottage cheese to melt and add the Mexican seasoning and the chicken. Stir to combine.

Spoon the filling into a bowl and stir in the shredded cheddar cheese. Set aside. Use a paper towel to wipe out the inner pot and return the pot to the base. Oil a trivet with cooking spray and fix in the upper position of the pot. Close the air fry lid and choose Air Fry. Adjust the temperature to 375°F and the time to 5 minutes. Press Start.

To assemble the quesadillas, place a tortilla on a clean flat surface. Brush the top with olive oil and sprinkle 1 teaspoon of Pecorino Romano cheese on top. Press the cheese down with the palm of your hand to stick to the tortilla. Spread about a ⅓ cup of filling over half the tortilla, leaving a ¼-inch border. Fold the other half over the filling and press gently. Repeat the process with the remaining tortillas, filling, and Pecorino Romano cheese.

Carefully transfer two quesadillas to the prepared rack. Close the air fry lid and choose Air Fry. Adjust the temperature to 375°F and the cooking time to 6 minutes. After 3 minutes, or when they are browned on top, use a spatula to flip the quesadillas. Continue cooking until browned on both sides.

Once ready, remove the trivet from the pot and use the spatula to transfer the quesadillas to the bottom of the pot to keep warm while you work on the other quesadillas. Return the empty rack to the pot and place the two remaining uncooked quesadillas on the trivet. Repeat the cooking process. Serve the quesadillas with guacamole.

289. Mexican Chicken & Wild Rice Bowls

Servings: 4 | Ready in about: 30 minutes

4 chicken breasts
2 cups chicken broth
2 ¼ packets Taco Seasoning
To Serve:
Grated cheese, of your choice
1 cup wild rice, rinsed
1 green bell pepper, seeded and diced
1 red bell pepper, seeded and diced

Chopped cilantro
1 cup salsa
Salt and black pepper to taste
1 cup sour cream

Avocado slices

Pour the chicken broth into the inner pot, add the chicken. Pour the taco seasoning over. Add the salsa and stir lightly with a spoon. Close the pressure lid, secure the pressure valve, and select Pressure on High for 15 minutes. Once the timer has ended, do a quick pressure release, and open the lid. Add the wild rice and peppers.

Use a spoon to push them into the sauce. Close the pressure lid, secure the pressure valve, and select Pressure Cook on High for 8 minutes. Once the timer has ended, do a quick pressure release, and open the lid. Gently stir the mixture, adjust the taste with salt and pepper. Stir in sour cream, close the air fry lid and select Broil. Cook for 2 minutes. Spoon the chicken into serving bowls. Top it with avocado slices, cilantro and some cheese. Serve.

290. Chicken with Cilantro Rice

Servings: 4 | Ready in about: 70 minutes

2 tbsp ghee
1 red onion, diced
1 yellow bell pepper, diced
1 tbsp cayenne powder
1 tsp ground cumin
1 tsp Italian herb mix
1 cup basmati rice
¾ cup chicken broth
½ cup tomato sauce
1 lb bone-in, skin-on chicken thighs
Chopped fresh cilantro for garnish
Lime wedges, for serving

Choose Sauté on your Instant Pot. Melt half of the ghee and cook the onion for 3 minutes, stirring occasionally, until softened. Include the yellow bell pepper, cayenne pepper, cumin, and herb mix and cook for 2 minutes more with frequent stirring. Pour the rice, broth, and tomato sauce into the pot. Place a trivet in the higher position of the pot, which is over the rice. Put the chicken on the trivet. Seal the pressure lid, choose Pressure Cook

Set the time to 30 minutes. When the time is over, perform a quick pressure release and carefully open the lid. Brush the chicken thighs with the remaining ghee. Close the air fry lid. Choose Broil and set the time to 5 minutes. Plate the chicken, garnish with cilantro, and serve with lime wedges.

291. Black Refried Beans & Chicken Fajitas

Servings: 4 | Ready in about: 40 minutes

1 large (27-oz) can black beans
1 garlic clove, crushed
1 bacon slice, halved widthwise
¼ cup water
4 tbsp olive oil, divided
1 lb chicken breasts, sliced
1 yellow bell pepper, sliced
1 red bell pepper, sliced
1 small onion, cut into 8 wedges
1 jalapeño pepper, sliced
1 tsp salt
1 tbsp Mexican seasoning mix
Corn tortillas to serve
Avocado slices to serve
Salsa to serve

Pour the beans with liquid into your Instant Pot. Stir in the garlic, bacon, water, and 2 tablespoons of olive oil. Seal the pressure lid, choose Pressure Cook on High and the cooking time to 5 minutes. In a large bowl, mix the chicken, yellow and red bell peppers, jalapeño, and onion. Drizzle with the remaining oil, sprinkle with salt and Mexican seasoning and toss to coat. Set aside. When the beans are ready, do a quick pressure release. Pour out the beans with liquid into a bowl. Remove and discard the bacon pieces and garlic clove. Fetch out about ¼ cup of the liquid and reserve it. Then, use a potato masher to break the beans into the remaining liquid until smooth while adding more liquid if needed. Cover the bowl with aluminum foil.

Add the vegetables and chicken to the air fry basket. Close the air fry lid. Choose Air Fry. Adjust the temperature to 375°F and the cooking time to 10 minutes. Press Start to begin browning. After 5 minutes, open the lid and use tongs to turn the vegetables and chicken. Continue cooking until the vegetables are slightly browned and the chicken tender. Wrap the chicken and beans in warm tortillas and garnish with the avocado and salsa to serve.

292. Wine Chicken with Mushrooms & Brussel Sprouts

Servings: 4 | Ready in about: 40 minutes

4 chicken thighs, bone-in skin-on
Salt and black pepper to taste
1 tbsp olive oil
½ small onion, sliced
½ cup dry white wine
⅓ cup chicken stock
1 cup halved Brussel sprouts
1 bay leaf
¼ tsp dried rosemary
1 cup sautéed Mushrooms
¼ cup heavy cream

Season the chicken on both sides with salt. On your Instant Pot, choose Sauté. Heat olive oil and add the chicken thighs. Fry for 4 to 5 minutes or until browned. Turn and lightly sear the other side, about 1 minute. Use tongs to remove the chicken into a plate and spoon out any thick coating of oil in your Instant Pot.

Sauté the onion in the pot and season with salt. Cook for about 2 minutes to soften and just beginning to brown for 2 minutes. Stir in the white wine and bring to a boil for 3 minutes or until reduced by about half. Mix in the chicken stock, brussel sprouts, bay leaf, rosemary, and several grinds of black pepper. Arrange the chicken thighs on top with skin-side up. Seal the pressure lid, choose Pressure Cook on High and the time to 5 minutes.

When the timer is over, perform a quick pressure release. Remove the bay leaf. Remove the chicken onto the trivet and stir the mushrooms into the sauce. Set a trivet in the pot. Close the air fry lid and choose Bake. Adjust the temperature to 375°F for12 minutes. When ready, transfer the chicken to a platter. Stir the heavy cream into the sauce. Spoon the sauce and vegetables over the chicken to serve.

293. Quick Chicken Fried Rice

Servings: 4 | Ready in about: 60 minutes

1 tbsp ghee
1 onion, diced
4 garlic cloves, minced

1 lb chicken breasts, diced
Salt black pepper to taste
2 cups chicken broth

¼ cup coconut aminos
1 cup long grain rice
1 (16-oz) bag frozen mixed vegetables

Press Sauté on your Instant Pot. Melt the ghee and sauté the onion for 3 minutes. Add and sauté the garlic until fragrant, about 1 minute. Put the chicken in the pot and season with the and black pepper. Cook for 5 minutes to brown the chicken. Pour the chicken broth, coconut aminos, and rice into the pot. Put the pressure lid together and lock the pressure release valve in the Seal position. Choose Pressure Cook on High, and set the time to 3 minutes. When done, perform a quick pressure and carefully open the lid. Pour the frozen vegetables into your Instant Pot. Choose Sauté to heat the vegetables through. Cook for 5 minutes while stirring occasionally. Serve.

294. Chicken Potato Pot Pie

Servings: 6 | Ready in about: 70 minutes

4 tbsp butter
1 onion, diced
2 garlic cloves, minced
2 lb boneless chicken breasts, cubed

2 potatoes, diced
1 cup chicken broth
½ tsp salt
½ tsp freshly ground black pepper

8 oz frozen sweetcorn
½ cup whipping cream
1 piecrust, at room temperature

Choose Sauté on your Instant Pot. Melt the ghee and sauté garlic and onion until softened, about 3 minutes. Add the chicken, potatoes, and broth to the pot. Season with salt and black pepper. Seal the pressure lid. Choose Pressure Cook on High, and the time to 10 minutes. When done cooking, do a quick pressure release. Select Sauté. Pour the frozen sweetcorn and whipping cream into the pot. Stir until the sauce thickens, about 3 minutes. Place the piecrust on top of vegetables and cream mixture, folding over the edges if necessary.

Cut out a small dent in the center of the pie to allow steam to escape when baking. Close the air fry lid. Choose Broil and set the time to 10 minutes. When ready, remove the inner pot from the pot and place it on a heat-resistant surface. Let the potpie rest for 10 to 15 minutes before serving.

295. Saucy Shredded Chicken

Servings: 4 | Ready in about: 35 minutes

4 chicken breasts, skinless
¼ cup Sriracha sauce
2 tbsp butter
1 tsp grated ginger

2 cloves garlic, minced
½ tsp Cayenne pepper
½ tsp red chili flakes
½ cup honey

½ cup chicken broth
Salt and black pepper to taste
Chopped scallion to garnish

In a bowl, pour the chicken broth. Mix in honey, ginger, sriracha sauce, red pepper flakes, cayenne pepper, and garlic. Put the chicken on a plate and season with salt and pepper. Select Sauté on your Instant Pot. Melt the butter and add the chicken. Brown on both sides for about 3 minutes. Add the chicken back, and pour the pepper sauce over. Close the pressure lid, secure the pressure valve, and select Pressure Cook on High for 20 minutes.

When ready, do a natural pressure release for 5 minutes and open the lid. Remove the chicken onto a cutting board and shred using two forks. Return the shredded chicken to the pot, close the air fry lid and select Air Fry mode. Adjust the time to 4 minutes at 385°F. When ready, transfer the chicken to a serving bowl, pour the sauce over, and garnish with the scallions. Serve with a side of sauteéd mushrooms.

POULTRY RECIPES

296. Chicken Shawarma Wrap

Servings: 4 | Ready in about: 35 minutes

1 ½ lb boneless skinless chicken breasts	2 tbsp freshly squeezed lemon juice	1 tsp smoked paprika
Salt and black pepper to taste	3 garlic cloves, minced	¼ tsp turmeric
2 tbsp olive oil	1 tsp ground cumin	¼ tsp cayenne pepper
2 tbsp yogurt	¼ tsp cinnamon powder	4 flat breads, halved
For the Sauce		
½ cup yogurt	1 tsp olive oil	2 tbsp Italian herb mix
½ tsp salt	1 small garlic clove, minced	1 tbsp chopped fresh cilantro
To Assemble		
2 large tomatoes, sliced	½ medium cucumber, sliced	

Season the chicken with salt on both sides, put in a plastic zipper bag, and set aside. In a bowl, evenly mix the olive oil, yogurt, lemon juice, garlic, cumin, cinnamon, paprika, turmeric, black pepper, and cayenne pepper. Pour the marinade over the chicken, zip up the bag, and massage the bag to coat the chicken well with the marinade. Refrigerate the chicken for 1 hour or more to marinate.

Cover the flatbread with foil and place it at the bottom of the pot. Grease a trivet with cooking spray and fix it in the pot. Close the air fry lid and choose Air Fry. Adjust the temperature to 390°F and the time to 4 minutes. Press Start to preheat the pot. Take the chicken out of the refrigerator and remove from the bag while holding each piece to allow excess liquid drip into the bag. Lay the chicken on the trivet in a single layer.

Close the air fry lid and choose Air Fry. Adjust the temperature to 390°F and the time to 16 minutes. Press Start. After 8 minutes, flip the chicken and close the lid. Cook to crisp and brown the other side for 8 minutes. When the breasts are ready, transfer to a cutting board, and cut into thin slices. Take out the bread from the pot.

Prepare the sauce: pour the yogurt into a small bowl. Add the salt, olive oil, garlic, and Italian herb mix. Whisk the ingredients to combine and stir in the parsley. Spread 1 to 2 tablespoons of yogurt sauce into half a side of flatbread. Spoon in some chicken and add the tomato and cucumber slices. Repeat the process for the remaining bread. Wrap the bread over the filling, repeat the assembling process for the remaining bread and serve.

297. Chicken Florentine

Servings: 4 | Ready in about: 30 minutes

4 chicken thighs, cut into 1-inch pieces	1 cup chopped sun dried tomatoes with herbs	¼ tsp red pepper flakes
1 tbsp olive oil	2 tbsp Italian Seasoning	6 oz softened cream cheese, cut into small cubes
1 ½ cups chicken broth	2 cups baby spinach	1 cup shredded Pecorino cheese
Salt to taste		

Pour the chicken broth into the pressure cooker, and add the Italian seasoning, chicken, tomatoes, salt, and red pepper flakes. Stir them with a spoon. Seal the lid and select Pressure Cook on High for 12 minutes. Once the timer has ended, do a quick pressure release. Stir in spinach, Parmesan, and cream cheese until the cheese melt and is fully incorporated. Close the air fry lid and cook on Broil for 5 minutes. Serve.

298. Herby Chicken Breasts

Servings: 4 | Ready in about: 15 minutes

4 boneless, skinless chicken breasts	¼ cup dry white wine	½ tsp mint
½ tsp salt	½ tsp rosemary	½ tsp sage

Sprinkle salt over the chicken and set it in your Instant Pot. Mix in mint, rosemary, and sage. Pour wine and 1 cup of water around the chicken. Seal the pressure lid, choose Pressure Cook on High, and set the timer to 6 minutes. Release the pressure naturally for 10 minutes.

299. Herbed Chicken & Biscuit Chili

Servings: 6 | Ready in about: 90 minutes

1 package refrigerated biscuits, at room temperature
1 tbsp olive oil
1 onion, chopped
2 garlic cloves, minced
1½ lb ground chicken
1 tbsp ground cilantro
1 tbsp dried oregano
4 cups chicken broth
⅛ tsp salt
⅛ tsp black pepper

Choose Sauté on your Instant Pot. Pour the oil, chicken, onion, and garlic into the inner pot and sauté until the onion is softened, about 3 minutes. Add the cilantro, oregano, broth, salt, and black pepper to the pot. Put the pressure lid together and lock in the Seal position. Choose Pressure Cook on High. Set the time to 10 minutes

When the time is over, perform a quick pressure release. Spread the biscuits in a single layer over the chili. Close the air fry lid. Choose Broil and set the time to 15 minutes. Choose Start. When ready, remove the pot from the pot and place it on a heat-resistant surface. Let the chili and biscuits rest for 10 to 15 minutes before serving.

300. Italian Chicken with Herby Dumplings

Servings: 4 | Ready in about: 40 minutes

For the Dumplings
1 large egg
¾ cup heavy cream
6 oz self-rising flour
1 tsp dried mixed herbs

For the Chicken
3 tbsp butter
3 tbsp flour
1 tsp Italian seasoning mix
3 cups chicken stock
1 ¼ lb skinless, chicken thighs, cubed
2 large celery stalks, chopped
3 large carrots, cut into coins
⅔ cup peas, frozen
1 cup frozen pearl onions

To make the dumplings, whisk the egg and heavy cream in a bowl until evenly combined and stir in the flour and mixed herbs until a stiff but soft dough forms. Refrigerate the dough while you make the chicken. On your Instant Pot, choose Sauté. Melt the butter, stir in the flour and Italian seasoning. Cook for 3 to 4 minutes, stirring occasionally, until the roux is golden brown. Pour in stock, whisking until combined. Cook until the sauce has slightly thickened. Add the chicken, celery, and carrots to the inner pot. Seal the pressure lid, choose Pressure Cook on High, and the cooking time to 6 minutes. Once ready, perform a quick pressure release.

Remove and discard the bay leaf. Stir in the peas and onion. Take out the dumpling from the fridge and drop in small spoonfuls into the chicken and vegetables. Seal the pressure lid, choose Pressure Cook on High and the cooking time to 2 minutes. After cooking, perform a quick pressure release and carefully open the lid. Close the air fry lid and choose Broil. Adjust the cooking time to 7 minutes. Ladle into bowls and serve.

301. Lemon and Paprika Chicken Thighs

Servings: 4 | Ready in about: 26 minutes

4 chicken thighs
1 ½ tbsp olive oil
½ tsp garlic powder
Salt and black pepper to taste
½ tsp red pepper flakes
½ tsp smoked paprika
1 small onion, chopped
2 cloves garlic, sliced
½ cup chicken broth
1 tsp Italian Seasoning
1 lemon, zested and juiced
1 ½ tbsp heavy cream
Lemon slices to garnish
Chopped parsley to garnish

Preheat your Instant Pot by selecting Sauté. Warm the olive oil and add the chicken thighs. Cook to brown e for about 3 minutes. Remove the chicken to a plate. Melt the butter and add garlic, onion, and lemon juice. Deglaze the bottom of the pot and cook for 1 minute. Add the Italian seasoning, broth, lemon zest, and the chicken. Close the pressure lid, secure the pressure valve, select Pressure on High for 10 minutes. When ready, do a quick pressure release. Open the lid. Stir in the heavy cream. Close the air fry lid and select Broil mode. Set the time to 5 minutes. Serve with the steamed kale and spinach mix. Garnish with the lemons slices and parsley.

302. Chicken with Tomato Salsa

Servings: 4 | Ready in about: 30 minutes

4 chicken thighs, skinless but with bone
4 tbsp olive oil
1 cup crushed tomatoes
1 large red bell pepper, diced
1 green bell pepper, seeded and diced
1 Red onion, diced
Salt and black pepper to taste
1 tbsp chopped basil
½ cup chicken broth
1 bay leaf
½ tsp dried oregano

Place the chicken on a clean flat surface and season with salt and pepper. On your Instant Pot, choose Sauté and heat the oil. Once heated, add the chicken to brown on both sides for 6 minutes. Then, add the onions and peppers. Cook for 5 minutes until nice and soft. Add bay leaf, salt, broth, pepper, and oregano. Stir using a spoon. Close the pressure lid, secure the pressure valve, and select Pressure Cook on High for 15 minutes.

Once the timer has ended, do a natural pressure release for 5 minutes. Discard the bay leaf. Stir in tomatoes, close the air fry lid, select Broil mode and cook for 25 minutes. Dish the chicken with the sauce into a serving bowl and garnish with the chopped basil. Serve over a bed of steamed squash spaghetti.

303. Tandoori Chicken Thighs

Servings: 4 | Ready in about: 45 minutes

1½ lb chicken thighs, boneless skinless
1 cup plain Greek yogurt
1½ tsp garlic puree
1 tbsp ginger puree
1 tsp sweet paprika
½ tsp chili pepper
½ tsp garam masala
½ tsp ground cumin
1 tsp turmeric powder
Salt and black pepper to taste
1 cup long grain white rice, rinsed
¾ cup coconut milk
¼ cup water
½ cup cooked lima beans
1 tbsp chopped fresh parsley

Season the chicken with salt and place it in a plastic zipper bag. Set aside and make the marinade. In a medium bowl, mix the yogurt, salt, garlic, ginger, paprika, chili pepper, garam masala, cumin, turmeric, and black pepper. Pour the marinade over the chicken. Zip the bag and rub the marinade on the chicken to coat properly. Set aside. Pour the rice into your Instant Pot and mix in the coconut milk, water, and some salt to taste. Seal the pressure lid, choose Pressure Cook on High and the cooking time to 3 minutes. After cooking, perform a natural pressure release for 6 minutes and then a quick pressure release to let out the remaining pressure.

Carefully open the lid. Stir in the lima beans and cover the rice with aluminum foil to prevent the rice from drying out. Oil a trivet with cooking spray. Place in the pot and slide the legs on the trivet under the foil. Remove the chicken from the marinade, hold for a while to allow the excess liquid drip back into the bag. Arrange the chicken on the greased rack in a single layer. Close the air fry lid and choose Broil. Adjust the cooking time to 16 minutes. After 8 minutes, open the lid and flip the chicken and close the lid. Cook until the second side is crisp and browned on the edges. Serve the chicken with rice and garnish with the parsley.

304. Pesto Chicken with Roasted Pepper Sauce

Servings: 4 | Ready in about: 23 minutes

4 chicken breasts
½ cup heavy cream
½ cup chicken broth
⅓ tsp minced garlic
Salt and black pepper to taste
⅓ tsp Italian Seasoning
¼ cup roasted red peppers, chopped
1 tbsp basil pesto
1 tbsp cornstarch

To your Instant Pot, add the chicken at the bottom. Pour the chicken broth and add Italian seasoning, garlic, salt, and pepper. Close the pressure lid, secure the pressure valve, and select Pressure Cook on High for 15 minutes. Once the timer has ended, do a natural pressure release for 5 minutes and open the lid. Use a spoon to remove the chicken onto a plate. Scoop out any fat or unwanted chunks from the sauce. In a bowl, add the cream, cornstarch, red peppers, and pesto. Mix them with a spoon. Pour the creamy mixture into the pot and close the air fry lid. Select Broil and cook for 4 minutes. Serve the chicken with sauce.

305. Hot Crispy Chicken with Potatoes

Servings: 4 | Ready in about: 35 minutes

4 bone-in skin-on chicken thighs	1 tsp dried oregano	¼ cup chicken stock
½ tsp salt	½ tsp dry mustard	1 tbsp olive oil
2 tbsp melted butter	½ tsp garlic powder	1 lb potatoes, quartered
2 tsp Worcestershire sauce	¼ tsp sweet paprika	2 carrots, sliced into rounds
2 tsp turmeric powder	2 dashes hot sauce	

Season the chicken on both sides with salt. In a small bowl, mix the melted butter, Worcestershire sauce, turmeric, oregano, dry mustard, garlic powder, sweet paprika, and hot sauce to be properly combined and stir in the chicken stock. On your Instant Pot, choose Sauté. Heat olive oil and add the chicken thighs and fry for 4 to 5 minutes or until browned. Turn and briefly sear the other side, about 1 minute. Remove from the pot. Add the potatoes and carrots to the pot and stir to coat with the fat. Pour in about half of the spicy sauce and mix to coat. Put the chicken thighs on top and drizzle with the remaining sauce. Seal the pressure lid, choose Pressure Cook and the cooking time to 3 minutes. After cooking, do a quick pressure release, and carefully open the lid.

Transfer the chicken to a trivet. Gently move the potatoes and carrots aside and fetch some of the sauce over the chicken. Mix the potatoes and carrots back into the sauce and carefully set a trivet in the pot. Close the air fry lid and choose Bake. Adjust the temperature to 375°F and the cooking time to 16 minutes. Press Start. When done, open the lid and transfer the potatoes, carrots, and chicken to a platter, drizzling with any remaining sauce.

306. Chicken Meatballs Primavera

Servings: 4 | Ready in about: 30 minutes

1 lb ground chicken	2 tbsp chopped basil + extra to garnish	2 cups chopped green beans
1 egg, cracked into a bowl	1 tbsp olive oil + ½ tbsp olive oil	½ lb chopped asparagus
6 tsp flour	1 ½ tsp Italian Seasoning	1 cup chopped tomatoes
Salt and black pepper to taste	1 red bell pepper, seeded and sliced	1 cup chicken broth

In a mixing bowl, add the chicken, egg, flour, salt, pepper, 2 tablespoons of basil, 1 tablespoon of olive oil, and Italian seasoning. Mix them well with hands and make 16 large balls out of the mixture. Set the meatballs aside. Select Sauté. Heat half teaspoon of olive oil, and add peppers, green beans, and asparagus. Cook for 3 minutes, stirring frequently. After 3 minutes, use a spoon the veggies onto a plate and set aside.

Pour the remaining oil ithe pot to heat. Fry the meatballs for 2 minutes on each side until brown lightly. Put the vegetables into the pot. Pour the chicken broth over it. Seal the lid and select Pressure Cook for 10 minutes. Do a quick pressure release. Close the air fry lid and select Air Fry. Cook for 5 minutes at 400°F until nice and crispy. Dish the meatballs with sauce into a serving bowl and garnish it with basil. Serve with over cooked pasta.

307. Whole Chicken with Lemon & Onion Stuffing

Servings: 6 | Ready in about: 55 minutes

4 lb whole chicken	Salt and black pepper to taste	1 yellow onion, peeled and quartered
1 tbsp herbes de Provence Seasoning	2 cloves garlic, peeled	1 lemon, quartered
1 tbsp olive oil	1 tsp garlic powder	1 ¼ cups chicken broth

Put the chicken on a clean flat surface and pat dry using paper towels. Sprinkle the top and cavity of the chicken with salt, pepper, Herbes de Provence, and garlic powder. Stuff the onion, lemon quarters, and garlic cloves into the cavity. In your Instant Pot, fit a trivet. Pour broth into the pot and place the chicken on the trivet. Seal the lid, and select Pressure Cook on High for 25 minutes. Once ready, do a natural pressure release for about 10 minutes. Close the air fry lid and broil the chicken for 5 minutes on Broil mode to ensure that it attains a golden brown color on each side. Dish the chicken on a bed of steamed mixed veggies. Right here, the choice is yours to whip up some good veggies together as your appetite tells you.

308. Cajun Roasted Chicken with Potato Mash

Servings: 4 | Ready in about: 70 minutes

2 bone-in chicken breasts
4 tsp Cajun seasoning
¾ cup chicken stock
3 Yukon Gold potatoes, scrubbed
3 tbsp melted butter
2 tbsp warm heavy cream

Pat the chicken dry with a paper towel and carefully slide your hands underneath the skin to slightly separate the meat from the skin. Then in a small bowl, combine salt and Cajun seasoning, and rub half of the mixture under the skin and cavity of the chicken. Pour the chicken stock into the inner pot of the pot. Fix a trivet in the pot and lay the chicken on the side in the center of a trivet. Also, arrange the potatoes around the chicken. Seal the pressure lid, choose Pressure Cook on High and the cooking time to 13 minutes. Mix the remaining spice mixture with 2 tablespoons of the melted butter, and set aside. When done pressure cooking, perform a natural pressure release for 10 minutes. Remove the potatoes and chicken onto a cutting board.

Pour the cooking juices into a bowl and return the trivet with chicken only to the pot. Baste the outer side of the chicken with half of the spice-butter mixture. Close the air fry lid and choose Air Fry. Adjust the temperature to 400°F and the cooking time to 16 minutes. After 8 minutes, open the lid and flip the chicken over. Baste this side with the remaining butter mixture and close the lid to continue cooking. With a potato masher, smoothly puree the potatoes, and add the remaining salt, melted butter, heavy cream, and 2 tablespoons of the reserved cooking juice. Stir to combine. Taste and adjust the seasoning with salt and pepper and cover the bowl with aluminum foil. After cooking, transfer the chicken to a cutting board, leaving a trivet in the pot.

Pour the remaining cooking sauce into your Instant Pot and choose Sauté. Place the bowl of potatoes on the trivet to keep warm as the sauce reduces. Press Start and boil the sauce for 2 to 3 minutes or until reduced by about half. Meanwhile, slice the chicken and lay the pieces on a platter. Remove the mashed potato from the pot and remove the trivet. Spoon the sauce over the chicken slices and serve with the creamy potatoes.

309. Chicken & Green Bean Coconut Curry

Servings: 8 | Ready in about: 32 minutes

4 chicken breasts
4 tbsp red curry paste
½ cup chicken broth
2 cups coconut milk
4 tbsp sugar
2 red bell pepper, sliced
2 yellow bell peppers, sliced
2 cup green beans, cut in half
2 tbsp lime juice

Add the chicken, red curry paste, salt, pepper, coconut milk, broth, and sugar in your Instant Pot. Close the pressure lid, secure the pressure valve, and select Pressure Cook on High for 15 minutes. Once the timer has ended, do a quick pressure release, and open the lid. Remove the chicken onto a cutting board and close the air fry lid. Select Broil mode. Add the bell peppers, green beans, and lime juice. Stir the sauce with a spoon and cook for 4 minutes. Slice the chicken with a knife, pour the sauce and vegetables over and serve warm.

310. Buffalo Chicken & Navy Bean Chili

Servings: 6 | Ready in about: 45 minutes

1 tbsp olive oil
1 shallot, diced
½ cup fennel, chopped
¼ cup minced garlic
1 tbsp smoked paprika
2 tsp chili powder
2 tsp ground cumin
1 (28 oz) can crushed tomatoes
1 ½ lb chicken sausage, sliced
1 (14 oz) can tomatoes with green chilies
¾ cup Buffalo wing sauce
2 (14 oz) cans navy beans, drained

Warm oil on Sauté in your Instant Pot. Add the sausages and brown for 5 minutes, turning frequently. Set aside on a plate. In the same fat, sauté onion, roasted red peppers, fennel, and garlic for 4 minutes until soft. Season with paprika, cumin, pepper, salt, and chili powder. Stir in crushed tomatoes, diced tomatoes with green chilies, buffalo sauce, and navy beans. Return the sausages to the pot. Seal the pressure lid, choose Pressure Cook on High, and set the timer to 30 minutes. When ready, do a quick pressure release. Spoon chili into bowls and serve.

311. Chicken Noodle Soup with Crispy Bacon

Servings: 8 | Ready in about: 33 minutes

5 oz dry egg noodles
4 chicken breasts
1 large white onion, chopped
8 bacon slices, chopped

4 cloves garlic, minced
Salt and black pepper to taste
2 medium carrots, sliced
2 cups sliced celery

½ cup chopped parsley
1 ½ tsp dried thyme
8 cups chicken broth

Turn on your Instant Pot and select Sauté. Add the chopped bacon and fry for 5 minutes until nicely brown and crispy. Remove to a paper towel to soak up excess oil and set aside. Add the onion and garlic to the pot and cook for 3 minutes until tender. Add the chicken breasts, noodles, carrots, celery, chicken broth, thyme, salt, and pepper. Seal the pressure lid and select Pressure Cook on High pressure. Adjust the time to 5 minutes. Once the timer has ended, do a quick pressure release, and open the lid. Use a wooden spoon to remove the chicken onto a plate. Shred the chicken with two forks and add it back to the soup. Stir in the bacon. Close the air fry lid and cook on Broil for 5 minutes. Ladle the soup into serving bowls and serve with a side of bread.

312. Coq au Vin

Servings: 4 | Ready in about: 60 minutes

4 chicken leg quarters, skin on
1½ tsp salt
1 tbsp olive oil
4 serrano ham slices, cut into thirds

¼ cup brown onion slices
1¼ cups dry red wine
⅓ cup chicken stock
1 ½ tsp tomato puree

½ tsp brown sugar
Black pepper to taste
½ cup sautéed mushrooms
¾ cup shallots, sliced

Season the chicken on both sides with 1 teaspoon of salt and set aside on a wire rack. On your Instant Pot, choose Sauté. Heat the olive oil, place the ham in the pot in a single layer and cook for 3 to 4 minutes or until browned. Remove the ham to a plate and set aside. Add the chicken quarters to the pot. Cook for 5 minutes or until the skin is golden brown. Turn the chicken over and cook further for 2 minutes. Remove to a plate.

Carefully pour out almost all the fat leaving about a tablespoon to cover the bottom of the pot. Then, stir in the sliced onion and cook until the onion begins to brown. Add ½ cup of red wine, stir, and scrape the bottom of the pan to let off any browned bits. Then, boil the mixture until the wine reduces by about 1/3, about 2 minutes.

Pour the remaining red wine, chicken stock, tomato puree, brown sugar, and a few grinds of black pepper into your Instant Pot. Boil the sauce for 1 minute, stirring to make sure the tomato paste is properly mixed. Add the chicken pieces with skin- side up, to the pot. Put the pressure lid in place and lock to seal. Choose Pressure Cook on High and the cooking time to 12 minutes. After cooking, perform a natural pressure release for 10 minutes.

Remove the chicken from the pot. Pour the sauce into a bowl and allow sitting until the fat rises to the top and starts firming up. Use a spoon to fetch off the fat on top of the sauce. Pour the sauce back to the pot and stir in the mushrooms and pearl onions. Place the chicken on the sauce with skin side up. Close the air fry lid and select Broil. Adjust the time to 7 minutes. When done, open the lid and transfer the chicken to a serving platter. Spoon the sauce with mushrooms and pearl onions all around the chicken and crumble the reserved ham on top.

313. Honey-Garlic Chicken

Servings: 4 | Ready in about: 30 minutes

4 chicken breasts, cut into chunks
1 onion, diced
4 garlic cloves, smashed

½ cup honey
3 tbsp soy sauce
2 tbsp lime juice

2 tsp sesame oil
1 tsp rice vinegar
1 tbsp cornstarch

Mix garlic, onion and chicken in your Instant Pot. In a bowl, combine honey, sesame oil, lime juice, soy sauce, 1 cup water, and rice vinegar. Pour over the chicken mixture. Seal the pressure lid, choose Pressure Cook on High, and set the timer to 15 minutes. When ready, release the pressure quickly. Mix 1 tbsp water and cornstarch until well dissolved. Stir into the sauce. Press Sauté. Simmer the sauce for 2 to 3 minutes as you stir until thickened.

314. White Wine Chicken

Servings: 4 | Ready in about: 9 hours

3 chicken legs, cut into drumsticks and thighs
8 oz Shiitake mushrooms, stems removed and cut into 4 pieces
3 skinny carrots, cut into 4 crosswise pieces each
2 bacon slices, chopped
1 ½ cups dry white wine
Salt and black pepper to taste
½ bunch thyme, divided
3 Shallots, peeled
3 tbsp butter, divided
2 cloves garlic, crushed
1 tbsp flour
3 tbsp chopped parsley for garnishing

Put the chicken on a clean flat surface and season on both sides with salt and pepper. In a plastic zipper bag, pour the wine. Add half of the thyme and chicken. Zip the bag and shake to coat the chicken well with the wine. Place it in the refrigerator for 6 to 8 hours. After 8 hours, turn on your Instant Pot on High and fry the bacon on Sauté mode for about 8 minutes. Remove the bacon without the fat onto a plate using a slotted spoon. Set aside.

Pour the mushroom into the pot, season with salt and cook for 5 minutes. Then, remove at the side of the bacon. Remove the chicken from the refrigerator onto a clean flat surface. Take out and discard the thyme but reserve the marinade. Pat the chicken dry with paper towels. Melt half of the butter in the pot on Sauté. Place the chicken in the butter in batches and fry until dark golden brown on each side, about 12 minutes.

Addin bacon, mushrooms, shallots, garlic, carrots, and salt. Cook for 4 minutes and top with the wine and remaining thyme. Seal the pressure lid and select Pressure Cook for 15 minutes. Add the flour and the remaining butter in a bowl, and smash them together with a fork. Once the timer has ended, do a quick pressure release. Discard the thyme. Add the flour mixture to the sauce in the pot, stir until well incorporated. Adjust the seasoning with salt and black pepper. Close the air fry lid and select Broil. Cook for 4 minutes. Top with parsley and serve.

315. Chicken Chili with Cannellini Beans

Servings: 4 | Ready in about: 40 minutes

3 chicken breasts, cubed
3 cups chicken broth
1 tbsp butter
1 white onion, chopped
29 oz canned Cannellini beans
1 tsp cumin powder
1 tsp dried oregano
½ cup heavy whipping cream
1 cup sour cream

On your Instant Pot, choose Sauté. Stir and let cook the chicken for 6 minutes. Stir in the cannellini beans, cumin powder, and oregano. Pour in the broth, stir, close the pressure lid, and secure the pressure valve. Select Pressure Cook on High for 10 minutes. Once the timer has ended, let the pot sit uncovered for 10 minutes, then do a quick pressure release. Stir in the whipping and sour cream. Close the air fry lid and select Broil mode. Cook for 2 minutes. Serve warm with a mix of steamed bell peppers and broccoli.

316. Spinach & Mushroom Chicken Stew

Servings: 4 | Ready in about: 56 minutes

4 chicken breasts, diced
1 ¼ lb Button mushrooms, halved
3 tbsp olive oil
1 large onion, sliced
5 cloves garlic, minced
Salt and black pepper to taste
1 ¼ tsp cornstarch
½ cup spinach, chopped
1 ½ cups chicken stock
1 tsp Dijon mustard
1 ½ cup sour cream
3 tbsp chopped parsley

On your Instant Pot, choose Sauté. Once the pot is ready, heat the olive oil then include the onion and sauté for 3 minutes until soft. Add the mushrooms, chicken, garlic, salt, pepper, Dijon mustard, and chicken broth. Stir well. Seal the lid and press Pressure Cooker for 15 minutes. Once done, do a natural pressure release for 5 minutes

Carefully open the lid. Stir the stew, remove the bay leaf, and scoop some of the liquid into a bowl. Add the cornstarch to the liquid and mix them until completely lump free. Pour the liquid into the sauce, stir it, and let the sauce thicken to your desired consistency. Top it with the sour cream, close the air fry lid and select Broil mode. Cook for 2 minutes. Garnish with the chopped parsley and serve with steamed green peas.

317. Cheesy Buffalo Chicken

Servings: 4 | Ready in about: 37 minutes

4 chicken breasts
½ cup Hot sauce
2 large white onion, finely chopped
2 cups finely chopped celery
1 tbsp olive oil
1 tsp dried thyme
3 cups chicken broth
1 tsp garlic powder
½ cup Blue cheese + extra for serving
4 oz cream cheese, cubed in small pieces
Salt and pepper, to taste

Put the chicken on a clean flat surface and season with pepper and salt. Set aside. Select Sauté. Heat in olive oil, add onion and celery. Sauté them, constant stirring, until they are nice and soft, for about 5 minutes. Add garlic powder and thyme. Stir and cook for about a minute, and add the chicken, hot sauce, and chicken broth.

Seal the pressure lid and select Pressure Cook on High for 15 minutes. Put the blue cheese and cream cheese in a bowl, and use a fork to mash them together. Set the resulting mixture aside. Once the timer has ended, do a quick pressure release. Take out the chicken onto a flat surface and use two forks to shred them. Return shredded chicken to the pot, close the air fry lid, select Broil mode and cook for 5 minutes. Add the cheese to the pot and stir until is slightly incorporated into the sauce. Dish the buffalo chicken soup into bowls. Sprinkle the remaining cheese over the soup and serve with sliced baguette.

318. Mediterranean Stuffed Chicken Breasts

Servings: 4 | Ready in about: 30 minutes

4 chicken breasts, skinless
Salt and black pepper to taste
1 cup baby spinach, frozen
½ cup crumbled Feta cheese
½ tsp dried oregano
½ tsp garlic powder
2 tbsp olive oil
2 tsp dried parsley
1 cup water

Wrap the chicken in plastic and put on a cutting board. Use a rolling pin to pound flat to a quarter-inch thickness. Remove the plastic wrap. In a bowl, mix spinach, salt, and feta cheese and scoop the mixture onto the chicken breasts. Wrap the chicken to secure the spinach filling in it. Use toothpicks to secure the wrap firmly from opening.

Gently season the chicken pieces with oregano, parsley, garlic powder, and pepper. Select Sauté on your Instant Pot. Heat the oil, add the chicken, and sear to golden brown on each side. Work in 2 batches. Remove the chicken onto a plate and set aside. Pour the water into the pot and scrape the bottom of the pot to let loose any chicken pieces or seasoning that is stuck to the bottom of the pot. Fit in a trivet.

Transfer the chicken onto the trivet. Seal the lid and select Pressure Cook on High for 10 minutes. Once the timer has ended, do a quick pressure release. Close the air fry lid and cook on Bake mode for 5 minutes at 390°F. Plate the chicken and serve with a side of sautéed asparagus and some slices of tomatoes.

319. BBQ Chicken Drumettes

Servings: 4 | Ready in about: 30 minutes

2 lb chicken drumettes
½ cup chicken broth
½ tsp dry mustard
½ tsp sweet paprika
½ tbsp cumin powder
½ tsp onion powder
¼ tsp Cayenne powder
1 stick butter, sliced in 5 pieces
BBQ sauce to taste

Pour the chicken broth into the inner pot of your Instant Pot and insert a trivet. In a zipper bag, pour in dry mustard, cumin powder, onion powder, cayenne powder, salt, and pepper. Add the chicken, close the bag and shake to coat the chicken well with the spices. You can toss the chicken in the spices in batches too. Then, remove the chicken from the bag and place on the trivet. Spread the butter slices on the drumsticks. Seal the lid and select Pressure Cook on High for 10 minutes. Once the timer has ended, do a quick pressure release, and open the lid. Remove the chicken onto a clean flat surface like a cutting board and brush them with the barbecue sauce using the brush. Return to a trivet and close the air fry lid. Cook for 10 minutes at 400°F on Air Fry mode.

320. Traditional Chicken Cordon Bleu

Servings: 4 | Ready in about: 35 minutes

2 boneless skinless chicken breasts	3 tbsp melted butter	4 thin slices Emmental cheese
¾ tsp salt	4 tsp Dijon mustard	⅔ cup panko bread crumbs
12 oz broccoli, cut into florets	4 thin ham slices	¼ cup grated Pecorino Romano cheese

Put the chicken breasts on a cutting board and slice through the breasts to form two thinner pieces from each breast to make 4 pieces in total. Season the chicken on both sides with ½ teaspoon of salt. Pour a cup of water into the inner pot. Put a trivet in the lower position of the pot and lay the broccoli florets on the trivet. After, put the chicken on the broccoli. Seal the pressure lid, choose Pressure Cook on High and the time to 1 minute.

After cooking, perform a quick pressure release. Take out the trivet and set aside. Pour the water out of the pot. Place the chicken on the cutting board and the broccoli into your Instant Pot. Put 1 tablespoon of melted butter on the broccoli florets and sprinkle with the remaining salt. Stir to coat the broccoli with the butter.

Smear 1 teaspoon of mustard on each chicken piece. Lay each ham slice on each chicken and each Emmental cheese slice on each ham. In a small bowl, combine the breadcrumbs, remaining butter, and the Pecorino Romano cheese. Sprinkle the breadcrumb mixture equally over the chicken. Open the air fry lid and carefully transfer the chicken pieces to a trivet. Close the air fry lid and choose Air Fry. Adjust the temperature to 400°F and the cooking time to 10 minutes. When done cooking, the crumbs should be crisp and have obtained a deep golden brown. Transfer the chicken pieces to a platter and serve with the broccoli.

321. Mexican Green Chili Chicken

Servings: 4 | Ready in about: 40 minutes

1 tbsp olive oil	1 ½ lb boneless skinless chicken breasts	¼ cup minced fresh cilantro
12 oz, baby plum tomatoes, halved	2 jalapeño peppers, seeded and chopped	Tortilla chips
¾ cup chicken stock	2 serrano peppers, cut into chunks	½ cup shredded Cheddar Cheese
½ tsp salt	2 large garlic cloves, minced	½ lime, juiced
½ tsp ground cumin	1 small onion, sliced	
1 tsp Mexican seasoning mix		

On your Instant Pot, choose Sauté. Heat the olive oil add the plum tomatoes. Cook without turning, for 3 to 4 minutes. Add the chicken stock while scraping the bottom of the pot to dissolve any browned bits. Stir in the cumin, Mexican seasoning, and salt. Add the chicken, jalapeños, serrano pepper, garlic, onion, and half the cilantro. Seal the pressure lid, choose Pressure Cook on High and the cooking time to 10 minutes.

Grease a trivet with cooking spray and fix it in the upper position of the pot. Cut out a circle of aluminum foil and place on the trivet. Lay on a single layer of tortilla chips, sprinkle with half of the Cheddar cheese and repeat with another layer of chips and cheese. Set aside. After cooking, perform a natural pressure release for 5 minutes. Take out the chicken from the pot and set aside. Then, with an immersion blender, purée the vegetables into the sauce.

Shred the chicken with two forks and return the pieces to the sauce. Add the remaining cilantro and the lime juice. Taste and adjust the seasoning and carefully transfer chips to the pot. Close the air fry lid and choose Air Fry. Adjust the temperature to 375°F and the time to 5 minutes. When done cooking, open the lid. Carefully take out the trivet and pour the chips into a platter. Serve the chili in bowls with the chips on the side.

322. Chicken Caesar Salad with Salted Croutons

Servings: 4 | Ready in about: 45 minutes

2 chicken breasts, skinless boneless	½ small Italian bread loaf, cubed	2 tbsp grated Parmigiano Reggiano
1 garlic clove, minced	⅓ cup Caesar dressing, divided	
1 tbsp unsalted butter	1 romaine lettuce heart, torn	
2 tbsp olive oil	1 oz grated Parmigiano Reggiano cheese	

Pour 1 cup of water into your Instant Pot. Put in a trivet in and place the chicken on the trivet. Seal the pressure lid, choose Pressure Cook, adjust the pressure to Low and the cooking time to 5 minutes. Once done cooking, perform a natural pressure release for 10 minutes. Carefully open the lid. Set aside. In a heatproof bowl, combine garlic, butter, and olive oil. Put the bowl in the air fry basket and place the basket in the pot.

Close the air fry lid and choose Air Fry. Adjust the temperature to 375°F and the cooking time to 2 minutes. Press Start to preheat the pot and melt the butter. When done preheating, take out the basket from the pot and the bowl from the basket. Pour the bread cubes into the bowl and toss to be well-coated in the butter and oil. Transfer the bread to the air fry basket and the basket into your Instant Pot.

Close the air fry lid and choose Air Fry. Adjust the temperature to 375°F and the cooking time to 10 minutes. After 5 minutes, open the lid and toss the bread. Close the lid and continue cooking until the croutons are golden brown. Remove the basket from the pot and lightly season the croutons with salt. Allow cooling. Cut the chicken into bite-size chunks. In a small bowl, toss the chicken with 3 tablespoons of Caesar dressing and set aside. Place the lettuce on a salad bowl, pour the remaining dressing over nad toss to coat well. Mix with chesse. Share the salad into bowls, top with chicken, then croutons, and sprinkle with extra cheese.

323. Tandoori Chicken with Cilantro Sauce

Servings: 4 | Ready in about: 9 hour

4 chicken thighs, skinless
½ cup Greek yogurt
1 tbsp olive oil
1 tbsp lemon juice
Cilantro Sauce:
A handful of fresh cilantro leaves
1 tsp cumin seeds
½ jalapeno pepper

1 tbsp red chili powder
2 tsp salt
1 tsp garam masala
½ tsp ground turmeric

2-3 garlic cloves
2 tsp honey
2 tsp lemon juice

½ tbsp grated fresh ginger
½ tbsp minced garlic
1 cup water
Cooking spray

¾ cup olive oil
salt to taste

In a large bowl, mix yogurt, lemon juice, garam masala, garlic, turmeric, red chili powder, vegetable oil, salt, and ginger. Use a paper towel to pat thighs. Place the thighs into a resealable plastic bag. Add in yogurt mixture and seal. Massage bag to ensure the marinade coats the chicken completely and place in the refrigerator for 12 hours. Take the chicken out of the refrigerator and set aside for 30 minutes before cooking. Add water into your Instant Pot. Apply a cooking spray to your steamer and set in the pot over the water. Remove chicken from marinade and arrange on the trivet. Seal the pressure lid, choose Pressure Cook on High, and set the timer to 15 minutes. When ready, release the pressure quickly. In a blender, blend cilantro, water, garlic, honey, cumin, jalapeno pepper, salt and lemon juice until smooth. Over the chicken, drizzle sauce before serving.

324. Indian Butter Chicken

Servings: 6 | Ready in about: 30 minutes

2 tbsp butter
1 large onion, minced
1 tbsp grated fresh ginger
1 tbsp minced fresh garlic
½ tsp ground turmeric

1 tbsp Kashmiri red chili powder
1 (14.5 oz) can coconut milk
2 lb boneless, skinless chicken legs
3 Roma tomatoes, pureed in a blender
½ cup chopped fresh cilantro, divided

2 tbsp Indian curry paste
2 tbsp dried fenugreek
2 tsp sugar
1 tsp garam masala
Salt to taste

Set your Instant Pot to Sauté and melt butter. Add in salt and onion. Cook for 2 to 3 minutes until fragrant. Stir in ginger, turmeric, garlic, and red chili powder to coat. Cook for 2 more minutes. Place water and coconut cream into separate bowls. Stir the water from the coconut milk can, pureed tomatoes, and chicken with the onion mixture. Seal the pressure lid, choose Pressure Cook on High, and set the timer to 8 minutes. When ready, release the pressure quickly. Stir sugar, coconut cream, fenugreek, curry paste, half the cilantro, and garam masala through the chicken mixture. Apply salt for seasoning. Simmer the mixture and cook for 10 minutes until the sauce thickens on Sauté. Garnish with the rest of the cilantro before serving.

325. Chicken & Veggie Tacos with Guacamole

Servings: 4 | Ready in about: 30 minutes

2 lb chicken breasts, sliced
½ cup chicken broth
1 yellow onion, sliced
1 green bell pepper, seeded and sliced
Tacos, Guacamole, sour cream, Salsa, cheese for assembling
1 yellow bell pepper, seeded and sliced
1 red bell pepper, seeded and sliced
2 tbsp cumin powder
2 tbsp chili powder
Salt to taste
½ Lime
Fresh cilantro, to garnish

Grease the inner pot with cooking spray and line the bottom with the peppers and onion. Lay the chicken on the bed of peppers. Sprinkle with salt, chili powder, and cumin powder. Squeeze some lime juice and pour in chicken broth. Seal the lid and select Pressure Cook on High for 15 minutes. Once ready, do a quick pressure release. Close the air fry lid and cook for 5 minutes on Bake at 390°F. Dish the chicken with the vegetables and juice onto a large serving platter. Add sour cream, cheese, guacamole, salsa, and tacos in one layer on the side of the chicken.

326. Chicken with Beans & Bacon

Servings: 4 | Ready in about: 45 minutes

1 tbsp olive oil
4 slices bacon, crumbled
4 boneless, skinless chicken thighs
1 onion, diced
4 garlic cloves, minced
1 tbsp tomato paste
1 tbsp oregano
1 tbsp ground cumin
1 tsp chili powder
½ tsp cayenne pepper
1 (14.5 oz) can whole tomatoes
1 cup chicken broth
1 cup cooked corn
1 red bell pepper, chopped
15 oz red kidney beans, drained
1 cup shredded Monterey Jack cheese
1 cup sliced red onion
¼ cup chopped cilantro

Warm oil on Sauté in your Instant Pot. Sear the chicken for 3 minutes for each side until browned. Set the chicken on a plate. In the same oil, fry bacon until crispy, about 5 minutes and set aside. Add in onions and cook for 2 to 3 minutes until fragrant. Stir in garlic, oregano, cayenne pepper, cumin, tomato paste, bell pepper, and chili powder and cook for 30 more seconds. Pour the chicken broth, salt, and tomatoes and bring to a boil.

Take back the chicken and bacon to the pot and ensure it is submerged in the liquid. Seal the pressure lid, choose Pressure Cook, and set the timer to 15 minutes. When ready, release the pressure quickly. Pour in the kidney beans. Press Sauté and bring the liquid to a boil. Cook for 10 minutes. Serve topped with cheese and cilantro.

327. Spicy Salsa Chicken with Feta

Servings: 6 | Ready in about: 30 minutes

2 lb boneless skinless chicken drumsticks
¼ tsp salt
1 ½ cups hot tomato salsa
1 onion, chopped
1 cup feta cheese, crumbled

Sprinkle salt over the chicken. Set in your Instant Pot. Stir in salsa to coat the chicken. Seal the pressure lid, choose Pressure Cook on High, and set the timer to 15 minutes. When ready, do a quick pressure release. Press Sauté and cook for 5 to 10 minutes as you stir until excess liquid has evaporated. Top with feta cheese and serve.

328. Paprika Buttered Chicken

Servings: 6 | Ready in about: 45 minutes

1 cup chicken stock
½ cup white wine
½ onion, thinly sliced
2 cloves garlic, minced
3.5-lb whole chicken
Salt and black pepper to taste
½ tsp dried thyme
3 tbsp butter, melted
½ tsp paprika

Into the pot, add onion, chicken stock, white wine, and garlic. Over the mixture, place a trivet. Apply pepper, salt, and thyme to the chicken. Lay onto trivet breast-side up. Seal the pressure lid, choose Pressure Cook on High, and set the timer to 26 minutes. When ready, release the pressure quickly. In a bowl, mix paprika and butter.

Remove the trivet with chicken from your pot. Get rid of onion and stock. Onto the chicken, brush butter mixture. Place it on the air fry basket and insert in the pot. Close the air fry lid, select Air Fry, and cook for 5 minutes at 400°F until the skin is crispy and browned. Let the chicken to cool for 5 minutes, then carve it to serve.

329. Chicken Cacciatore

Servings: 4 | Ready in about: 40 minutes

1 lb chicken drumsticks, boneless, skinless
2 tsp olive oil
2 tsp salt
1½ tsp freshly ground black pepper
1 carrot, chopped
1 red bell pepper, chopped
1 yellow bell pepper, chopped

1 onion, chopped
4 garlic cloves, thinly sliced
2 tsp dried oregano
1 tsp dried basil
1 tsp dried parsley
1 pinch red pepper flakes

1 (28 oz) can diced tomatoes
½ cup dry red wine
¾ cup chicken stock
1 cup black olives, pitted and sliced
2 bay leaves

Warm oil on Sauté in your Instant Pot. Add pepper and salt to the chicken drumsticks. In batches, sear the chicken for 5-6 minutes until golden brown. Set aside on a plate. Drain the cooker and remain with 1 tbsp of fat. In the hot oil, sauté onion, garlic, and bell peppers for 4 minutes until softened. Add red pepper flakes, basil, parsley, and oregano, and cook for 30 more seconds. Season with salt and pepper. Stir in tomatoes, olives, chicken stock, red wine and bay leaves. Return chicken to the pot. Seal the pressure lid, choose Pressure Cook on High, and set the timer to 15 minutes. When ready, release the pressure quickly. Divide chicken between four serving bowls. Top with tomato mixture before serving.

330. Pesto Stuffed Chicken with Green Beans

Servings: 4 | Ready in about: 20 minutes

4 chicken breasts
1 tbsp butter
1 tbsp olive oil
For pesto:
1 cup fresh basil
1 garlic clove, smashed

¼ cup dry white wine
¾ cup chicken stock
1 tsp salt

2 tbsp pine nuts
¼ cup Parmesan cheese

1 cup green beans, trimmed and cut into 1-inch pieces

¼ cup extra virgin olive oil

In a bowl, mix fresh basil, pine nuts, garlic, salt, pepper and Parmesan and place in food processor. Add in oil and process until the desired consistency is attained. Adjust seasoning. Apply a thin layer of pesto to one side of each chicken breast. Tightly roll into a cylinder and fasten closed with small skewers. Press Sauté. Add oil and butter. Cook chicken rolls for 1 to 2 minutes per side until browned. Add in wine cook until the wine has evaporated, about 3-4 minutes. Add stock and salt into your Instant Pot. Top the chicken with green beans. Seal the pressure lid, choose Pressure Cook on High, and set the timer to 5 minutes. When ready, release the pressure quickly. Serve chicken rolls with cooking liquid and green beans.

331. Spicy Chicken Wings with Lemon

Servings: 4 | Ready in about: 40 minutes

2 tbsp olive oil
8 chicken wings
½ tsp chili powder

½ tsp garlic powder
½ tsp onion powder
½ dried oregano

½ tsp cayenne pepper
½ cup chicken broth
2 lemons, juiced

Coat the chicken wings with olive oil. Season with chili powder, onion powder, oregano, garlic powder, and cayenne pepper. In the steel pot of your Instant Pot, add your wings and chicken broth. Seal the pressure lid, choose Pressure Cook on High, and set the timer to 4 minutes. When ready, do a quick pressure release. Onto a greased baking sheet, place the wings in a single layer and drizzle over the lemon juice. Place in the pot and close the air fry lid. Select Bake for 5 minutes at 400 F until the skin is crispy. Serve.

332. Hawaiian-Style Chicken Sliders with Salad

Servings: 12 | Ready in about: 2 hour

Mango Slaw:
¼ cup apple cider vinegar
¼ cup olive oil
Hawaiian-Style Chicken:
1 cup brown sugar
½ cup chicken broth
½ cup soy sauce
½ cup honey

1 small pineapple, chopped
4 cups arugula

¼ cup orange juice
2 garlic cloves, minced
2 tbsp grated fresh ginger
1 tsp freshly ground black pepper

¼ cup chopped fresh cilantro
4 green onions, sliced

6 chicken breasts, halved
2 tbsp cornstarch
2 tbsp water
12 Hawaiian bread rolls

In a bowl, mix oil and vinegar. Add pineapple, green onions, cilantro, and arugula and toss to coat. Refrigerate for 1 hour while the bowl is covered. In your Instant Pot, mix brown sugar, soy sauce, garlic, pepper, ginger, honey, chicken broth, and orange juice. Press Sauté. Allow the liquid to a simmer. Cook until the honey and brown sugar dissolves. Arrange chicken into the sauce and toss to coat. Seal the pressure lid, choose Pressure Cook.

Set the timer to 16 minutes. When ready, release the pressure quickly. Transfer chicken to a cutting board and shred it. In a small bowl, mix water and cornstarch. Stir into the sauce in the cooker. Set cooker to Sauté. Cook sauce for 2 to 3 minutes until it begins to thicken. Stir in the shredded chicken. Halve the loaf of Hawaiian rolls. Set the halves, cut-side up, onto the air fry basket. Close the air fry lid. Select Bake set the temperature to 400°F, and set the time to 3 minutes. When ready, remove, transfer the shredded chicken to the bottom half of the rolls and apply a topping of salad. Replace the top half of the rolls and cut into individual sliders before serving.

333. Sage Chicken Thighs

Servings: 4 | Ready in about: 35 minutes

2 lb chicken thighs
2 tbsp olive oil
1 ½ cups diced tomatoes

¾ cup yellow onions
2 tsp minced garlic
½ cup balsamic vinegar

3 tsp chopped fresh sage
1 cup chicken broth
2 tbsp chopped parsley

With paper towels, pat dry the chicken and season with salt and pepper. Select Sauté mode. Warm the olive and add the chicken with the skin side down. Cook to golden brown on each side, for about 9 minutes. Remove onto a clean plate. Add garlic, onions, and tomatoes to the pot and sauté for 3 minutes, stirring occasionally. Pour the chicken broth, sage, and balsamic vinegar. Stir them using a spoon. Add the chicken back to the pot. Seal the lid and select Pressure Cook for 15 minutes. When ready, do a quick pressure release. Close the air fry lid and cook on Air Fry for 5 minutes at 400°F. Garnish with parsley and serve with roasted tomatoes and potatoes.

334. Chicken with BBQ Sauce

Servings: 6 | Ready in about: 20 minutes

2 lb boneless skinless chicken breasts
1 tsp salt

1½ cups barbecue sauce
1 small onion, minced

1 cup carrots, thinly sliced
4 garlic cloves

Apply a seasoning of salt to the chicken and place in the inner pot of the pot. Add onion, carrots, garlic and barbeque sauce. Toss the chicken to coat. Seal the pressure lid, choose Pressure Cook on High, and set the timer to 15 minutes. Once ready, do a quick release. Use two forks to shred chicken and stir into the sauce.

335. Pulled Chicken & Peach Salsa

Servings: 4 | Ready in about: 40 minutes

15 oz canned peach chunks
4 boneless, skinless chicken thighs
14 oz canned diced tomatoes

2 cloves garlic, minced
½ tsp cumin
½ tsp salt

Cheddar shredded cheese
Fresh chopped mint leaves

Strain canned peach chunks. Reserve the juice and set aside. To your Instant Pot, add chicken, tomatoes, cumin, garlic, peach juice, and salt. Seal the pressure lid, choose Pressure Cook on High, and set the timer to 15 minutes. When ready, do a quick pressure release. Shred chicken. Transfer to a serving plate. Add peach chunks to the cooking juices and mix until well combined. Pour the peach salsa over the chicken. Top with mint and cheese.

336. Thyme Chicken with Veggies

Servings: 4 | Ready in about: 40 minutes

4 skin-on, bone-in chicken legs	½ cup dry white wine	3 tomatoes, thinly sliced
2 tbsp olive oil	1¼ cups chicken stock	1 tbsp honey
4 cloves garlic, minced	1 cup carrots, thinly sliced	4 slices lemon
1 tsp fresh chopped thyme	1 cup parsnip, thinly sliced	Fresh thyme, chopped for garnish

Season the chicken with pepper and salt. Warm oil on Sauté in your Instant Pot. Arrange chicken legs into the hot oil. Cook for 3 to 5 minutes each side until browned. Place in a bowl and set aside. Cook thyme and garlic in the chicken fat for 1 minute until soft and lightly golden. Add wine into the pot to deglaze, scrape the pot's bottom to get rid of any brown bits of food. Simmer the wine for 2 to 3 minutes until slightly reduced in volume.

Add stock, carrots, parsnips, tomatoes, pepper and salt into the pot. Lay trivet onto veggies. Into the pot's steamer basket, arrange chicken legs. Set the steamer basket onto the trivet. Drizzle the chicken with honey then top with lemon slices. Seal the pressure lid, choose Pressure Cook, and set the timer to 12 minutes. Release pressure quickly. Place the chicken to a bowl. Drain the veggies and place them around the chicken. Garnish with thyme.

337. Chicken Chickpea Chili

Servings: 4 | Ready in about: 25 minutes

1 tbsp olive oil	1 tsp ground cumin	2 tbsp chili powder
3 large serrano peppers, diced	1 tsp minced fresh garlic	½ cup chopped fresh cilantro
1 onion, diced	1 tsp salt	½ cup shredded Monterey Jack cheese
1 jalapeño pepper, diced	2 (14.5 oz) cans chickpeas, drained	1 lime, cut into six wedges
1 lb chicken breasts, cubed	2 ½ cups water, divided	

Warm oil on Sauté in your Instant Pot. Add in onion, serrano peppers, and jalapeno pepper and cook for 5 minutes until tender. Add salt, cumin and garlic for seasoning. Stir chicken with vegetable mixture. Cook for 3 to 6 minutes until no longer pink. Add 2 cups water and chickpeas. Seal the pressure lid, choose Pressure Cook. Set the timer to 5 minutes. Release pressure quickly. Stir chili powder with remaining ½ cup water. Press Sauté. Cook the chili until slightly thickened. Garnish with cheese and cilantro. Over the chili, squeeze a lime wedge.

338. Chicken in Tikka Masala Sauce

Servings: 4 | Ready in about: 40 minutes

2 lb boneless, skinless chicken thighs,	1 tbsp garam masala	3 tomatoes, chopped
2 tbsp olive oil	2 tsp curry powder	½ cup natural yogurt
½ onion, chopped	1 tsp ground coriander	1 lemon, juiced
2 garlic cloves, minced	½ tsp ground cumin	3 cups cooked basmati rice
3 tbsp tomato puree	⅛ tsp jalapeño pepper, chopped	¼ cup fresh chopped cilantro leaves
1 tsp fresh ginger, minced	29 oz canned tomato sauce	4 lemon wedges

Set your Instant Pot to Sauté. Warm oil. Add garlic and onion and cook for 3 minutes until soft. Stir in tomato puree, garam masala, cumin, curry powder, ginger, coriander, and jalapeño. Cook for 30 seconds until fragrant. Stir in tomato sauce and tomatoes. Simmer the mixture as you scrape the bottom to get rid of any browned bits. Stir in chicken to coat. Seal the pressure lid, choose Pressure Cook on High, and set the timer to 10 minutes. When ready, release the pressure quickly. Press Sauté and simmer the sauce and cook for 3 to 5 minutes until thickened. Stir lemon juice and yogurt through the sauce. Serve garnished with lemon wedges and cilantro.

339. Sticky Orange Chicken

Servings: 4 | Ready in about: 30 minutes

2 chicken breasts, cubed
½ cup honey
½ cup orange juice
⅓ cup soy sauce
⅓ cup chicken stock
⅓ cup hoisin sauce
1 garlic clove, minced
2 tsp cornstarch
2 tsp water
1 cup diced orange
3 cups hot cooked quinoa

Arrange the chicken to the bottom of your Instant Pot. In a bowl, mix honey, soy sauce, garlic, hoisin sauce, chicken stock, and orange juice, until the honey is dissolved. Pour the mixture over the chicken. Seal the pressure lid, choose Pressure Cook on High, and set the timer to 7 minutes. When ready, release the pressure quickly. Take the chicken from the pot and set in a bowl. Press Sauté. In a bowl, mix water with cornstarch, pour into the liquid in the pot and cook for 3 minutes until thick. Stir orange and chicken into the sauce until coated. Serve.

340. Salsa Verde Chicken

Servings: 4 | Ready in about: 50 minutes

1 jalapeño pepper, deveined and sliced
½ cup capers
¼ cup parsley
1 lime, juiced
1 tsp salt
¼ cup extra virgin olive oil
4 boneless skinless chicken breasts
2 cups water
1 cup quinoa, rinsed

In a blender, mix olive oil, salt, lime juice, jalapeño pepper, capers, and parsley and blend until smooth. Arrange chicken breasts in the bottom of the pot pot. Over the chicken, add salsa verde mixture. In a bowl that can fit in the cooker, mix quinoa and water. Set a trivet onto chicken and sauce. Set the bowl onto the trivet. Seal the pressure lid, choose Pressure Cook on High, and set the timer to 20 minutes. When ready, release the pressure quickly. Remove the quinoa bowl and trivet. Using two forks, shred chicken into the sauce. Stir to coat. Divide the quinoa, between plates. Top with chicken and salsa verde before serving.

341. Cajun Chicken with Rice & Peas

Servings: 4 | Ready in about: 30 minutes

4 chicken breasts, sliced
1 garlic clove, minced
½ tsp paprika
¼ tsp dried oregano
¼ tsp dried thyme
⅛ tsp cayenne pepper
⅛ tsp ground white pepper
Salt to taste
1 tbsp oil olive
1 onion, chopped
1 tbsp tomato puree
2 cups chicken broth, divided
1 cup long grain rice
1 celery stalk, diced
1 cup frozen green peas

Season chicken with garlic powder, oregano, white pepper, thyme, paprika, cayenne pepper, and salt. Warm the oil on Sauté in your Instant Pot. Add in onion and cook for 4 minutes until fragrant. Mix in tomato puree. Add ¼ cup chicken stock into the pot to deglaze the pan, scrape the pan's bottom to get rid of browned bits of food. Mix in celery, rice, and the seasoned chicken. Add in the remaining broth to the chicken mixture. Seal the pressure lid, choose Pressure Cook on High, and set the timer to 8 minutes. Once ready, do a quick release. Mix in green peas, cover with the lid and let sit for 5 minutes. Serve warm.

342. Crumbed Sage Chicken Scallopini

Servings: 4 | Ready in about: 12 minutes

4 chicken breasts
3 oz breadcrumbs
2 tbsp grated Parmesan cheese
2 oz flour
2 eggs, beaten
1 tbsp fresh, chopped sage

Place some plastic wrap underneath and on top of the chicken. Using a rolling pin beat the meat until it becomes fragile. In a bowl, combine Parmesan, sage, and breadcrumbs. Dip the chicken in the egg first, and then in the sage mixture. Spray with cooking oil and place the meat in your Instant Pot. Cook for 7 minutes on Air Fry at 390°F.

343. Asian-Style Chicken

Servings: 4 | Ready in about: 35 minutes

1 lb chicken, cut in stripes
2 tomatoes, cubed
3 green peppers, cut in stripes
1 tbsp cumin powder
1 large onion
2 tbsp oil
1 tbsp mustard
1 pinch ginger
1 pinch fresh and chopped coriander

Heat the oil in a deep pan. Add in the mustard, onion, ginger, cumin and green chili peppers. Sauté the mixture for 2-3 minutes. Then, add the tomatoes, coriander, and salt and keep stirring. Coat the chicken with oil, salt, and pepper and cook for 25 minutes on Air Fry mode at 380°F. Remove the chicken and pour the sauce over.

344. Chicken Meatballs in Tomato Sauce

Servings: 5 | Ready in about: 35 minutes

1 lb ground chicken
3 tbsp red hot sauce
1 egg
⅓ cup crumbled blue cheese
¼ cup bread crumbs
¼ cup Pecorino cheese
1 tbsp ranch dressing
1 tsp dried basil
15 oz canned tomato sauce
1 cup chicken broth
2 tbsp olive oil
A handful of parsley, chopped

In a bowl, mix ground chicken, egg, pecorino, basil, pepper, salt, ranch dressing, blue cheese, 3 tbsp hot sauce, and bread crumbs. Shape the mixture into meatballs. Warm oil on Sauté in your Instant Pot. Add in the meatballs and cook for 2 to 3 minutes until browned on all sides. Add in tomato sauce and broth. Seal the pressure lid. Choose Pressure Cook on High, and set the timer to 7 minutes. When ready, release the pressure quickly. Remove meatballs carefully and place to a serving plate. Top with parsley and serve.

345. Chicken in Pineapple Gravy

Servings: 4 | Ready in about: 25 minutes

1 tbsp olive oil
4 boneless, skinless chicken thighs,
¼ cup pineapple juice
2 tbsp ketchup
2 tbsp Worcestershire sauce
1 garlic clove, minced
1 tsp cornstarch
2 tsp water
A handful of fresh cilantro, chopped

Warm oil on Sauté in your Instant Pot. In batches, sear chicken in oil for 3 minutes until golden brown. Set aside on a plate. Mix, pineapple juice, Worcestershire sauce, garlic, and ketchup. Add to the pot to deglaze, scrape the bottom to get rid of any browned bits of food. Place the chicken into the sauce and stir well to coat. Seal the pressure lid, choose Pressure Cook, and set the timer to cook for 5 minutes. When ready, release the pressure quickly. In a bowl, mix water and cornstarch until well dissolved. Set to Sauté. Stir the cornstarch slurry into the sauce. Cook for 2 minutes until the sauce is well thickened. Set in serving bowls and cilantro to serve.

346. Za'atar Chicken with Lemony Couscous

Servings: 4 | Ready in about: 40 minutes

4 chicken thighs
2 tbsp za'atar mix
1 tbsp ground sumac
sea Salt and black pepper to taste
2 tbsp butter
2 ½ cups chicken stock, divided
1 onion, thinly sliced
1 garlic clove, minced
1½ cups couscous
Juice from 1 lemon
Fresh parsley, chopped

Season the chicken with salt, sumac, za'atar, and pepper. On your Instant Pot, choose Sauté. Melt butter and sear the chicken in batches for 5 minutes per batch until lightly browned. Set aside. In the pot, add ¼ cup chicken stock to deglaze, scrape the bottom to get rid of any browned bits of food. Add garlic and onion to the stock. Cook for 3 minutes until soft. Add the remaining chicken stock into the pan. Add lemon juice and couscous. Add in chicken. Seal the pressure lid, choose Pressure Cook on High, and set the timer to 5 minutes. Naturally release the pressure for 5 minutes. Transfer the couscous and chicken to a serving plate. Add parsley to garnish.

347. Juicy Orange Chicken

Servings: 6 | Ready in about: 50 minutes

2 tbsp olive oil
6 chicken breasts, cubed
⅓ cup chicken stock
¼ cup soy sauce

2 tbsp brown sugar
1 tbsp lemon juice
1 tbsp garlic powder
1 tsp chili sauce

1 cup orange juice
Salt and black pepper to taste
2 cups cooked gnocchi

Warm oil on Sauté in your Instant Pot. In batches, sear chicken in the oil for 5 minutes until browned. Set aside in a bowl. In your pot, mix orange juice, water, sugar, chili sauce, garlic powder, vinegar, and soy sauce. Stir in chicken to coat. Seal the pressure lid, choose Pressure Cook on High, and set the timer to 7 minutes. When ready, release the pressure quickly. Take ¼ cup liquid from the pot to a bowl. Stir in cornstarch to dissolve. Mix into sauce in the pot until the color is consistent. Press Sauté. Cook sauce for 5 minutes until thickened. Season with pepper and salt. Serve the chicken with gnocchi.

348. Creamy Chicken and Quinoa Soup

Servings: 6 | Ready in about: 30 minutes

2 tbsp butter
1 cup red onion, chopped
1 cup carrots, chopped
1 cup celery, chopped

4 chicken breasts, cubed
4 cups chicken broth
6 oz quinoa, rinsed
1 tbsp fresh parsley, chopped

Salt and black pepper to taste
4 oz mascarpone cheese, softened
1 cup milk
1 cup heavy cream

Melt butter on Sauté in your Instant Pot. Add carrot, onion, and celery and cook for 5 minutes until tender. Add chicken broth to the pot. Mix in parsley, quinoa and chicken. Add pepper and salt for seasoning. Seal the pressure lid, choose Pressure Cook on High, and set the timer to 5 minutes. When ready, release the pressure quickly. Press Sauté. Add mascarpone cheese to the soup and stir well to melt completely. Mix in heavy cream and milk. Simmer the soup for 3 to 4 minutes until thickened and creamy.

349. Honey-Garlic Chicken & Okra

Servings: 4 | Ready in about: 25 minutes

6 garlic cloves, grated
¼ cup tomato puree
½ cup soy sauce
⅓ cup honey
2 tbsp rice vinegar

1 tbsp olive oil
4 chicken breasts, sliced
1 cup rice, rinsed
½ tsp salt
2 cups water

2 cups frozen okra
1 tbsp cornstarch
1 tbsp water
2 tsp toasted sesame seeds
4 spring onions, thinly sliced

In your Instant Pot, mix garlic, tomato puree, vinegar, soy sauce, ginger, honey, and oil. Toss in chicken to coat. In an ovenproof bowl, mix water, salt and rice. Set a trivet on top of chicken. Lower the bowl onto the trivet. Seal the pressure lid, choose Pressure Cook on High, and set the timer to 10 minutes. Release pressure naturally for 5 minutes, release the remaining pressure quickly. Use a fork to fluff the rice. Lay okra onto the rice. Allow the okra steam in the residual heat for 3 minutes. Take the trivet and bowl from the pot. Set the chicken to a plate. Press Sauté. In a bowl, mix 1 tbsp of water and cornstarch until smooth. Stir into the sauce and cook until thickened. Divide the rice, chicken, and okra between bowls. Drizzle sauce over and top with spring onions and sesame seeds.

350. Chicken with Prunes

Servings: 6 | Ready in about: 55 minutes

1 whole chicken, 3 lb
½ cup pitted prunes
3 minced cloves of garlic
2 tbsp capers

2 bay leaves
2 tbsp red wine vinegar
2 tbsp olive oil
1 tbsp dried oregano

¼ cup packed brown sugar
1 tbsp chopped fresh parsley
Salt and black pepper to taste

In a large and deep bowl, mix the prunes, olives, capers, garlic, olive oil, bay leaves, oregano, vinegar, salt, and pepper. Spread the mixture on the bottom of a baking tray, and place the chicken. Preheat your Instant Pot to 400° F. Sprinkle a little bit of brown sugar on top of the chicken, close the air fry lid and cook for 45-55 minutes on Air Fry mode. When ready, garnish with fresh parsley.

351. Herby Chicken with Asparagus Sauce

Servings: 4 | Ready in about: 1 hour

1 (3 ½ lb) Young Whole Chicken	2 lemons, zested and quartered	1 cup chicken stock
4 garlic cloves, minced	Salt and black pepper to taste	1 tbsp soy sauce
1 tsp olive oil	2 tbsp olive oil	1 fresh thyme sprig
4 fresh thyme, minced	8 oz asparagus, trimmed and chopped	1 tbsp flour
3 fresh rosemary, minced	1 onion, chopped	Chopped parsley to garnish

Rub all sides of the chicken with garlic, rosemary, black pepper, lemon zest, minced thyme, and salt. Into the chicken cavity, insert lemon wedges. Warm oil on Sauté in your Instant Pot. Add in onion and asparagus, and cook for 5 minutes until softened. Mix in chicken stock, 1 thyme sprig, black pepper, soy sauce, and salt.

Into the inner pot, set trivet over asparagus mixture. On top of the trivet, place your chicken with breast-side up. Seal the pressure lid, choose Pressure Cook on High, and set the timer to 20 minutes. Once ready, do a quick release. Remove the chicken to a serving platter. In the inner pot, sprinkle flour over asparagus mixture and blend the sauce with an immersion blender until desired consistency. Top the chicken with asparagus sauce and parsley.

352. Creamy Chicken Pasta with Pesto Sauce

Servings: 8 | Ready in about: 30 minutes

3½ cups water	Salt and black pepper to taste	¼ cup cream cheese, softened
4 chicken breast, cubed	2 cups fresh collard greens, trimmed	1 garlic clove, minced
8 oz macaroni pasta	1 cup cherry tomatoes, halved	¼ cup Asiago cheese, grated
1 tbsp butter	½ cup basil pesto sauce	Freshly chopped basil for garnish

To your Instant Pot, add water, chicken, 2 tsp salt, butter, and macaroni, and stir well to mix and be submerged in water. Seal the pressure lid, choose Pressure Cook on High, and set the timer to 2 minutes. When ready, release the pressure quickly. Press Start, open the lid, get rid of ¼ cup water from the pot. Set to Sauté the pot. Mix in collard greens, pesto sauce, garlic, remaining 1 tsp salt, cream cheese, tomatoes, and black pepper. Cook for 1 to 2 minutes as you stir, until sauce is creamy. Place the pasta into serving plates. Top with cheese and basil.

353. Cajun Shredded Chicken & Wild Rice

Servings: 6 | Ready in about: 45 minutes

6 chicken thighs, skinless	1 tsp Cajun seasoning	2 onions, diced
1 tsp salt	1/8 tsp smoked paprika	2 garlic cloves, crushed
½ tsp ground red pepper	2 tbsp olive oil	3 cups chicken broth, divided
½ tsp onion powder	1 cup pumpkin, peeled and cubed	1 ½ cups wild rice
½ tsp ground white pepper	2 celery stalks, diced	

Season the chicken with salt, onion powder, Cajun seasoning, ground white pepper, ground red pepper, and smoked paprika. Warm oil on Sauté in your Instant Pot. Stir in celery and pumpkin and cook for 5 minutes. Set the vegetables on a plate. In batches, sear chicken in oil for 3 minutes each side until golden brown. Set on a plate.

In the pot, add 1/4 cup chicken stock to deglaze the pan, scrape away any browned bits from the bottom. Add garlic and onion and cook for 2 minutes until fragrant. Take back the celery and pumpkin to the pot. Add the wild rice and remaining chicken stock. Place the chicken over the rice mixture. Seal the pressure lid, choose Pressure Cook, and set the timer to 10 minutes. When ready, release the pressure quickly. Serve.

354. Chicken & Zucchini Pilaf

Servings: 4 | Ready in about: 40 minutes

2 tsp olive oil	2 garlic cloves, minced	2 cups chicken stock
1 zucchini, chopped	1 tbsp chopped fresh rosemary	1 lb boneless and skinless chicken legs
1 cup leeks, chopped	2 tsp chopped fresh thyme leaves	1 cup rice, rinsed

Set your Instant Pot to Sauté. Warm oil. Add in zucchini and cook for 5 minutes. Stir in thyme, leeks, rosemary, pepper, salt and garlic. Cook the mixture for 3-4 minutes. Add ½ cup chicken stock into the pot to deglaze. When liquid stops simmering, add in the remaining stock, rice, and chicken with more pepper and salt. Seal the pressure lid, choose Pressure Cook for 5 minutes. Once ready, do a quick release.

355. Lettuce Chicken Carnitas Wraps

Servings: 6 | Ready in about: 50 minutes

2 tbsp canola oil	¼ cup soy sauce	3 tbsp cornstarch
2 lb chicken thighs, boneless, skinless	2 tbsp maple syrup	Salt and black pepper to taste
1 cup pineapple juice	1 tbsp rice vinegar	12 large lettuce leaves
⅓ cup water	1 tsp chili-garlic sauce	2 cups canned pinto beans, rinsed

Warm oil on Sauté in your Instant Pot. In batches, sear chicken in the oil for 5 minutes until browned. Set aside in a bowl. Into your pot, mix chili-garlic sauce, pineapple juice, soy sauce, vinegar, maple syrup, and water. Stir in chicken to coat. Seal the pressure lid, choose Pressure Cook on High, and set the timer to 7 minutes.

Release pressure naturally for 10 minutes. Shred the chicken with two forks. Take ¼ cup liquid from the pot to a bowl. Stir in cornstarch to dissolve. Mix the cornstarch mixture with the mixture in the pot and return the chicken. Select Sauté and cook for 5 minutes until the sauce thickens. Add pepper and salt for seasoning. Transfer beans into lettuce leaves. Apply a topping of chicken carnitas and serve.

356. Chicken & Sweet Potato Corn Chowder

Servings: 8 | Ready in about: 40 minutes

4 chicken breasts, diced	1 sweet potato, peeled and cubed	2 cups cheddar cheese, shredded
3 garlic cloves, minced	4 oz canned diced green chiles, drained	2 cups creme fraiche
1 cup chicken stock	2 tsp chili powder	Salt and black pepper to taste
19 oz corn kernels, frozen	1 tsp ground cumin	Cilantro leaves, chopped

Mix chicken, corn, chili powder, cumin, chicken stock, sweet potato, green chiles, and garlic in your Instant Pot of the pot. Seal the pressure lid, choose Pressure Cook on High, and set the timer to 10 minutes. When ready, release the pressure quickly. Set the chicken to a cutting board and use two forks to shred it. Return to pot and stir well into the liquid. Stir in cheese and creme fraiche. Season with pepper and salt. Cook for 2 to 3 minutes until cheese is melted. Place chowder into plates and top with cilantro.

357. Basil & Cheddar Stuffed Chicken

Servings: 4 | Ready in about: 25 minutes

2 large chicken breasts, skinless	A handful of fresh basil leaves	Salt and pepper to taste
4 slices cheddar cheese	4 cherry tomatoes, halved	2 tbsp olive oil

With a sharp knife, cut a slit into the side of each chicken breast. Put 2 slices of cheese, 3-4 basil leaves, and 4 cherry tomato halves into each slit. Use toothpicks to keep the chicken breasts closed. Season the meat with salt and pepper, and brush with some olive oil. Grease the air fry basket with the remaining olive oil. Place the chicken breasts in the basket. Close the air fry lid and cook for 12 minutes at 390°F. After 6 minutes, turn the breasts over. Once ready, leave to sit the chicken breasts, then slice each one in half and serve with salad.

358. Hot Chicken Wings

Servings: 4 | Ready in about: 25 minutes

8 chicken wings
1 tbsp ranch salad mix
1 tbsp garlic powder
1 tbsp onion powder
1 tbsp cayenne pepper
½ tsp paprika

Combine the paprika, ranch salad mix, onion powder, garlic powder, and cayenne pepper in a bowl. Pour the seasoning all over the chicken and oil with cooking spray. Place in the air fry basket, close the air fry lid and cook for 15 minutes at 380°F. After half of the cooking time, shake the wings. Oil the chicken again with cooking spray and continue cooking until the wings are crispy. Serve hot.

359. Sriracha Chicken with Black Beans

Servings: 4 | Ready in about: 25 minutes

½ cup soy sauce
½ cup chicken broth
3 tbsp honey
2 tbsp tomato paste
1 tbsp sriracha
1 (1 inch) piece fresh ginger, grated
3 garlic cloves, grated
4 boneless, skinless chicken drumsticks
1 tbsp cornstarch
1 tbsp water
2 tbsp toasted sesame seeds, divided
1 tbsp sesame oil
2 cups canned black beans
2 green onions, thinly sliced

In your Instant Pot, mix the soy sauce, honey, ginger, tomato paste, chicken broth, sriracha, and garlic. Stir well until smooth. Toss in the chicken to coat. Seal the pressure lid, choose Pressure Cook on High, and set the timer to 3 minutes. Release the pressure immediately. Open the lid and press Sauté. In a bowl, mix water and cornstarch until no lumps remain. Stir into the sauce and cook for 5 minutes until thickened. Stir sesame oil and 1 ½ tbsp sesame seeds through the chicken mixture. Garnish with extra sesame seeds and green onions. Serve with beans.

360. Winter Chicken Thighs with Cabbage

Servings: 4 | Ready in about: 35 minutes

1 tbsp lard
4 slices pancetta, diced
4 chicken thighs, boneless skinless
Salt and ground black pepper to taste
1 cup chicken broth
1 tbsp Dijon mustard
1 lb green cabbage, shredded
Fresh parsley, chopped

Warm lard on Sauté in your Instant Pot. Fry pancetta for 5 minutes until crisp. Set aside. Season chicken with pepper and salt. Sear in the pot for 2 minutes each side until browned. In a bowl, mix mustard and chicken broth. To the pot, add pancetta and chicken broth mixture. Seal the pressure lid, choose Pressure Cook. Set the timer to 6 minutes. When ready, release the pressure quickly. Open the lid, mix in green cabbage, seal again, and cook on High Pressure for 2 minutes. When ready, release the pressure quickly. Serve with parsley.

361. Saucy Chicken Breasts

Servings: 4 | Ready in about: 45 minutes

4 chicken breasts
Salt and ground black pepper to taste
2 tbsp olive oil
2 tbsp soy sauce
2 tbsp tomato paste
2 tbsp honey
2 tbsp minced garlic
½ cup chicken broth
1 tbsp cornstarch
1 tbsp water
½ cup chives, sliced

Season the chicken with pepper and salt. Warm oil on Sauté in your Instant Pot. Add in chicken and cook for 5 minutes until lightly browned. In a bowl, mix garlic, soy sauce, honey, and tomato paste. Pour the mixture over the chicken. Stir in ½ cup broth. Seal the pressure lid, choose Pressure Cook, and set the timer to 12 minutes. When ready, release the pressure quickly. Set the chicken to a bowl. Mix water and cornstarch to create a slurry. Briskly stir the mixture into the sauce that is remaining in the pan for 2 minutes until thickened. Serve the chicken with the sauce and chives.

362. Cordon Bleu Chicken

Servings: 4 | Ready in about: 40 minutes

4 skinless and boneless chicken breasts	3 tbsp all-purpose flour	1 tsp chicken bouillon granules
4 slices ham	4 tbsp butter	½ cup dry white wine
4 slices Swiss cheese	1 tsp paprika	1 cup heavy whipping cream

Pound the chicken breasts and put a slice of ham and then a slice of swiss cheese on each of the breasts. Fold the edges over the filling and secure the sides with toothpicks. In a medium bowl, combine the paprika and the flour and coat the chicken pieces. Close the air fry lid and fry the chicken for 20 minutes on Air Fry mode at 380°F.

Meanwhile, in a large skillet over medium heat, melt the butter and add the bouillon and the wine. Reduce the heat to low. Add in the heavy cream and let simmer for 20-25 minutes. When the chicken is done, remove to a serving platter and drizzle with the sauce. Serve hot.

363. Chicken with Tomatoes & Capers

Servings: 4 | Ready in about: 45 minutes

4 chicken legs	2 garlic cloves, minced	¼ cup fresh basil
Sea salt and black pepper to taste	⅓ cup red wine	2 pickles, chopped
2 tbsp olive oil	2 cups diced tomatoes	
1 onion, diced	⅓ cup capers	

Sprinkle pepper and salt over the chicken. Warm oil on Sauté in your Instant Pot. Add in onion and cook for 3 minutes until fragrant. Add in garlic and cook for 30 seconds until softened. Mix the chicken with vegetables and cook for 6 to 7 minutes until lightly browned. Add red wine to the pan to deglaze and stir in tomatoes. Seal the pressure lid, choose Pressure Cook on High, and set the timer to 12 minutes. When ready, release the pressure quickly. To the chicken mixture, add basil, capers and pickles. Serve the chicken poured with the tomato sauce.

364. Chicken Burgers with Avocado

Servings: 8 | Ready in about: 15 minutes

1 lb ground chicken	1 small red potato, shredded	Salt and pepper to taste
1 red onion, chopped	A pinch of ground cumin	1 Avocado, sliced
1 egg, beaten	A pinch of ground chili	½ cup mayonnaise
4 buns, halved	Fresh cilantro, chopped	1 tomato, sliced

Mix the chicken, onion, egg, potato, cumin, chili, cilantro, salt, and pepper in a large bowl with your hands until you have an even burger mixture. Shape the mixture into 8 patties. Grease the air fry basket with cooking spray. Arrange the burgers onto the basket. Close the air fry lid and cook for 10 minutes, at 360°F. After 5 minutes, shake the patties. To assemble your burgers, spread mayonnaise on the bottom of each half of the buns, top with a chicken patty, then put over a tomato slice. Cover with the other half of the buns and arrange on a serving platter.

365. Shredded Chicken with Lentils & Rice

Servings: 4 | Ready in about: 45 minutes

1 tsp olive oil	3 cups chicken broth, divided	½ cup dried lentils
1 garlic clove, minced	4 boneless, skinless chicken thighs	Salt and ground black pepper to taste
1 small yellow onion, chopped	1 cup white rice	Chopped fresh parsley for garnish

Set your Instant Pot to Sauté. Warm oil. Add in onion and garlic and cook for 3 minutes until soft. Add in broth, rice, lentils, and chicken. Season with pepper and salt. Seal the pressure lid, choose Pressure Cook on High, and set the timer to 15 minutes. Once ready, do a quick release. Remove and shred the chicken in a large bowl. Set the lentils and rice into serving plates, top with shredded chicken and parsley and serve.

366. Greek-Style Chicken with Potatoes

Servings: 4 | Ready in about: 40 minutes

- 4 potatoes, peeled and quartered
- 4 cups water
- 2 lemons, zested and juiced
- 1 tbsp olive oil
- 2 tsp fresh oregano
- Salt to taste
- ¼ tsp freshly ground black pepper
- 2 Serrano peppers, chopped
- 4 boneless skinless chicken drumsticks
- 3 tbsp finely chopped parsley
- 1 cup packed watercress
- 1 cucumber, thinly sliced
- ½ cup cherry tomatoes, quartered
- ¼ cup Kalamata olives, pitted
- ¼ cup hummus
- ¼ cup feta cheese, crumbled
- Lemon wedges, for serving

In the cooker, add water and potatoes. Set trivet over them. In a baking bowl, mix lemon juice, olive oil, black pepper, oregano, zest, salt, and red pepper flakes. Add chicken drumsticks in the marinade and stir to coat. Set the bowl with chicken on the trivet in the pot. Seal the lid, select Pressure and set the time to 15 minutes on High.

When ready, do a quick pressure release. Take out the bowl with chicken and the trivet from the pot. Drain potatoes and add parsley and salt. Split the potatoes among four serving plates and top with watercress, cucumber slices, hummus, cherry tomatoes, chicken, olives, and feta cheese. Garnished with a lemon wedge.

367. Crunchy Chicken Schnitzels

Servings: 4 | Ready in about: 25 minutes

- 4 chicken breasts, boneless
- 1 cup flour
- 2 eggs, beaten
- 1 cup breadcrumbs
- Salt and pepper to taste
- 2 tbsp fresh parsley, chopped
- 4 slices cold butter
- 4 slices lemon
- Cooking spray

Combine the breadcrumbs with the parsley in a dish and set aside. Season the chicken with salt and pepper. Coat in flour. Dip the coated chicken into the beaten egg followed by breadcrumbs. Spray the schnitzels with cooking spray. Put them into the air fry basket, close the air fry lid and cook for 10 minutes at 380°F. After 5 minutes, turn the schnitzels over. Arrange the schnitzels on a serving platter and place the butter and lemon slices over to serve.

368. Chicken Fajitas with Avocado

Servings: 4 | Ready in about: 30 minutes

- 4 chicken breasts,
- 1 taco seasoning
- 1 tbsp olive oil
- 1 (24 oz) can diced tomatoes
- 3 bell peppers, julienned
- 1 shallot, chopped
- 4 garlic cloves, minced
- Juice of 1 lemon
- salt and pepper to taste
- 4 flour tortillas
- 2 tbsp cilantro, chopped
- 1 avocado, sliced

In a bowl, mix taco seasoning and chicken until evenly coated. Warm oil on Sauté in your Instant Pot. Sear chicken for 2 minutes per side until browned. To the chicken, add tomatoes, shallot, lemon juice, garlic, and bell peppers. Season with pepper and salt. Seal the pressure lid, choose Pressure Cook, and set the timer to 4 minutes. When ready, release the pressure quickly. Move the bell peppers and chicken to tortillas. Add avocado slices and serve.

369. Rosemary Lemon Chicken

Servings: 2 | Ready in about: 60 minutes

- 2 chicken breasts
- 1 tsp minced ginger
- 2 rosemary sprigs
- ½ lemon, cut into wedges
- 1 tbsp soy sauce
- ½ tbsp olive oil
- 1 tbsp oyster sauce
- 3 tbsp brown sugar

Place ginger, soy sauce, and olive oil in a bowl. Add the chicken and coat well. Cover the bowl and refrigerate for 30 minutes. Transfer the marinated chicken to the air fry basket. Close the air fry lid and cook for about 6 minutes on Air Fry at 390°F. Mix the oyster sauce, rosemary, and brown sugar in a bowl. Pour the sauce over the chicken. Arrange the lemon wedges in the dish. Return to the and cook for 13 more minutes on Air Fry mode.

370. Chicken Stroganoff with Fetucini

Servings: 4 | Ready in about: 35 minutes

2 large boneless skinless chicken breasts
1½ tsp salt
2 tbsp butter
½ cup sliced onion
1 tbsp flour
½ cup dry white wine
2 cups chicken stock
8 oz fettucini
½ tsp Worcestershire sauce
1 cup sautéed mushrooms
¼ cup heavy cream
2 tbsp chopped fresh dill to garnish

Season the chicken on both sides with salt and set aside. Choose Sauté. Melt the butter and sauté the onion until brown, about 3 minutes. Mix in the flour to make a roux, about 2 minutes and gradually pour in the dry white wine while stirring and scraping the bottom of the pot to release any browned bits. Allow the white wine to simmer and to reduce by two-thirds. Pour in 1 ½ cups water, chicken stock, 1 tablespoon of salt, and fettucini. Mix and arrange the chicken on top of the fettucini. Lock the pressure lid to Seal. Choose Pressure Cook on High and the cooking time to 5 minutes. When done, perform a quick pressure release.

Transfer the chicken breasts to a cutting board to cool slightly, and then cut into bite-size chunks. Return the chicken to the pot and stir in the Worcestershire sauce and mushrooms. Add the heavy cream and cook until the mixture stops simmering. Ladle the stroganoff into bowls and garnish with dill.

371. Turkey Stuffed Potatoes

Servings: 4 | Ready in about: 30 minutes

2 cups vegetable broth
1 tsp chili powder
1 tsp ground cumin
½ tsp onion powder
½ tsp garlic powder
1 lb turkey breasts
4 potatoes
2 tbsp fresh cilantro, chopped
1 Fresno chili pepper, chopped

In your Instant Pot, combine chicken broth, cumin, garlic powder, onion powder, and chili powder. Toss in turkey to coat. Place a trivet over the turkey. Use a fork to pierce the potatoes and set them on the trivet. Seal the pressure lid, choose Pressure Cook on High, and set the timer to 20 minutes. When ready, release the pressure quickly. Remove the trivet. Place the potatoes on a plate. Place turkey in a mixing bowl and use two forks to shred. Half each potato lengthwise. Stuff with shredded turkey. Top with cilantro, onion, and fresno pepper and serve.

372. Greek-Style Chicken

Servings: 6 | Ready in about: 45 minutes

1 whole chicken (3 lb), cut in pieces
3 garlic cloves, minced
½ cup olive oil
½ cup white wine
1 tbsp fresh rosemary
1 tbsp chopped fresh oregano
1 tbsp fresh thyme
Juice from 1 lemon
Salt and black pepper, to taste

In a large bowl, combine the garlic, rosemary, thyme, olive oil, lemon juice, oregano, salt, and pepper. Mix all ingredients very well and spread the mixture into the air fry basket. Stir in the chicken. Sprinkle with wine and cook for 45 minutes on Air Fry mode at 380°F.

373. Buttermilk Chicken Thighs

Servings: 6 | Ready in about: 4 hours 40 minutes

1 ½ lb chicken thighs
1 tsp cayenne pepper
2 cups flour
1 tbsp paprika
1 tbsp baking powder
2 cups buttermilk

Rinse and pat dry the chicken thighs. Place the chicken thighs in a bowl. Add cayenne pepper, 2 tsp salt, black pepper, and buttermilk, and stir to coat well. Refrigerate for 4 hours. In another bowl, mix the flour, paprika, 1 tsp salt, and baking powder. Dredge the chicken thighs, one at a time, in the flour, and then place on a lined dish. Close the air fry lid and cook for 18 minutes on Air Fry, flipping once halfway through.

374. Tuscany-Style Turkey Soup

Servings: 4 | Ready in about: 40 minutes

1 lb hot turkey sausage	1 red onion, chopped	9 oz refrigerated tortellini
2 tbsp olive oil	½ cup dry white wine	1 Parmesan cheese rind
2 tbsp melted butter	4 cups chicken broth	2 cups chopped spinach
3 celery stalks, chopped	½ tsp fennel seeds	4 Italian bread slices
3 garlic cloves, chopped	1 (15-oz) can cannellini beans, rinsed	½ cup grated Parmesan cheese

On the pot, choose Sauté. Heat olive oil and cook the sausage for 4 minutes until golden brown. Stir in the celery, garlic, and onion, season with salt and cook for 2 to 3 minutes, stirring occasionally. Pour in the wine and bring the mixture to a boil until the wine reduces by half. Scrape the bottom of the pot to let off any browned bits. Add the chicken stock, fennel seeds, tortellini, Parmesan rind, cannellini beans, and spinach.

Lock the pressure lid into place and to seal. Select Pressure. Adjust the pressure to High and the cooking time to 5 minutes. Brush the butter on the bread slices, and sprinkle with half of the cheese. Once the timer is over, perform a natural pressure release for 5 minutes. Grease a trivet with cooking spray and fix in the pot.

Lay the bread slices on the trivet. Close the air fry lid and choose Broil. Adjust the time to 5 minutes. When the bread has browned and crisp, transfer from the trivet to a cutting board and let cool for a couple of minutes. Cut the slices into cubes. Ladle the soup into bowls and sprinkle with the remaining cheese. Top with croutons.

375. Chicken Tenders with Broccoli & Rice

Servings: 3 | Ready in about: 60 minutes

1 lb chicken tenderloins	1 cup chopped broccoli	1 can condensed cream chicken soup
1 package instant long grain rice	2 cups water	1 tbsp minced garlic

Place the chicken quarters in your Instant Pot. Season with salt, pepper and a tbsp of oil and cook for 30 minutes on Roast at 390°F. In a bowl, mix rice, water, minced garlic, soup, and broccoli. Combine the mixture very well. Remove the chicken from the pot and place it on a platter to drain. Spread the rice mixture on the bottom of the dish and place the chicken on top of the rice. Close the air fry lid and cook for 30 minutes on Roast at 390°F.

376. Asian Turkey Lettuce Cups

Servings: 4 | Ready in about: 45 minutes

¾ cup olive oil	1 cup coconut milk	1 lb turkey breasts, cut into strips
4 cloves garlic, minced	3 tbsp rice wine vinegar	1 romaine lettuce, leaves separated
3 tbsp maple syrup	3 tbsp soy sauce	⅓ cup chopped peanuts
2 tbsp pineapple juice	1 tbsp Thai-style chili paste	¼ cup chopped fresh cilantro leaves

In your Instant Pot, mix peanut butter, garlic, rice wine vinegar, soy sauce, pineapple juice, honey, coconut milk, and chili paste until smooth. Add turkey strips and ensure they are submerged in the sauce. Seal the pressure lid, choose Pressure Cook on High, and set the timer to 12 minutes. When ready, release the pressure quickly. Place the turkey at the center of each lettuce leaf. Top with cilantro and chopped peanuts.

377. Honey-Glazed Chicken Kabobs

Servings: 4 | Ready in about: 20 minutes

4 chicken breasts, skinless and cubed	Juice from 1 Lime	Salt and pepper to taste
4 tbsp honey	½ tsp ground paprika	

In a bowl, combine honey, soy sauce, lime juice, paprika, salt, and pepper. Add in chicken cubes and toss to coat. Load 8 small skewers with honey-glazed chicken. Lay the kabobs into the air fry basket, close the air fry lid and cook for 15 minutes at 360°F. After 8 minutes, turn the kabobs over. Drizzle the remaining honey sauce and serve.

378. Turkey and Brown Rice Salad with Peanuts

Servings: 4 | Ready in about: 60 minutes

4 cups water	3 tsp peanut oil, divided	A pinch of sugar
1 cup brown rice	3 tbsp apple cider vinegar	½ cup peanuts, toasted
2¼ tsp salt	⅛ tsp freshly ground black pepper	3 celery stalks, thinly sliced
1 lb turkey tenderloins	¼ tsp celery seeds	1 apple, cored and cubed

Pour the water into the inner pot. Stir in the brown rice and 1 teaspoon of salt. Lock the pressure lid into the Seal position. Choose Pressure Cook on High and the cooking time to 10 minutes. Season the turkey on both sides with salt. Set aside. After cooking the brown rice, perform a natural pressure release for 10 minutes. Spoon the rice into a bowl to cool completely. Put the turkey in the air fry basket and brush with 2 teaspoons of peanut oil. Fix in the basket. Close the air fry lid and choose Bake. Adjust the temperature to 375°F and the cooking time to 12 minutes. Pour the remaining peanut oil and the vinegar into a jar with a tight-fitting lid. Add the black pepper, celery seeds, salt, and sugar. Close the jar and shake until the ingredients properly combined.

When the turkey is ready, transfer to a plate to cool for several minutes. Cut it into bite-size chunks and add to the rice along with the peanuts, celery, and apple. Pour half the dressing over the salad and toss gently to coat, adding more dressing as desired.Proceed to serve the salad.

379. Tom Yum Wings

Servings: 2 | Ready in about: 4 hours 20 minutes

8 chicken wings	2 tbsp potato starch	2 tbsp tom yum paste
1 tbsp water	2 tbsp cornstarch	½ tsp baking powder

Combine the tom yum paste and water, in a small bowl. Place the wings in a large bowl, add the tom yum mixture and coat well. Cover the bowl and refrigerate for 4 hours. Combine the baking powder, cornstarch, and potato starch. Dip each wing in the starch mixture. Place on a lined baking dish in the pot and cook for 7 minutes on Air Fry at 370°F. Flip over and cook for 5 to 7 minutes more. Serve.

380. Korean-Style Barbecued Satay

Servings: 4 | Ready in about: 4h 15 minutes

1 lb boneless,skinless chicken tenders	2 tsp sesame seeds, toasted	½ cup soy sauce
4 cloves garlic, chopped	1 tsp fresh ginger, grated	⅓ cup sesame oil
4 scallions, chopped	½ cup pineapple juice	1 pinch black pepper

Skew each tender and trim any excess fat. Mix the other ingredients in one large bowl. Add the skewered chicken and place in the fridge for 4 to 24 hours. Preheat your Instant Pot to 370°F. Using a paper towel, pat the chicken dry. Fry for 10 minutes on Air Fry mode.

381. Basil Chicken Thighs with Mushrooms

Servings: 6 | Ready in about: 25 minutes

½ lb mushrooms, halved	2 garlic cloves, minced	½ cup chopped basil
½ cup green olives, pitted	6 chicken thighs, boneless	1 tbsp tomato paste
¼ cup chopped parsley	2 carrots, peeled and chopped	salt and pepper to taste
1 onion, chopped	1 tbsp olive oil	1 tsp oregano

Season the thighs with salt and pepper. Heat the olive oil in your Instant Pot on Sauté. Stir in the mushrooms, onions and carrots, and sauté for 3 minutes. Add the garlic and cook for 1 minute. Add the remaining ingredients and secure the lid. Select Pressure Cook and cook on High for 10 minutes. Once it goes off, perform a quick pressure release and serve immediately.

382. Turkey Meatballs with Rigatoni

Servings: 4 | Ready in about: 40 minutes

2 tbsp canola oil
1 lb ground turkey
1 large egg
¼ cup bread crumbs
2 cloves garlic, minced
1 tsp dried oregano
3 cups tomato sauce
8 oz rigatoni
2 tbsp grated Grana Padano cheese

In a bowl, combine ground turkey, bread crumbs, cumin, garlic, and egg. Season with oregano, salt, red pepper flakes, and pepper. Form the mixture into meatballs with well-oiled hands. Warm the oil on Sauté in your Instant Pot. Cook the meatballs for 3 to 4 minutes until browned on all sides. Remove to a plate. Add rigatoni to the pot and cover with tomato sauce. Pour water into the pot enough to cover the pasta. Stir well. Throw in the meatballs. Seal the pressure lid, choose Pressure Cook on High, and set the timer to 10 minutes. When ready, release the pressure quickly. Serve topped with Grana Padano cheese.

383. Creamy Turkey Enchilada Casserole

Servings: 6 | Ready in about: 70 minutes

1 tbsp butter
1 yellow onion, diced
2 garlic cloves, minced
1 lb boneless, skinless turkey breasts
2 cups enchilada sauce
¼ tsp salt
¼ tsp freshly ground black pepper
1 (15-oz) can pinto beans, drained
8 tortillas, each cut into 8 pieces
1 (16-oz) bag frozen corn
2 cups shredded Monterey Jack cheese

Choose Sauté on your Instant Pot. Melt the butter and cook the onion and garlic for 3 minutes, stirring occasionally. Put the turkey and enchilada sauce in the pot and season with salt and black pepper. Stir to combine. Seal the pressure lid, choose Pressure Cook on High, and set the time to 15 minutes.

When done cooking, perform a quick pressure release and carefully open the lid. Shred the turkey with two long forks while being careful not to burn your hands. Mix in the pinto beans, tortilla pieces, corn, and half of the cheese to the pot. Sprinkle the remaining cheese evenly on top of the casserole. Close the air fry lid. Choose Broil and set the time to 5 minutes. Press Start. When ready, allow the casserole to sit for 5 minutes before serving.

384. Herby Chicken Thighs

Servings: 4 | Ready in about: 40 minutes + marinating time

4 chicken thighs
3 cups chicken broth
3 garlic cloves, crushed
1 cup olive oil, divided
3 tbsp lemon juice
1 tbsp fresh basil, thyme and rosemary, chopped
¼ cup apple cider vinegar
Salt to taste

In a large bowl, combine olive oil, lemon juice, apple cider, garlic, basil, rosemary, thyme, and salt. Douse the thighs into this mixture and refrigerate for 1 hour. Remove the Pressure Cook from the refrigerator, and pat dry using paper towel. Pour the chicken broth into the Instant Pot. Set the steamer insert, and place the chicken on it. Secure the lid, press Pressure Cook and cook for 15 minutes. When done, allow a natural release for 10 minutes. Carefully open the lid. Remove the chicken and the broth. Grease the pot with oil, add back the chicken and press Sauté. Brown for 5 minutes, flipping once. Serve hot.

385. Sticky Drumsticks

Servings: 4 | Ready in about: 50 minutes

1 lb chickendrumsticks
2 tbsp honey
2 tsp dijon mustard

Combine the honey, mustard, salt, and pepper in a large bowl. Add in the chicken and toss to coat. Cover and put in the fridge for 30 minutes. Preheat your Instant Pot to 380°F. Grease the air fry basket with cooking spray. Arrange the drumsticks on the basket. Cook for 20 minutes on Air Fry mode. After 10 minutes, shake the drumsticks.

386. Sweet Garlicky Chicken Wings

Servings: 4 | Ready in about: 20 minutes

16 chicken wings	¼ cup honey	4 garlic cloves, minced
¼ cup butter	½ tsp salt	¾ cup potato starch

Rinse and pat dry the wings, and place them in a bowl. Add the starch to the bowl, and mix to coat the chicken. Place the chicken in a baking dish that has been previously coated lightly with cooking oil. Close the air fry lid and cook for 5 minutes on Air Fry mode at 390°F. Whisk the rest of the ingredients in a bowl. Pour the sauce over the wings and cook for another 10 minutes.

387. Spicy Buttered Turkey

Servings: 6 | Ready in about: 25 minutes

6 turkey breasts, boneless and skinless	Salt and black pepper to taste	1 stick butter, melted
2 cups panko breadcrumbs	½ tsp cayenne pepper	

In a bowl, combine the panko breadcrumbs, pepper, cayenne pepper, and salt. Brush the butter over the turkey breast. Coat the turkey with the panko mixture. Arrange on a lined air fry basket. Close the air fry lid and cook for 15 minutes at 390°F on Air Fry, flipping the meat after 8 minutes.

388. Thyme Turkey Nuggets

Servings: 2 | Ready in about: 20 minutes

8 oz boneless, skinless turkey breast	1 cup breadcrumbs	½ tsp dried parsley
1 egg, beaten	1 tbsp dried thyme	Salt and pepper, to taste

Mince the turkey in a food processor. Transfer to a bowl. Stir in the thyme and parsley, and season with salt and pepper. Take a nugget-sized piece of the turkey mixture and shape it into a ball, or another form. Dip it in the breadcrumbs, then egg, then in the breadcrumbs again. Place the nuggets onto a prepared baking dish. Close the air fry lid and cook for 10 minutes on Air Fry mode at 350°F.

389. Lemon Turkey Risotto

Servings: 4 | Ready in about: 40 minutes

2 boneless turkey breasts, cut into strips	½ tsp sea salt	Salt and black pepper to taste
2 lemons, zested and juiced	1½ tbsp olive oil	¼ cup chopped fresh parsley, or to taste
1 tbsp dried oregano	1 onion, diced	8 lemon slices
2 garlic cloves, minced	2 cups chicken broth	
	1 cup Arborio rice, rinsed	

In a ziplock back, mix turkey, oregano, sea salt, garlic, juice and zest of two lemons. Marinate for 10 minutes. Warm oil on Sauté in your Instant Pot. Add onion and cook for 3 minutes until fragrant. Add rice and chicken broth and season with pepper and salt. Empty the ziplock having the chicken and marinade into the pot. Seal the pressure lid, choose Pressure Cook on High, and set the timer to 12 minutes. When ready, release the pressure quickly. Divide the rice and turkey between 4 serving bowls. Garnish with lemon slices and parsley.

390. Glazed Chicken Thighs

Servings: 4 | Ready in about: 35 minutes

4 boneless chicken thighs	1 tbsp lemon juice	¼ cup olive oil
3 sweet potatoes, wedged	2 cup water	¼ tsp cayenne pepper
2 garlic cloves, crushed	1 tsp ground ginger	Salt to taste

In a small bowl, add the olive oil, lemon juice, garlic, ground ginger, cayenne pepper, and a pinch of salt. Brush each chicken piece with the mixture. Grease the Instant Pot with the remaining mixture. Add the potatoes to the cooker and place the chicken. Add water and secure the lid. Press Pressure Cook and cook for 15 minutes. Release the steam naturally for 10 minutes and serve immediately.

391. Spicy Chicken Wings

Servings: 2 | Ready in about: 25 minutes

10 chicken wings
2 tbsp hot chili sauce
½ tbsp lime juice
½ tbsp honey
Salt and black pepper to taste

Mix the lime juice, honey, and chili sauce. Toss the mixture over the chicken wings. Put the wings in the fryer's basket, close the air fry lid and cook for 25 minutes on Air Fry mode at 350°F. Shake the basket every 5 minutes.

392. Spicy Turkey Casserole

Servings: 5 | Ready in about: 45 minutes

1 tbsp olive oil
½ sweet onion, diced
3 cloves garlic, minced
1 jalapeno pepper, minced
1 lb turkey breast, cubed
2 (14 oz) cans fire-roasted tomatoes
1 ½ cups water
1 cup salsa
2 bell peppers, cut into thick strips
2 tsp ancho chili powder
2 tsp chili powder
1 tsp ground cumin
Sea salt to taste
5 tbsp fresh oregano, chopped

Warm the oil on Sauté in your Instant Pot. Add in garlic, onion and jalapeño and cook for 5 minutes until fragrant. Stir turkey into the pot and cook for 5-6 minutes until browned. Add in salsa, tomatoes, bell peppers, and water. Apply a seasoning of sea salt, ancho chili powder, cumin, and chili powder. Seal the pressure lid, choose Pressure Cook, and set the timer to 10 minutes. When ready, release the pressure quickly. Top with oregano and serve.

393. Greek Turkey Meatballs

Servings: 6 | Ready in about: 30 minutes

1 onion, minced and divided
½ cup plain bread crumbs
⅓ cup feta cheese, crumbled
2 tsp salt, divided
½ tsp dried oregano
¼ tsp ground black pepper
1 lb ground turkey
1 egg, lightly beaten
1 tbsp olive oil
1 carrot, minced
½ celery stalk, minced
3 cups tomato puree

In a mixing bowl, thoroughly combine half the onion, oregano, ground turkey, salt, bread crumbs, pepper, and egg and stir until everything is well incorporated. Heat oil on Sauté, and cook celery, remaining onion, and carrot for 5 minutes until soft. Pour in 2 cups water and tomato puree. Adjust the seasonings. Roll the mixture into meatballs and drop into the sauce. Seal the pressure lid, choose Pressure Cook, and set the timer to 5 minutes. When done, release pressure naturally for 10 minutes. Serve topped with feta cheese.

394. Pulled Chicken

Servings: 4 | Ready in about: 50 minutes

4 chicken breasts, boneless
14 oz can tomatoes, diced
¼ tsp garlic powder
Salt and black pepper to taste
2 cups chicken broth

Combine the chicken and broth in your Instant Pot. Secure the lid, and select Pressure Cook. Cook on High for 20 minutes. Once completed, perform a quick pressure release and carefully open the lid. Remove the chicken from the cooker and shred it onto a plate. Discard the excess cooking liquid. Set the Instant Pot to Sauté. Stir in all of the remaining ingredients, including the shredded chicken. Secure the lid and cook for 5 minutes on Pressure Cook. Use the natural pressure release for 10 minutes and serve immediately.

395. Mexican Stuffed Bell Peppers

Servings: 4 | Ready in about: 35 minutes

1 ½ cups water
2 tbsp organic butter
4 oz green chilies, chopped
1 lb ground turkey
4 large bell peppers, cleaned out
1 cup shredded cheddar
½ cup corn kernels
1 onion, chopped
2 tsp minced garlic
1 tsp oregano
Salt and black pepper to taste

Melt the butter in your Instant Pot on Sauté. Cook the onion until soft. Add garlic, and cook for 1 minute. Add turkey and cook for another 3 minutes. Stir in oregano, salt and pepper. Transfer the mixture to a large bowl. Add the cheese, chilies, and corn. Stuff the bell peppers with this mixture. Pour the water in your Instant Pot, and arrange the stuffed peppers on the rack. Secure the lid, select Pressure Cook, and cook on High for 7 minutes. When ready, do a natural pressure release for 10 minutes. Serve warm.

396. Pekin-Inspired Chicken Thighs

Servings: 4 | Ready in about: 35 minutes

4 chicken thighs, boneless
½ cup chicken stock
1 tbsp vinegar
5 tbsp organic soy sauce
5 tbsp chili sauce
4 garlic cloves, minced

Whisk together all of the remaining ingredients, in a bowl. Arrange the chicken at the bottom of the Instant Pot and pour this mixture over the chicken thighs. Secure the lid, and select Pressure Cook. Cook on High for 15 minutes. When ready, release the pressure naturally for 10 minutes and serve hot with rice or mashed potatoes.

397. Paprika Chicken Breasts

Servings: 4 | Ready in about: 35 minutes

1 onion, diced
4 garlic cloves, minced
¼ cup white wine
¼ tsp paprika
1 ½ lb chicken breasts, chopped
1 lemon, juicedf
1 tbsp butter
3 tsp quinoa flour
½ cup broth

Melt the butter in your Instant Pot on Sauté. Add onion and cook for 3 minutes. Add garlic and cook for 1 minute. Stir in all of the remaining ingredients, except the flour. Secure the lid and cook on Pressure Cook for 15 minutes. Once completed, release the pressure quickly. Stir in the flour and cook on Sauté until it thickens.

398. Party Chicken Legs

Servings: 4 | Ready in about: 60 minutes

4 chicken legs
½ cup white wine
½ cup chopped celery
2 tbsp chopped parsley
2 tbsp vinegar
Juice and zest of 1 lemon
3 garlic cloves, chopped
¼ cup chopped shallots
¼ cup chopped carrots
½ tbsp olive oil

Heat the oil in your Instant Pot on Sauté. Add the legs, and brown them on all sides. Set aside. Place the remaining ingredients to the cooker and stir to combine. Add back the legs. Secure the lid, select Pressure Cook, and cook on High for 45 minutes. Release the pressure quickly and serve with rice or potatoes.

399. Italian Turkey Polpette

Servings: 4 | Ready in about: 25 minutes

1 lb ground turkey
28 oz can diced tomatoes
1 tsp Italian seasoning
1 tsp garlic powder
⅓ cup breadcrumbs
1 tsp dried basil
¼ cup chicken stock
1 tsp dried oregano
1 tsp dried thyme
2 tbsp onion, diced
Salt and black pepper to taste

Combine the turkey, basil, oregano, thyme, breadcrumbs, salt, and pepper, in a big bowl. Make meatballs out of the mixture. In your Instant Pot, combine the remaining ingredients. Place the meatballs inside and secure the lid. Press Pressure Cook and cook on High for 10 minutes. When ready, perform a quick pressure release and serve immediately or chilled.

400. Louisville-Style Fried Chicken

Serves: 4 | Total Time: 65 minutes

4 boneless, skinless chicken thighs	1 ½ tbsp Cajun seasoning	1 large egg
¾ cup sour cream	1 tsp dried thyme	
⅓ cup hot sauce	1 cup flour	

Combine chicken, sour cream, hot sauce, and ½ tablespoon Cajun seasoning in a large bowl. Toss to coat. Cover the bowl and refrigerate for at least 30 minutes.

Preheat your Instant Pot Duo Crisp to 375°F. Whisk flour with ½ tablespoon Cajun seasoning in a large bowl. Whisk egg in a bowl. Remove chicken from marinade and season with the rest of the Cajun seasoning and thyme. Dip in beaten egg, then dredge in flour and press to coat. Lightly spray with cooking oil and transfer to the air fry basket. Close the fry lid and Air Fry for 10 minutes, then use tongs to flip the chicken. Cook for another 10 minutes until the chicken is golden and cooked through. Serve warm.

401. BBQ Chicken Enchiladas

Serves: 4 | Total Time: 25 minutes

1 ½ cups barbecue sauce	1 cup grated sharp cheddar cheese	2 tbsp chopped parsley
4 cups grated cooked chicken	½ cups Parmesan cheese	
8 flour tortillas	⅓ cup diced red onion	

Preheat your Instant Pot Duo Crisp to 350°F. Combine 1 cup of barbecue sauce and all of the chicken in a large bowl until coated. Take ¼ cup chicken and place it in the middle of one tortilla. Top with 2 tablespoons of cheddar cheese, Parmesan cheese, parsley, and roll the tortilla around the chicken. Transfer to one of two round baking dishes. Repeat for all of the tortillas. Brush tortillas with the rest of the sauce and top with the rest of the cheese and onion. Place in the air fry basket and close the fry lid. Air Fry for 15 minutes. The cheese will be melted, and the sauce will be bubbling. Serve warm and enjoy!

402. Chicken Nacho Bake

Serves: 4 | Total Time: 15 minutes

50 tortilla chips	2 cups grated cheddar cheese	½ cup diced red onion
3 cups shredded cooked chicken breasts	½ cup sliced pickled jalapeño peppers	2 tbsp chopped parsley

Line the air fry basket with foil. Add half of the tortilla chips in the basket, then layer 1 cup of chicken, parsley, 1 cup of cheddar cheese, ¼ cup jalapenos, and ¼ cup onion. Repeat the layers. Place the basket in the air fryer basket and close the lid. Air Fry for 7 minutes. The cheese will be melted, and toppings are heated through. Serve.

403. Sticky Turkey Drumsticks

Servings: 4 | Ready in about: 35 minutes

6 turkey drumsticks	1 tsp black pepper	½ cup soy sauce
½ cup water	2 tsp brown sugar	½ tsp garlic powder

Combine all of the spices together and rub this mixture onto the turkey. Whisk together the water and soy sauce in your Instant Pot. Add the drumsticks, and secure the lid. Select Pressure Cook, and cook on High for 25 minutes. When ready, release the pressure quickly, carefully open the lid and serve.

404. Chicken Teriyaki

Serves: 4 | Total Time: 25 minutes + marinating time

¾ cup teriyaki sauce
4 chicken thighs, cubed
Salt and black pepper to taste
1 cup pineapple chunks
1 red bell pepper, cubed
¼ yellow onion, cubed
4 cups broccoli florets, steamed
2 tbsp chopped parsley

Put chicken in a large bowl, then add ½ teriyaki sauce, salt, and pepper. Cover and refrigerate for 1 hour. Preheat your Instant Pot Duo Crisp to 400°F. To prepare the kebab, place a chicken cube on a skewer, then a chunk of pineapple, bell pepper, and onion. Repeat the pattern. Brush the kebabs with the rest of the teriyaki, then transfer them to the air fry basket. Close the fry lid and Air Fry for 5 minutes, then turn the kebabs. Cook for another 5 minutes, then turn the kebabs again. Cook for 5 more minutes or until the chicken is cooked and the vegetables are tender. Sprinkle with parsley. Serve with broccoli and enjoy!

405. German-Inspired Chicken

Serves: 4 | Total Time: 25 minutes

4 chicken breasts, sliced in half lengthwise
2 cups mini twist pretzels
½ cup mayonnaise
2 tbsp honey
2 tbsp yellow mustard
Salt and black pepper to taste
1 tbsp chopped fresh parsley
4 lemon wedges

Preheat your Instant Pot Duo Crisp to 375°F. Add pretzels to a food processor and pulse ten times. Transfer to a shallow plate. Combine mayonnaise, honey, and mustard in a bowl. Season chicken with salt and pepper, then brush all over with honey mustard sauce. Next, press the chicken into the pretzel crumbs until coated. Lightly spray the chicken with cooking oil and transfer it to the air fry basket. Close the fry lid and Air Fry for 6 minutes, then flip with tongs. Cook for another 6 minutes until the edges are golden. Sprinkle with parsley. Serve warm with lemon wedges. Enjoy!

406. Teriyaki Chicken Wings

Servings: 6 | Ready in about: 35 minutes

2 lb chicken wings
3 cups chicken broth
2 scallions, finely chopped
2 tbsp olive oil
2 garlic cloves, crushed
1 tsp ginger, grated
1 tbsp honey
½ cups Worcestershire sauce

Add the wings and broth to your Instant Pot. Seal the lid and press Pressure Cook. Cook for 20 minutes. Then perform a quick release. Remove the chicken and the broth. Grease the cooker with oil, and add scallions and garlic. Press Sauté and cook for 3 minutes, stirring constantly. Add Worcestershire sauce, honey, and ginger. Cook for a minute, and add the chicken wings. Stir, and continue to cook for 2 - 3 minutes. Serve topped with scallions.

407. Simple Chicken Wings with Yogurt Dip

Servings: 4 | Ready in about: 40 minutes

2 lb chicken wings
2 cups chicken broth
For the yogurt sauce:
1 cup of yogurt
2 tbsp of olive oil
1 tsp of salt

2 garlic cloves, crushed
1 tsp fresh dill, chopped

Press Sauté on your Instant Pot and heat the olive oil. Add the wings and brown for 8 minutes, flipping once. Then, add the chicken broth, secure the lid and press Pressure Cook for 15 minutes. Once ready, allow for a natural release for 10 minutes. To prepare the yogurt sauce, combine the yogurt, dill and garlic. Let the wings cool for a while and top with the yogurt mixture.

408. Special Chicken Cordon Bleu

Serves: 4 | Total Time: 30 minutes

4 chicken breasts	8 Gruyère cheese slices	1 egg, beaten
Salt and black pepper to taste	1 tsp dried thyme	2 cups panko bread crumbs
8 deli ham slices	2 tbsp cilantro, chopped	

Preheat your Instant Pot Duo Crisp to 375°F. Cut each chicken breast in half lengthwise, then pound it with a mallet to ¼-inch thickness. Season both sides with thyme, salt, and pepper. Top each breast with a slice of ham and a slice of cheese. Roll the chicken and secure it with toothpicks.

Set up two bowls. In the first bowl, add beaten egg. In the second bowl, add bread crumbs. Dip one chicken roll in the egg, shaking off any excess. Then press the chicken in the bread crumbs and coat. Lightly spray with cooking spray and transfer to the air fry basket. Close the fry lid and Air Fry for 8 minutes, then flip the chicken. Cook for another 7 minutes or until the chicken is golden brown. Serve warm sprinkled with cilantro and enjoy!

409. Chicken & Broccoli Bake

Serves: 4 | Total Time: 40 minutes

1 lb chicken breasts, cubed	1 cup chopped broccoli florets	2 tbsp Parmesan cheese
Salt and black pepper to taste	1 cup chicken broth	2 tbsp chopped cilantro
1 cup instant white rice	1 cup grated sharp cheddar cheese	

Preheat your Instant Pot Duo Crisp to 400°F. Place chicken in a baking pan and season with salt and pepper. Place the pan in the air fry basket and close the fry lid. Bake for 3 minutes. Stir the chicken and cook for another 3 minutes. Stir once again and cook for 4 minutes. Stir in rice, broccoli, broth, Parmesan cheese, and cheddar cheese. Cover the pan with foil that is long enough to tuck under the bottom to ensure that the foil does not blow off the top from the air. Return the pan to the basket and Bake for 20 minutes. Rice will be tender. Serve warm sprinkled with cilantro and enjoy!

410. Kiddo Chicken Tenders

Serves: 4 | Total Time: 25 minutes

1 lb chicken breast tenderloins	1 cup grated Parmesan cheese	½ tsp dried oregano
2 tbsp mayonnaise	1 cup panko bread crumbs	Salt and black pepper to taste
2 tbsp English mustard	½ tsp garlic powder	

Preheat your Instant Pot Duo Crisp to 400°F. Add chicken, mayonnaise, and mustard to a large bowl and toss to coat. Mix together Parmesan, bread crumbs, garlic powder, oregano, salt, and pepper in a bowl. Transfer chicken to bread crumb bowl and press until the chicken is coated. Lightly spray the chicken with cooking oil and transfer it to the air fry basket. Close the fry lid and Air Fry for 6 minutes, then flip using tongs. Cook for another 6 minutes until the tenders are crispy on the edges and golden. Serve warm.

411. Buttered Swiss Chard & Chicken

Servings: 6 | Ready in about: 25 minutes

2 lb chicken meat, dark and white meat, cut in pieces		
1.5 lb swiss chard, chopped	2 tbsp olive oil	1 tsp sea salt
3 cups chicken broth	1 tbsp organic butter	

Chop the Swiss chard and drain it in a colander. Grease the Instant Pot with oil. Add the Pressure Cook and pour in chicken broth. Season with salt and secure the lid. Press Pressure Cook and cook for 15 minutes. When done, perform a quick release. Carefully open the lid and ddd the Swiss chard and butter. Seal the lid again. Select Pressure Cook and cook for 2 minutes minutes. Once it beeps, perform a quick pressure release. Serve warm.

412. School Chicken Popcorns

Serves: 4 | Total Time: 25 minutes

Salt and black pepper to taste
1 ½ tsp garlic powder
1 tbsp mayonnaise
½ tsp mustard powder
1 tsp dried oregano
1 lb chicken breasts, cubed
1 cup panko bread crumbs

Preheat your Instant Pot Duo Crisp to 350°F. Mix salt, pepper, mustard powder, and mayonnaise in a large bowl, then add chicken cubes. Toss to coat. In a resealable bag, add bread crumbs, salt, pepper, oregano, and garlic powder. Transfer the chicken into the bag, seal, and then toss to coat completely. Lightly spray the chicken with cooking oil and transfer it to the air fry basket. Close the fry lid and Air Fry for 6 minutes, then turn the chicken pieces. Cook for another 6 minutes or until the chicken is golden and cooked through. Serve warm and enjoy!

413. Cheddar Chicken Patties

Serves: 4 | Total Time: 25 minutes

1 lb ground chicken
1 cup grated mozzarella cheese
½ cup bread crumbs
1 garlic clove, minced
¾ cup chopped shallots
Salt and black pepper to taste
2 tbsp mayonnaise
1 cup panko bread crumbs

Preheat your Instant Pot Duo Crisp to 400°F. Mix chicken in a large bowl with the mozzarella, plain bread crumbs, garlic, shallots, salt, and pepper. Divide into 4 equal portions and shape into patties that are ½-inch thick. Brush ½ tablespoon of mayonnaise on each patty, then press into panko to coat. Lightly spray with cooking oil. Place the patties in the air fry basket and close the fry lid. Air Fry for 8 minutes. Flip the patties and cook for another 6-8 minutes until the patties are golden. Serve warm and enjoy!

414. Cheesy Chicken Taquitos

Serves: 4 | Total Time: 15 minutes

1 ½ cups grated cooked chicken
5 oz cream cheese, softened
1 cup grated Mexican-blend cheese
12 corn tortillas
1 cup tomato salsa

Preheat your Instant Pot Duo Crisp to 350°F. Combine chicken, cream cheese, and Mexican-blend cheese in a large bowl. Add 3 tablespoons of the chicken mixture to each tortilla. Roll, then lightly spray with cooking oil. Transfer tortillas to the air fry basket with the seam side down. Close the fry lid and Air Fry for 4 minutes, then flips the taquitos. Cook for another 4 minutes or until the taquitos are crispy and brown. Serve warm drizzled with tomato salsa.

415. Easy Turkey Quinoa

Servings: 4 | Ready in about: 25 minutes

1 ½ lb turkey tenderloins
⅔ cup chicken broth
1 ¼ cups quinoa
1 onion, sliced
½ tsp salt

Combine all ingredients in your Instant Pot. Close and secure the lid and select Pressure Cook. Cook on High for 8 minutes. Once if goes off, release the pressure naturally, for 10 minutes. Serve hot and enjoy!

416. Amazing Turkey Burgers

Servings: 4 | Ready in about: 20 minutes

1 lb ground turkey
1 tbsp olive oil
¼ cup breadcrumbs
1 egg
1 tbsp chopped parsley
¼ tsp garlic powder
1 ½ cups chicken broth
Salt and black pepper to taste

Combine the turkey, parsley, breadcrumbs, garlic powder, egg, salt, and pepper, in a bowl. Make 4 patties out of the mixture. Heat the oil in your Instant Pot on Sauté. Add the patties, and cook until browned on all sides. Transfer to a plate. Pour the broth in the Instant Pot, and arrange the patties on the rack. Secure the lid, select Pressure Cook, and cook for 5 minutes on High. When ready, release the pressure quickly and serve hot.

417. Mediterranean Chicken Thighs

Serves: 4 | Total Time: 35 minutes

½ cup mayonnaise
4 chicken thighs
Salt and black pepper to taste

½ cup cherry tomatoes
½ cup roasted red peppers, chopped
2 tsp Italian seasoning

1 cup Italian bread crumbs

Preheat your Instant Pot Duo Crisp to 370°F. Brush mayonnaise on both sides of the chicken, then season with salt, pepper, and Italian seasoning. In a resealable bag, add bread crumbs, then add thighs. Shake until well coated. Lightly spray with cooking oil and transfer to the air fry basket. Close the fry lid and Air Fry for 15 minutes, then use tongs to flip the chicken. Cook for another 10 minutes or until the skin is crispy and golden. Serve with cherry tomatoes and roasted red peppers on the side and enjoy!

418. Ranch Chicken Wings

Serves: 4 | Total Time: 25 minutes + marinating time

2 lb chicken wings, flats, and drums separated
1 cup pickle juice
Salt and black pepper to taste

2 tsp smoked paprika
2 tsp dry ranch seasoning

2 tbsp chopped parsley

Add chicken wings in a large bowl, then cover with pickle juice. Cover and refrigerate for 1 hour. Preheat your Instant Pot Duo Crisp to 400°F. Combine salt, pepper, smoked paprika, and ranch seasoning in a large bowl. Transfer the wings to the seasoning bowl and toss to coat. Arrange the wings in a single layer in the air fry basket and close the fry lid. Air Fry for 10 minutes, then flip the wings. Cook for another 10 minutes. Let cool for 5 minutes. Serve warm with sprinkled parsley.

419. Breaded Chicken Drumsticks

Serves: 4 | Total Time: 30 minutes

8 chicken drumsticks
Salt and black pepper to taste
¼ cup dry ranch seasoning

½ tsp dried coriander
½ cup panko bread crumbs
½ cup grated Parmesan cheese

½ cup sweet chili sauce

Preheat your Instant Pot Duo Crisp to 375°F. Season chicken with salt, pepper, coriander, and ranch seasoning. In a resealable plastic bag, add bread crumbs and Parmesan. Add chicken and shake to coat. Lightly spray the chicken with cooking oil and transfer it to the air fry basket. Close the fry lid and Air Fry for 10 minutes, then use tongs to flip the chicken. Cook for another 10 minutes. Serve with sweet chili sauce and enjoy!

420. Veggie & Chicken Stir-Fry

Servings: 6 | Ready in about: 40 minutes

8 chicken thighs, boneless and skinless
½ lb Brussels sprouts
3 medium-sized zucchinis, sliced

1 cup of chicken stock
½ cauliflower head, chopped
3 tomatoes, diced

1 onion, sliced
2 tbsp of olive oil

Press Sauté and add the onion. Fry for 2 minutes and add the vegetables. Continue to cook for another 5 minutes, stirring constantly. Add the remaining ingredients, and seal the lid. Set the steam release handle and press Pressure Cook. When ready, allow for a naturally pressure release for 10 minutes. Serve hot.

421. Nevada´s Chicken Thighs

Serves: 4 | Total Time: 45 minutes + marinating time

1 cup sour cream	1 lb chicken thighs	1 tsp dried thyme
2 tbsp seasoned salt	1 cup flour	¼ cup cornstarch

Mix sour cream and 1 tablespoon seasoned salt in a large bowl, then add chicken. Cover the bowl and refrigerate for 30 minutes. Preheat your Instant Pot Duo Crisp to 375°F. In another bowl, combine flour, cornstarch, the rest of the seasoned salt, and thyme. Dip the chicken in the flour mixture to coat completely. Spray with cooking oil and transfer to the air fry basket. Close the fry lid and Air Fry for 15 minutes, then flip the chicken. Cook for another 15 minutes or until the chicken is crispy and brown. Serve warm and enjoy!

422. Chicken with Apple Sauce

Servings: 6 | Ready in about: 30 minutes

1 shallot, chopped	2 apples, sliced	½ tsp dill
2 tbsp organic butter	1 cup chicken broth	2 lb chicken, chopped

Set your Instant Pot on Sauté and melt the butter. Add the chicken and cook until no longer pink, 6-8 minutes. Stir in the remaining ingredients. Secure the lid, and select Pressure Cook. Cook on High for 15 minutes. Serve.

423. Parmesan Broccoli & Chicken Meal

Servings: 4 | Ready in about: 20 minutes

3 cups shredded chicken	⅓ cup grated Parmesan cheese	Salt and black pepper to taste
2 cups broccoli florets	1 ½ cups chicken broth	

Place the chicken and broth into your Instant Pot. Secure the lid, select Pressure Cook, and cook for 10 minutes on High. When done, do a quick pressure release. Carefully open the lid and stir in all of the broccoli and season with salt and pepper. Set on Sauté and cook for 2 minutes. Serve with freshly grate Parmesan cheese.

424. Zesty Chicken Thighs

Servings: 3 | Ready in about: 50 minutes

1 lb chicken thighs	Salt and chili powder to taste	2 tbsp olive oil
3 cups chicken broth	2 tsp lime zest	¾ cup tomato puree

Season the thighs with salt and chili powder. Heat oil on Sauté, add the thighs and brown them lightly on both sides. Remove from the pot. Add tomato puree and lime zest. Cook for 10 minutes until a thick sauce. Return the chicken thighs, and pour in the chicken broth. Seal the lid and cook on Pressure Cook mode for 25 minutes. Once off, perform a quick release, and serve hot with rice or salad.

425. Mustardy Shredded Turkey

Servings: 4 | Ready in about: 60 minutes

12 oz chicken broth	¼ tsp pepper	2 tbsp apple cider vinegar
1 tbsp mustard	1 tbsp tomato paste	2 tbsp brown sugar
2 turkey thighs	½ tsp garlic powder	2 tsp coriander

Mix the seasonings, except the broth and the turkey, in a small bowl. Rub the seasoning mixture onto the turkey. Pour the broth in the Instant Pot, and add the turkey. Secure the lid, select Pressure Cook, and cook on High for 45 minutes. When ready, do a quick release. Transfer the turkey in a plate and shred it. Whisk together the remaining ingredients and bring the mixture to a boil on Sauté. Stir in the shredded turkey. Cook for 3 minutes.

426. Fast Chicken Breasts

Serves: 4 | Total Time: 25 minutes

3 chicken breasts
2 tbsp olive oil
Salt and black pepper to taste
1 tsp garlic powder
1 tsp paprika
1 tsp dried oregano
1 tsp dried thyme

Preheat your Instant Pot Duo Crisp to 375°F. Butterfly. the chicken, breasts lengthwise while keeping both halves connected. Drizzle with oil, then season with salt, oregano, thyme, garlic powder, paprika, and pepper. Place the chicken in the air fry basket and close the fry lid. Air Fry for 8 minutes. Flip the chicken, then cook for another 7 minutes until the chicken is golden and cooked through. Serve warm.

427. Fiery Chicken Sliders

Serves: 4 | Total Time: 35 minutes

4 boneless, skinless chicken thighs
½ tbsp dry ranch seasoning
¼ cup buffalo sauce
¼ tsp chili powder
5 pepper jack cheese slices
4 sandwich buns
2 tsp melted butter

Preheat your Instant Pot Duo Crisp to 375°F. Season chicken with ranch seasoning and chili powder and brush it with melted butter. Transfer to the air fry basket and close the fry lid. Air Fry for 10 minutes. Flip chicken and Cook for another 10 minutes until the edges on the chicken are brown. Drizzle the chicken with buffalo sauce, then add a slice of cheese. Place on buns. Serve warm.

428. Texas-Style Chicken Drumsticks

Serves: 4 | Total Time: 30 minutes

1 tsp chili powder
1 tsp garlic powder
1 tsp dried thyme
1 tsp dried oregano
Salt and black pepper to taste
½ tsp onion powder
8 chicken drumsticks
1 cup barbecue sauce

Preheat your Instant Pot Duo Crisp to 375°F. Mix salt, chili powder, garlic powder, thyme, oregano, pepper, and onion powder in a large bowl. Add drumsticks to the spice mixture and toss to coat. Brush the drumsticks with ¾ cup barbecue sauce to coat. Transfer chicken to the air fry basket and close the fry lid. Air Fry for 25 minutes, turning the chicken twice or until chicken is brown and cooked through. Brush the drumsticks with the remaining barbecue sauce and serve warm.

429. Jamaican Chicken Wings

Serves: 4 | Total Time: 25 minutes + marinating time

2 lb chicken wings, flats, and drums separated
¼ cup Jamaican jerk marinade
1 tsp onion powder
1 tsp garlic powder
1 tbsp soy sauce
2 tbsp honey
1 tsp salt

Mix jerk seasoning, onion powder, garlic powder, soy sauce, honey, and salt in a large bowl. Add chicken and toss to coat. Cover the bowl and refrigerate for at least an hour.

Preheat your Instant Pot Duo Crisp to 400°F. Arrange the chicken in a single layer in the air fry basket and close the fry lid. Air Fry for 10 minutes, then flip the chicken. Cook for another 10 minutes. Let cool for at least 5 minutes. Serve and enjoy!

MEAT RECIPES

430. Ground Beef Stuffed Empanadas

Servings: 2 | Ready in about: 60 minutes

1 tbsp olive oil
1 garlic clove, minced
½ white onion, chopped
¼ lb ground beef
6 green olives, pitted and chopped
¼ tsp cumin powder
¼ tsp paprika
⅛ tsp cinnamon powder
2 small tomatoes, chopped
8 square gyoza wrappers
1 egg, beaten

Choose Sauté on your Instant Pot. Put the oil, garlic, onion, and beef in the preheated pot and cook for 5 minutes, stirring occasionally, until the fragrant and the beef is no longer pink. Stir in the olives, cumin, paprika, and cinnamon and cook for an additional 3 minutes. Add the tomatoes and cook for 1 more minute. Spoon the beef mixture into a plate and allow cooling for a few minutes.

Meanwhile, put the air fry basket in the pot. Close the air fry lid, choose Air Fry, set the temperature to 400°F, and the time to 5 minutes. Lay the gyoza wrappers on a flat surface. Place 1 to 2 tablespoons of the beef mixture in the middle of each wrapper. Brush the edges of the wrapper with egg and fold in half to form a triangle. Pinch the edges together to seal. Place 4 empanadas in a single layer in the preheated basket. Close the air fry lid. Choose Air Fry, set the temperature to 400°F, and set the time to 7 minutes. Once the timer is done, remove the empanadas from the basket and transfer to a plate. Repeat with the remaining empanadas.

431. Winter Pot Roast with Biscuits

Servings: 6 | Ready in about: 75 minutes

2 tbsp olive oil
1 (3-lb) chuck roast
Salt and black pepper to taste
⅔ cup dry red wine
⅔ cup beef broth
1 tsp dried oregano leaves
1 bay leaf
1 small red onion, peeled and quartered
1 lb small butternut squash, diced
2 carrots, cut into 1-inch pieces
¾ cup frozen pearl onions
6 refrigerated biscuits

On the pot, choose Sauté. Heat the olive oil until shimmering. Season the beef on both sides with salt and add to the pot. Cook undisturbed for 3 minutes or until deeply browned. Flip the roast over and brown the other side for 3 minutes. Transfer the beef to a wire rack. Pour the oil out of the pot and add in the wine. Scrape the bottom of the pot to let off any browned bits. Bring to a boil and cook for 2 minutes or until the wine has reduced by half.

Mix in the beef broth, oregano, bay leaf, black pepper, and red onion. Stir to combine and add the beef with its juices. Seal the pressure lid and choose Pressure Cook on High and the cooking time to 35 minutes. After cooking, perform a quick pressure release. Carefully open the pressure lid. Add the butternut squash, carrots, and pearl onions to the pot. Seal the pressure lid and choose Pressure Cook on High and the time to 2 minutes.

After cooking, perform a quick pressure release, and open the lid. Transfer the beef to a cutting board and cover with aluminum foil. Put a trivet in the upper position of the pot and cover it with a circular piece of aluminum foil. Put the biscuits on the trivet and put a trivet in the pot. Close the air fry lid and choose Bake. Adjust the temperature to 300°F and the cooking time to 15 minutes. After 8 minutes, open the lid and flip the biscuits over.

After baking, remove the trivet and biscuits. Allow the biscuits to cool for a few minutes. While the biscuits cook, remove the foil from the beef and cut it against the grain into slices. Remove and discard the bay leaf and transfer the beef to a serving platter. Spoon the vegetables and the sauce over the beef. Serve with the biscuits.

432. Smoky Horseradish Spare Ribs

Servings: 4 | Ready in about: 55 minutes

1 spare rack ribs
1 tsp salt
1 cup smoky horseradish sauce

Season all sides of ribs with salt and cut into 3 pieces. Cut a trivet into 3 pieces. Pour 1 cup of water into your Instant Pot. Fix in a trivet and put the ribs on top, bone-side down. Seal the pressure lid, choose Pressure Cook on High and the time to 18 minutes. After cooking, perform a quick pressure release and carefully open the lid.

Take out the trivet with ribs and pour out the water from the pot. Set a trivet and ribs in the pot. Close the air fry lid and choose Air Fry. Adjust the temperature to 400°F and the cooking time to 20 minutes. After 10 minutes, open the lid and turn the ribs. Lightly baste the bony side of the ribs with the smoky horseradish sauce and close the lid to cook further. After 4 minutes, open the lid and turn the ribs again. Baste the meat side with the remaining sauce and close the lid to cook until the ribs are done.

433. Steak with Chips

Servings: 4 | Ready in about: 50 minutes

4 potatoes, cut into wedges	1 tbsp olive oil	1 tsp ground black pepper
1 tsp sweet paprika	1 tsp salt, divided	4 rib-eye steaks

Put the air fry basket in your Instant Pot. Close the air fry lid. Choose Air Fry, set the temperature to 390°F, and set the time to 5 minutes. Meanwhile, rub all over with olive oil. Put the potatoes in the preheated air fry basket and season with ½ teaspoon of salt and ½ teaspoon of black pepper and sweet paprika.

Close the air fry lid. Choose Air Fry, set the temperature to 400°F, and set the time to 35 minutes. Season the steak on both sides with the remaining salt and black pepper. When done cooking, remove potatoes to a plate. Grease the air fry basket with cooking spray and put the steaks in the basket. Close the air fry lid. Choose Air Fry, set the temperature to 400°F, and set the time to 8 minutes. When ready, check the steaks for your preferred doneness and cook for a few more minutes if needed. Take out the steaks from the basket and rest for 5 minutes. Serve the steaks with the potato wedges and the steak sauce.

434. Beef & Broccoli Sauce

Servings: 4 | Ready in about: 35 minutes

2 lb chuck roast, boneless and cut into thin strips		
4 cloves garlic, minced	1 tbsp olive oil	1 tbsp cornstarch
7 cups broccoli florets	1 cup beef broth	¾ cup soy sauce

Open the lid of your Instant Pot and select Sauté. Add the olive oil, and once heated, add the beef and minced garlic. Cook the meat until brown. Stir in soy sauce and beef broth. Seal the lid and select Pressure Cook on High for 10 minutes. Once the timer has ended, do a quick pressure release and remove the meat and set aside. Fetch out a quarter of the liquid into a bowl, add the cornstarch, and mix it until it is well dissolved. Pour the mixture into the pot and place a trivet. Place the broccoli florets on it and seal the lid. Select Steam for 5 minutes.

When ready, do a quick pressure release and open the lid. Remove the trivet, stir the sauce, add the meat and close the air fry lid. Cook for 5 minutes on Broil mode. The sauce should be thick enough when you finish cooking. Dish the beef broccoli sauce into a serving bowl and serve with a side of cooked pasta.

435. Greek Beef Gyros

Servings: 4 | Ready in about: 55 minutes

1 lb beef sirloin, cut into thin strips	2 tbsp olive oil	4 slices pita bread
1 onion, thinly sliced	2 tsp dry oregano	1 cup Greek yogurt
⅓ cup beef broth	1 clove garlic, minced	2 tbsp fresh dill, chopped
2 tbsp fresh lemon juice	Salt and black pepper to taste	

In your Instant Pot, mix beef, beef broth, oregano, garlic, lemon juice, pepper, onion, olive oil, and salt. Seal the pressure lid, choose Pressure Cook on High, and set the timer to 30 minutes. Release pressure naturally for 15 minutes. Divide the beef mixture between the pita bread slices, top with yogurt and dill, and roll up to serve.

436. Thai Roasted Beef

Servings: 2 | Ready in about: 4 hours 20 minutes

1 lb ground beef	4 garlic cloves, chopped	2 tbsp cilantro, chopped
2 tbsp soy sauce	1 tsp brown sugar	2 tbsp basil, chopped
Thumb-sized piece of ginger, chopped	Juice of 1 lime	2 tbsp oil
3 chilies, deseeded and chopped	2 tbsp mirin	2 tbsp fish sauce

Place all ingredients, except beef, salt, and pepper, in a blender. Pulse until smooth. Season the beef with salt and pepper. Place the meat and Thai mixture in a zipper bag. Shake well to combine and let marinate in the fridge for about 4 hours. Place the beef in the air fry basket and cook for about 12 minutes, or a little more for well done, on Air Fry mode at 350°F. Let sit for 5 minutes before serving.

437. Sweet Gingery Beef & Broccoli

Servings: 4 | Ready in about: 70 minutes

1 tbsp olive oil	½ cup coconut aminos	2 tbsp cornstarch
2 lb skirt steak, cut into strips	⅔ cup dark brown sugar	1 head broccoli, trimmed into florets
4 garlic cloves, minced	½ tsp ginger puree	3 scallions, thinly sliced

Choose Sauté on your Instant Pot. Pour the oil and beef into the pot and brown the beef strips on both sides, about 5 minutes in total. Remove the beef from the pot and set aside. Add the garlic to the oil and sauté for 1 minute or until fragrant. Stir in the coconut aminos, ½ cup of water, brown sugar, and ginger to the pot. Mix evenly and add the beef. Seal the pressure lid, choose Pressure Cook on High, and set the time to 10 minutes.

In a small bowl, whisk combine the cornstarch and 3 tbsp water. When done cooking, perform a quick pressure release. Choose Sauté. Pour in the cornstarch mixture and stir continuously until the sauce becomes syrupy. Add the broccoli, stir to coat in the sauce, and cook for another 5 minutes. Top with scallions and serve.

438. Honey Short Ribs with Rosemary Potatoes

Servings: 4 | Ready in about: 105 minutes

4 bone-in beef short ribs, silver skin	1 onion, chopped	2 tbsp minced fresh rosemary
Salt and black pepper to taste	2 tbsp honey	3 garlic cloves, minced
2 tbsp olive oil	½ cup beef broth	2 potatoes, cut into 1-inch pieces

Choose Sauté on your Instant Pot. Season the short ribs on all sides with ½ teaspoon of salt and ½ teaspoon of pepper. Heat 1 tablespoon of olive oil and brown the ribs on all sides, about 10 minutes total. Stir in the onion, honey, broth, 1 tablespoon of rosemary, and garlic. Seal the pressure lid, choose Pressure Cook on High, and set the time to 40 minutes.. In a large bowl, toss the potatoes with the remaining oil, rosemary, salt, and black pepper.

When the ribs are ready, perform a quick pressure release and carefully open the lid. Fix a trivet in the higher position of the pot, which is over the ribs. Put the potatoes on the trivet. Close the air fry lid. Choose Bake set the temperature to 350°F, and set the time to 15 minutes. Once the potatoes are tender and roasted, use tongs to pick the potatoes and the short ribs into a plate. Set aside. Choose Sauté and set to High. Simmer the sauce for 5 minutes and spoon the sauce into a bowl. Allow sitting for 2 minutes and scoop off the fat that forms on top. Serve the ribs with the potatoes and sauce.

439. Sticky BBQ Baby Back Ribs

Servings: 4 | Ready in about: 35 minutes

3 lb rack baby back ribs, cut into quarters		
1 ½ tbsp smoked paprika	2 tsp garlic powder	1 cup barbecue sauce
3 tbsp brown sugar	1 cup beer	

In a bowl, mix the paprika, brown sugar, garlic, salt, and black pepper. Season all sides of the ribs with the rub. Pour the beer into your Instant Pot, put the ribs in the air fry basket, and place the basket in the pot. Seal the pressure lid, choose Pressure Cook on High, and set the time to 10 minutes.

When done cooking, perform a quick pressure release, and carefully the open the lid. Close the air fry lid. Choose Air Fry, set the temperature to 400°F, and the time to 15 minutes. After 10 minutes, open the lid, and brush the ribs with the barbecue sauce. Close the lid to cook further for 5 minutes.

440. Peanut Sauce Beef Satay

Servings: 4 | Ready in about: 60 minutes

- 1 lb flank steak
- ½ tsp salt

For the Cucumber Relish
- ½ cucumber
- ½ cup rice vinegar

For the Sauce
- 1 tbsp coconut oil
- 1 tbsp onion, minced
- 1 tsp garlic, minced

- 1 tbsp lime juice
- 1½ tsp red curry paste

- ¼ cup water
- 2 tbsp sugar

- 1 cup coconut milk
- 2 tsp red curry paste
- 1 tsp brown sugar

- 1 tbsp coconut aminos
- 1 tbsp coconut oil

- 1 tsp salt
- 1 serrano chile, cut into thin rounds

- ⅓ cup water
- ½ cup peanut butter
- 1 tbsp lime juice

Season the steak with salt. Put in a resealable plastic bag. In a small bowl, whisk the lime juice, curry paste, coconut aminos, and coconut oil. Pour the marinade over the steak, seal the bag, and massage the bag to coat the meat. Let sit for 20 minutes. Cut the cucumber into ¼-inch slices, then into quarters. In a bowl, whisk the vinegar, water, sugar, and salt until the sugar and salt dissolve. Add the cucumber pieces. Refrigerate until needed.

To make the sauce, on the pot, choose Sauté. Heat the coconut oil until shimmering and sauté the onion and garlic in your Instant Pot. Cook for 1 to 2 minutes or until fragrant. Stir in the coconut milk, curry paste, and brown sugar. Seal the pressure lid, choose Pressure Cook on High and the cooking time to 1 minute.

After cooking, perform a quick pressure release. Pour in the water and mix. Remove the meat from the marinade, holding the meat above the bag for a while to drain the excess marinade, put on the trivet, and put the trivet with the steak in the sauce. Close the air fry lid, choose Broil, adjust the cooking time to 14 minutes, and press Start to begin cooking. After about 7 minutes, open the lid and turn the steak. Close the lid and begin broiling.

Transfer the steak to a cutting board and allow resting for a few minutes. While the steak cools, mix the peanut butter and lime juice into the sauce. Taste and adjust the seasoning. Cut the steak into thin slices and serve with the peanut sauce and cucumber relish.

441. Classic Carbonnade Flamande

Servings: 4 | Ready in about: 70 minutes

- 2 lb brisket, cut into 2 or 3 pieces
- 1 tbsp olive oil
- 1 large onion, sliced

- 8 fluid oz stout
- ¼ tsp dried rosemary leaves
- ¼ cup beef broth

- ½ tsp Dijon-style mustard
- ½ tsp brown sugar to taste
- 2 tbsp chopped fresh chervil

Season the brisket with salt. On the pot, choose Sauté. Heat the olive oil in your Instant Pot until shimmering and sear the brisket. Cook, without turning, for 4 minutes or until browned. Use tongs to turn the beef and move to the side. Add the onion on the other side. Cook, stirring, for 1 to 2 minutes or until slightly softened. Pour in the stout, scraping off any browned bits from the bottom of the pot. Simmer and cook until the stout has reduced by about half. Stir in the rosemary and broth. Seal the pressure lid, choose Pressure Cook on High and the cooking time to 35 minutes. After cooking, perform a natural pressure release for 10 minutes.

Remove the beef onto a cutting board. Scoop off any excess fat on the sauce and stir in the mustard and brown sugar. Choose Sauté. Simmer the sauce and cook until reduced to a thin gravy. Taste and adjust the seasoning. Slice the beef and return to the sauce to reheat. Serve over mashed potatoes or noodles and garnish with chervil.

442. Beef Carnitas

Servings: 4 | Ready in about: 55 minutes

2 ½ lb bone-in country ribs	2 tbsp beef stock	1 small onion, cut into 8 wedges
¼ cup orange juice	1 tbsp lime juice	3 garlic cloves, smashed and peeled

Season the ribs with salt on all sides. In your Instant Pot, combine the orange juice, stock, and lime juice. Drop in the onion and garlic. Stir. Put the ribs in your Instant Pot. Seal the pressure lid, choose Pressure Cook on High and the cooking time to 25 minutes. After cooking, do a natural pressure release for 12 minutes. Transfer the ribs to a plate to cool slightly. Remove and discard the bones. Run the juice in the pot through a fat separator and set aside for a few minutes. Pour the sauce back into the pot and reserve the fat. Oil a trivet with cooking spray and lay the ribs in a single layer on the trivet. Baste with the reserved fat. Put the trivet in the pot. Close the air fry lid and choose Air Fry. Adjust the temperature to 375°F for 6 minutes. After crisping, put the beef back in the sauce and shred the meat. Stir the beef into the sauce. Serve the carnitas with flatbread or on rice.

443. Beef Congee (Chinese Rice Porridge)

Servings: 6 | Ready in about: 1 hour

1 cup jasmine rice	6 cups beef stock	2 lb ground beef
2 cloves garlic, minced	1 cup kale, roughly chopped	Salt and black pepper to taste
1 (1 inch) piece fresh ginger, minced	1 cups water	Fresh cilantro, chopped

Run cold water and rinse rice. Add garlic, rice, and ginger into your Instant Pot. Pour in water and stock and spread the beef on top of rice. Seal the pressure lid, choose Pressure Cook on High, and set the timer to 30 minutes. Once ready, release pressure naturally for 10 minutes. Stir in kale to obtain the desired consistency. Add pepper and salt for seasoning. Divide into serving plates and top with cilantro.

444. Pineapple Appetizer Ribs

Servings: 4 | Ready in about: 30 minutes

2 lb cut spareribs	5 oz canned pineapple juice	Salt and black pepper to taste
7 oz salad dressing	2 cups water	

Sprinkle the ribs with salt and pepper and place them in a saucepan. Pour water and cook the ribs for around 12 minutes on high heat. Drain the ribs and arrange them in your Instant Pot. Sprinkle with garlic salt. Close the air fry lid and cook for 15 minutes at 390°F on Air Fry mode. Prepare the sauce by combining the salad dressing and the pineapple juice. Serve the ribs with this delicious dressing sauce!

445. Beef & Cabbage Stew

Servings: 4 | Ready in about: 30 minutes

1 cup rice	4 cloves garlic, minced	¼ cup Plain vinegar
1 large head cabbage, cut in chunks	2 tbsp butter	2 tbsp Worcestershire sauce
1 lb ground beef	1 bay leaf	1 tbsp paprika powder
Salt and black pepper to taste	1 cup diced tomatoes	1 tbsp dried oregano
½ cup chopped onion	1 ½ cup beef broth	Chopped parsley to garnish

Set your Instant Pot on Sauté. Melt the butter and add the beef. Brown it for about 6 minutes and add in the onions, garlic, and bay leaf. Stir and cook for 2 more minutes. Stir in the oregano, paprika, salt, pepper, rice, cabbage, vinegar, broth, and Worcestershire sauce. Cook for 3 minutes, stirring occasionally. Add the tomatoes but don't stir. Seal the lid and select Pressure Cook mode on High for 5 minutes. Once the timer is done, let the pot sit closed for 5 minutes and then do a quick pressure. Open the lid. Stir the sauce, remove the bay leaf, and adjust the seasoning with salt. Dish the cabbage sauce in serving bowls and serve with bread rolls.

446. Short Ribs with Egg Noodles

Servings: 4 | Ready in about: 65 minutes

4 lb bone-in short ribs	6 oz egg noodles	1 garlic clove, minced
Salt and black pepper to taste	2 tbsp prepared horseradish	3 tbsp melted unsalted butter
Low-sodium beef broth	6 tbsp Dijon mustard	1 ½ cups panko bread crumbs

Season the short ribs on all sides with 1½ teaspoons of salt. Pour 1 cup of broth into in your Instant Pot. Put a trivet in the lower position in your Instant Pot, and place the short ribs on top. Seal the pressure lid, choose Pressure Cook on High and the time to 25 minutes. After cooking, perform a natural pressure release for 5 minutes, then a quick pressure release, and carefully open the lid. Remove the trivet and short ribs. Pour the cooking liquid into a measuring cup to get 2 cups. If lesser than 2 cups, add more broth and season with salt and pepper. Add the egg noodles and the remaining salt. Stir and submerge the noodles as much as possible. Seal the pressure lid, choose Pressure Cook on High and the cooking time to 4 minutes.

In a bowl, combine the horseradish, mustard, garlic, and pepper. Brush the sauce on all sides of the short ribs and reserve any extra sauce. In another bowl, mix the butter and breadcrumbs. Coat the ribs with the crumbs. Put the ribs back on the trivet. After cooking, do a quick pressure release. Stir the noodles, which may not be quite done but will continue cooking. Return the trivet and beef to the pot in the upper position. Close the air fry lid and choose Bake. Adjust the temperature to 400°F and the cooking time to 15 minutes. After 8 minutes, open the lid and turn the ribs over. Close the lid and continue cooking. Serve the beef and noodles with extra sauce.

447. Pot Roast with Broccoli

Servings: 4 | Ready in about: 35 minutes

2 lb beef chuck roast	1 cup beef broth	2 red bell peppers, seeded and quartered
3 tbsp olive oil, divided into 2	1 packet onion soup mix	
Salt to taste	1 cup chopped broccoli	1 yellow onion, quartered

Season the chuck roast with salt and set aside. Select Sauté on your Instant Pot. Add the olive oil, and once heated, add the chuck roast. Sear for 5 minutes on each side. Then, pour in the beef broth. In a zipper bag, add broccoli, onions, peppers, the remaining olive oil, and onion soup. Close the bag and shake the mixture to coat the vegetables well. Use tongs to remove the vegetables into the pot and stir with a spoon. Seal the lid and select Pressure Cook on High for 18 minutes. Once the timer has stopped, do a quick pressure release, and open the pressure lid. Make cuts on the meat inside the pot and close the air fry lid. Cook on Air Fry for 10 minutes at 380°F until nice and crispy. Serve with the vegetables and a drizzle of the sauce in the pot.

448. Cheeseburgers in Hoagies

Servings: 4 | Ready in about: 65 minutes

1 tbsp olive oil	2 tbsp Worcestershire sauce	3 slices Provolone cheese
1 (14 oz) can French onion soup	2 Cups beef broth	3 hoagies, halved
1 lb chuck beef roast	Salt and black pepper to taste	3 tsp mayonnaise
1 onion, sliced	1 tsp garlic powder	

Season the beef with garlic powder, salt, and pepper. On your Instant Pot, select Sauté. Heat the olive oil and brown the beef on both sides for about 5 minutes. Remove the meat onto a plate. To the pot, add the onions and cook until soft. Then, pour the beef broth and stir while scraping the bottom of every stuck bit. Add the onion soup, Worcestershire sauce, and beef. Seal the lid and select Pressure Cook on High for 20 minutes.

Once the timer has stopped, do a natural pressure release for 10-15 minutes, and then a quick pressure release to let out any remaining steam. Use two forks to shred the meat. Close the air fry lid and cook on Bake for 10 minutes at 350°F. When ready, open the lid and strain the juice of the pot through a sieve into a bowl. Assemble the burgers by slathering mayo on halved hoagies, spoon the shredded meat over and top each hoagie with cheese.

449. Tasty Baby Porcupine Meatballs

Servings: 4 | Ready in about: 30 minutes

1 cup rice
1 lb ground beef
1 onion, chopped
1 green bell pepper, finely chopped
1 tsp celery salt
2 tbsp Worcestershire sauce
1 garlic clove, minced
2 cups of tomato juice
1 tsp oregano

Combine the rice, ground beef, onion, celery, salt, green peppers, and garlic. Shape into balls of 1 inch each. Arrange the balls on the air fry basket of your Instant Pot. Close the air fry lid and cook for 15 minutes at 390°F. After 8 minutes, shape the balls. Heat the tomato juice, cloves, oregano, and Worcestershire sauce in a saucepan over medium heat. Pour in the meatballs, bring to a boil, and simmer for 10 minutes, stirring often.

450. Beef & Green Bell Pepper Pot

Servings: 4 | Ready in about: 55 minutes

2 lb beef chuck roast, cut in 4 pieces
1 tbsp onion powder
1 tbsp garlic powder
1 tbsp Italian Seasoning
1 cup beef broth
1 medium white onion, sliced
1 green bell pepper, seeded and sliced
1 red bell pepper, seeded and sliced
2 tbsp olive oil

Rub the beef with pepper, salt, garlic powder, Italian seasoning, and onion powder. Select Sauté on your Instant Pot. Heat 1 tbsp oil, add the beef pieces and sear them on both sides until brown, for about 5 minutes. Use a pair of tongs to remove them onto a plate after. Pour the beef broth and fish sauce into the pot to deglaze the bottom while you use a spoon to scrape any stuck beef bit at the bottom. Add the meat back to the pot.

Seal the lid and select Pressure Cook on High for 30 minutes. Once the timer has stopped, do a quick pressure release, and open the pot. Use two forks to shred the beef inside the pot. Close the air fry lid and select Broil mode for 10 minutes. When ready, set aside the meat and discard the liquid. Wipe clean the pot. Select Sauté, heat the remaining oil, add the beef with onions and peppers. Sauté them for 3 minutes and season with salt and pepper. Turn off the pot and dish the stir-fried beef into serving plates.

451. Beef Soup with Tortillas

Servings: 8 | Ready in about: 30 minutes

2 tbsp olive oil
6 green bell pepper, diced
2 medium yellow onion, chopped
3 lb ground beef, grass-fed
Salt and black pepper to taste
3 tbsp chili powder
2 tbsp cumin powder
2 tsp paprika
1 tsp garlic powder
1 tsp cinnamon
1 tsp onion powder
6 cups chopped tomatoes
½ cup chopped green chilies
3 cups bone broth
3 cups milk

Topping:
Chopped Jalapenos, cilantro and green onions, sliced Avocados, lime juice

Select Sauté on your Instant Pot. Pour in the oil and add the yellow onion and green peppers. Sauté until they are soft for about 5 minutes. Include the ground beef, stir the ingredients, and let the beef cook for about 8 minutes until it browns. Add the chili powder, cumin powder, black pepper, paprika, cinnamon, garlic powder, onion powder, and green chilies. Give them a good stir. Top with tomatoes, milk, and bone broth. Seal the lid and select Pressure Cook on High for 20 minutes. Once the timer has ended, do a quick pressure release. Adjust the taste with salt and pepper. Dish the taco soup into serving bowls and add the toppings. Serve with a side of tortillas.

452. Beef & Pepperoncini Peppers

Servings: 4 | Ready in about: 55 minutes

14 oz jar pepperoncini peppers, with liquid
2 lb beef roast, cut into cubes
1 pack brown gravy mix
1 pack Italian salad dressing mix

Place the beef, pepperoncini peppers, brown gravy mix, Italian salad dressing mix, and ½ cup water in your Instant Pot. Seal the lid and select Pressure Cook on High for 35 minutes. Once the timer has stopped, do a quick pressure release, and open the pot. Close the air fry lid and cook on Bake mode for 15 to 20 minutes at 380°F, until nice and tender. Shred the beef and serve the beef sauce on plates with a side of a veggie mash.

453. Beef and Bell Pepper with Onion Sauce

Servings: 6 | Ready in about: 62 minutes

2 lb round steak pieces, 6 to 8 pieces	½ yellow bell pepper, finely chopped	Salt and black pepper to taste
½ green bell pepper, finely chopped	1 yellow onion, finely chopped	¼ cup flour
½ red bell pepper, finely chopped	2 cloves garlic, minced	2 tbsp olive oil

Wrap the steaks in plastic wrap, place on a cutting board, and use a rolling pin to pound flat of about 2-inch thickness. Remove the plastic wrap and season with salt and pepper. Mix the chopped peppers, onion, and garlic in a bowl. Spoon the bell pepper mixture onto the flattened steaks and roll them to have the peppers inside.

Use some toothpicks to secure the beef rolls and dredge the steaks in all-purpose flour while shaking off any excess flour. Place them on a plate. Select Sauté on your Instant Pot and heat the oil. Add the beef rolls and brown them for about 6 minutes. Pour ½ cup water over the meat, seal the lid and select Pressure Cook for 20 minutes. Once the timer has stopped, do a natural pressure release for 10 minutes. Close the air fry lid and cook for 10 minutes on Broil mode. When ready, remove the meat to a plate and spoon the sauce from the pot over. Serve the stuffed meat rolls with a side of steamed veggies.

454. Asian Beef Curry

Servings: 4 | Ready in about: 40 minutes

1 ½ lb beef brisket, cut in cubes	2 star anises	1 Potato, peeled and chopped
1 tbsp olive oil	1 large carrot, chopped	1 tbsp sugar
2 cloves garlic, minced	1 medium onion, chopped	2 tsp oyster sauce
¼-inch ginger, peeled and sliced	2 tbsp red curry paste	2 tsp flour
2 bay leaves	1 cup milk	3 tbsp water

Select Sauté on your Instant Pot. Heat oil, add garlic, ginger, and red curry paste. Stir-fry them for 1 minute. Stir in onion and beef. Cook for 4 minutes. Add the carrots, bay leaves, potato, star anises, sugar, and water. Stir. Seal the lid and select Pressure Cook on High for 25 minutes. Once the timer goes off, do a quick pressure release.

In a bowl, add the flour and 4 tablespoons of milk. Mix well with a spoon and pour it into your Instant Pot along with the oyster sauce and remaining milk. Stir it gently not to break the potato. Close the air fry lid and cook on Broil mode for about 3 minutes, until the sauce thickens and meat is tender. After, turn off the pot. Spoon the sauce into soup bowls and serve with a side of rice.

455. Meatballs with Spaghetti Sauce

Servings: 6 | Ready in about: 20 minutes

2 lb ground beef	Salt and black pepper to taste	1 cup grated Parmesan cheese
1 cup breadcrumbs	1 tsp dried oregano	2 eggs, cracked into a bowl
1 onion, finely chopped	3 tbsp milk	4 cups spaghetti sauce
2 cloves garlic, minced	1 cup water	1 tbsp olive oil

In a bowl, add beef, onion, breadcrumbs, parmesan, eggs, garlic, milk, salt, oregano, and pepper. Mix well with hands and shape bite-size balls. Open your Instant Pot and add the spaghetti sauce, water, and meatballs. Close the lid, secure the pressure valve, and select Steam mode on High pressure for 6 minutes. Once the timer is done, do a natural pressure release for 5 minutes, then do a quick pressure release to let out any extra steam, and open the lid. Dish the meatball sauce over cooked pasta and serve.

456. Beef & Garbanzo Bean Chili

Servings: 10 | Ready in about: 45 minutes

1 lb garbanzo beans, soaked overnight	6 garlic cloves, minced	1 tsp dried oregano
1 tbsp olive oil	¼ cup chili powder	1 tsp garlic powder
2 onions, finely chopped	2 tbsp ground cumin	¼ tsp cayenne pepper
2 ½ lb ground beef	2 tsp salt	2 ½ cups beef broth
1 small jalapeño with seeds, minced	1 tsp smoked paprika	1 (6 oz) can tomato puree

Add the garbanzo beans to your Instant Pot and pour in cold water to cover 1 inch. Seal the pressure lid, choose Pressure Cook on High, and set the timer to 20 minutes. When ready, release the pressure quickly. Drain beans and rinse with cold water. Set aside. Wipe clean the pot and set it to Sauté. Warm olive oil, add in onion and cook for 3 minutes until soft. Add jalapeño, ground beef, and minced garlic and stir-fry for 5 minutes.

Stir in chili powder, kosher salt, garlic powder, paprika, cumin, oregano, and cayenne pepper, and cook until soft, about 30 seconds. Pour beef broth, garbanzo beans, and tomato paste into the pot. Seal the pressure lid, choose Pressure Cook on High, and set the timer to 20 minutes. When ready, release pressure naturally for about 10 minutes. Open the lid, press Sauté, and cook as you stir until desired consistency is attained. Serve.

457. Beef & Cheese Stuffed Mushrooms

Servings: 3 | Ready in about: 10 minutes

6 white mushrooms, stems removed	½ cup vegetable broth	1 cup shredded Cheddar cheese
2 cups cooked leftover beef, cubed	2 oz cream cheese, softened	1 tsp olive oil

In a bowl, add the beef, cream cheese, and cheddar cheese. Use a spoon to mix them. Spoon the beef mixture into the mushrooms and place the mushrooms in the inner pot of your Instant Pot. Drizzle them with olive oil, and add the broth. Seal the lid and select Pressure Cook on High for 3 minutes. Once the timer is off, do a quick pressure release and open the pressure lid, discard the liquid, and remove the mushrooms. Place a trivet and lay the mushrooms on it. Close the air fry lid and cook for 2 to 3 minutes on Air Fry mode at 350°F. Remove the stuffed mushrooms onto a plate and serve hot.

458. Beef Stew with Beer

Servings: 4 | Ready in about: 60 minutes

2 lb beef stewed meat, cut into bite-size pieces		
Salt and black pepper to taste	2 tbsp Worcestershire sauce	2 cups beef broth
¼ cup flour	2 cloves garlic, minced	1 medium bottle beer
3 tbsp butter	1 packet dry onion soup mix	1 tbsp tomato paste

In a zipper bag, add beef, salt, all-purpose flour, and pepper. Close the bag up and shake it to coat the meat well with the mixture. Select Sauté on your Instant Pot. Melt the butter, and brown the beef on both sides for 5 minutes. Pour the broth to deglaze the bottom of the pot. Stir in tomato paste, beer, Worcestershire sauce, and the onion soup mix. Seal the lid and select Pressure Cook on High for 25 minutes. Once the timer is done, do a natural pressure release for 10 minutes, and then a quick pressure release to let out any remaining steam. Open the pressure lid and close the air fry lid. Cook on Broil mode for 10 minutes. Spoon the beef stew into serving bowls and serve over a bed of vegetable mash with steamed greens.

459. Cheddar Cheeseburgers

Servings: 4 | Ready in about: 20 minutes

1 lb ground beef	4 burger buns	4 Cheddar cheese slices
1 (1 oz) packet dry onion soup mix	4 tomato slices	4 small leaves lettuce
Mayonnaise, Mustard, Ketchup for garnish		

In a bowl, add beef and onion mix, and mix well with hands. Shape in 4 patties and wrap each in foil paper. Pour 1 cup of water into the inner steel insert of your Instant Pot, and fit in the steamer rack. Place the wrapped patties on the trivet. Seal the lid and cook for 10 minutes on Pressure Cook. Once ready, do a quick pressure release.

Use a set of tongs to remove the wrapped beef onto a flat surface and carefully unwrap the patties. In each half of the buns, put a lettuce leaf, then a beef patty, a slice of cheese, and a slice of tomato. Top it with the other halves of buns. Serve with some ketchup, mayonnaise, and mustard.

460. Beef Pho with Swiss Chard

Servings: 6 | Ready in about: 1 hour 10 minutes

2 tbsp coconut oil	9 cups water	10 oz sirloin steak
1 yellow onion, quartered	2 lb Beef Neck Bones	A handful of fresh cilantro, chopped
¼ cup minced fresh ginger	2 ½ tsp kosher salt	2 scallions, chopped
2 tsp coriander seeds	8 oz rice noodles	2 jalapeño peppers, sliced
2 tsp ground cinnamon	3 tbsp sugar	2 cups Swiss chard, chopped
2 tsp ground cloves	2 tbsp fish sauce	Freshly ground black pepper to taste

Melt the oil on Sauté in your Instant Pot. Add ginger and onions and cook for 4 minutes until the onions are softened. Stir in cloves, cinnamon and coriander seeds and cook for 1 minute until soft. Add in water, salt, beef meat and bones. Seal the pressure lid, choose Pressure Cook for 30 minutes. Release pressure quickly. Transfer the meat to a large bowl. Cover with it enough water and soak for 10 minutes. Drain the water and slice the beef. In hot water, soak rice noodles for 8 minutes until softened and pliable. Drain and rinse with cold water. Drain liquid from cooker into a separate pot through a fine-mesh strainer. Get rid of any solids.

Add fish sauce and sugar to the broth. Transfer into the pot and simmer on Sauté. Place the noodles in four separate soup bowls. Top with steak slices, scallions, swiss chard, sliced jalapeño pepper, cilantro, red onion, and pepper. Spoon the broth over each bowl to serve.

461. Spiced Beef Chili

Servings: 4 | Ready in about: 40 minutes

2 lb ground beef	2 cups chopped tomatoes	5 tsp chili powder
2 tbsp olive oil	2 cups beef broth	2 tbsp Worcestershire sauce
1 large red bell pepper, chopped	2 carrots, cut into little bits	2 tsp paprika
1 large yellow bell pepper, chopped	2 tsp onion powder	½ tsp cumin powder
1 white onion, chopped	2 tsp garlic powder	2 tbsp chopped parsley

Select Sauté on your Instant Pot and add the olive oil and ground beef. Cook the meat until brown, stirring occasionally, for about 8 minutes. Top with the remaining ingredients and mix well. Seal the lid, and cook on Pressure Cook on High for 15 minutes. Once the timer has ended, do a quick pressure release, and open the lid. Stir the stew and close the air fry lid. Cook on Broil mode for 10 minutes. Dish into serving bowls. Serve.

462. Spiced Beef Shapes

Servings: 12 | Ready in about: 40 minutes

1 ½ lb ground beef	2 tsp paprika	1 tbsp chopped parsley
½ cup minced onion	2 tsp coriander seeds	2 tsp cumin
2 tbsp chopped mint leaves	½ tsp cayenne pepper	½ tsp ground ginger
3 garlic cloves, minced	1 tsp salt	24 skewers, soaked in water

Combine all ingredients in a large bowl. Make sure to mix well with your hands until the herbs and spices are evenly distributed and the mixture is well incorporated. Shape the beef mixture into 12 shapes around 2 skewers. Close the air fry lid and cook for 12 - 15 minutes on Air Fry mode at 330°F, or until preferred doneness. Serve.

463. Meatloaf with Cheesy Mashed Potatoes

Servings: 6 | Ready in about: 45 minutes

Meatloaf:
1 ½ lb ground beef
1 onion, diced
1 egg

1 potato, grated
¼ cup tomato puree
1 tsp garlic powder

1 tsp salt
1 tsp ground black pepper

Mashed Potatoes:
4 potatoes, chopped
2 cups water

½ cup milk
2 tbsp butter

Salt and black pepper to taste
1 cup ricotta cheese

In a bowl, combine ground beef, eggs, 1 tsp pepper, garlic powder, potato, onion, tomato puree, and 1 tsp salt to obtain a consistent texture. Shape the mixture into a meatloaf and place onto an aluminum foil. Arrange potatoes onto your Instant Pot and pour water over them. Place a trivet onto potatoes and set the foil sheet with meatloaf onto the trivet. Seal the pressure lid, choose Pressure Cook on High, and set the timer to 22 minutes. When ready, release the pressure quickly. Place the meatloaf on a cutting board to cool before slicing. Drain the liquid out of the pot. Mash potatoes in the pot with pepper, milk, ricotta cheese, salt, and butter until smooth and all the liquid is absorbed. Plate the potatoes and lean a meatloaf slice to one side of the potato pile before serving.

464. Beef & Vegetable Stew

Servings: 4 | Ready in about: 70 minutes

2 lb brisket, cut into 2-inch pieces
4 cups beef broth
1 tbsp Dijon mustard
1 tbsp olive oil

1 lb small potato, quartered
¼ lb carrots, cut into 2-inch pieces
1 large red onion, quartered
3 cloves garlic, minced

1 bay leaf
2 fresh thyme sprigs
2 tbsp cornstarch
3 tbsp chopped cilantro to garnish

Pour broth, cornstarch, mustard, ½ teaspoon salt, and ½ teaspoon pepper in a bowl. Whisk them and set aside. Season the beef with salt and pepper. On your Instant Pot, select Sauté. Add the olive oil, and once heated, add the beef strips. Flip halfway through to brown evenly. That should take 7 to 10 minutes. Add potato, carrots, onion, garlic, thyme, mustard mixture, and bay leaf. Stir once more. Seal the lid and select Pressure Cook for 35 minutes. Once the timer has ended, do a quick pressure release. Remove the bay leaf. Close the air fry lid and cook for 10 minutes on Broil mode. Serve the soup with a bread of your choice.

465. Beef Roast with Peanut Satay Sauce

Servings: 4 | Ready in about: 40 minutes

1 lb beef roast, cut into cubes
Salt and black pepper to taste

½ cup coconut milk, light
½ cup Peanut Satay sauce

2 cups diced carrots

Place the beef into your Instant Pot. In a bowl, mix in coconut milk, salt, pepper, and satay sauce. Pour over the beef. Add the carrots too. Seal the lid and select Pressure Cook on High for 15 minutes. Once the timer has ended, do a natural pressure release for 10 minutes. Give it a stir and close the air fry lid. Cook for 10 minutes on Bake mode at 400°F. Use a spoon to dish the meat into a serving plate, and serve with a side of steamed greens.

466. Beef & Cherry Tagine

Servings: 4 | Ready in about: 1 hour 20 minutes

2 tbsp olive oil
1 onion, chopped
1 ½ lb stewing beef, trimmed
1 tsp ground cinnamon
½ tsp paprika

½ tsp turmeric
½ tsp salt
¼ tsp ground ginger
¼ tsp ground allspice
1-star anise

1 cup water
1 tbsp honey
1 cup dried cherries, halved
¼ cup toasted almonds, slivered

Set your Instant Pot to Sauté. Warm olive oil. Add in onions and cook for 3 minutes until fragrant. Mix in beef and cook for 2 minutes each side until browned. Stir in anise, cinnamon, turmeric, allspice, salt, paprika, and ginger. Cook for 2 minutes until aromatic. Add in honey and water. Seal the lid, choose Pressure Cook for 50 minutes. Meanwhile, in a bowl, soak dried cherries in hot water until softened. Once ready, release pressure naturally for 15 minutes. Drain cherries and stir into the tagine. Top with toasted almonds before serving.

467. Caribbean Ropa Vieja

Servings: 6 | Ready in about: 1 hour 10 minutes

Salt and black pepper to taste	1 red onion, halved and thinly sliced	1 tsp ground cumin
2 lb beef skirt steak	1 green bell pepper, thinly sliced	1 cup tomato sauce
3 ½ cups beef stock	1 red bell pepper, thinly sliced	1 cup dry red wine
2 bay leaves	¼ cup minced garlic	1 tbsp vinegar
¼ cup olive oil	1 tsp dried oregano	¼ cup cheddar cheese, shredded

Season the skirt steak with pepper and salt. Add water to your Instant Pot. Mix in bay leaves and flank steak. Seal the pressure lid, choose Pressure Cook on High, and set the timer to 35 minutes. When ready, release the pressure quickly. Remove skirt steak to a cutting board and allow to sit for about 5 minutes. When cooled, shred the beef using two forks. Drain the pressure cooker, and reserve the bay leaves and 1 cup liquid.

Warm the oil on Sauté. Add onion, red bell pepper, cumin, garlic, green bell pepper, and oregano and continue cooking for 5 minutes until vegetables are softened. Stir in reserved liquid, tomato sauce, bay leaves and red wine. Return shredded beef to the pot with vinegar. Season with pepper and salt. Seal the pressure lid, choose Pressure Cook on High, and set the timer to 15 minutes. Release pressure naturally for 10 minutes. Serve with cheese.

468. Chipotle Beef Brisket

Servings: 4 | Ready in about: 1 hour 10 minutes

2 tsp smoked paprika	½ tsp garlic powder	2 tbsp olive oil
½ tsp dried oregano	1 tsp chipotle powder	1 cup beef broth
1 tbsp Worcestershire sauce	¼ tsp cayenne pepper	¼ cup red wine
½ tsp ground cumin	2 lb beef brisket	A handful of parsley, chopped

In a bowl, combine oregano, cumin, cayenne pepper, garlic powder, paprika, Worcestershire sauce and chipotle powder. Rub the seasoning mixture on the beef to coat. Warm olive oil on Sauté in your Instant Pot. Add in beef and cook for 3 to 4 minutes on each side until browned completely. Pour in beef broth and red wine. Seal the pressure lid, choose Pressure Cook on High, and set the timer to 50 minutes. Release the Pressure naturally for 10 minutes. Place the beef on a cutting board and Allow cooling for 10 minutes before slicing. Arrange the beef slices on a serving platter, pour the cooking sauce over and scatter with parsley to serve.

469. Brisket Chili con Carne

Servings: 6 | Ready in about: 1 hour 25 minutes

1 tbsp ground black pepper	1 tsp chili powder	1 cup beef broth
2 tsp salt	½ tsp garlic salt	2 bay leaves
1 tsp sweet paprika	½ tsp onion powder	2 tbsp Worcestershire sauce
1 tsp cayenne pepper	1 (4 lb) beef brisket	14 oz canned black beans, drained

In a bowl, combine pepper, paprika, chili powder, cayenne pepper, salt, onion powder and garlic salt. Rub onto brisket pieces to coat. Add the brisket to your Instant Pot. Cover with Worcestershire sauce and water. Seal the pressure lid, choose Pressure Cook, and set the timer to 50 minutes. Release pressure naturally for 10 minutes. Transfer the brisket to a cutting board. Drain any liquid present in the using a fine-mesh strainer. Get rid of any solids and fat. Slice brisket, arrange the slices onto a platter, add the black beans on the side, and spoon the cooking liquid over.

470. Short Ribs with Mushrooms & Asparagus Sauce

Servings: 6 | Ready in about: 1 hour 15 minutes

3 ½ lb boneless beef short ribs, cut into pieces
Salt and black pepper to taste
3 tbsp olive oil
1 onion, diced
1 cup dry red wine
1 tbsp tomato puree
2 carrots, peeled and chopped
2 garlic cloves, minced
5 sprigs parsley, chopped
2 sprigs rosemary, chopped
3 sprigs oregano, chopped
4 cups beef stock
10 oz mushrooms, quartered
1 cup asparagus, chopped
1 tbsp cornstarch

Apply a seasoning of black pepper and salt to the ribs. Warm oil on Sauté in your Instant Pot. In batches, add the short ribs to the oil and cook for 3 to 5 minutes each side until browned. Set aside on a bowl. Add onions to the hot oil and cook for 3 to 5 minutes until soft. Add tomato puree and red wine into the pot to deglaze, scrape the bottom to get rid of any browned beef bits. Cook for 2 minutes until wine reduces slightly.

Return the ribs to pot and top with carrots, oregano, rosemary, and garlic. Add in beef broth. Seal the pressure lid, choose Pressure Cook on High, and set the timer to 35 minutes. Release pressure naturally for 10 minutes. Transfer ribs to a plate. Strain and get rid of herbs and vegetables, and return cooking broth to the pot. Add mushrooms and asparagus to the broth. Press Sauté and cook for 2 to 4 minutes until vegetables are soft.

In a bowl, mix ¼ cup cold water and cornstarch until cornstarch dissolves completely. Add the cornstarch mixture into the broth as you stir for 1 to 3 minutes until the broth thickens slightly. Season the sauce with black pepper and salt. Pour the sauce over ribs, add chopped parsley for garnish before serving.

471. Meatballs with Marinara Sauce

Servings: 6 | Ready in about: 35 minutes

1½ lb ground beef
⅓ cup warm water
¾ cup grated Parmigiano-Reggiano
½ cup bread crumbs
1 egg
2 tbsp fresh parsley
¼ tsp garlic powder
¼ tsp dried oregano
Salt and black pepper to taste
½ cup capers
1 tsp olive oil
3 cups marinara sauce

In a large bowl, mix ground beef, garlic powder, pepper, oregano, bread crumbs, egg, and salt. Shape into meatballs. Warm the oil on Sauté in your Instant Pot. Add meatballs to the oil and brown for 2-3 minutes and all sides. Pour water and marinara sauce over the meatballs. Seal the pressure lid, choose Pressure Cook, and set the timer to 10 minutes. When ready, release the pressure quickly. Top with capers and Parmigiano-Reggiano cheese.

472. Beef Stew with Veggies

Servings: 6 | Ready in about: 1 hour 15 minutes

¼ cup flour
1 tsp paprika
2 lb beef chuck, cubed
2 tbsp olive oil
2 tbsp butter
1 onion, diced
3 garlic cloves, minced
1 cup dry red wine
2 cups beef stock
1 tbsp dried Italian seasoning
2 tsp Worcestershire sauce
4 cups potatoes, diced
2 celery stalks, chopped
3 cups carrots, chopped
3 tomatoes, chopped
2 bell pepper, thinly sliced
Salt and black pepper to taste
2 tbsp fresh parsley

In a bowl, mix black pepper, beef, flour, paprika, and salt. Toss the ingredients and ensure the beef is coated. Warm butter and oil on Sauté. Add in beef and cook for 8- 10 minutes until browned. Set aside on a plate. To the same fat, add garlic, onion, and celery, bell peppers, and cook for 4-5 minutes until tender.

Deglaze with wine, scrape the bottom to get rid of any browned beef bits. Pour in salt, beef stock, Worcestershire sauce, and Italian seasoning. Return beef to the pot. Add carrots, tomatoes, and potatoes. Seal the pressure lid, choose Pressure Cook on High, and set the timer to 35 minutes. Release pressure naturally for 10 minutes. Serve on plates and scatter over the parsley.

473. Beef & Pumpkin Stew

Servings: 6 | Ready in about: 35 minutes

2 tbsp canola oil	1 tsp garlic powder	3 carrots, sliced
2 lb stew beef, cut into 1-inch chunks	1 tsp salt	½ butternut pumpkin, sliced
1 cup red wine	3 whole cloves	2 tbsp cornstarch
1 onion, chopped	1 bay leaf	3 tbsp water

Warm oil on Sauté in your Instant Pot. Add beef and brown for 5 minutes on each side. Deglaze the pot with wine, scrape the bottom to get rid of any browned beef bits. Add in onion, salt, bay leaf, cloves, and garlic powder. Seal the pressure lid, choose Pressure Cook on High, and set the timer to 15 minutes. When ready, release the pressure quickly. Add in pumpkin and carrots without stirring. Seal the pressure lid again, choose Pressure Cook on High, and set the timer to 5 minutes. When ready, release the pressure quickly. In a bowl, mix water and cornstarch until cornstarch dissolves completely. Mix into the stew. Allow the stew to simmer while uncovered on Keep Warm for 5 minutes until you attain the desired thickness.

474. Braised Short Ribs with Creamy Sauce

Servings: 6 | Ready in about: 1 hour 55 minutes

3 lb beef short ribs	1 celery stalk, chopped	¼ cup red wine vinegar
Salt and black pepper to taste	3 garlic cloves, chopped	2 bay leaves
2 tbsp olive oil	2 cups beef broth	¼ tsp red pepper flakes
1 onion, chopped	1 (14.5 oz) can diced tomatoes	2 tbsp chopped parsley
1 large carrot, chopped	½ cup dry red wine	1/2 cup cheese cream

Season your short ribs with 1 tsp black pepper and salt. Warm olive oil on Sauté in your Instant Pot. Add in short ribs and sear for 3 minutes each side until browned. Set aside on a bowl. Drain everything only to be left with 1 tbsp of the remaining fat from the pot. Set on Sauté, and stir-fry garlic, carrot, onion, and celery in the hot fat for 4 to 6 minutes until fragrant. Stir in broth, wine, red pepper flakes, vinegar, tomatoes, bay leaves, pepper, and salt.

Turn the pot to Sauté on Low and bring the mixture to a boil. With the bone-side up, lay short ribs into the braising liquid. Seal the pressure lid, choose Pressure Cook on High, and set the timer to 40 minutes. When ready, release the pressure quickly. Set the short ribs on a plate. Get rid of bay leaves. Using an immersion blender, blitz the liquid for 1 minute. Add cream cheese, pepper and salt and blend until smooth. Arrange the ribs onto a serving plate, pour the sauce over and top with parsley.

475. Italian-Style Pot Roast

Servings: 5 | Ready in about: 1 hour 30 minutes

2 ½ lb beef brisket, trimmed	1 cup beef broth	4 oz pancetta, chopped
2 tbsp olive oil	¾ cup dry red wine	6 carrots, chopped
1 onion, chopped	2 fresh thyme sprigs	1 bay leaf
3 garlic cloves, minced	2 fresh rosemary sprigs	A handful of parsley, chopped

Warm olive oil on Sauté in your Instant Pot. Fry the pancetta for 4-5 minutes until crispy. Set aside. Season the beef with pepper and salt and add it to the pot and brown for 5 to 7 minutes for each. Remove and set aside on a plate. In the same oil, fry garlic and onion for 3 minutes until softened. Pour in red wine and beef broth to deglaze the bottom, scrape the bottom of the pot to get rid of any browned bits of food.

Return the beef and pancetta to the pot and add rosemary sprigs and thyme. Seal the pressure lid, choose Pressure Cook on High, and set the timer to 50 minutes. When ready, release the pressure quickly. Add carrots and bay leaf to the pot. Seal the pressure lid again, choose Pressure Cook on High, and set the timer to 4 minutes. When ready, release the pressure quickly. Get rid of the thyme, bay leaf and rosemary sprigs. Place beef on a serving plate and sprinkle with parsley to serve.

476. BBQ Sticky Baby Back Ribs with

Servings: 6 | Ready in about: 40 minutes

2 tbsp olive oil	1 tbsp mustard powder	1/3 cup ketchup
1 rack baby back ribs, cut into bones	1 tbsp smoked paprika	1 cup barbecue sauce
Salt and black pepper to taste	1 tbsp dried oregano	½ cup apple cider

In a bowl, thoroughly combine salt, mustard powder, smoked paprika, oregano, and black pepper. Rub the mixture over the ribs. Warm oil on Sauté in your Instant Pot. Add in the ribs and sear for 1 to 2 minutes for each side until browned. Pour apple cider and barbecue sauce into your Instant Pot. Turn the ribs to coat. Seal the pressure lid, choose Pressure Cook for 30 minutes. When ready, release the pressure quickly. Place the air fry basket in the pot. Close the air fry lid, choose Air Fry, set the temperature to 390°F, and the time to 5 minutes.

Place the ribs with the sauce in the air fry basket. Close the air fry lid. Preheat the unit by selecting Air Fry, setting the temperature to 390°F, and setting the time to 7 minutes. When ready, the ribs should be sticky with a dark brown color. Transfer the ribs to a serving plate. Baste with the sauce to serve.

477. Swedish Meatballs with Mashed Cauliflower

Servings: 6 | Ready in about: 1 hour

¾ lb ground beef	1 tbsp water	½ tsp red wine vinegar
¾ lb ground pork	Salt and black pepper to taste	1 ¾ cup heavy cream, divided
1 large egg, beaten	4 tbsp butter, divided	1 head cauliflower, cut into florets
½ onion, minced	2 cups beef stock	¼ cup sour cream
¼ cup bread crumbs	3 tbsp flour	¼ cup fresh chopped parsley

In a mixing bowl, mix ground beef, onion, salt, bread crumbs, ground pork, egg, water, and pepper. Shape meatballs. Warm 2 tbsp of butter on Sauté in your Instant Pot. Add meatballs and cook until browned, about 5-6 minutes. Set aside. Pour beef stock in the pot to deglaze, scrape the pan to get rid of browned bits of food.

Stir vinegar and flour with the liquid in your Instant Pot until smooth. Bring to a boil. Stir ¾ cup heavy cream into the liquid. Arrange meatballs into the gravy. Place trivet onto meatballs. Arrange cauliflower florets onto the trivet. Seal the pressure lid, choose Pressure Cook on High, and set the timer to 8 minutes. When ready, release the pressure quickly. Set the cauliflower in a mixing bowl. Add in the remaining 1 cup heavy cream, pepper, sour cream, salt, and 2 tbsp butter and use a potato masher to mash the mixture until smooth. Spoon the mashed cauliflower onto serving bowls. Top with gravy and meatballs. Add parsley for garnishing.

478. Hot Pork Carnitas Lettuce Cups

Servings: 6 | Ready in about: 30 minutes + overnight refrigerated

3 lb pork shoulder	1 ½ cup water	1 tsp garlic powder
2 tbsp olive oil	1 onion, chopped	1 tsp white pepper
1 head lettuce, leaves removed	½ tsp Cayenne pepper	2 tsp dried oregano
2 Limes, cut in wedges	½ tsp coriander powder	1 tsp red pepper flakes
2 carrots, grated	1 tsp cumin powder	Salt to taste

In a bowl, add onion, cayenne, coriander, garlic, cumin, white pepper, dried oregano, red pepper flakes, and salt. Mix them well with a spoon. Drizzle over the pork and rub to coat. Then, wrap the meat in plastic wrap and refrigerate overnight. On the next day, open your Instant Pot lid, and select Sauté. Pour 2 tablespoons of olive oil in the pot and while heating, take the pork out from the fridge, remove the wraps and place it in your Instant Pot.

Brown it on both sides for 6 minutes and then pour the water. Seal the lid and select Pressure Cook for 15 minutes. Once ready, do a quick pressure release. Shred the pork. Close the air fry lid, and select Bake mode. Set for 10 minutes at 350°F. When ready, turn off the heat and begin assembling. Arrange double layers of lettuce leaves on a flat surface, make a bed of grated carrots in them, and spoon the pulled pork on them. Serve with lime.

479. Tomatillo & Sweet Potato pork Chili

Servings: 6 | Ready in about: 70 minutes

1 ½ lb pork roast, cut into 1-inch cubes
1 lb tomatillos, husks removed
2 tbsp olive oil, divided into 2
1 bulb garlic, tail sliced off, peeled
2 green chilies
3 cups chicken broth
1 green bell pepper, roughly chopped
Salt and black pepper to taste
½ tsp cumin powder
1 tsp dried oregano
1 bay leaf
1 bunch cilantro, chopped
2 sweet potatoes, peeled and cut into ½-inch cubes

Put the garlic bulb in a baking dish. Drizzle a bit of 1 portion of olive oil over the garlic bulb. Place the green bell peppers, onion, green chilies, and tomatillos on the dish in a single layer. Close the air fry lid and cook for 15 minutes at 400°F on Air Fry. Set aside to cool. Place the garlic in a blender. Add green bell pepper, tomatillos, onions, and green chilies. Pulse for a few minutes not to be smooth but slightly chunky.

Now, open the lid of your Instant Pot, and select Sauté. Pour in the remaining olive oil and while is heating, season the pork cubes with salt and pepper. Then, brown the pork, for about 5 minutes. Stir in oregano, cumin, bay leaf, pour in the blended green sauce, potatoes, and add the chicken broth. Stir well. Seal the lid and select Pressure Cook on High for 25 minutes. Once the timer has ended, let the pot sit closed for 10 minutes.

After, do a natural pressure release for 5 minutes, and then a quick pressure release to let the remaining steam out. Open the pot. Remove and discard the bay leaf, add half of the cilantro, adjust with salt and pepper, and stir. Close the air fry lid to give it nice and tender taste. Cook on Broil mode for 10 minutes. Dish the chili into serving bowls and garnish it with the remaining chopped cilantro. Serve topped with a side of chips or crusted bread.

480. Beer-Braised Short Ribs with Mushrooms

Servings: 4 | Ready in about: 1 hour

2 lb beef short ribs
1 tsp smoked paprika
½ tsp dried oregano
½ tsp cayenne pepper
1 tbsp olive oil
1 small onion, sliced
4 garlic cloves, smashed
1 cup beer
⅓ cup beef broth
1 cup crimini mushrooms, sliced
1 tbsp soy sauce
1 bell pepper, diced

In a small bowl, combine pepper, paprika, cayenne pepper, salt, and oregano. Rub the seasoning mixture on all sides of the short ribs. Warm oil on Sauté in your Instant Pot. Add mushrooms and cook until browned, about 6-8 minutes. Set aside. Add short ribs to the pot, and cook for 3 minutes for each side until browned. Set aside on a plate. Throw in garlic and onion to the oil and stir-fry for 2 minutes until fragrant.

Add in beer to deglaze, scrape the pot's bottom to get rid of any browned bits of food. Bring to a simmer and cook for 2 minutes until reduced slightly. Stir in soy sauce, bell pepper and beef broth. Dip short ribs into the liquid in a single layer. Seal the pressure lid, choose Pressure Cook on High, and set the timer to 40 minutes. Release pressure naturally for about 10 minutes. Divide the ribs with the sauce into bowls and top with fried mushrooms.

481. Beef & Turnip Chili

Servings: 6 | Ready in about: 30 minutes

1 tbsp olive oil
1 yellow onion, chopped
4 garlic cloves, minced
2 tbsp tomato puree
1 tbsp chili powder
2 tsp ground cumin
1 tsp dried oregano
½ tsp ground turmeric
1 pinch cayenne pepper
1 lb ground beef meat
1 (28 oz) can whole tomatoes
2 cups beef stock
1 lb turnips, peeled and cubed
2 tomatoes, chopped
1 bell pepper, chopped

Warm oil on Sauté in your Instant Pot. Add in onion and garlic and cook for 3 minutes until softened. Stir in chili powder, turmeric, cumin, tomato puree, oregano, and cayenne pepper for 2 to 3 minutes until very soft. Add beef and cook for 5 minutes until browned. Mix in tomatoes, turnips, bell pepper, and beef stock. Seal the pressure lid, choose Pressure Cook on High, and set the timer to 15 minutes. When ready, release the pressure quickly. Serve.

482. Sweet-Garlic Pork Tenderloin

Servings: 4 | Ready in about: 30 minutes

2 lb pork tenderloin
2 tbsp olive oil
¼ cup honey
½ cup chicken broth
Salt and black pepper to taste
1 clove garlic, minced
1 tsp sage powder
1 tbsp Dijon mustard
¼ cup Balsamic vinegar
1 tbsp Worcestershire sauce
½ tbsp cornstarch
4 tbsp water

Season the pork with salt and pepper. Select Sauté in your Instant Pot. Heat the oil and brown the pork on both sides for about 4 minutes in total. Remove the pork to a plate and set aside. Add in honey, chicken broth, balsamic vinegar, garlic, Worcestershire sauce, mustard, and sage. Stir the ingredients and return the pork to the pot. Seal the lid and select Pressure Cook on High for 15 minutes. Once the timer has ended, do a quick pressure release.

Remove the pork to a plate and wrap it in aluminum foil. Mix the cornstarch with water and pour it into the pot. Select Sauté mode, stir the mixture and cook until it thickens. Then, turn the pot off after the desired thickness is achieved. Unwrap the pork and use a knife to slice it with 3 to 4-inch thickness. Arrange the slices on a serving platter and spoon the sauce all over it. Serve with a syrupy sautéed Brussels sprouts and red onion chunks.

483. Crispy Pork Fajitas

Servings: 5 | Ready in about: 1 hour 30 minutes

1 tbsp ground cumin
2 tsp dried oregano
1 tsp paprika
1 tsp onion powder
1 tsp salt
1 tsp ground black pepper
1/2 tsp ground cinnamon
3 lb boneless pork shoulder
¾ cup vegetable broth
¼ cup pineapple juice
1 lime, juiced
4 cloves garlic, crushed
2 bay leaves
5 corn tortillas, warmed
½ cup queso Cotija, crumbled

In a bowl, combine cumin, paprika, pepper, onion powder, oregano, salt, and cinnamon. Toss in pork to coat. Place the pork in your Instant Pot and allow settling for 15 to 30 minutes. Add in chicken broth, garlic, lime juice, bay leaves, and pineapple juice. Seal the pressure lid, choose Pressure Cook, and set the timer to 50 minutes. When ready, release pressure naturally for 15 minutes, then release the remaining pressure quickly.

Transfer the pork to a rimmed baking sheet and use two forks to shred the meat. Reserve the juices in a bowl. Place the Cook & air fry basket into the inner pot. Close the air fry lid and choose Air Fry. Adjust the temperature to 380°F and the time to 4 minutes to preheat. Add the baking sheet to the air fry basket. Close the air fry lid. Select Air Fry. Adjust the temperature to 375°F and the cook time to 10 minutes. After 5 minutes, open the lid and toss the meat. Continue cooking until the pork is done. Skim and get rid of fat from the liquid remaining. Dispose of the bay leaves. Over the pork, pour the liquid and serve alongside warm corn tortillas and queso fresco.

484. Ranch Flavored Pork Roast with Gravy

Servings: 4 | Ready in about: 25 minutes

2 lb pork roast, cut into 2-inch slabs
1 tbsp Italian Seasoning
1 tbsp Ranch Dressing
1 tsp red wine vinegar
2 cloves garlic, minced
Salt and black pepper to taste
1 small onion, chopped
1 tbsp olive oil
2 tsp onion powder
½ tsp paprika
2 cups vegetable broth
2 tbsp cornstarch

Season the pork roast with salt and pepper, and set aside. In a bowl, add Italian seasoning, ranch dressing, red wine vinegar, garlic, onion powder, and paprika. Open in your Instant Pot, select Sauté, and heat the oil. Sauté the onion, until translucent. Pour the gravy mixture and broth over and add the pork. Seal the lid and select Pressure Cook on High for 15 minutes. Once the timer has ended, do a quick pressure release, and open the pot.

Remove the pork roast with a slotted spoon onto a serving plate. Mix the cornstarch with 2 tbsp of water in a small bowl and add it to the sauce. Select Sauté. Stir and cook the sauce for 4 minutes until thickens. Once the gravy is ready, turn off the pot and spoon the sauce over the pork. Serve with a turnip mash.

485. Stewed Beef with Portobello Mushrooms

Servings: 5 | Ready in about: 40 minutes

2 cups Portobello mushrooms, quartered		
1 lb boneless chuck steak, cut into chunks	1 cup pancetta, chopped	4 shallots, sliced
¼ cup flour	½ cup red burgundy wine	3 garlic cloves, crushed
1 tsp salt	1¼ cup beef broth	A handful of parsley, chopped
1 tsp ground black pepper	1 carrot, diced	

Toss beef with black pepper, salt, and flour in a large bowl to coat. Set Sauté on your Instant Pot. Cook pancetta for 5 minutes until brown and crispy. Pour in approximately half the beef and cook for 5 minutes each side until browned all over. Transfer the pancetta and beef to a plate. Sear remaining beef and transfer to the plate. Add in beef broth and wine to deglaze the pan, scrape the pan's bottom to get rid of any browned bits of food. Return beef and pancetta to cooker. Stir in garlic, carrot, shallots, and mushrooms. Seal the pressure lid, choose Pressure Cook, and set the timer to 30 minutes. When ready, release the pressure quickly. Garnish with parsley.

486. Peppercorn Meatloaf

Servings: 8 | Ready in about: 35 minutes

4 lb ground beef	1 onion, diced	1 tsp ground peppercorns
1 tbsp basil	1 tbsp Worcestershire sauce	10 whole peppercorns, for garnishing
1 tbsp oregano	3 tbsp ketchup	1 cup breadcrumbs
1 tbsp parsley	½ tsp salt	

Place the beef in a large bowl. Add all of the ingredients except the whole peppercorns and the breadcrumbs. Mix with your hand until well combined. Stir in the breadcrumbs. Put the meatloaf on a lined baking dish. Insert in your Instant Pot, close the air fry lid and cook for 25 minutes on Air Fry mode at 350°F. Garnish the meatloaf with the whole peppercorns and let cool slightly before serving.

487. Classic Beef Bourguignon

Servings: 4 | Ready in about: 45 minutes

2 lb stewing beef, cut into large chunks	3 tsp tomato paste	1 cup red wine
Salt and black pepper to taste	½ lb mushrooms, sliced	2 cups beef broth
2 ½ tbsp olive oil	2 carrots, peeled and chopped	1 bunch thyme
¼ tsp red wine vinegar	1 onion, sliced	½ cup cognac
¼ cup pearl onion	2 cloves garlic, crushed	2 tbsp flour

Select Sauté on your Instant Pot. Season the beef with salt, pepper, and a light sprinkle of flour. Heat the oil and brown the meat on all sides. Pour in the cognac and stir to deglaze the bottom. Add in thyme, red wine, broth, paste, garlic, mushrooms, onion, and pearl onions. Seal the lid and select Pressure Cook for 25 minutes. Once the timer is off, do a quick pressure release. Close the air fry lid and cook for 10 minutes on Broil at 390 F. When ready, remove the thyme, adjust the taste with salt and pepper, and add the vinegar. Stir the sauce and serve hot.

488. Ranch Pork with Mushroom Sauce

Servings: 4 | Ready in about: 22 minutes

4 pork loin chops	1 oz Ranch Dressing seasoning mix	Chopped parsley to garnish
1 (15 oz) can mushroom soup cream	½ cup chicken broth	

Add pork, mushroom soup cream, ranch dressing and seasoning mix, and chicken broth inside your Instant Pot. Seal the lid and select Pressure Cook on High for 10 minutes. Once the timer has ended, do a natural pressure release for 10 minutes, then a quick pressure release to let the remaining steam out. Close the air fry lid and cook for 5 minutes on Broil mode, until tender. Serve with well-seasoned sautéed cremini mushrooms, and the sauce.

489. Mississippi Pot Roast with Potatoes

Servings: 6 | Ready in about: 1 hour 40 minutes

1 tbsp canola oil	1 onion, finely chopped	6 cups beef broth
2 lb chuck roast	1 tsp onion powder	½ cup pepperoncini juice
2 tsp salt	1 tsp garlic powder	10 pepperoncini
½ tsp black pepper	½ tsp dried thyme	5 potatoes, peeled and sliced
¼ cup butter	½ tsp dried parsley	2 bay leaves

Warm oil on Sauté in your Instant Pot. Season chuck roast with pepper and salt, then sear in the hot oil for 2 to 4 minutes for each side until browned. Set aside. Melt butter and cook the onion for 3 minutes until fragrant. Sprinkle with dried parsley, onion powder, dried thyme, and garlic powder and stir for 30 seconds. Into the pot, stir bay leaves, beef broth, pepperoncini juice, and pepperoncini. Nestle chuck roast down into the liquid. Seal the pressure lid, choose Pressure Cook on High, and set the timer to 60 minutes. Release pressure naturally for about 10 minutes. Set the chuck roast to a cutting board and use two forks to shred. Serve immediately.

490. Beef & Bacon Chili

Servings: 6 | Ready in about: 1 hour

2 lb stewing beef, trimmed	2 bell peppers, diced	1 chipotle in adobo sauce, chopped
Salt and black pepper to taste	3 garlic cloves, minced	2 cups beef broth
4 oz smoked bacon, cut into strips	1 tbsp ground cumin	29 oz canned whole tomatoes
2 tsp olive oil, divided	1 tsp chili powder	15 oz canned kidney beans, drained
1 onion, diced	½ tsp cayenne pepper	

Set Sauté on your Instant Pot and fry the bacon until crispy, about 5 minutes. Set aside. Rub the beef with ½ tsp black pepper and 1 tsp salt. In the bacon fat, brown beef for 5-6 minutes. Transfer to a plate.

Warm the oil. Add in garlic, peppers and onion and cook for 3 to 4 minutes until soft. Stir in cumin, cayenne pepper, the extra pepper and salt, chopped chipotle, and chili powder and cook for 30 seconds until soft. Return beef and bacon to the pot with vegetables and spices. Add in tomatoes and broth. Seal the pressure lid, choose Pressure Cook on High, and set the timer to 45 minutes. When ready, release the pressure quickly. Stir in beans. Let simmer on Keep Warm for 10 minutes until flavors combine.

491. Traditional Beef Stroganoff

Servings: 6 | Ready in about: 1 hour 15 minutes

¼ cup flour	1 onion, chopped	8 oz sour cream
Salt and black pepper to taste	2 garlic cloves, minced	1 tbsp chopped fresh parsley
2 lb beef stew meat	1 cup beef broth	1 cup long-grain rice, cooked
2 tbsp olive oil	3 cups fresh mushrooms, chopped	

In a large bowl, combine salt, pepper and flour. Add beef and massage to coat beef in flour mixture. Warm oil on Sauté in your Instant Pot. Brown the beef for 4 to 5 minutes. Add garlic and onion and cook for 3 minutes until fragrant. Add beef broth to the pot. Seal the pressure lid, choose Pressure Cook on High, and set the timer to 35 minutes. When ready, release the pressure quickly. Stir mushrooms and sour cream into the beef mixture. Seal the pressure lid again, choose Pressure Cook on High, and set the timer to 2 minutes. When ready, release the pressure quickly. Season the stroganoff with pepper and salt. Scoop over cooked rice before serving.

492. Italian Beef Sandwiches with Pesto

Servings: 4 | Ready in about: 1 hour

1 ½ lb beef steak, cut into strips	1 tbsp olive oil	1 cup beef broth
Salt and black pepper to taste	¼ cup dry red wine	1 tbsp oregano

1 tsp onion powder	4 hoagie rolls, halved	½ cup sliced pepperoncini peppers
1 tsp garlic powder	8 slices mozzarella cheese	4 tbsp pesto

Sprinkle pepper and salt to season the beef cubes and bring to room temperature. Warm oil on Sauté in your Instant Pot. Add in the beef and sear for 2 to 3 minutes for each side until browned. Add wine into the pot to deglaze, scrape the bottom to get rid of any browned beef bits. Stir garlic powder, beef broth, onion powder, and oregano into the pot. Seal the pressure lid, choose Pressure Cook on High, and set the timer to 25 minutes. Release pressure naturally for 10 minutes. Spread each bread half with pesto, put beef on top, place pepperoncini slices over, add mozzarella cheese slices and cover with the second half of bread to serve.

493. Pork Tenderloin with Garlic and Ginger

Servings: 4 | Ready in about: 23 minutes

2 lb pork tenderloin	3 tbsp grated ginger	2 tsp cornstarch
½ cup soy sauce	2 cloves garlic, minced	Chopped scallions to garnish
¼ cup sugar	2 tbsp sesame oil	Sesame seeds to garnish

In your Instant Pot, add soy sauce, sugar, half cup of water, ginger, garlic, and sesame oil. Use a spoon to stir them. Add in the pork. Seal the lid and select Pressure Cook on High for 12 minutes. Once the timer has ended, do a quick pressure release, and open the pot. Remove the pork and set aside. In a bowl, mix the cornstarch with 2 tbsp water until smooth and pour it into the pot. Bring back the pork. Close the air fry lid and press Broil. Cook for 5 minutes until the sauce has thickened. Stir the sauce, every 1-2 minutes to avoid burning. Once the sauce is ready, serve the pork with a side endive salad. Spoon the sauce all over it.

494. Pork Sandwiches with Slaw

Servings: 8 | Ready in about: 20 minutes

2 lb chuck roast	1 tsp garlic powder	Salt to taste
¼ cup sugar	1 white onion, sliced	2 tbsp apple cider vinegar
1 tsp Spanish paprika	2 cups beef broth	
Assembling:		
4 Buns, halved	4 tbsp mayonnaise	1 cup white cabbage, shredded
1 cup white Cheddar cheese, grated	1 cup red cabbage, shredded	

Place the pork roast on a clean flat surface and sprinkle with paprika, garlic powder, sugar, and salt. Use your hands to rub the seasoning on the meat. Open your Instant Pot, add beef broth, onions, pork, and apple cider vinegar. Seal the lid and select Pressure Cook on High for 12 minutes. Once ended, do a quick pressure release. Remove the roast to a cutting board, and use two forks to shred them. Return to the pot, close the air fry lid, and cook for 3 minutes on Air Fry at 300°F. In the buns, spread the mayo, add the shredded pork, some cooked onions from the pot, and shredded red and white cabbage. Top with the cheese.

495. BBQ Pork Ribs

Servings: 2 | Ready in about: 45 minutes

½ lb rack baby back ribs	¼ cup beef broth	3 tbsp apple cider vinegar
Salt and pepper to season	½ cup Barbecue sauce	

Select Sauté on your Instant Pot. Heat the oil. Season the ribs with salt and pepper. Cook them to brown, for 1 to 2 minutes per side. Pour the barbecue sauce, broth, and apple cider vinegar over the ribs and use tongs to flip so they are well coated. Close the lid and pressure valve and set to Pressure Cook on High for 30 minutes. Once the timer goes off, do a natural pressure release for 12 minutes. Close the air fry lid and set to Air Fry mode for 5 minutes at 350°F. Make sure the sauce is thick enough. Use a knife to slice the ribs and over the sauce all over it. Serve the ribs with a generous side of steamed but crunchy green beans.

496. Cuban-Style Pork

Servings: 8 | Ready in about: 2 hour 30 minutes

½ cup orange juice
¼ cup lime juice
¼ cup canola oil
¼ cup chopped fresh cilantro
1 tsp red pepper flakes
8 cloves garlic, minced
1 tbsp ground cumin
1 tbsp fresh oregano
3 lb pork shoulder

In a bowl, mix orange juice, olive oil, cumin, salt, pepper, oregano, lime juice, and garlic. Add to a plastic bag alongside the pork. Seal and massage the bag to ensure the marinade covers the pork completely. Place in the refrigerator for 1 hour. In your Instant Pot, set the removed pork from bag. Add the marinade on top. Seal the pressure lid, choose Pressure Cook on High, and set the timer to 50 minutes. Release pressure naturally for 15 minutes. Transfer the pork to a cutting board. Use a fork to break into smaller pieces. Skim and get rid of the fat from liquid in the cooker. Serve the liquid with pork and sprinkle with cilantro.

497. Mediterranean Tender Pork Roast

Servings: 6 | Ready in about: 60 minutes

3 lb pork roast, cut into 3-inch pieces
1 tsp Cavender's Greek seasoning
1 tsp onion powder
1 cup beef broth
½ cup Kalamata olives, pitted
¼ cup fresh lemon juice

Put the pork chunks in the inner pot of your Instant Pot. In a bowl, add greek seasoning, onion powder, beef broth, lemon juice, olives, and salt to taste. Mix using a spoon and pour the sauce over the pork. Seal the lid and select Pressure Cook on High for 35 minutes. Once the timer is off, do a natural pressure release for 10 minutes. Open the pot. Use two forks to shred the roast inside to pot and close the air fry lid. Cook on Broil mode for 10 minutes, until nice and tender. Serve with a green salad, potatoes or rice.

498. Garlicky Braised Pork Neck Bones

Servings: 6 | Ready in about: 40 minutes

3 lb pork neck bones
4 tbsp olive oil
Salt and black pepper to taste
2 cloves garlic, smashed
1 tbsp tomato paste
1 tsp dried thyme
1 white onion, sliced
½ cup red wine
1 cup beef broth

Open your Instant Pot and select Sauté. Warm the olive oil. Season the pork neck bones with salt and pepper. After, place them in the oil to brown on all sides. Work in batches. Each batch should cook in about 5 minutes. Remove them onto a plate. Add the onion and season with salt to taste. Stir and cook the onions until soft for 5 minutes. Add garlic, thyme, pepper, and tomato paste. Cook for 2 minutes, constantly.

Pour in the red wine to deglaze the bottom. Add the pork neck bones back to the pot and pour the beef broth over it. Seal the lid and select Pressure Cook for 10 minutes. Once the timer has ended, do a quick pressure release. Close the air fry lid and cook on Broil mode for 5 minutes, until nice and tender. Dish the pork neck into a serving bowl and serve with the red wine sauce spooned over and a right amount of broccoli mash.

499. Sweet & Sour Pork

Servings: 4 | Ready in about: 40 minutes

1 lb pork loin, cut into chunks
2 tbsp white wine
15 oz canned peaches
¼ cup beef stock
2 tbsp sweet chili sauce
2 tbsp honey
2 tbsp soy sauce
2 tbsp cornstarch
¼ cup water

Into your Instant Pot, mix soy sauce, beef stock, white wine, juice from the canned peaches, and sweet chili sauce. Stir in pork to coat. Seal the pressure lid, choose Pressure Cook on High, and set the timer to 5 minutes. Release pressure naturally for 10 minutes. Remove the pork to a serving plate. Chop the peaches into small pieces.

In a bowl, mix water and cornstarch until cornstarch dissolves completely. Stir the mixture into your Instant Pot. Press Sauté and cook for 5 more minutes until you obtain the desired thick consistency. Add in the chopped peaches and stir well. Serve the pork topped with peach sauce and enjoy.

500. Garlick & Ginger Pork with Coconut Sauce

Servings: 6 | Ready in about: 45 minutes

3 lb shoulder roast
1 tbsp olive oil
Salt and black pepper to season
2 cups coconut milk
1 tsp Coriander powder
1 tsp cumin powder
3 tbsp grated ginger
3 tsp minced garlic
½ cup beef broth
1 onion, peeled and quartered
Parsley leaves (unchopped), to garnish

In a bowl, add coriander, salt, pepper, and cumin. Use a spoon to mix them. Season the pork with the spice mixture. Rub the spice onto meat, with hands. Open the lid of your Instant Pot, add olive oil, pork, onions, ginger, garlic, broth and coconut milk. Seal the lid and select Pressure Cook on High for 30 minutes. Once the timer has stopped, do a quick pressure release. Give it a good stir and close the air fry lid. Cook for 10 minutes on Broil mode, until you perfect texture and creaminess. Dish the meat with the sauce into a serving bowl, garnish it with the parsley and serve with a side of bread or cooked shrimp.

501. Pork Chops with Broccoli and Gravy

Servings: 6 | Ready in about: 45 minutes

Pork Chops:
1 tsp garlic powder
1 tsp onion powder
Gravy:
3 tbsp flour
1 tsp red pepper flakes
6 boneless pork chops
1 broccoli head, broken into florets
½ cup heavy cream
1 cup chicken stock
¼ cup butter, melted
¼ cup milk
Salt and black pepper to taste

Combine salt, garlic powder, red pepper flakes, onion powder, and black pepper. Rub the mixture to the pork chops. Place stock and broccoli into the pot. Lay the pork chops on top. Seal the pressure lid, choose Pressure Cook on High, and set the timer to 15 minutes. When ready, release the pressure quickly. Transfer the pork chops and broccoli to a plate. Press Sauté and simmer the liquid remaining in the pot. Mix cream and flour. Pour into the simmering liquid and cook for 5 to 7 minutes until thickened and bubbly. Season with pepper and salt. Top the chops with gravy before, drizzle melted butter over broccoli and serve.

502. Pork Chops with Squash Purée

Servings: 4 | Ready in about: 45 minutes

2 tbsp olive oil
2 sprigs thyme, chopped
2 sprigs rosemary, chopped
4 pork chops
1 cup mushrooms, chopped
4 cloves garlic, minced
1 cup chicken broth
1 tbsp soy sauce
1 lb butternut squash, cubed
1 tbsp olive oil
1 tsp cornstarch

Set to Sauté your Instant Pot and heat 1 tbsp of olive oil. Add in the pork chops and sear for 1 minute for each side until lightly browned. Add in garlic and mushrooms and cook for 5-6 minutes until tender. Stir in rosemary and thyme for 1 minute. Pour in soy sauce and broth. Transfer pork chops to a wire trivet and place it into the pressure cooker. Over the chops, place a cake pan. Add butternut squash in the pot and drizzle with 1 tbsp olive oil.

Seal the pressure lid, choose Pressure Cook on High, and set the timer to 10 minutes. When ready, release the pressure quickly. Remove the pan and trivet from the pot. Stir cornstarch into the mushroom mixture. Cook for 2 minutes until the sauce thickens. Transfer the mushroom sauce to an immersion blender and blend until you attain the desired consistency. Scoop sauce into a cup with a pour spout. Smash the squash into a purée. Set pork chops on a plate and ladle squash puree next to them. Top the pork chops with gravy.

503. Pork Tenderloin with Sweet Pepper Sauce

Servings: 4 | Ready in about: 35 minutes

1 roasted red bell pepper, cut into strips	½ cup dry white wine	2 medium garlic cloves, finely minced
1 ¼ pork tenderloin, cut into 2 pieces	1 lb russet potatoes, quartered	6 pickled pimientos, quartered
Salt and black pepper to taste	¼ cup chicken stock	2 tsp pickling liquid from the peppers
2 tbsp olive oil	1 thyme sprig	2 tbsp unsalted butter

Season the pork pieces with salt and black pepper on all sides. On your Instant Pot, choose Sauté. Pour in the oil into the pot and heat until shimmering. Add the pork, sear for 4-5 minutes until browned on all sides. Remove the pork to a plate. Pour in the wine into the pot and scrape off any browned bits at the bottom.

Let the wine cook until reduced by one-third. Stir in the potatoes, chicken stock, thyme, and garlic. Return the pork to the pot. Seal the pressure lid, choose Pressure Cook on High and the cook time to 20 minutes. After cooking, perform a natural pressure release for 10 minutes. Carefully open the pressure lid.

Remove the pork and allow resting while you finish the sauce. Remove and discard the thyme. Choose Sauté. Cook the potatoes for 2 to 4 minutes or until tender. Stir in the roasted pepper, pimiento, and the pickling liquid. Taste and adjust the seasoning. Right before serving, turn off the heat and stir in the butter. Slice the tenderloin and lay the pieces on a platter. Ladle the peppers and potatoes around the pork and spoon the sauce over.

504. The Crispiest Roast Pork

Servings: 4 | Ready in about: 50 minutes

4 pork tenderloins	½ tsp white pepper	1 tsp salt
1 tsp five spice seasoning	¾ tsp garlic powder	Cooking spray

Place the pork, white pepper, garlic powder, five seasoning, and salt into a bowl and toss to coat. Leave to marinate at room temperature for 30 minutes. Place the pork into the air fry basket, greased with cooking spray, close the air fry lid and cook for 20 minutes at 360°F. After 10 minutes, turn the tenderloins. Serve hot.

505. Pork Carnitas Wraps

Servings: 12 | Ready in about: 1 hour 15 minutes

2 tsp grapeseed oil	2 limes, juiced	1 avocado, sliced
1 (4 to 5 lb) boneless pork shoulder	2 tbsp sweet smoked paprika	Fresh cilantro leaves, chopped
1 onion, sliced	1 tbsp dried oregano	2 tsp ground black pepper
2 garlic cloves, minced	1 tbsp salt	12 corn tortillas, warmed
2 oranges, juiced	2 jalapeños, sliced	

Warm oil on Sauté in your Instant Pot. Add in pork and cook for 5 minutes until golden. Transfer the pork to a plate. Add garlic and onions to the inner pot and cook for 2 to 3 minutes until soft. Add lime and orange juices into the pot to deglaze, scrape the bottom to get rid of any browned bits of food. Stir in pepper, paprika, salt and oregano. Return the pork to pot. Stir to coat in seasoning and liquid. Seal the pressure lid, choose Pressure Cook.

Set the timer to 35 minutes. When ready, release the pressure quickly. Press Sauté. When the liquid starts to simmer, use two forks to shred the pork. Cook for 10 more minutes until liquid is reduced by half. Serve in warmed tortillas topped with jalapeños, avocado slices and cilantro.

506. Savory Pork Loin with Celery Sauce

Servings: 4 | Ready in about: 35 minutes

2 lb pork loin roast	1 medium onion, diced	3 carrots, chopped
Salt and black pepper to taste	2 tbsp butter	1 cup vegetable broth
3 cloves garlic, minced	3 stalks celery, chopped	2 tbsp Worcestershire sauce

½ tbsp sugar
1 tsp yellow mustard

2 tsp dried basil
2 tsp dried thyme

1 tbsp cornstarch
¼ cup water

Select Sauté on your Instant Pot, and heat oil. Season the pork with salt and pepper. Sear the pork to golden brown on both sides, about 4 minutes. Then, add the garlic and onions, and cook them until soft, for about 4 minutes. Top with the celery, carrots, broth, Worcestershire sauce, mustard, thyme, basil, and sugar. Seal the lid and select Pressure Cook on High for 15 minutes. Once the timer is off, do a quick pressure release.

Next, add the cornstarch to the water in a bowl, and mix with a spoon, until nice and smooth. Add it to the pot, close the air fry lid, and cook on Broil mode, for 3 - 5 minutes, until the sauce becomes a slurry with a bit of thickness, and the pork is nice and tender. Adjust the seasoning, and ladle to a serving platter. Serve.

507. Chunky Pork Meatloaf with Mashed Potatoes

Servings: 4 | Ready in about: 55 minutes

1 tbsp olive oil
1 cup chopped white onion
2 garlic cloves, minced
12 oz pork meatloaf
2 tsp salt
½ tsp black pepper

3 tbsp chopped fresh cilantro
¼ tsp dried rosemary
12 individual saltine crackers, crushed
1¾ cups full cream milk, divided
2 large eggs
1 tsp yellow mustard

1 tsp Worcestershire sauce
½ cup heavy cream
2 lb potatoes, cut into large chunks
3 tbsp unsalted butter
¼ cup barbecue sauce

Select Sauté in your Instant Pot. Heat the olive oil until shimmering and sauté the onion and garlic in the oil. Cook for about 2 minutes until the onion softens. Transfer the onion and garlic to a plate and set aside. In a bowl, crumble the meatloaf mix into small pieces. Sprinkle with 1 teaspoon of salt, the pepper, cilantro, and thyme. Add the sautéed onion and garlic. Sprinkle the crushed saltine crackers over the meat and seasonings.

In a small bowl, beat ¼ cup of milk, the eggs, mustard, and Worcestershire sauce. Pour the mixture on the layered cracker crumbs and gently mix the ingredients in the bowl with your hands. Shape the meat mixture into an 8-inch round. Cover a trivet with aluminum foil and carefully lift the meatloaf on the trivet. Pour the remaining 1½ cups of milk and the heavy cream into the inner pot. Add the potatoes, butter, and remaining salt. Place a trivet with meatloaf over the potatoes in the upper position in the pot. Seal the pressure lid, choose Pressure Cook on High and the cook time to 25 minutes.

After cooking, perform a quick pressure release, and carefully open the pressure lid. Brush the meatloaf with the barbecue sauce. Close the air fry lid, choose Broil and adjust the cook time to 7 minutes. Press Start to begin grilling. When the top has browned, remove the trivet, and transfer the meatloaf to a serving platter. Mash the potatoes in the pot. Slice the meatloaf and serve with the mashed potatoes.

508. Pulled Pork Tacos

Servings: 5 | Ready in about: 1 hour 25 minutes

3 tbsp sugar
3 tsp taco seasoning
1 tsp ground black pepper
2 lb pork shoulder, cut into chunks

1 cup beer
1 cup vegetable broth
¼ cup plus 2 tbsp lemon juice
¼ cup mayonnaise

2 tbsp honey
2 tsp mustard
3 cups shredded cabbage
5 taco tortillas

In a bowl, combine sugar, taco seasoning, and black pepper. Rub the mixture onto pork pieces to coat well. Allow to settling for 30 minutes. Into the pot, add 1/4 cup lemon juice, broth, pork and beer. Seal the pressure lid, choose Pressure Cook on High, and set the timer to 50 minutes.

Meanwhile in a large bowl, mix mayonnaise, mustard, 2 tbsp lemon juice, cabbage and honey until well coated. Release pressure naturally for 15 minutes before doing a quick release. Transfer the pork to a cutting board and Allow cooling before using two forks to shred. Skim and get rid of fat from liquid in the pressure cooker. Return pork to the pot and mix with the liquid. Top the pork with slaw on taco tortillas before serving.

509. Italian Sausage with Potato Mash & Gravy

Servings: 4 | Ready in about: 40 minutes

2 lb potatoes, peeled and halved	Salt and black pepper to taste	3 tbsp balsamic vinegar
4 Italian sausages	4 tbsp milk	1 onion, sliced thinly
1 cup water + 2 tbsp water	¼ cup + 2 tbsp + 2 tbsp butter	1 cup + 2 tbsp beef broth
⅓ cup green onion, sliced	1 tbsp cornstarch	

Put the potatoes in in your Instant Pot and pour in 1 cup water. Seal the lid and select Steam for 15 minutes. Do a quick pressure release and remove the potatoes to a bowl. Add in a quarter cup butter and use a masher to mash them until the butter is well mixed. Slowly add the milk and mix it using a spoon. Add the green onions, season with pepper and salt and fold it in with the spoon. Set aside.

Pour out the liquid in your Instant Pot, and use paper towels to wipe inside the pot dry. Select Sauté and melt two tablespoons of butter. Brown the sausages on each side for 3 minutes. Remove to the potato mash and cover with aluminium foil to keep warm. Set aside. Back into the pot, add the two tablespoons of the beef broth to deglaze the bottom of the pot while stirring and scraping the bottom with a spoon. Add the remaining butter and onions. Sauté the onions until translucent, then pour in the balsamic vinegar. Stir for another minute.

In a bowl, mix the cornstarch with water and pour into the pot. Add the remaining beef broth. Allow the sauce to thicken and adjust the seasoning. Turn off the heat once a slurry is formed. Dish the mashed potatoes and sausages in serving plates. Spoon the gravy over it and serve immediately with steamed green beans.

510. Red Pork & Chickpea Stew

Servings: 6 | Ready in about: 40 minutes

1 tbsp olive oil	½ cup sweet paprika	2 red bell peppers, chopped
1 (3 lb) boneless pork shoulder, cubed	2 tsp salt	6 cloves garlic, minced
1 white onion, chopped	1 tbsp chilli powder	1 tbsp cornstarch
15 oz canned chickpeas, drained	1 bay leaf	

Set on Sauté. Add pork and oil and allow cooking for 5 minutes until browned. Add in the onion, paprika, bay leaf, salt, 1 ½ cups water, chickpeas, and chili powder. Seal the pressure lid, choose Pressure Cook for 8 minutes. Do a quick release. Discard bay leaf. Remove 1 cup of cooking liquid from the pot. Add to a blender alongside garlic, 1 tbsp water, cornstarch, and red bell peppers. Blend well until smooth. Pour in the pot and mix well.

511. Char Siew Pork Ribs

Servings: 6 | Ready in about: 4 hours 55 minutes

2 lb pork ribs	2 tbsp hoisin sauce	4 garlic cloves, minced
2 tbsp char siew sauce	2 tbsp sesame oil	1 tbsp soy sauce
2 tbsp minced ginger	1 tbsp honey	

Whisk together all marinade ingredients, in a small bowl. Coat the ribs well with the mixture. Place in a container with a lid, and refrigerate for 4 hours. Place the ribs in the basket but do not throw away the liquid from the container. Close the air fry lid and cook for 40 minutes on Air Fry at 350°F. Stir in the liquid, increase the temperature to 350°F, and cook for 10 minutes.

512. Baby Back Ribs with BBQ Sauce

Servings: 4 | Ready in about: 45 minutes

2 lb baby back pork ribs	2 tbsp honey	1 tsp mustard
4 cups orange juice	½ cup ketchup	2 tsp paprika
Juice from 1 lemon	Juice from ½ lemon	½ tsp cayenne pepper
For BBQ sauce:	1 tbsp Worcestershire sauce	Salt to taste

Mix all the BBQ sauce ingredients in a bowl until well incorporated. Set aside. Place ribs in your Instant Pot. Add in lemon juice and orange juice. Seal the pressure lid, choose Pressure Cook on High, and set the timer to 20 minutes. Release pressure naturally for 15 minutes. Preheat oven to 400° F. Line the sheet pan with aluminum foil. Transfer the ribs to a baking dish. Do away with the cooking liquid. Onto both sides of ribs, brush barbecue sauce. Place in the pot, close the air fry lid, and select Bake at 390 F. Cook for 10 minutes until browned and caramelized. Set the ribs aside and cut into individual bones to serve.

513. Spicy Pork Roast with Peanut Sauce

Servings: 6 | Ready in about: 30 minutes

3 lb pork roast	½ cup soy sauce	1 tsp ginger puree
1 cup Hot water	1 tbsp plain vinegar	2 chilies, deseeded, chopped
1 red bell pepper, seeded and sliced	½ cup peanut butter	Chopped Peanuts to garnish
Salt and black pepper to taste	1 tbsp lime juice	Chopped green onions to garnish
1 large white onion, sliced	1 tbsp garlic powder	Lime Wedges to garnish

Add the soy sauce, vinegar, peanut butter, lime juice, garlic powder, chilies, and ginger puree, to a bowl. Whisk together and even. Add a few pinches of salt and pepper, and mix it. Open your Instant Pot, and place the pork in. Pour the hot water and peanut butter mixture over it. Seal the lid and select Pressure Cook for 15 minutes. Once the timer has stopped, do a quick pressure release. Use two forks to shred it, inside the pot, and close the air fry lid. Cook on Broil mode for 4 - 5 minutes, until the sauce thickens. On a bed of cooked rice, spoon the meat with some sauce and garnish it with the chopped peanuts, green onions, and the lemon wedges.

514. Jamaican Pulled Pork with Mango Sauce

Servings: 6 | Ready in about: 1 hour 15 minutes

1 ½ tsp onion powder	1 tsp cayenne pepper	3 lb pork shoulder
1 tsp sea salt	1 tsp ground allspice	1 mango, cut into chunks
1 tsp dried thyme	½ tsp ground nutmeg	1 tbsp olive oil
1 tsp ground black pepper	½ tsp ground cinnamon	2 tbsp fresh cilantro, finely minced

In a bowl, combine onion powder, thyme, allspice, cinnamon, sugar, pepper, sea salt, cayenne, and nutmeg. Coat the pork shoulder with olive oil. Season with seasoning mixture. Warm oil on Sauté in your Instant Pot. Add in the pork and cook for 5 minutes until browned completely. To the pot, add ½ cup water and mango chunks. Seal the pressure lid, choose Pressure Cook on High, and set the timer to 45 minutes. Release pressure naturally for 15 minutes, then release the remaining pressure quickly. Transfer the pork to a cutting board and allow cooling. To make the sauce, pour the cooking liquid in a food processor and pulse until smooth. Use two forks to shred the pork and arrange on a serving platter. Serve the pulled pork topped with mango salsa and fresh cilantro.

515. Pork Chops with Cremini Mushroom Sauce

Servings: 4 | Ready in about: 35 minutes

4 pork chops	1 tsp garlic powder	1 cup beef broth
1 tbsp olive oil	1 (10 oz) can mushroom soup	1 sprig fresh thyme
3 cloves garlic, minced	8 oz Cremini mushrooms, sliced	Chopped parsley to garnish
Salt and black pepper to taste	1 small onion, chopped	

Select Sauté on your Instant Pot. Add oil, mushrooms, garlic, and onion. Sauté them, stirring occasionally until nice and translucent, for 3 minutes. Season the pork chops with salt, garlic powder, and pepper, and add them to the pot followed by the thyme and broth. Seal the lid and select Pressure Cook on High for 10 minutes. Once the timer has ended, do a natural pressure release for about 10 minutes. Close the air fry lid and cook on Broil mode for 5 minutes. When ready, add the mushroom soup. Stir it until the mixture thickens a little bit. Dish the pork and gravy into a serving bowl and garnish with parsley. Serve.

516. Ragu with Pork & Rigatoni

Servings: 6 | Ready in about: 70 minutes

4 oz sweet and hot Italian sausage, casings removed	1 medium carrot, peeled and chopped	2 tbsp tomato paste
1 lb boneless pork shoulder	1 celery stalk, diced	2 tsp dried Italian herb mix
1 tsp salt	½ cup dry red wine	1 cup water, divided
2 tbsp olive oil	⅛ tsp red pepper flakes	12 oz rigatoni
1 medium onion, chopped	1 (28-oz) can crushed tomatoes	½ cup grated Parmesan + for serving
2 garlic cloves, minced or pressed		

Season the pork shoulder with ½ teaspoon of salt. On your Instant Pot, choose Sauté. Heat in the olive oil until shimmering and add the pork. Sear on one side for 4 minutes or until browned. Then, add the sausage, the onion, garlic, carrot, and celery. Sauté for 2 minutes or until the vegetables just start softening. Stir in the wine, use a wooden spoon to scrape the bottom of any browned bits. Cook for 2 to 3 minutes until the wine has reduced by half. Add the red prepper flakes, tomatoes, tomato paste, remaining salt, and the dried herbs. Stir to combine. Seal the pressure lid. Choose Pressure Cook on High, and the cook time to 20 minutes.

After cooking, perform a natural pressure release for 10 minutes, then a quick pressure release. Carefully open the lid. Mix the sauce and shred the pork with two forks and break the sausage apart. Add the water and the rigatoni. Seal the pressure lid again and choose Pressure Cook on High and the cook time to 4 minutes. After cooking, perform a quick pressure release, and carefully open the lid. Sprinkle the cheese over the sauce and pasta. Close the air fry lid and choose Broil. Adjust the time to 7 minutes. Press Start to broil the cheese. After cooking, open the lid. The cheese should be brown and crispy. Cool slightly and serve.

517. Juicy Barbecue Pork Chops

Servings: 4 | Ready in about: 100 minutes

3 tbsp brown sugar	2 tsp garlic powder	1 tbsp olive oil
1 tbsp salt	1 tbsp freshly ground black pepper	1½ cups chicken broth
1 ½ tbsp smoked paprika	4 bone-in pork chops	4 tbsp barbecue sauce

Choose Sauté on your Instant Pot. In a small bowl, mix the brown sugar, salt, paprika, garlic powder, and black pepper. Season both sides of the pork with the rub. Heat the oil in the preheated pot and sear the pork chops, one at a time, on both sides, about 5 minutes per chop. Set aside. Pour the chicken broth into the pot.

With a wooden spoon, scrape the bottom of the pot of any browned bits. Place the air fry basket in the upper position of the pot. Put the pork chops in the basket and brush with 2 tablespoons of barbecue sauce. Seal the pressure lid, choose Pressure Cook and set to High. Set the time to 5 minutes, then cooking. When the timer is done, perform a natural pressure release for 10 minutes, then a quick pressure release, and carefully open the lid. Apply the remaining barbecue sauce on both sides of the pork and close the air fry lid. Choose Broil and set the time to 3 minutes. When ready, check for your desired crispiness and remove the pork from the basket.

518. Sticky Pork Ribs

Serves: 4 | Total Time: 30 minutes

1 (2-lb) rack pork spareribs	Salt and black pepper to taste	½ tsp cayenne pepper
¼ cup brown sugar	1 tbsp chili powder	2 tbsp chopped parsley
1 tbsp cumin powder	1 tsp garlic powder	

Preheat your Instant Pot Duo Crisp to 400°F. Cut the ribs into two racks so that the pieces will fit in the air fry basket. To make the dry rub, combine brown sugar, cumin, salt, black pepper, chili powder, garlic powder, and cayenne in a small bowl. Rub the seasoning on both sides of the ribs until well coated. Place one rack of ribs in the air fry basket and close the fry lid. Air Fry for 20 minutes until cooked through and no longer pink. Repeat for the other rack. Allow ribs to rest at least 5 minutes before cutting. Serve sprinkled with parsley, and enjoy!

519. Bolognese-Style Pizza

Servings: 4 | Ready in about: 70 minutes

4 pizza crusts
½ cup canned crushed tomatoes
1 yellow bell pepper, sliced
½ lb ground pork, cooked and crumbled
1 cup shredded mozzarella cheese
1 tsp red chili flakes, divided

Place a trivet in your Instant Pot. Close the air fry lid, choose Air Fry, set the temperature to 400°F, and the time to 5 minutes. Grease one side of a pizza crust with cooking spray and lay on the preheated rack, oiled side up. Close the air fry lid. Choose Air Fry, set the temperature to 400°F, and set the time to 4 minutes. baking. Remove the crust from the trivet and flip. Top the crust with 2 tablespoons of crushed tomatoes, a quarter of bell pepper, 2 ounces of ground pork, ¼ cup of mozzarella cheese, and ¼ tablespoon of red chili flakes. Close the air fry lid. Choose Broil and set the time to 3 minutes. Choose Start to continue baking. When done baking and crispy, remove the pizza from the trivet. Repeat with the remaining pizza crusts and ingredients. Serve.

520. Apple & Onion Topped Pork Chops

Servings: 3 | Ready in about: 25 minutes

Topping:
1 small onion, sliced
2 tbsp olive oil
1 tbsp apple cider vinegar
2 tsp thyme
¼ tsp brown sugar
1 cup sliced apples

Meat:
¼ tsp smoked paprika
1 tbsp olive oil
3 pork chops
1 tbsp apple cider vinegar
Salt and black pepper to taste

Place all topping ingredients in a baking dish and then in your Instant Pot. Cook for 4 minutes on Air Fry. Place the pork chops in a bowl. Add olive oil, vinegar, paprika, and season with salt and pepper. Stir to coat them well. Remove the topping from the dish. Add the pork chops in the dish, close the air fry lid and cook for 10 minutes on Air Fry mode at 350°F. Place the topping on top, return to the pot and cook for 5 more minutes.

521. Honey Barbecue Pork Ribs

Servings: 2 | Ready in about: 4 h 35 minutes

1 lb pork ribs
½ tsp five spice powder
1 tsp salt
3 garlic cloves, chopped
1 tsp black pepper
1 tsp sesame oil
1 tbsp honey, plus more for brushing
4 tbsp barbecue sauce
1 tsp soy sauce

Chop the ribs into smaller pieces and place in a large bowl. In a separate bowl, whisk together all of the other ingredients. Add to the bowl with the pork, and mix until the pork is thoroughly coated. Cover the bowl, place it in the fridge, and let it marinade for about 4 hours. Place the ribs in the basket of your Instant Pot. Close the air fry lid and cook for 15 minutes on Air Fry at 350°F. Brush the ribs with some honey and cook for 15 minutes.

522. Pork Chops with Plum Sauce

Servings: 4 | Ready in about: 20 minutes

4 pork chops
1 tsp cumin seeds
Salt and black pepper to taste
2 cups firm plums, pitted and sliced
1 tbsp vegetable oil
¾ cup vegetable stock

Sprinkle salt, cumin, and pepper on the pork chops. Set your Instant Pot to Sauté. Warm oil. Add the chops and cook for 3 to 5 minutes until browned and set aside on a bowl. Arrange plum slices on the bottom of the pot. Place the pork chops on top of the plumes. Add any juice from the plate over the pork and apply stock around the edges. Seal lid and cook on High pressure for 8 minutes. When ready, do a quick pressure release. Transfer the pork chops to a serving plate and spoon over the plum sauce before serving.

523. Philippine-Style Pork Chops

Servings: 6 | Ready in about: 20 minutes + marinating time

2 lb pork chops	2 tbsp soy sauce	1 tbsp peppercorns
2 bay leaves	5 garlic cloves, coarsely chopped	1 tbsp peanut oil

Combine the bay leaves, soy sauce, garlic, salt, peppercorns, and oil in a bowl. Rub the mixture onto meat. Wrap the pork with a plastic foil and refrigerate for 2 hours. Place the pork in your Instant Pot, close the air fry lid and cook for 20 minutes on Air Fry at 390°F, flipping the chops, and cook for another 10 minutes. Discard bay leaves.

524. Teriyaki Pork Noodles

Servings: 4 | Ready in about: 60 minutes

8 oz egg noodles	Salt and black pepper to taste	1 cup teriyaki sauce
1 lb green beans, trimmed	1 pork tenderloin, trimmed and cut into 1-inch pieces	Cooking spray
1 tbsp olive oil		Sesame seeds, for garnish

Pour the egg noodles and cover with enough water in your Instant Pot. Seal the pressure lid, choose Pressure Cook on High, and set the time to 2 minutes. In a large bowl, toss the green beans with the olive oil, salt, and black pepper. In another bowl, toss the pork with the teriyaki sauce. When the egg noodles are ready, perform a quick pressure release, and carefully open the lid. Fix a trivet in the pot, which will be over the egg noodles. Grease a trivet with cooking spray and place the pork on the trivet. Also, lay the green beans around the pork. Close the air fry lid. Choose Broil and set the time to 12 minutes. When done cooking, check for your desired crispiness. Serve the pork and green beans over the drained egg noodles and garnish with sesame seeds.

525. Italian Sausage with Garlic Mash

Servings: 6 | Ready in about: 30 minutes

1 ½ cups water	2 garlic cloves, smashed	¼ cup milk, at room temperature
6 Italian sausages	4 large potatoes, cut into chunks	Salt and ground black pepper to taste
1 tbsp olive oil	⅓ cup butter, melted	1 tbsp chopped chives

Select Sauté on your Instant Pot and heat olive oil. Cook for 8-10 minutes, turning periodically until browned. Set aside. Wipe the pot with paper towels. Add in water and set a trivet over. Place potatoes on the trivet. Seal the pressure lid, choose Pressure Cook, and set the timer to 12 minutes. When ready, release the pressure quickly.

Remove the trivet from the pot. Drain water from the pot. Return potatoes to pot. Add in salt, butter, pepper, garlic, and milk and use a hand masher to mash until no large lumps remain. Using an immersion blender, blend potatoes on Low for 1 minute until fluffy and light. Avoid over-blending to ensure the potatoes do not become gluey! Transfer the mash to a serving plate, top with sausages and scatter chopped chives over to serve.

526. Potato & Ground Pork Chili

Servings: 6 | Ready in about: 55 minutes

1 tbsp olive oil	6 potatoes, peeled and sliced	1 cup chicken broth
1 small onion, diced	1cup carrots, chopped	1 tbsp ground cumin
2 garlic cloves, minced	1 cups corn kernels, roasted	1 tbsp chili powder
1 lb ground pork	1 cups tomato puree	Salt and black pepper to taste
2 bell peppers, chopped	1 cups diced tomatoes	

Warm the olive on Sauté and stir-fry onions and garlic until soft, for about 3 minutes. Stir in pork and cook until thoroughly browned, about 5-6 minutes. Add the remaining ingredients, and stir to combine. Seal the pressure lid, choose Pressure Cook on High, and set the timer to 25 minutes. Once ready, do a quick release. Set to Sauté. Cook uncovered for 15 more minutes. Serve warm.

527. Vietnamese Pork Soup

Servings: 4 | Ready in about: 40 minutes

2 tbsp olive oil	½ tsp coriander seeds	2 tsp salt
2 yellow onions, halved	10 black peppercorns	8 oz rice noodles
1 piece fresh ginger, halved lengthwise	2-star anise	1 lime, cut into wedges
2 tsp fennel seeds	8 cups water	A handful of fresh cilantro leaves
1 tsp red pepper flakes	1 lb pork tenderloin, cut into thin strips	

Set your Instant Pot to Sauté. Warm oil. Add ginger and onions and cook for 4 minutes. Add in red pepper flakes, fennel seeds, star anise, peppercorns, and coriander seeds. Cook for 1 minute as you stir. Add water, salt and pork into your Instant Pot. Seal the pressure lid, choose Pressure Cook on High, and set the timer to 60 minutes.

Release the pressure naturally for 10 minutes. Soak rice noodles in hot water for 8 minutes until softened and pliable. Stop the cooking process by draining and rinsing with cold water. Separate the noodles into soup bowls. Remove the pork from the cooker and ladle among bowls. Strain the broth to get rid of solids. Pour it over the pork and noodles. Season with red pepper flakes. Garnish with lime wedges and cilantro leaves.

528. Sweet Potato Gratin with Peas & Prosciutto

Servings: 4 | Ready in about: 30 minutes

1 ½ lb sweet potatoes, quartered	½ cup heavy cream, or more to taste	¾ cup frozen peas, thawed
½ tsp salt or to taste	1 cup shredded Provolone cheese	½ cup grated Pecorino Romano
⅛ tsp freshly ground black pepper	10 oz prosciutto, cooked and diced	3 tbsp chopped fresh chives

Pour 1 cup of water into the inner pot and put a trivet in your Instant Pot. Place the sweet potatoes on the trivet. Seal the pressure lid, choose Pressure Cook on High and the cook time to 4 minutes. After cooking, perform a quick pressure release, and carefully open the lid. Remove the trivet. Empty the water out of the pot.

Put the potatoes back in the pot and season with the salt and pepper. Use a large fork to break the potatoes into pieces about ½ inch on a side. Mix in the heavy cream, Provolone cheese, and prosciutto. Gently stir in the peas. Sprinkle the mixture with the Pecorino Romano. Close the air fry lid and choose Bake. Adjust the temperature to 400°F and the cook time to 10 minutes. When the top of the gratin has browned, sprinkle with chives and serve.

529. Chorizo Stuffed Yellow Bell Peppers

Servings: 4 | Ready in about: 40 minutes

4 large yellow bell peppers	1 small onion, diced	1 cup shredded Mexican blend cheese
2 tsp olive oil	⅔ cup diced fresh tomatoes	Salt and black pepper to taste
¾ lb chorizo	1 ½ cups cooked rice	

Cut about ¼ inch off the top of each pepper. Cut through the ribs inside the peppers and pull out the core and remove as much of the ribs as possible. On your Instant Pot, choose Sauté. Heat the oil until shimmering and cook in the chorizo while breaking the meat with a spatula. Cook until just starting to brown, about 2 minutes. Add the onion and sauté until the vegetables soften and the chorizo has now browned, about 3 minutes.

Turn the pot off and scoop the chorizo and vegetables into a medium bowl. Add the tomatoes, rice, and ½ cup of cheese to the bowl. Mix to combine well. Spoon the filling mixture into the bell peppers to the brim. Clean the inner pot with a paper towel and return the pot to the base. Pour 1 cup of water into your Instant Pot and fix in a trivet. Put the peppers on the trivet and cover the tops loosely with a piece of foil.

Seal the pressure lid and choose Pressure Cook and the time to 12 minutes. After cooking, perform a quick pressure release and carefully open the lid. Remove the foil from the top of the peppers and sprinkle the remaining ½ cup of cheese on the peppers. Close the air fry lid, choose Broil, adjust the time to 5 minutes, and press Start to broil the cheese. After 4 minutes, open the lid and check the peppers. The cheese should have melted and browned a bit. If not, close the lid and continue cooking. Let the peppers cool for several minutes before serving.

530. Sausage with Noodles and Braised Cabbage

Servings: 4 | Ready in about: 35 minutes

3 oz serrano ham, diced
1 small onion, sliced
⅓ cup dry white wine
1 cup chicken stock
1 tsp salt
¼ tsp black pepper
5 oz wide egg noodles
4 cups shredded green cabbage
1½ lb smoked sausage, cut into 4 pieces

On your Instant Pot, choose Sauté. Put the ham in the pot and cook for 6 minutes until crisp. Using a slotted spoon, transfer the ham to a paper towel-lined plate to drain, leaving the fat in the pot. Sauté the onion to the pot for about 2 minutes or until the onion starts to soften. Pour in the wine and simmer until the wine reduces slightly while scraping the bottom of the pot with a wooden spoon to let off any browned bits.

Pour in the chicken stock, salt, black pepper, and noodles. Stir, while pushing the noodles as much as possible into the sauce. Put the cabbage on top of the noodles and the sausages on the cabbage. Lock the pressure lid into place and seal. Choose Pressure Cook on High and the cook time to 3 minutes. When the cooking time is over, do a quick pressure release, and carefully open the lid. Stir the noodles and cabbage and adjust the taste with seasoning. Grease a trivet with cooking spray and fix in the pot. Transfer the sausages to the trivet. Choose Bake. Adjust the temperature to 390°F and the cook time to 8 minutes. After 4 minutes, open the lid and check the sausages. When browned, turn the sausages, close the lid, and cook to brown the other side. Ladle the cabbage and noodles into a bowl and top with the bacon. Serve with the sausages.

531. Italian Sausage & Cannellini Stew

Servings: 6 | Ready in about: 45 minutes

1 tbsp olive oil
1 lb Italian sausages, halved
1 celery stalk, chopped
1 carrot, chopped
1 onion, chopped
1 sprig fresh sage
1 sprig fresh rosemary
1 bay leaf
1 cup Cannellini Beans, soaked
2 cups vegetable stock
3 cups fresh spinach
1 tsp salt

Warm oil on Sauté in your Instant Pot. Add in sausage pieces and sear for 5 minutes until browned. Set aside on a plate. To the pot, add celery, onion, bay leaf, sage, carrot, and rosemary. Cook for 3 minutes to soften slightly. Stir in vegetable stock and beans. Arrange seared sausage pieces on top of the beans. Seal the pressure lid, choose Pressure Cook on High, and set the timer to 10 minutes. Release pressure naturally for 20 minutes. Once ready, do a quick release. Get rid of bay leaf, rosemary and sage. Mix in spinach and serve.

532. Calzones with Sausage and Mozzarella

Servings: 4 | Ready in about: 35 minutes

2 tbsp olive oil
1 green bell pepper, chopped
2 or 3 Italian sausages
1 lb frozen bread dough
¼ cup tomato sauce
1 cup shredded mozzarella cheese

On your Instant Pot, choose Sauté. Heat 1 tbsp of olive oil and sauté the bell pepper for 1 minute or until just starting to soften. Remove the pepper into a plate and set aside. Brown the sausages for 2 to 3 minutes on one side. Turn the sausages and brown the other side. Add ¾ cup of water to the inner pot. Seal the pressure lid. Choose Pressure Cook for 4 minutes. After cooking, perform a quick pressure release and carefully open the pressure lid.

Remove the sausages from the pot onto a cutting board and cool for several minutes. Discard the water in the pot. When the sausages have cooled, slice into ¼-inch rounds. Cut 4 pieces of parchment paper and divide the dough into 4 equal pieces. One at a time and on a piece of parchment, use your hands to press each dough into a circle.

Make the calzones. One after the other, spread 1 tablespoon of tomato sauce over half a dough circle, leaving a ½-inch clear border. Arrange the sausage rounds in a single layer and sprinkle a quarter of the green peppers over the top. Top with a quarter cup of cheese. Use the parchment to pull the other side of the dough over the filling and pinch the edges together to seal. Repeat the process with another dough.

Cut the parchment around each calzone, so it is about ½ inch larger than the calzone. Brush the calzones with some of the remaining olive oil. With a large spatula, transfer the two calzones to the trivet set it in the pot. Close the air fry lid and choose Bake. Adjust the temperature to 400°F and the cook time to 12 minutes.

After 6 minutes, check the calzones, which will be a dark golden brown. Remove the trivet and turn the calzones over. Remove the parchment paper and brush the tops with a little olive oil. Return the trivet to the pot. Close the lid and continue cooking for the last 6 minutes. While the first two calzones bake, assemble the remaining two. When the first set of calzones are done, transfer to a wire rack to cool and bake the second batch.

533. Sausage with Celeriac & Potato Mash

Servings: 4 | Ready in about: 45 minutes

1 tbsp olive oil
4 pork sausages
1 onion
2 cups vegetable broth
½ cup water
4 potatoes, peeled and diced
1 cup celeriac, chopped
2 tbsp butter
¼ cup milk
Salt and black pepper to taste
1 tbsp heavy cream
1 tsp Dijon mustard
½ tsp dry mustard powder
Fresh flat-leaf parsley, chopped

Warm oil on Sauté in your Instant Pot. Add in sausages and cook for 1 to 2 minutes for each side until browned. Set the sausages to a plate. To the same pot, add onion and cook for 3 minutes until fragrant. Add sausages on top of onions and pour water and broth over them. Place a trivet over onions and sausages. Put potatoes and celeriac in the steamer basket and transfer it to the trivet. Seal the pressure lid, choose Pressure Cook for 11 minutes.

When ready, release the pressure quickly. Transfer potatoes and celeriac to a bowl and set sausages on a plate and cover them with aluminum foil. Using a potato masher, mash potatoes and celeriac together with black pepper, milk, salt and butter until mash becomes creamy and fluffy. Adjust the seasonings. Set the pot to Sauté. Add the onion mixture and bring to a boil. Cook for 5 to 10 minutes until the mixture is reduced and thickened. Into the gravy, stir in dry mustard, salt, pepper, mustard and cream. Place the mash in 4 bowls in equal parts, top with a sausage or two, and gravy. Add parsley for garnishing.

534. Beer-Braised Hot Dogs with Peppers

Servings: 6 | Ready in about: 15 minutes

1 tbsp olive oil
6 sausages pork sausage links
1 green bell pepper, sliced into strips
1 red bell pepper, sliced into strips
1 yellow bell pepper, sliced into strips
2 spring onions, sliced
1 ½ cups beer
6 hot dog rolls

Warm oil on Sauté in your Instant Pot. Add in sausage links and sear for 5 minutes until browned. Set aside on a plate. Into the pot, pile peppers. Lay the sausages on top. Add beer into the pot. Seal the pressure lid, choose Pressure Cook on High, and set the timer to 5 minutes. When ready, release the pressure quickly. Serve sausages in buns topped with onions and peppers.

535. Sunday Beef Skewers

Serves: 4 | Total Time: 25 minutes

1 ½ lb sirloin steak, cubed
1 white onion, quartered
1 yellow bell pepper, cubed
1 red bell pepper, cubed
1 zucchini, cubed
1 tsp ground cumin
Salt and black pepper to taste
2 tbsp olive oil

Preheat your Instant Pot Duo Crisp to 400°F. Assemble kebabs. Start by placing one cube of steak on a skewer, then add one onion piece, then one yellow pepper piece, a red pepper piece, and then a zucchini piece. Follow this pattern three times per skewer. Season with cumin, salt, and pepper and drizzle with oil. Arrange the kebabs in a single layer in the air fry basket and close the fry lid. Air Fry for 5 minutes, then flip the kebabs. Cook for another 5 minutes or until the meat is brown and the vegetables are tender Serve and enjoy!

536. Sweet Carrots with Crumbled Bacon

Servings: 8 | Ready in about: 30 minutes

3 slices bacon, crumbled
4 lb carrots, peeled and sliced
½ cup fresh orange juice
¼ cup olive oil
3 tbsp honey
1 tsp salt
2 tsp cornstarch
1 tbsp cold water

Fry the bacon in your Instant Pot on Sauté until crisp, 5 minutes; set aside. In a bowl, mix salt, olive oil, orange juice, and maple syrup. Add the mixture and carrots to the pot and mix well to coat. Seal the pressure lid, choose Pressure Cook on High, and set the timer to 6 minutes. When ready, release the pressure quickly. Transfer carrots to a serving dish. Press Sauté. In a bowl, mix cold water and cornstarch until cornstarch dissolves completely. Add to the liquid remaining in the pressure cooker. Simmer sauce as you stir for 2 minutes to obtain a thick and smooth consistency. Ladle sauce over the carrots and scatter over the crumbled bacon.

537. Holiday Honey-Glazed Ham

Servings: 10 | Ready in about: 30 minutes

½ cup apple cider
¼ cup honey
1 tbsp Dijon mustard
¼ cup brown sugar
2 tbsp orange juice
2 tbsp pineapple juice (optional)
½ tsp ground cinnamon
¼ tsp grated nutmeg
1 pinch ground cloves
1 (5 lb) ham, bone-in

Set on Sauté in your Instant Pot. Mix in apple cider, mustard, pineapple juice, cloves, cinnamon, brown sugar, honey, orange juice, and nutmeg. Cook until sauce becomes warm and the sugar and spices are completely dissolved. Lay ham into the sauce. Seal the pressure lid, choose Pressure Cook, and set the timer to 10 minutes.

When ready, release the pressure quickly. Line aluminum foil to a baking sheet. Transfer the ham to the prepared baking sheet. On Sauté, cook the remaining liquid for 4 to 6 minutes until you have a thick and syrupy glaze. Brush the glaze onto ham. Set the glazed ham in the pot, close the air fry lid, and press Bake. Cook for 3 to 5 minutes at 400 F until the glaze is caramelized. Place the ham on a cutting board and slice. Transfer to a serving bowl and drizzle glaze over the ham.

538. Tasty Ham with Collard Greens

Servings: 4 | Ready in about: 10 minutes

20 oz collard greens, washed and cut
2 cubes of chicken bouillon
4 cups water
½ cup diced sweet onion
2 ½ cups diced ham

Place the ham at the bottom of the inner pot. Add collard greens and onion. Add chicken cubes to the water and dissolve it. Pour the mixture into your Instant Pot. Close the lid, secure the pressure valve, to seal properly. Select Steam mode on High pressure for 5 minutes. Once the timer has ended, do a quick pressure release, and open the lid. Spoon the vegetables and the ham with sauce into a serving bowl. Serve.

539. Crunchy Cashew Lamb Rack

Servings: 4 | Ready in about: 30 minutes

3 oz chopped cashews
1 tbsp chopped rosemary
1 ½ lb rack of lamb
1 garlic clove, minced
1 tbsp breadcrumbs
1 egg, beaten
1 tbsp olive oil
Salt and black pepper to taste

Combine the olive oil with the garlic and brush this mixture onto the lamb. Combine the rosemary, cashews, and breadcrumbs, in a small bowl. Brush the egg over the lambs, and then coat it with the cashew mixture. Place the lamb in your Instant Pot, close the air fry lid and cook for 25 minutes on Air Fry at 390°F. Then increase to 390°F, and cook for 5 more minutes. Cover with a foil and let sit for a couple of minutes before serving.

540. Holiday Apricot-Lemon Ham

Servings: 12 | Ready in about: 1 hour

¼ cup water
5 lb smoked ham
¾ cup apricot jam
½ cup brown sugar
Juice from 1 Lime
2 tsp mustard
½ tsp ground cardamom
¼ tsp ground nutmeg
Black pepper to taste

Into your Instant Pot, add water and ham to the steel pot of a pressure cooker. In a bowl, combine jam, lemon juice, cardamom, pepper, nutmeg, mustard, and brown sugar. Pour the mixture over the ham. Seal the pressure lid, choose Pressure Cook on High, and set the timer to 10 minutes. When ready, release the pressure quickly. Transfer the ham to a cutting board. Allow to sit for 10 minutes. Press Sauté. Simmer the liquid and cook for 4 to 6 minutes until thickened into a sauce. Slice ham and place onto a serving bowl. Drizzle with sauce before serving.

541. Winter Minestrone with Pancetta

Servings: 6 | Ready in about: 40 minutes

2 tbsp olive oil
2 oz pancetta, chopped
1 onion, diced
1 parsnip, peeled and chopped
2 carrots, peeled and sliced into rounds
2 celery stalks,
2 garlic cloves, minced
1 tbsp dried basil
1 tbsp dried thyme
1 tbsp dried oregano
6 cups chicken broth
2 cups green beans, chopped
1 (15 oz) can diced tomatoes
1 (15 oz) can chickpeas, rinsed
1 ½ cups small shaped pasta
Salt and ground black pepper to taste
½ cup grated Parmesan cheese

Warm oil on Sauté in your Instant Pot. Add onion, carrots, garlic, pancetta, celery, and parsnip, and cook for 5 minutes until they become soft. Stir in basil, oregano, green beans, broth, tomatoes, pepper, salt, thyme, vegetable broth, chickpeas, and pasta. Seal the pressure lid, choose Pressure Cook on High, and set the timer to 6 minutes. Release pressure naturally for 10 minutes then release the remaining pressure quickly. Ladle the soup into bowls and serve garnished with grated Parmesan cheese.

542. Herbed Lamb Chops

Servings: 4 | Ready in about: 30 minutes

4 lamb chops
1 garlic clove, peeled
1 tbsp plus
2 tsp olive oil
½ tbsp oregano
½ tbsp thyme

Coat the garlic clove with 1 tsp of olive oil and cook in your Instant Pot for 10 minutes on Air Fry. Mix the herbs and seasonings with the remaining olive oil. Using a towel, squeeze the hot roasted garlic clove into the herb mixture and stir to combine. Coat the lamb chops with the mixture well, and place in the pot. Close the air fry lid and cook for about 8 to 12 minutes on Air Fry mode at 390°F, until crispy on the outside.

543. Aromatic Pork Chops

Serves: 4 | Total Time: 25 minutes

5 boneless pork chops
Salt and black pepper to taste
2 cups croutons
½ tsp dried thyme
¼ tsp dried sage
¼ tsp dried parsley
¼ tsp dried oregano
1 lemon, sliced
1 large egg, whisked

Preheat your Instant Pot Duo Crisp to 400°F. Season pork chops on both sides with salt and pepper. Add croutons, thyme, parsley, oregano, and sage to a food processor. Pulse five times to break down the croutons but keep a few medium-sized pieces. Pour into a bowl.

In another bowl, add the egg. Dip the pork chop into the egg, then dip into the crouton mixture to coat both sides. Spray with cooking oil. Transfer the pork chops to the air fry basket and close the fry lid. Air Fry for 14 minutes, flipping once until the chops are golden. Serve with lemon slices on the side and enjoy!

544. Lamb Chops & Creamy Potato Mash

Servings: 8 | Ready in about: 40 minutes

8 lamb cutlets	1 tbsp olive oil	5 potatoes, peeled and chopped
Salt to taste	1 tbsp tomato puree	⅓ cup milk
3 sprigs rosemary leaves, chopped	1 green onion, chopped	4 cilantro leaves, for garnish
3 tbsp butter, softened	1 cup beef stock	

Rub rosemary leaves and salt to the lamb chops. Warm oil and 2 tbsp of butter on Sauté in your Instant Pot. Add in the lamb chops and cook for 1 minute for each side until browned. Set aside on a plate. In the pot, mix tomato puree and green onion. Cook for 2-3 minutes. Add beef stock into the pot to deglaze, scrape the bottom to get rid of any browned bits of food. Return lamb cutlets alongside any accumulated juices to the pot.

Set a trivet on lamb cutlets. Place steamer basket on the trivet. Arrange potatoes in the steamer basket. Seal the pressure lid, choose Pressure Cook, and set the timer to 4 minutes. When ready, release the pressure quickly. Remove the trivet and steamer basket from pot. In a high speed blender, add potatoes, milk, salt, and remaining tbsp butter. Blend well until you obtain a smooth consistency. Divide the potato mash between serving dishes. Lay lamb chops on the mash. Drizzle with cooking liquid obtained from pressure cooker. Apply cilantro for garnish.

545. Spicy-Sweet Pork Ribs

Serves: 4 | Total Time: 35 minutes

3 lb pork back ribs	½ tsp dried thyme	⅓ cup honey
Salt and black pepper to taste	½ cup sweet chili sauce	1 tbsp lemon juice

Preheat your Instant Pot Duo Crisp to 400°F. Cut the ribs into 2 racks so that they fit in the air fry basket. Season the ribs with thyme, salt, and pepper. Place the ribs meat side down in the air fry basket and close the fry lid. Air Fry for 15 minutes. While the ribs are cooking, prepare the sauce. Mix sweet chili sauce, honey, and lemon juice in a small bowl. When the ribs are done, pour sauce on both sides of the racks. Place the ribs meat side up in the basket and cook for 10 minutes or until the ribs have browned. Serve warm and enjoy!

546. Mustard & Brown Sugar Pork Loin

Serves: 4 | Total Time: 40 minutes

1 lb boneless pork loin	¼ cup brown sugar	1 tsp paprika
1 tbsp olive oil	1 tbsp lemon juice	
¼ cup Dijon mustard	Salt and black pepper to taste	

Coat pork loin with oil. Prepare sauce in a small bowl by combining mustard, lemon juice, brown sugar, paprika, salt, and pepper, then brush it on both sides of the pork. Let sit for 15 minutes. Preheat your Instant Pot Duo Crisp to 400°F. Transfer the loin to the air fry basket and close the fry lid. Air Fry for 20 minutes. Allow loin to rest for 10 minutes before slicing. Serve warm and enjoy!

547. BBQ Short Ribs

Serves: 4 | Total Time: 30 minutes

4 lb beef short ribs	Salt and black pepper to taste	½ cup barbecue sauce
2 tbsp olive oil	1 tsp hot paprika	2 tbsp chopped parsley

Preheat your Instant Pot Duo Crisp to 375°F. In a large bowl, add short ribs then, drizzle with oil. Season both sides with hot paprika, salt, and pepper. Transfer the ribs to the air fry basket and close the fry lid. Air Fry for 20 minutes. Remove the ribs and brush with barbecue sauce, then cook again for another 5 minutes or until the sauce is dark and brown. Serve sprinkled with parsley, and enjoy!

548. Empanadas Argentinas

Serves: 4 | Total Time: 40 minutes

2 tbsp olive oil	⅓ cup salsa	2 boiled eggs, quartered
1 lb ground beef	2 refrigerated piecrusts	2 pitted green olives, minced
¼ cup taco seasoning	1 cup grated Colby-jack cheese	

Warm the olive oil in your Instant Pot on Sauté. Brown beef for 10 minutes until completely cooked. Add the taco seasoning and salsa. Bring the mixture to a boil, then simmer for 5 minutes. Remove from the pot. Cut out 3 circles from each pie crust. Combine the scraps and roll out to ½-inch thickness. Cut out 2 circles for a total of 8 circles. Place ¼ cup of the meat mixture, boiled eggs, and olives on the lower half of each circle, then top with 2 tablespoons of cheese. With a little water on your finger, gently rub the edges of the pastry and fold over the filling into a half-circle. Press and seal with a fork. Lightly spray with cooking oil.

Preheat your Instant Pot Duo Crisp to 370°F. Place the empanadas in the air fry basket and close the fry lid. Air Fry for 6 minutes. Flip the empanadas and cook for another 6 minutes. The crust will be golden. Serve and enjoy!

549. Veggie Steak Rolls

Serves: 4 | Total Time: 35 minutes

2 tbsp olive oil	1 cup chopped spinach	8 provolone cheese slices
½ onion, chopped	½ red bell pepper, sliced	Salt and black pepper to taste
½ cup chopped bella mushrooms	1 lb flank steak	2 garlic cloves, minced

Warm the olive oil in your instant Pot on Sauté. Cook the onion for 2 minutes. When the onions are soft and aromatic, add garlic, pepper, mushrooms, and spinach. Cook for another 5 minutes to soften the mushrooms and wilt the spinach. Butterfly the steak but keep the two halves connected. Top the steak with cheese and vegetables. Roll the filling in the steak and secure with 8 toothpicks or 8 pieces of twine, all evenly placed. Carve the steak into four rolls. Lightly spray with cooking oil and season with salt and pepper.

Preheat your Instant Pot Duo Crisp to 400°F. Place the rolls in the air fryer basket and close the lid. Air Fry for 12 minutes. The steak will be browned on the edges. Serve warm and enjoy!

550. American Cheeseburgers

Serves: 4 | Total Time: 15 minutes

| 1 lb ground beef | 4 cheddar cheese slices | 4 hamburger buns |
| Salt and black pepper to taste | ½ tsp onion powder | |

Preheat your Instant Pot Duo Crisp to 360°F. Divide the beef and shape into 4 equal patties. Season with onion powder, salt, and pepper on both sides. Place in the air fry basket and close the fry lid. Air Fry for 5 minutes. Flip the patties and cook for another 5 minutes. Add a slice of cheddar cheese to each patty and serve warm on a bun.

551. Sausage Stuffed Bell Peppers

Serves: 4 | Total Time: 25 minutes

1 (10-oz) can diced tomatoes and green chilies, drained

| ½ lb cooked Italian sausage | 1 tsp salt | 1 cup grated Italian-blend cheese |
| 2 tsp allspice | 3 bell peppers, trimmed and seeded | 2 tbsp chopped parsley |

Preheat your Instant Pot Duo Crisp to 320°F. Combine sausage, tomatoes with chilies, allspice, and salt in a large bowl. Stuff each pepper with ¼ of the sausage mixture, then top with ¼ cup cheese. Lightly spray with cooking oil and sprinkle with parsley. Place in the air fry basket and close the fry lid. Bake for 15 minutes until the cheese is melted and the peppers are tender. Serve immediately.

552. Peppery Flank Steak Rolls

Serves: 4 | Total Time: 25 minutes

1 lb flank steak
4 pepper jack cheese slices
1 green bell pepper, chopped
½ red bell pepper, chopped
2 tbsp dried oregano
¼ cup chopped onion
Salt and black pepper to taste
2 tbsp chopped parsley

Preheat your Instant Pot Duo Crisp to 400°F. Butterfly the steak but keep the two halves connected. Top the steak with cheese, then peppers, oregano, and onion. Roll the filling in the steak and secure with 8 toothpicks or 8 pieces of twine, all evenly placed. Carve the steak into four rolls. Lightly spray with cooking oil and season with salt and pepper. Place the rolls in the air fryer basket and close the lid. Air Fry for 12 minutes. The steak will be browned on the edges. Serve warm sprinkled with parsley, and enjoy!

553. Quick Pork Chops

Serves: 4 | Total Time: 20 minutes

4 boneless pork chops
Salt and black pepper to taste
½ tsp Tajín seasoning
½ tsp mustard powder
4 tbsp butter, sliced
1 tbsp dried thyme

Preheat your Instant Pot Duo Crisp to 400°F. Season pork chops with thyme, Tajín seasoning, mustard powder, salt, and pepper, then top with ½ tablespoon of butter. Transfer the pork chops to the air fry basket and close the fry lid. Air Fry for 6 minutes. Turn the chops and cook for another 6 minutes. The chops will be golden on the top and edges. While the chops are still hot, add the rest of the butter on top and let rest for 5 minutes. Serve warm.

554. Pancetta & Cheese Pinwheels

Serves: 5 | Total Time: 25 minutes

4 oz cream cheese, softened
1 tbsp dry ranch seasoning
¼ cup grated cheddar cheese
¼ cup Parmesan cheese
1 puff pastry dough sheet
6 cooked pancetta slices, crumbled

Preheat your Instant Pot Duo Crisp to 320°F. Line the basket with parchment paper. Combine cream cheese, ranch seasoning, Parmesan cheese, and cheddar cheese in a bowl. Unfold the puff pastry and carefully spread the cream cheese mixture. Sprinkle with pancetta. Roll the dough from the long side. Press the edges to seal the log. Cut into 10 pieces and transfer to the air fry basket. Close the fry lid and Bake for 6-8 minutes, then flip each piece. Cook for another 5 minutes. Allow cooling for 5 minutes. Serve warm and enjoy!

555. Monsieur Burgers

Serves: 4 | Total Time: 20 minutes

1 lb ground beef
½ cup crumbled blue cheese
8 cooked bacon slices, crumbled
½ tsp dried oregano
1 tsp balsamic vinegar
Salt and black pepper to taste
4 pretzel buns

Preheat your Instant Pot Duo Crisp to 370°F. Combine ground beef, blue cheese, balsamic vinegar, bacon, and oregano in a large bowl. Divide into 4 portions and shape into patties. Season with salt and pepper and lightly spray with cooking oil. Place in the air fry basket and close the fry lid. Air Fry for 8 minutes. Flip the burgers and cook for another 7 minutes. Place on pretzel buns and serve.

556. Buttered Rib Eye Steak

Serves: 4 | Total Time: 20 minutes + marinating time

4 rib eye steaks
Salt and black pepper to taste
2 tbsp butter, melted
1 tbsp parsley, chopped
1 tbsp chipotle paste

Rub the steaks with chipotle paste, salt, and pepper and set aside to marinate for 15 minutes.

Preheat your Instant Pot Duo Crisp to 400°F. Place the steaks in the air fry basket and drizzle melted butter over them. Close the fry lid and Air Fry for 8 minutes, then flip. Cook for another 6-8 minutes. Edges will be firm. Check for an internal temperature of at least 160°F. Top with parsley. Let rest before cutting. Serve and enjoy!

557. Mama Polpette

Serves: 6 | Total Time: 25 minutes

1 lb ground beef
⅓ cup Italian bread crumbs
1 large egg

2 tsp Italian seasoning
¼ cup grated Pecorino cheese
Salt and black pepper to taste

1 tsp dried thyme

Preheat your Instant Pot Duo Crisp to 400°F. Combine all of the ingredients in a large bowl. Shape into meatballs. Place the meatballs in the air fry basket and close the fry lid. Air Fry for 15 minutes, shaking the basket twice or until the meatballs are browned. Serve warm and enjoy!

558. Italian Meatloaf

Serves: 4 | Total Time: 50 minutes

1 lb ground beef
1 large egg
3 tbsp Italian bread crumbs

1 tsp ground fennel seeds
½ lemon, zested
1 shallot, chopped

Salt and black pepper to taste
2 tbsp ketchup
2 tbsp brown sugar

Preheat your Instant Pot Duo Crisp to 350°F. Combine beef, egg, bread crumbs, lemon zest, fennel seeds, shallot, pepper, and salt in a large bowl. Shape into a loaf. Combine ketchup and brown sugar in a small bowl. Brush on the loaf. Place the meatloaf in the air fry basket and close the fry lid. Bake for 40 minutes. Serve warm and enjoy!

559. Sirloin Bites with Sriracha Mayo

Serves: 4 | Total Time: 15 minutes

3 lb sirloin steak, cubed
Salt and black pepper to taste
½ tsp garlic powder

½ tsp shallot powder
½ tsp porcini powder
½ cup mayonnaise

3 tbsp sriracha

Preheat your Instant Pot Duo Crisp to 400°F. Season steak with salt, pepper, garlic powder, shallot powder, and porcini powder. Place in the air fry basket and close the fry lid. Air Fry for 8-10 minutes, shaking the basket twice.

While the steak is cooking, combine mayonnaise and sriracha in a small bowl. Place along with the steak bites when done. Serve warm and enjoy!

560. Pepperoni Calzones

Serves: 4 | Total Time: 25 minutes

1 refrigerated pizza dough
7 oz pepperoni slices
½ tsp red chili flakes

½ cup ricotta cheese
1 cup grated mozzarella cheese
1 tbsp grated Parmesan cheese

1 egg, whisked

Preheat your Instant Pot Duo Crisp to 350°F. Line the basket with parchment paper. Unroll the dough on a flat surface, then cut into 4 equal portions. On the bottom half of each calzone dough, arrange 7 slices of pepperoni topped with 2 tablespoons of ricotta, Parmesan cheese, chili flakes, and ¼ cup mozzarella.

Fold the top half of the dough over the fillings. Press and seal the edges with a fork. Brush with egg. Bake the calzones for 10 minutes, then turn them over. Bake for another 5 minutes until the dough is firm and golden. Serve warm and enjoy!

FISH & SEAFOOD

561. Herb Salmon with Barley & Haricot Verts

Servings: 4 | Ready in about: 50 minutes

1 cup pearl barley
2 cups water
4 salmon fillets
8 oz green beans haricot verts
1 tbsp olive oil
Salt and black pepper to taste
4 tbsp melted butter
½ tbsp brown sugar
½ tbsp freshly squeezed lemon juice
½ tsp dried rosemary
2 garlic cloves, minced
½ tsp dried thyme

Pour the barley and water into your Instant Pot and mix to combine. Place in a trivet. Lay the salmon fillets on the trivet. Seal the pressure lid, choose Pressure Cook on High and set the time to 2 minutes. In a bowl, toss the green beans with olive oil, pepper, and salt. In another bowl, mix pepper, salt, butter, brown sugar, lemon juice, rosemary, garlic, and rosemary. When done cooking the rice and salmon, perform a quick pressure release.

Gently pat the salmon dry with a paper towel, then coat with the buttery herb sauce. Position the haricots vert around the salmon. Close the air fry lid, choose Broil and set the time to 7 minutes. When ready, remove the salmon from the trivet, and serve with the barley and haricots vert.

562. Lemon Cod Goujons & Rosemary Chips

Servings: 4 | Ready in about: 100 minutes

2 eggs
1 cup arrowroot starch
1 cup flour
½ tbsp cayenne powder
1 tbsp cumin powder
Salt and black pepper to taste
4 cod fillets, cut into strips
Zest and juice from 1 lemon
2 potatoes, cut into chips
2 tbsp olive oil
3 tbsp fresh rosemary, chopped
4 lemon wedges to serve

In a bowl, whisk the eggs, lemon zest, and lemon juice. In another bowl, combine the arrowroot starch, flour, cayenne powder, cumin, black pepper, and salt. Coat each cod strip in the egg mixture, and then dredge in the flour mixture, coating well on all sides. Place the coated fish in the greased basket and oil with cooking spray.

Close the air fry lid. Choose Air Fry, set the temperature to 375°F, and the time to 15 minutes. Toss the potatoes with oil and season with salt and pepper. After 15 minutes, check the fish making sure the pieces are as crispy as desired. Remove the fish from the basket. Pour the potatoes into the basket.

Close the air fry lid, choose Air Fry, set the temperature to 400°F, and the time to 24 minutes. After 12 minutes, open the lid, and shake the fries. Return the basket to the pot and close the lid to continue cooking until crispy. When ready, sprinkle with fresh rosemary. Serve the fish with the potatoes and lemon wedges.

563. Autumn Succotash with Basil-Crusted Fish

Servings: 4 | Ready in about: 65 minutes

1 tbsp olive oil
½ small onion, chopped
1 garlic clove, minced
1 red chili, seeded and chopped
1 cup frozen corn
1 cup frozen mixed beans
1 cup butternut squash, cubed
1 bay leaf
¼ tsp cayenne pepper
¼ cup chicken stock
½ tsp Worcestershire sauce
1 tsp salt, divided
4 white fish fillets, at least 1 inch thick
¼ cup mayonnaise
1 tbsp Dijon-style mustard
1 ½ cups breadcrumbs
1 large tomato, seeded and chopped
¼ cup chopped fresh basil

Press Sauté on your Instant Pot. Heat the oil and sauté the onion, garlic, and red chili pepper in the oil for 4 minutes or until the vegetables are soft. Stir in the corn, squash, mixed beans, bay leaf, cayenne, stock, Worcestershire sauce, and ½ teaspoon salt. Seal the pressure lid, choose Pressure Cook and the cook time to 5 minutes. Season the fish fillets with the remaining salt. In a small bowl, mix the mayonnaise and mustard. Pour the breadcrumbs and basil into another bowl. Use a brush to spread the mayonnaise mixture on all sides of the fish and dredge each piece in the basil breadcrumbs to be properly coated.

Once the succotash is ready, perform a quick pressure release and carefully open the pressure lid. Stir in the tomato and remove the bay leaf. Set a trivet in the upper position of the pot, line with aluminum foil, and carefully lay the fish in a trivet. Oil the top of the fish with cooking spray. Close the air fry lid and choose Bake. Adjust the temperature to 375°F and the time to 8 minutes. After 4 minutes, open the lid. Turn them over and oil the other side with cooking spray. Close the lid and continue cooking. Serve the fillets with the succotash.

564. Farfalle Tuna Casserole with Cheese

Servings: 4 | Ready in about: 60 minutes

1 tbsp olive oil	1 (12-oz) can full cream milk	2 (5- to 6-oz) cans tuna, drained
1 medium onion, chopped	1 cup vegetable broth	1 cup chopped green beans
1 large carrot, chopped	2 cups shredded Monterey Jack cheese	2 ½ cups panko breadcrumbs
6 oz farfalle	2 tsp cornstarch	3 tbsp butter, melted

On your Instant Pot, choose Sauté. Heat the oil until shimmering and sauté the onion and carrots for 3 minutes, stirring, until softened. Add the farfalle, ¾ cup of milk, broth, and salt to the pot. Stir to combine and submerge the farfalle in the liquid with a spoon. Seal the pressure lid, choose Pressure Cook, and the cook time to 5 minutes. After cooking, do a quick pressure release and carefully open the pressure lid.

Choose Sauté and adjust to Less for low heat. Pour the remaining milk on the farfalle. In a medium bowl, mix the cheese and cornstarch evenly and add the cheese mixture by large handfuls to the sauce while stirring until the cheese melts and the sauce thickens. Add the tuna and green beans, gently stir. Heat for 2 minutes. In another bowl, mix the crumbs and melted butter. Spread the crumbs over the casserole. Close the air fry lid and press Broil. Adjust the time to 5 minutes. When ready, the topping should be crisp and brown. Serve immediately.

565. Crispy Cod on Lentils

Servings: 4 | Ready in about: 65 minutes

1 tbsp olive oil	4 cups vegetable broth	1 tsp lemon zest
2 cups lentils, soaked	1 cup panko breadcrumbs	1 lemon, juiced
1 yellow bell pepper, diced	4 tbsp melted butter	1 tsp salt
1 red bell pepper, diced	¼ cup minced fresh cilantro	4 cod fillets

Choose Sauté on your Instant Pot. Combine the oil, lentils, bell peppers in the pot and cook for 1 minute. Mix in the broth. Seal the pressure lid, choose Pressure Cook, and set the time to 6 minutes. In a bowl, combine the breadcrumbs, butter, cilantro, lemon zest, lemon juice, and salt. Spoon the breadcrumb mixture on the cod fillet.

When cooking ended, perform a quick pressure release. Fix a trivet in the pot, which will be over the lentils. Lay the cod fillets on the trivet. Close the air fry lid. Choose Air Fry, set the temperature to 350°F, and set the time to 12 minutes. When ready, share the lentils into four serving plates, and top with salmon.

566. Traditional Mahi Mahi

Servings: 4 | Ready in about: 10 minutes

4 Mahi Mahi fillets, fresh	Salt and black pepper	1 ½ tbsp maple syrup
4 cloves garlic, minced	2 tbsp chili powder	1 lime, juiced
1 ¼ -inch ginger, grated	1 tbsp Sriracha sauce	1 cup water

Place mahi mahi on a plate and season with salt and pepper on both sides. In a bowl, add garlic, ginger, chili powder, sriracha sauce, maple syrup, and lime juice. Use a spoon to mix it. Brush the mixture on the fillet. Then, open your Instant Pot, pour in the water and fit a trivet at the bottom of the pot. Put the fillets on the trivet. Close the lid, secure the pressure valve, and select Steam mode on High pressure for 5 minutes. Once ready, do a quick pressure release, and open the lid. Remove the mahi mahi onto serving plates. Serve with steamed or braised asparagus. For a crispier taste, cook them for 2 minutes on Air Fry mode at 300°F.

567. Tuna Salad with Asparagus & Potatoes

Servings: 4 | Ready in about: 60 MinutesUTES

1½ lb potatoes, quartered
3 tbsp olive oil
Salt and black pepper to taste
8 oz asparagus, cut into three
2 tbsp red wine vinegar, divided
½ cup pimento stuffed green olives
½ cup chopped roasted red peppers
2 tbsp chopped fresh parsley
2 cans tuna, drained

Pour 1 cup water into your Instant Pot and set in a trivet. Place the potatoes on the trivet. Seal the pressure lid. Choose Pressure Cook on High and the cook time to 4 minutes. After pressure cooking, perform a quick pressure release and carefully open the pressure lid. Take out a trivet, empty the water, and return the pot to the base. Arrange the potatoes and asparagus on the air fry basket. Drizzle some olive oil on them and season with salt.

Place the basket in the pot. Close the air fry lid, choose Air Fry, adjust the temperature to 375°F, and the cook time to 12 minutes. After 8 minutes, open the lid, and check the veggies. The asparagus will have started browning and crisping. Gently toss with the potatoes and close the lid. Continue cooking for the remaining 4 minutes.

Pour the asparagus and potatoes into a salad bowl. Sprinkle with some red wine vinegar and mix to coat. In a bowl, pour the remaining oil, remaining vinegar, salt, and pepper. Whisk to combine. Add in the roasted red peppers, olives, parsley, and tuna. Drizzle the dressing over the salad and mix to coat. Serve.

568. Cajun Salmon with Creamy Grits

Servings: 4 | Ready in about: 100 minutes

¾ cup corn grits
1 ½ cups coconut milk
1 ½ cups vegetable stock
3 tbsp butter, divided
Salt to taste
½ tbsp Cajun seasoning
1 tbsp packed brown sugar
4 salmon fillets, skin removed
Cooking spray

Pour the grits into a heatproof bowl. Add the coconut milk, stock, 1 tablespoon of butter, and salt. Stir and cover the bowl with foil. Pour the water into your Instant Pot. Put in a trivet and place the bowl on top. Seal the pressure lid, choose Pressure Cook and the cook time to 15 minutes. In a bowl combine Cajun, brown sugar, and salt. Oil the fillets on one side with cooking spray and place one or two at a time with sprayed-side down into the spice mixture. Oil the other sides and turn over to coat that side in the seasoning. Repeat the process with the remaining fillets. Once the grits are ready, perform a natural pressure release for 10 minutes.

Remove the trivet and bowl from the pot. Add the remaining butter to the grits and stir to combine well. Cover again with aluminum foil and return the bowl to the pot (without a trivet). Fix a trivet in the upper position of the pot and put the salmon fillets on the trivet. Close the air fry lid and choose Bake. Adjust the temperature to 400°F and the cook time to 12 minutes. After 6 minutes, open the lid and use tongs to turn the fillets over. Close the lid and continue cooking. When the salmon is ready, take out a trivet. Remove the bowl of grits and take off the foil. Stir and serve immediately with the salmon.

569. Mediterranean-Style Steamed Cod

Servings: 4 | Ready in about: 20 minutes

1 lb cherry tomatoes, halved
1 bunch fresh thyme sprigs
4 fillets cod
1 tsp olive oil
1 clove garlic, pressed
1 cup white rice
1 cup Kalamata olives
2 tbsp pickled capers
1 tbsp olive oil, divided

Line a parchment paper to the steamer basket of your Instant Pot. Place about half the tomatoes in a single layer on the paper. Sprinkle with thyme, reserving some for garnish. Arrange cod fillets on the top of tomatoes. Sprinkle with a little bit of olive oil. Spread the garlic, pepper, salt, and remaining tomatoes over the fish. In the pot, mix rice and water. Lay a trivet over the rice and 2 cups water. Lower steamer basket onto the trivet. Seal the pressure lid, choose Pressure Cook on High, and set the timer to 7 minutes. When ready, release the pressure quickly. Remove the steamer basket and trivet from the pot. Use a fork to fluff rice. Plate the fish fillets and apply a garnish of olives, reserved thyme, pepper, remaining olive oil, and capers. Serve with rice.

570. Mackerel en Papillote with Vegetables

Servings: 6 | Ready in about: 25 minutes + marinating time

3 whole mackerel, cut into 2 pieces
1 lb asparagus, trimmed
1 carrot, cut into sticks
1 celery stalk, cut into sticks
½ cup butter, at room temperature
6 medium tomatoes, quartered
1 large brown onion, sliced thinly
1 Orange Bell pepper, cut into sticks
Salt and black pepper to taste
2 ½ tbsp Pernod
3 cloves garlic, minced
2 lemons, cut into wedges

Cut out 6 pieces of parchment paper a little longer and wider than a piece of fish with kitchen scissors. Then, cut out 6 pieces of foil slightly longer than the parchment papers. Lay the foil wraps on a flat surface and place each parchment paper on each aluminium foil. In a bowl, add tomatoes, onions, garlic, bell pepper, pernod, butter, asparagus, carrot, celery, salt, and pepper. Use a spoon to mix them.

Place each fish piece on the layer of parchment and foil wraps. Spoon the vegetable mixture on each fish. Wrap the fish and place the packets in the refrigerator for 2 hours. Remove the fish to a flat surface. Pour in your Instant Pot 1 cup water and fit a trivet. Put the packets on the trivet. Seal the lid and select Steam for 3 minutes. Once the timer has ended, do a quick pressure release, and open the lid. Remove the trivet with the fish packets onto a flat surface. Carefully open the foil and using a spatula. Return the packets to the pot, on top of the trivet. Close the air fry lid and cook on Air Fry for 3 minutes at 300°F. Then, remove to serving plates. Serve with lemon.

571. Italian-Style Flounder

Servings: 4 | Ready in about: 70 minutes

3 slices prosciutto, chopped
½ small red onion, chopped
Salt and black pepper to taste
2 (6-oz) bags baby kale
½ cup whipping cream
4 flounder fillets
3 tbsp unsalted butter, melted
2 tbsp chopped fresh parsley
1 cup panko breadcrumbs

On your Instant Pot, choose Sauté. Add the prosciutto and cook until crispy, about 6 minutes. Stir in the red onions and cook for about 2 minutes or until the onions start to soften. Sprinkle with salt. Fetch the kale into your Instant Pot and cook, stirring frequently until wilted and most of the liquid has evaporated, about 4-5 minutes. Mix in the whipping cream. Lay the flounder fillets over the kale in a single layer. Brush 1 tablespoon of the melted butter over the fillets and sprinkle with the remaining salt and black pepper. Close the air fry lid and choose Bake. Adjust the temperature to 300°F and the cook time to 3 minutes.

Combine the remaining butter, parsley and breadcrumbs in a bowl. When done, open the air fry lid. Spoon the breadcrumbs mixture on the fillets. Close the air fry lid and choose Bake. Adjust the temperature to 400°F and the cook time to 6 minutes. After about 4 minutes, open the lid and check the fish. The breadcrumbs should be golden brown and crisp. If not, close the lid and continue to cook for an additional two minutes.

572. Haddock with Sanfaina

Servings: 4 | Ready in about: 40 minutes

4 haddock fillets
¼ tsp salt
3 tbsp olive oil
½ small onion, sliced
1 jalapeño pepper, seeded and minced
2 large garlic cloves, minced
1 eggplant, cubed
1 bell pepper, chopped
1 (14.5-oz) can diced tomatoes, drained
1 bay leaf
½ tsp dried basil
⅓ cup sliced green olives
¼ cup chopped fresh chervil, divided
3 tbsp capers, divided

Season the fish on both sides with salt, place in the refrigerator, and make the sauce. Press Sauté on your Instant Pot. Melt the butter until no longer foaming. Add onion, eggplant, bell pepper, jalapeño, and garlic. Sauté for 5 minutes. Stir in the tomatoes, bay leaf, basil, and olives. Remove the fish from the refrigerator and lay on the vegetables in the pot. Seal the pressure lid, choose Pressure Cook, adjust the pressure to Low and the cook time to 3 minutes. After cooking, do a quick pressure release. Remove and discard the bay leaf. Transfer the fish to a serving platter and spoon the sauce over. Sprinkle with the chervil and capers. Serve and enjoy!

FISH & SEAFOOD

573. Paprika & Garlic Salmon

Servings: 4 | Ready in about: 10 minutes

4 (5 oz) salmon fillets
2 tsp cumin powder
1 ½ tsp paprika
2 tbsp chopped parsley
2 tbsp olive oil
2 tbsp hot water
1 tbsp maple syrup
2 cloves garlic, minced
1 lime, juiced

In a bowl, add cumin, paprika, parsley, olive oil, hot water, maple syrup, garlic, and lime juice. Mix with a whisk. Set aside. Open your Instant Pot and pour in 1 cup water. Fit in a trivet. Place salmon on the trivet. Seal the lid and select Steam for 3 minutes. Once the timer has ended, do a quick pressure release and open the pot. Close the air fry lid and cook on Air Fry mode for 3 minutes at 300°F. Use a set of tongs to transfer the salmon to a serving plate and drizzle the lime sauce all over it. Serve with steamed swiss chard.

574. Spicy Tangy Salmon with Wild Rice

Servings: 4 | Ready in about: 50 minutes

1 cup wild rice
1 cup vegetable stock
4 skinless salmon fillets
A bunch of asparagus, cut diagonally
3 tbsp olive oil, divided
Salt and black pepper to taste
2 limes, juiced
2 tbsp honey
1 tsp sweet paprika
2 jalapeño peppers, seeded and diced
4 garlic cloves, minced
2 tbsp chopped fresh parsley

Pour the brown rice and vegetable stock in your Instant Pot. Stir to combine. Put a trivet in the pot and lay the salmon fillets on the trivet. Seal the pressure lid, choose Pressure Cook on High, and set the time to 2 minutes. In a bowl, toss the broccoli with 1 tablespoon of olive oil and season with the salt and black pepper.

In another bowl, evenly combine the remaining oil, the lime juice, honey, paprika, jalapeño, garlic, and parsley. When done cooking, do a quick pressure release, and carefully open the pressure lid. Pat the salmon dry with a paper towel and coat the fish with the honey sauce while reserving a little for garnishing. Arrange the asparagus around the salmon. Close the air fry lid, choose Broil and set the time to 7 minutes. When ready, remove the salmon. Dish the salmon with asparagus and rice. Garnish with parsley and remaining sauce.

575. Salmon with Dill Chutney

Servings: 2 | Ready in about: 15 minutes

2 salmon fillets
For Chutney
¼ cup fresh dill
Juice from ½ lemon
Juice from ½ lemon

Sea salt to taste
¼ cup extra virgin olive oil
¼ tsp paprika

In a food processor, blend all the chutney ingredients until creamy. To your Instant Pot, add 1 cup water and place a trivet. Arrange salmon fillets skin-side down on the trivet. Drizzle lemon juice over salmon and apply a seasoning of paprika. Seal the lid, choose Pressure Cook, and set the timer to 3 minutes. When ready, release the pressure quickly. Season the fillets with pepper and salt, transfer to a serving plate and top with the dill chutney.

576. Steamed Sea Bass with Turnips

Servings: 4 | Ready in about: 15 minutes

1 lemon, sliced
4 sea bass fillets
4 sprigs thyme
1 white onion, sliced into thin rings
2 turnips, sliced
2 tsp olive oil

Add 1 cup water to your Instant Pot. Set in a trivet. Line a parchment paper to the bottom of steamer basket. Place lemon slices in a single layer on the trivet. Arrange fillets on the top, cover with onion and thyme sprigs and top with turnip slices. Drizzle olive oil over the mixture. Put steamer basket onto the trivet. Seal lid and cook on Low for 8 minutes. When ready, release pressure quickly. Serve over the delicate onion rings and thinly sliced turnips.

577. Monk Fish with Greens

Servings: 4 | Ready in about: 22 minutes

2 tbsp olive oil
4 monk fish fillets, cut in 2 pieces each
½ cup chopped green beans
2 cloves garlic, sliced
1 cup kale leaves
½ lb baby bok choy, chopped largely
1 lemon, zested and juiced
Salt and white pepper to taste

Pour the coconut oil, garlic, red chili, and green beans in your Instant Pot. Stir fry for 5 minutes on Sauté. Add the kale leaves, and cook them to wilt, about 3 minutes. Place the fish on a plate and season with salt, white pepper, and lemon zest. After, remove the green beans and kale into a plate and set aside. Back to the pot, add the olive oil and fish. Brown the fillets on each side for about 2 minutes and then add the bok choy in. Pour the lemon juice over the fish and gently stir. Cook for 2 minutes. Spoon the fish with bok choy over the green beans and kale.

578. Alaskan Cod with Fennel & Beans

Servings: 4 | Ready in about: 25 minutes

2 Alaskan cod fillets, cut into 4 pieces each
4 tbsp olive oil
2 cloves garlic, minced
2 small onions, chopped
½ cup olive brine
3 cups chicken broth
½ cup tomato puree
1 head fennel, quartered
1 cup pinto beans, soaked, drained
1 cup green olives, pitted and crushed
½ cup basil leaves
Lemon slices to garnish

Heat the olive oil on Sauté in your Instant Pot and add the garlic and onion. Stir-fry until the onion softens. Pour in chicken broth and tomato puree. Let simmer for about 3 minutes. Add fennel, olives, beans, salt, and pepper. Seal the lid and select Steam mode on High pressure for 10 minutes. Once ready, do a quick pressure release. Transfer the beans to a plate with a slotted spoon. Add the cod pieces to the cooker. Close the lid again, secure the pressure valve, and select Steam mode on Low pressure for 3 minutes. Once the timer has ended, do a quick pressure release. Remove the cod to soup plate, top with beans and basil, and spoon the broth over. Serve.

579. Fish Finger Sandwich

Servings: 4 | Ready in about: 20 minutes

4 cod fillets
2 tbsp flour
10 capers
4 bread rolls
2 oz breadcrumbs
4 tbsp pesto sauce
4 lettuce leaves
Salt and black pepper to taste

Season the fillets with some salt and pepper, and coat them with the flour, and then dip in the breadcrumbs. You should get at the layer of breadcrumbs, that's why we don't use eggs for this recipe. Arrange the fillets onto a baking mat. Close the air fry lid and cook for about 10 to 15 minutes on Air Fry mode at 390°F. Cut the bread rolls in half. Place a lettuce leaf on top of the bottom halves. Place the fillets over. Spread a tsp of pesto sauce on top of each fillet. Top with the remaining halves.

580. Pistachio Crusted Salmon

Servings: 1 | Ready in about: 15 minutes

1 salmon fillet
1 tsp mustard
3 tbsp pistachios
Pinch of sea salt
Pinch of garlic powder
Pinch of black pepper
1 tsp lemon juice
1 tsp grated Parmesan cheese
1 tsp olive oil

Whisk the mustard and lemon juice together. Season the salmon with salt, pepper, and garlic powder. Brush the olive oil on all sides. Brush the mustard-lemon mixture on top of the salmon. Chop the pistachios finely, and combine them with the Parmesan cheese. Sprinkle them on top of the salmon. Place the salmon in the air fry basket with the skin side down. Close the air fry lid and cook for 10 minutes on Air Fry mode at 350°F.

581. Smoked Salmon Pilaf with Walnuts

Servings: 4 | Ready in about: 60 minutes

½ cup walnut pieces	1 cup basmati rice	1 smoked salmon fillet, flaked
1 tbsp ghee	1 cup frozen corn, thawed	2 tsp prepared horseradish
4 green onions, chopped	1 tsp salt	1 medium tomato, seeded and diced

Pour the walnuts into a heatproof bowl. Put the air fry basket in the inner pot and the bowl in the basket. Close the air fry lid and choose Air Fry. Adjust the temperature to 375°F and the time to 5 minutes. Press Start to begin toasting the walnuts. After the cooking time is over, carefully take the bowl and basket out of the pot and set aside.

On the pot, choose Sauté. Add the ghee to melt and sauté the white part of the green onions for about a minute, or until starting to soften. Stir in rice and corn, stirring occasionally for 2 minutes or until starting to be fragrant. Add 2 cups water and salt. Seal the pressure lid, choose Pressure Cook on High and the time to 3 minutes. After cooking, perform a natural pressure release for 10 minutes, and carefully open the lid. Fluff the rice gently with a fork. Stir in the flaked salmon, green parts of the green onions, and the horseradish. Add the tomato and allow sitting a few minutes to warm through. Spoon the pilaf into bowls and top with walnuts. Serve.

582. Parmesan Tilapia

Servings: 4 | Ready in about: 15 minutes

¾ cup grated Parmesan cheese	2 tsp paprika	¼ tsp garlic powder
1 tbsp olive oil	1 tbsp chopped parsley	4 tilapia fillets

Mix parsley, Parmesan, garlic, salt, and paprika, in a shallow bowl. Brush the olive oil over the fillets, and then coat them with the Parmesan mixture. Place the tilapia onto a lined baking sheet, and then into your Instant Pot. Close the air fry lid and cook for about 4 to 5 minutes on all sides on Air Fry mode at 350°F. Serve.

583. Tuna Patties

Servings: 2 | Ready in about: 50 minutes

5 oz of canned tuna	¼ cup flour	2 eggs
1 tsp lime juice	½ cup milk	1 tsp chili powder, optional
1 tsp paprika	1 small onion, diced	½ tsp salt

Place all ingredients in a bowl, and mix to combine. Make two large patties, or a few smaller ones, out of the mixture. Place them on a lined sheet and refrigerate for 30 minutes. Close the air fry lid and cook the patties for about 6 minutes on each side on Roast mode at 350°F.

584. Cod Cornflakes Nuggets

Servings: 4 | Ready in about: 25 minutes

1 ¼ lb cod fillets, cut into chunks	1 egg	1 cup cornflakes
½ cup flour	1 tbsp water	1 tbsp olive oil

Add the oil and cornflakes in a food processor, and process until crumbed. Season the fish chunks with salt and pepper. Beat the egg along with 1 tbsp water. Dredge the chunks in flour first, then dip in the egg, and coat with cornflakes. Arrange on a lined sheet. Close the air fry lid and cook at 350°F for 15 minutes on Air Fry mode.

585. Cajun Salmon with Lemon

Servings: 1 | Ready in about: 10 minutes

1 salmon fillet	Juice of ½ lemon	2 lemon wedges
¼ tsp brown sugar	1 tbsp Cajun seasoning	1 tbsp chopped parsley, for garnishing

Meanwhile, combine the sugar and lemon and coat the salmon with this mixture thoroughly. Coat the salmon with the Cajun seasoning as well. Place a parchment paper into your Instant Pot, close the air fry lid and cook the salmon for 7 minutes on Air Fry mode at 350°F. Serve with lemon wedges and chopped parsley.

586. Quick & Easy Fried Salmon

Servings: 1 | Ready in about: 13 minutes

| 1 salmon fillet | 1 tbsp soy sauce | ¼ tsp garlic powder |

Combine the soy sauce with the garlic powder. Brush the mixture over the salmon. Place the salmon onto a sheet of parchment paper and inside your Instant Pot. Close the air fry lid and cook for 10 minutes on Air Fry at 350°F, until crispy on the outside and tender on the inside.

587. Scottish Seafood Curry

Servings: 8 | Ready in about: 45 minutes

Seafood
½ lb squid, cut into 1-inch rings
½ lb sscallop meat
½ lb langoustine tall meat
½ lb mussels

Curry
4 tbsp olive oil	2 tbsp garlic paste	1 tsp shrimp paste
2 cups shellfish stock	1 ½ tbsp chili powder	1 ½ cups coconut milk
2 curry leaves	1 ½ tbsp chili paste	1 cup milk
2 tbsp shallot puree	2 tbsp lemongrass paste	1 tbsp Grants Scotch Whiskey
3 tbsp yellow curry paste	½ tsp turmeric powder	2 tbsp fish curry powder
2 tbsp ginger paste	2 tsp shrimp powder	Salt to taste

Vegetables
| ¼ cup diced tomatoes | ¼ cup chopped okra |
| ¼ cup chopped onion | ¼ cup chopped eggplants |

Add olive oil, shallot paste, yellow curry paste, ginger puree, garlic paste, lemongrass paste, chili paste, shrimp paste, and curry leaves. Stir-fry for 10 minutes on Sauté mode, until well combined and aromatic. Next, add turmeric powder, fish curry powder, and shrimp powder. Stir-fry for another minute. Pour in the shellfish stock and close the air fry lid. Cook on Broil mode for 15 minutes. Open the lid, and add the scallops, squid, chopped onion, okra, tomatoes, and aubergine. Stir lightly. Close the pressure lid, secure the pressure valve, and select

Steam mode on High pressure for 5 minutes. Once ready, do a quick pressure release. Add in milk, coconut milk, whiskey, and salt. Stir carefully not to mash the aubergine. Select Sauté and add mussels and langoustine. Stir carefully. Simmer the sauce for 3 minutes. Dish the seafood with sauce and veggies into serving bowls. Serve.

588. White Wine Black Mussels

Servings: 4 | Ready in about: 45 minutes

1 ½ lb black mussels, cleaned and de-bearded
3 tbsp olive oil	1 white onion, chopped finely	1 cup dry white wine
3 large chilies, seeded and chopped	10 tomatoes, chopped	3 cups vegetable broth
3 cloves garlic, peeled and crushed	4 tbsp tomato paste	⅓ cup fresh basil leaves

Heat the olive oil on Sauté and stir-fry the onion, chilies, and garlic, and cook for 2 minutes, stirring frequently. Stir in the tomatoes and tomato paste, and cook for 2 more minutes. Pour in the wine and vegetable broth. Let simmer for 5 minutes. Add the mussels, close the lid, secure the pressure valve, and press Steam for 3 minutes. Once the timer has ended, do a natural pressure release for 15 minutes. Remove and discard any unopened mussels. Add half of the basil and stir. Close the air fry lid and cook on Broil for 5 minutes. Dish the mussels with sauce and garnish it with the remaining basil. Serve with crusted bread.

589. Mushroom & Shrimp Egg Wrappers

Servings: 4 AS AN APPETIZER | Ready in about: 70 minutes

2 tbsp coconut aminos	1 large carrot, peeled and grated	¼ tsp freshly ground black pepper
1 tbsp dry white wine	1 tsp ginger puree	½ cup sautéed mushrooms, chopped
2 tsp plain vinegar	2 garlic cloves, minced	8 oz shrimp, peeled and chopped
3 cups shredded cabbage	1 tsp sugar	1 tsp arrowroot starch
3 green onions, chopped	2 tsp peanut oil	10 egg roll wrappers

Mix the coconut aminos, white wine, and vinegar in your Instant Pot. Stir in the cabbage, green onions, carrot, ginger, garlic, sugar, and peanut oil. Seal the pressure lid, choose Pressure Cook, and the cook time to 2 minutes. After cooking, do a quick pressure release. Stir in the pepper, mushrooms, and shrimp. Choose Sauté and simmer the shrimp and mushrooms for about 5 minutes until almost all of the liquid has dried up. Spoon the filling into a bowl and set aside to cool. Wipe out the inner pot with a paper towel and return the pot to the base. In a bowl, combine the arrowroot and 1 tbsp water. Lay an egg roll wrapper on a clean flat surface with a corner side facing you. Dip your index finger in the starch mixture and lightly moisten the edges of the wrapper.

With a slotted spoon, fetch a ¼ cup of filling onto the wrapper, just below the center. Fold the bottom corner of the wrapper over the filling, tuck under the filling, roll once and fold both sides in. Continue rolling up tightly and repeat the process with the remaining wrappers. Close the air fry lid and choose Air Fry. Adjust the temperature to 390°F and the time to 5 minutes. Lay 5 egg rolls in the air fry basket and oil with the cooking spray. Flip and oil the other sides. When the pot is ready, fix the basket in the inner pot. Close the air fry lid and choose Air Fry. Adjust the temperature to 390°F and the cook time to 15 minutes.

After 6 minutes, open the lid and check the egg rolls, which should be golden brown and crisp on top. Otherwise, close the lid and cook for 2 minutes more. Flip the rolls with tongs and cook further for 5 to 6 minutes or until crisp on the other side too. Repeat the frying process for the remaining egg rolls. When ready, use tongs to remove the egg rolls into a plate. Allow cooling for a few minutes before serving.

590. Sausage & Shrimp Paella

Servings: 4 | Ready in about: 70 minutes

1 tbsp melted butter	½ cup dry white wine	1 tsp turmeric powder
1 lb andouille sausage, sliced	1 cup Spanish rice	1 lb baby squid, cut into ¼-inch rings
1 white onion, chopped	2 cup chicken stock	1 lb jumbo shrimp, deveined
4 garlic cloves, minced	1½ tsp sweet paprika	1 red bell pepper, diced

Choose Sauté on your Instant Pot. Melt the butter and add the sausage. Cook until browned on both sides, about 3 minutes while stirring frequently. Remove the sausage to a plate and set aside. Sauté the onion and garlic in the same fat for 3 minutes until fragrant and pour in the wine. Use a wooden spoon to scrape the bottom of the pot of any brown bits and cook for 2 minutes or until the wine reduces by half. Stir in the rice and chicken stock.

Season with paprika, turmeric, black pepper, and salt. Seal the pressure lid, choose Pressure Cook and set to High. Set the time to 5 minutes, then When done cooking, do a quick pressure release and carefully open the lid. Choose Sauté. Add the squid and shrimp to the pot and stir gently without mashing the rice. Seal the pressure lid again and cook for 6 minutes, until the shrimp are pink and opaque. Return the sausage to the pot and mix in the bell pepper. Warm through for 2 minutes. Dish the paella and serve immediately.

591. Spaghetti with Arugula & Scallops

Servings: 4 | Ready in about: 50 minutes

1¼ lb scallops, peeled and deveined	¼ cup white wine	½ tsp red chili flakes or to taste
1½ tsp salt, divided	10 oz spaghetti	1 tsp grated lemon zest
1 tbsp melted butter	2½ cups water	1 tbsp lemon juice
2 large garlic cloves, minced, divided	⅓ cup tomato puree	6 cups arugula

FISH & SEAFOOD

Arrange the scallops in the air fry basket. Season with ½ teaspoon salt, melted butter, and 1 minced garlic clove. Toss to coat and put the basket in the inner pot. Close the air fry lid, choose Air Fry, adjust the temperature to 400°F and the cook time to 6 minutes. After 3 minutes, open the lid and use tongs to turn the scallops. Close the lid and resume cooking. Remove onto a plate and set aside.

On your Instant Pot, choose Sauté. Pour in the white wine and simmer for 1 to 2 minutes until reduced by half. Add the spaghetti, water, remaining salt, garlic, puréed tomato, and chili flakes. Stir to combine. Lock the pressure lid into place and set to Seal. Choose Pressure Cook on High and the cook time to 5 minutes. After cooking, perform a quick pressure release and carefully open the lid. Stir in the lemon zest, juice, and arugula until wilted and soft. Add the scallops and heat through for a few minutes. Serve immediately.

592. Crabmeat with Broccoli Risotto

Servings: 4 | Ready in about: 80 minutes

1 lb broccoli, cut into 1-inch pieces	1 small onion, chopped	2 cups vegetable stock
1 tbsp olive oil	1 cup short grain rice	8 oz lump crabmeat
2 tbsp ghee	⅓ cup white wine	⅓ cup grated Pecorino Romano cheese

Choose Air Fry your Instant Pot. Adjust the temperature to 375°F and the time to 2 minutes. Add the broccoli in the air fry basket and drizzle with the olive oil. Season with ½ teaspoon of salt and toss. Put the basket in the inner pot. Close the air fry lid, choose Air Fry, adjust the temperature to 375°F and the cook time to 10 minutes.

After 5 minutes, open the lid and stir the broccoli, then resume cooking. When done, take out the basket and set aside. Choose Sauté. Melt the ghee. Add and sauté the onion for 5 minutes until softened. Stir in the rice for 1 minute. Add in wine and cook for 3 minutes, stirring often, until the liquid has almost completely evaporated. Pour in vegetable stock and the remaining salt. Stir to combine. Seal the pressure lid, choose Pressure Cook on High, and the cook time to 8 minutes. After cooking, perform a quick pressure release and carefully open the pressure lid. Gently stir in the crabmeat, and cheese. Taste and adjust the seasoning. Serve immediately.

593. Creamy Crab Soup

Servings: 4 | Ready in about: 45 minutes

2 lb crabmeat lumps	2 celery stalk, diced	3 tsp Worcestershire sauce
6 tbsp butter	1 ½ cup chicken broth	3 tsp old bay Seasoning
6 tbsp flour	¾ cup heavy cream	¾ cup Muscadet
1 white onion, chopped	½ cup Half and Half cream	Lemon juice to serve
3 tsp minced garlic	2 tsp hot sauce	Chopped dill to serve

Melt the butter on Sauté in your Instant Pot and mix in the all-purpose flour, in a fast motion to make a rue. Add celery, onion, and garlic. Stir and cook until soft and crispy, for 3 minutes. While stirring, gradually add the half and half cream, heavy cream, and broth. Let simmer for 2 minutes. Add Worcestershire sauce, old bay seasoning, Muscadet, and hot sauce. Stir and let simmer for 15 minutes. Add the crabmeat and mix it well into the sauce. Close the air fry lid and cook on Broil mode for 10 minutes to soften the meat. Dish into serving bowls, garnish with dill and drizzle squirts of lemon juice over. Serve with a side of garlic crusted bread.

594. Prawn Toast

Servings: 2 | Ready in about: 12 minutes

6 prawns, shells removed, chopped	3 white slices of bread	1 egg white, whisked
1 large spring onion, finely sliced	½ cup sweet corn	1 tbsp black sesame seeds

In a bowl, place the prawns, corn, spring onion and the black sesame seeds. Add the whisked egg white, and mix the ingredients. Spread the mixture over the bread slices. Place the prawns in the air fry basket and sprinkle with oil. Close the air fry lid and fry the prawns until golden, for 8-10 minutes at 390°F on Air Fry mode. Serve.

595. Seafood Gumbo

Servings: 4 | Ready in about: 90 minutes

1 lb jumbo shrimp	1½ tsp Cajun seasoning	1 small banana pepper, minced
8 oz lump crabmeat	1 medium onion, chopped	3 cups chicken broth
1½ tsp salt divided	1 small red bell pepper, chopped	1 cup jasmine rice
¼ cup olive oil, plus 2 tsp	2 celery stalks, chopped	¾ cup water
⅓ cup all-purpose flour	2 garlic cloves, minced	2 green onions, finely sliced

Lay the shrimp in the air fry basket. Season with salt and some olive oil. Toss to coat and fix the basket in the inner pot. Close the air fry lid and choose Air Fry. Adjust the temperature to 400°F and the cook time to 6 minutes. After 3 minutes, open the lid and toss the shrimp. Close the lid and resume cooking. When ready, the shrimp should be opaque and pink. Remove the basket and set aside. Choose Sauté. Heat the remaining olive oil. Whisk in the flour with and cook the roux that forms for 5 minutes, stirring constantly, until the roux has the color of peanut butter. Stir in the Cajun, onion, bell pepper, celery, garlic, and banana pepper for about 5 minutes until the mixture slightly cools. Add the chicken broth and crabmeat, stir. Put the rice into a heatproof bowl.

Add water and salt. Cover the bowl with foil. Put a trivet in the pot and set the bowl on the trivet. Seal the lid, choose Pressure Cook, and the time to 6 minutes. After cooking, perform a natural pressure for 10 minutes. Take out the trivet and bowl. Stir the shrimp into the gumbo to heat it up for 3 minutes. Fluff the rice and divide into bowls. Spoon the gumbo around the rice and garnish with the green onions.

596. Trout with Tomato Sauce & Spinach

Servings: 4 | Ready in about: 30 minutes + marinating time

1 lb trout fillets	3 cups fish stock	2 tomatoes, peeled and diced
5 oz fresh spinach, torn	¼ cup olive oil	1 tbsp thyme, dried
3 tbsp lemon juice	3 garlic cloves, crushed	½ tbsp rosemary, fresh

In a large bowl, combine the olive oil, thyme, rosemary, lemon juice. Stir well and submerge the fillets in the mixture. Refrigerate for 45 minutes. Remove from the fridge, drain the fillets and keep the marinade. Grease the stainless steel cooking insert of the Instant Pot with 1/4 cup of the marinade. Add the fillets, fish stock and seal the lid. Set the steam release handle, press Pressure Cook button and cook for 10 minutes.

When ready, do a quick release. Remove the fish and set aside. Pour the remaining marinade into the pot. Press Sauté and add tomatoes. Cook until the tomatoes soften; then remove. Grease the bottom with olive oil, add garlic and spinach. Cook for 7 minutes. Transfer to a plate. Add the fish and top with with tomato sauce.

597. Potato Chowder with Peppery Prawns

Servings: 4 | Ready in about: 80 minutes

4 slices serrano ham, chopped	16 oz frozen corn	16 prawns, peeled and deveined
4 tbsp minced garlic, divided	2 cups vegetable broth	2 tbsp olive oil
1 onion, chopped	1 tsp dried rosemary	½ tsp red chili flakes
2 Yukon Gold potatoes, chopped	Salt and black pepper to taste	¾ cup heavy cream

Choose Sauté on your Instant Pot. Add 1 tbsp the olive oil and cook serrano ham, 2 tbsp garlic, and onion, stirring occasionally, for 5 minutes. Fetch out one-third of the serrano ham into a bowl for garnishing. Add the potatoes, corn, broth, rosemary, salt, and pepper to the pot. Seal the lid, hit Pressure Cook and cook for 10 minutes.

In a bowl, toss the prawns in the remaining garlic, salt, black pepper, the remaining olive oil, and the red chili flakes. When done cooking, do a quick pressure release and carefully open the pressure lid. Stir in the heavy cream and fix a trivet the pot over the chowder. Spread the prawn in a trivet. Close the air fry lid. Choose Broil and set the time to 8 minutes. When the timer has ended, remove the trivet from the pot. Ladle the corn chowder into serving bowls and top with the prawns. Garnish with the reserved ham and serve immediately.

598. Mussel Chowder with Oyster Crackers

Servings: 4 | Ready in about: 75 minutes

3 (6-oz) cans chopped mussels, drained, liquid reserved
2 cups oyster crackers
2 tbsp melted ghee
¼ cup grated Pecorino Romano cheese
½ tsp garlic powder
1 tsp salt, divided
2 thick pancetta slices, cut into thirds
2 celery stalks, chopped
1 medium onion, chopped
1 tbsp flour
¼ cup white wine
1 cup clam juice
1 lb parsnips, cut into chunks
1 bay leaf
1 ½ cups heavy cream
2 tbsp chopped fresh chervil

In a bowl, pour the oyster crackers. Drizzle with melted ghee, add the cheese, garlic powder, and salt. Toss to coat the crackers. Transfer to the air fry basket. Once the pot is ready, open the pressure lid and fix the basket in your Instant Pot. Close the lid and choose Air Fry. Adjust the temperature to 375°F and the cook time to 6 minutes. After 3 minutes, open the lid and mix the crackers with a spoon. Close the lid and resume cooking until crisp and lightly browned. Take out the basket and let it cool. On the pot, choose Sauté. Add the pancetta and cook for 5 minutes, turning once or twice, until crispy. Remove the pancetta to a paper towel-lined plate. Set aside.

Sauté the celery and onion in the pancetta grease for 1 minute or until the vegetables start softening. Mix the flour into the vegetables to coat evenly and pour the wine over the veggies. Cook for about 1 minute or until reduced by about one-third. Pour in the clam juice, the reserved mussel liquid, parsnips, remaining salt, and bay leaf. Seal the pressure lid, choose Pressure Cook and the cook time to 4 minutes. After cooking, perform a natural pressure release for 10 minutes. Stir in mussels and heavy cream. Choose Sauté. Simmer the chowder and heat the mussels. Remove and discard the bay leaf after. Spoon the soup into bowls and crumble the pancetta over the top. Garnish with the chervil and a handful of oyster crackers, serving the remaining crackers on the side.

599. White Wine Mussels

Servings: 5 | Ready in about: 15 minutes

1 cup white wine
2 lb mussels, cleaned and debearded
Juice from 1 lemon

In your Instant Pot, mix ½ cup water and wine. Put the mussels into a steamer basket. Insert a trivet in the pot and lower steamer basket onto the trivet. Seal lid and cook on Pressure Cook for 1 minute. When ready, release the pressure quickly. Remove unopened mussels. Coat the mussels with the wine mixture. Serve with French fries.

600. Mustardy Halibut

Servings: 4 | Ready in about: 10 minutes

1 tbsp organic mustard
4 halibut fillets

Pour 2 cups of water into your Instant Pot. Brush the fish fillets with mustard. Arrange the fish in the steaming basket. Secure the lid, and select Pressure Cook. Cook on high for 3 minutes. When ready, release the pressure quickly.

601. Parsley Oyster Stew

Servings: 4 | Ready in about: 12 minutes

2 cups heavy cream
2 cups chopped celery
2 cups bone broth
3 (10 oz) jars shucked oysters in liqueur
3 Shallots, minced
3 tbsp olive oil
Salt and white pepper to taste
3 cloves garlic, minced
3 tbsp chopped parsley

To your Instant Pot, add oil, garlic, shallot, and celery. Stir-fry them for 2 minutes on Sauté and add the heavy cream, broth, and oysters. Stir once or twice. Close the lid, secure the pressure valve, and select Steam mode on High pressure for 3 minutes. Once the timer has stopped, do a quick pressure release, and open the lid. Season with salt and white pepper. Close the air fry lid and cook for 5 minutes on Broil mode. Stir and dish the oyster stew into serving bowls. Garnish with parsley and top with some croutons.

FISH & SEAFOOD

602. Penne all'Arrabbiata with Seafood & Chorizo

Servings: 4 | Ready in about: 50 minutes

1 tbsp olive oil	1 (24-oz) jar Arrabbiata sauce	8 oz shrimp, peeled and deveined
1 onion, diced	3 cups fish broth	8 oz scallops
16 oz penne	1 chorizo, sliced	12 clams, cleaned and debearded

Choose Sauté on your Instant Pot. Heat the oil and add the chorizo, onion, and garlic. Sauté them for about 5 minutes. Stir in the penne, Arrabbiata sauce, and broth. Season with the black pepper and salt and mix. Seal the pressure lid, choose Pressure Cook on High and set the time to 2 minutes. Do a quick pressure release. Choose Sauté. Stir in the shrimp, scallops, and clams. Put the pressure lid together and set to the Vent position. Cover and cook for 5 minutes, until the clams have opened and the shrimp and scallops are opaque and cooked through. Discard any unopened clams. Spoon the seafood and chorizo pasta into serving bowls and serve warm.

603. Rosemary Salmon with Spinach

Servings: 4 | Ready in about: 25 minutes

1 lb salmon filets, boneless	1 garlic cloves, finely chopped	Salt and black pepper to taste
1 lb fresh spinach, torn	1 tbsp lemon juice	
3 tbsp olive oil	1 tbsp fresh rosemary, chopped	

Grease the bottom of the Instant Pot with 2 tbsp. olive oil. Place the salmon filets and season with rosemary, salt and pepper. Drizzle with lemon juice, add half cup of water and seal the lid. Set the steam release handle and press the Pressure Cook button. Cook on High for 4 minutes. When done, press CANCEL and turn off the Instant Pot.

In a large pot, place the torn spinach and cover with water. Bring to a boil and cook for 2 -3 minutes or until tender. Drain in a colander. Remove the salmon from the Instant Pot and place the spinach at the bottom. Pour half cup of water and add garlic. Top with salmon and press Sauté. Cook for 7 - 8 minutes more, and serve immediately.

604. Simple Coconut Shrimp

Serves: 4 | Total Time: 20 minutes

1 cup coconut four	½ cup panko bread crumbs	1 tbsp finely chopped cilantro
1 tsp salt	1 cup grated coconut flakes	
2 large eggs	1 lb large shrimp, peeled and deveined	

Preheat your Instant Pot Duo Crisp to 375°F. Set up three bowls. In the first bowl, combine coconut flour, and salt. In the second bowl, whisk the eggs. In the third bowl, combine bread crumbs and coconut flakes. First, dip the shrimp in the flour and shake off the excess. Next, dip the shrimp in the egg and shake off the drips. After that, coat the shrimp in the bread crumb mixture. Lightly spray with cooking oil and transfer to the air fry basket. Close the fry lid and Air Fry for 5 minutes, then flip the shrimp. Lightly spray with cooking oil and cook for another 5 minutes or until the shrimp is opaque. Serve immediately sprinkled with cilantro.

605. Lemony Sea Bream

Servings: 4 | Ready in about: 50 minutes

2 pieces sea bream, cleaned	4 tbsp olive oil	1 tsp Italian seasoning
4 cups fish stock	½ tbsp garlic powder	sea salt to taste
4 tbsp lemon juice	1 tsp rosemary sprigs	

In a small bowl, combine olive oil, lemon juice, rosemary, Italian seasoning, sea salt and garlic powder. Brush the fish and wrap tightly with plastic foil. Refrigerate for 30 minutes before cooking. Pour in the fish stock in your Instant Pot. Adjust the steamer insert and place the fish. Secure, set the steam release handle and select Pressure Cook for 8 minutes. Once ready, do a quick release and serve immediately.

606. Fish & Chips with Spinach

Servings: 4 | Ready in about: 35 minutes

4 medium-sized mackerels, skin on	¼ cup olive oil	juice of 1 lemon
1 lb fresh spinach, torn	2 garlic cloves, crushed	Salt to taste
4 sweet potatoes, peeled and sliced	1 tbsp rosemary, dried, chopped	

Grease the bottom of the Instant Pot with 4 tbsp. of olive oil. Press Sauté button and add garlic and rosemary. Stir-fry for a minute and add the spinach. Sprinkle with salt and cook for 5 more minutes, stirring occasionally. Remove the spinach from the cooker and set aside. Add the remaining olive oil to the pot and make a lay in the potatoes. Place the fish and drizzle with lemon juice and salt. Pour in 1 cup of water and Secure the lid. Adjust the steam release handle and press Pressure Cook. Cook for 8 minutes. Release the steam naturally, for 10 minutes and transfer the fish and the potatoes to a serving plate. Serve with spinach.

607. Tilapia Taco Bowls

Serves: 4 | Total Time: 25 minutes

2 cups grated cabbage	5 tilapia fillets	1 minced garlic clove
½ cup mayonnaise	2 tsp chili powder	Salt and black pepper to taste
1 lime, juiced	1 tbsp lime zest	

Combine cabbage, mayonnaise, and half of the lime juice. Cover the slaw and refrigerate. Preheat your Instant Pot Duo Crisp to 400°F. Season tilapia with chili powder, lime zest, garlic, salt, and pepper. Lightly spray with cooking oil. Place tilapia in the air fry basket and close the fry lid. Air Fry for 6 minutes. Flip the fish and cook for another 6 minutes until the fish is flaky and opaque. Let cool for 5 minutes. Chop into bite-sized pieces. In each bowl, add ½ cup slaw from the refrigerator and top with ¼ of the fish. Sprinkle with the rest of the lime juice. Serve warm.

608. Elegant Shrimp Burgers

Serves: 4 | Total Time: 20 minutes

10 oz shrimp, peeled and deveined	1 shallot, minced	Salt and black pepper to taste
¼ cup mayonnaise	½ cup panko bread crumbs	4 hamburger buns
½ jalapeño pepper, minced	½ tsp Old Bay Seasoning	1 avocado, thinly sliced

Preheat your Instant Pot Duo Crisp to 400°F. Pulse shrimp in a food processor four times until broken down. Transfer the shrimp to a large bowl and combine with mayonnaise, jalapeño, shallot, bread crumbs, Old Bay, salt, and pepper. Divide the mixture into 4 parts and shape it into patties. The patties will feel wet but maintain their shape. Place the patties in the air fry basket and close the fry lid. Air Fry for 5 minutes. Flip the patties carefully and cook for another 5 minutes or until the patties are brown. Transfer to buns and serve warm topped with avocado slices.

609. Paella Señorito

Servings: 5 | Ready in about: 25 minutes

¼ cup olive oil	1 tsp paprika	¼ cup frozen green peas
1 onion, chopped	1 tsp turmeric	2 cups fish broth
1 red bell pepper, diced	Salt and ground white pepper to taste	1 lb shrimp, peeled and deveined
2 garlic cloves, minced	1 cup bomba rice	1 lemon, cut into wedges

Warm oil on Sauté in your Instant Pot. Add in bell pepper and onion and garlic and cook for 3 minutes until soft. Add paprika, white pepper, salt, and turmeric and cook for 1 minute. Stir in fish broth and rice. Add shrimp in the rice mixture. Seal the lid, choose Pressure Cook, and set timer to 5 minutes. When ready, release the pressure quickly. Stir in green peas and let sit for 5 minutes until green peas are heated through. Garnish with lemon.

610. Cheesy Shrimp Stew

Servings: 4 | Ready in about: 35 minutes

1 ½ lb tomatoes, chopped	1 onion, chopped	1 cup shredded cheddar cheese
1 ½ lb shrimp, peeled and deveined	2 tbsp olive oil	½ cup clam juice
¼ cup chopped cilantro	1 jalapeño, diced	2 garlic cloves, minced

Set your Instant Pot to Sauté. Heat the olive oil, and sauté the onion for 3 minutes. Add garlic, and cook for 1 minute. Stir in tomatoes, clam juice, jalapeño, and cilantro. Secure the lid and select Pressure Cook. Cook on high for 9 minutes. Release the pressure naturally for 10 minutes. Stir in cilantro and shrimp, seal the lid and cook on Pressure Cook for 1 minute. Once done, perform a quick release. Stir in cheddar and serve.

611. Chorizo & Shrimp Boil

Servings: 4 | Ready in about: 30 minutes

3 red potatoes	4 chorizo sausages, sliced	Salt to taste
3 ears corn, cut into 1½-inch rounds	1 lb shrimp, peeled and deveined	1 lemon, cut into wedges
1 cup white wine	2 tbsp of seafood seasoning	¼ cup butter, melted

To your Instant Pot, add all ingredients except butter and lemon wedges. Do not stir. Pour in 2 cups water. Seal the pressure lid, choose Pressure Cook, and set the timer to 2 minutes. When ready, release the pressure quickly. Drain the mixture through a colander. Transfer to a serving platter. Serve with melted butter and lemon wedges.

612. Crab Cakes

Servings: 4 | Ready in about: 55 minutes

½ cup cooked crab meat	¼ cup chopped red pepper	2 tbsp chopped parsley
¼ cup chopped red onion	3 tbsp mayonnaise	Old Bay seasoning, as desired
1 tbsp chopped basil	Zest of ½ lemon	Cooking spray
¼ cup chopped celery	¼ cup breadcrumbs	

Place all ingredients in a large bowl and mix well until thoroughly incorporated. Make 4 large crab cakes from the mixture and place on a lined sheet. Refrigerate for 30 minutes. Spay the air basket with cooking spray and arrange the crab cakes in it. Close the air fry lid and cook for 7 minutes on each side on Air Fry at 390°F.

613. Seared Scallops with Butter-Caper Sauce

Servings: 6 | Ready in about: 18 minutes

2 lb sea scallops, foot removed	4 tbsp capers, drained	1 cup dry white wine
10 tbsp butter, unsalted	4 tbsp olive oil	3 tsp lemon zest

Melt the butter to caramel brown on Sauté in your Instant Pot. Fetch the butter out into a bowl. Heat the oil in the pot, add the scallops and sear them until golden brown, about 5 minutes; reserve. Pour the white wine in the pot to deglaze the bottom while using a spoon to scrape the bottom of the pot of any scallop bits. Add the capers, butter, and lemon zest. Stir the mixture once gently. Spoon the sauce with capers over the scallops. Serve.

614. Delicious Coconut Shrimp

Servings: 2 | Ready in about: 30 minutes

8 large shrimp	¼ tsp salt	1 tbsp honey
½ cup breadcrumbs	¼ tsp pepper	½ tsp cayenne pepper
8 oz coconut milk	½ cup orange jam	¼ tsp hot sauce
½ cup shredded coconut	1 tsp mustard	

Combine breadcrumbs, cayenne, shredded coconut, salt, and pepper in a bowl. Dip the shrimp in the coconut milk, then in the coconut crumbs. Arrange in the lined air fry basket, close the air fry lid and cook for 20 minutes on Air Fry at 350°F. Whisk the jam, honey, hot sauce, and mustard. Serve the shrimp with the sauce.

615. Tomato & Alaskan Cod Fillets

Servings: 4 | Ready in about: 20 minutes

2 cups cherry tomatoes
4 Alaskan cod fillets
2 tbsp organic butter, melted
Salt and pepper, to taste

Place the cherry tomatoes in a baking dish. Top with the cod fillets. Drizzle the butter over the fish, and season with salt and pepper. Place the dish in the Instant Pot. Secure the lid, and select Pressure Cook. Cook on High for 5 minutes. Once it goes off, do a natural pressure release for 5 minutes and serve immediately.

616. Chipotle Salmon

Servings: 4 | Ready in about: 10 minutes

1 lemon, sliced
2 tbsp chipotle chili pepper
4 salmon fillets
Juice of 1 lemon
Salt and black pepper to taste

Pour 2 cups of water into your Instant Pot. Season the salmon with the lemon juice, salt and black pepper. Top with chili pepper and lemon slices. Secure the lid and select Pressure Cook. Cook on high for 4 minutes. When done, release the pressure quickly and serve.

617. Shrimp & Chickpea Stew

Servings: 5 | Ready in about: 35 minutes

1 lb shrimp, cleaned and deveined
3 cups fish broth
1 cup scallions, chopped
1 carrot, chopped
1 cup chickpeas, soaked
½ tbsp Italian seasoning

Add all ingredients in the Instant Pot. Secure the lid and adjust the steam release handle. Press Pressure Cook and cook on High for 14 minutes. When done, allow for a natural pressure release for 10 minutes. Open the lid after 10 minutes and serve warm.

618. Blaze Salmon Fillets

Servings: 4 | Ready in about: 15 minutes

1 ½ cups water
4 salmon fillets
1 tsp organic mustard
1 tsp garlic powder
1 garlic clove, minced
1 tbsp lemon juice

Whisk together the lemon juice, mustard, garlic powder, and minced garlic. Brush this mixture over the salmon. Pour the water into your Instant Pot. Arrange the salmon fillets on the rack. Secure the lid, and select Pressure Cook. Cook on High for 4 minutes. When ready, perform a quick pressure release and serve immediately.

619. Steamed Salmon with Broccoli

Servings: 4 | Ready in about: 10 minutes

10 oz broccoli florets
4 salmon fillets
1 ½ cups water
1 tsp garlic powder
Salt and black pepper to taste

Season the salmon with garlic powder, salt, and pepper. Sprinkle the broccoli with salt and pepper, as well. Pour the water into your Instant Pot. Arrange the salmon n the steaming basket and scatter the broccoli around the fillets. Secure the lid, and select Pressure Cook. Cook on High for 2 minutes. Release the pressure quickly. Serve.

620. Lisboa-Style Octopus

Servings: 4 | Ready in about: 20 minutes

10 oz octopus
3 tbsp lime juice
2 tsp garlic powder

1 ½ cups water
1 tsp chopped cilantro
2 tbsp olive oil

Salt and black pepper to taste

Place the octopus in your Instant Pot. Sprinkle with olive oil, salt, pepper, and garlic powder. Pour the water around it (not on it!). Secure the lid and select Pressure Cook. Cook on high for 8 minutes. Once if goes off, perform a quick pressure release, open the lid and sprinkle lime juice over and cilantro.

621. Diavolo Shrimp

Serves: 4 | Total Time: 15 minutes

1 lb shrimp, peeled and deveined
½ cup lime juice
2 tbsp olive oil

2 tbsp sriracha
Salt and black pepper to taste
2 tbsp chopped parsley

1 lemon, juiced

Preheat your Instant Pot Duo Crisp to 375°F. Combine all of the ingredients in a cake pan. Place the pan in the air fry basket and close the fry lid. Air Fry for 5 minutes. Stir the mixture and cook for another 5 minutes or until the shrimp is opaque. Drizzle with lemon juice and sprinkle with parsley. Serve warm.

622. Cape Cod Scallops

Serves: 4 | Total Time: 20 minutes

Salt and black pepper to taste
8 (1-oz) sea scallops
4 tbsp butter, melted

4 tsp minced garlic
1 tbsp dry white wine
½ lemon, zested and juiced

2 tbsp chopped parsley

Preheat your Instant Pot Duo Crisp to 375°F. Season scallops with salt and pepper, then lightly spray with cooking oil. Arrange in a single layer in the air fry basket and close the fry lid. Air Fry for 6 minutes, then turn the scallops. Cook for another 6 minutes or until they are firm and opaque. While the scallops are cooking, prepare the garlic-lemon butter. Mix butter, garlic, lemon zest, white wine, and lemon juice in a small bowl. When the scallops are done, serve drizzled with the butter and sprinkled with parsley.

623. Rustic Fish Nuggets

Serves: 4 | Total Time: 25 minutes

3 cod fillets, cut into nudges
Salt and black pepper to taste

½ tsp dried dill
½ tsp lemon zest

2 large eggs
1 cup bread crumbs

Preheat your Instant Pot Duo Crisp to 350°F. Set up two small bowls. In the first bowl, whisk the eggs. In the second bowl, combine bread crumbs, dill, lemon zest, salt, and pepper. Dip each nugget into the eggs and shake off excess drips. Next, roll the nugget in the bread crumbs. Repeat until you have coated all of the nuggets. Place the nuggets in the air fry basket and lightly spray with cooking oil. Close the fry lid and Air Fry for 6 minutes, then flip the nuggets. Cook for another 6 minutes or until the nuggets are golden. Serve warm and enjoy!

624. Dill & Potato-Crusted Cod

Serves: 4 | Total Time: 25 minutes

4 skinless cod fillets
2 tbsp olive oil
Salt and black pepper to taste

1 tsp dried dill
1 tsp garlic powder
1 tsp shallot powder

1 tsp dried parsley
2 cups mashed potato flakes

Preheat your Instant Pot Duo Crisp to 350°F. Brush cod fillets with some olive oil, and season with salt and dill. Mix mashed potato flakes, salt, pepper, garlic powder, shallot powder, and dried parsley in a large bowl. Coat each fillet with the potato mixture, then lightly brush with the remaining olive oil. Place fillets in the air fry basket and close the fry lid. Air Fry for 8 minutes. Flip the fillets and cook for another 7 minutes or until the cod is golden.

625. Tomato Pollock Stew

Servings: 4 | Ready in about: 30 minutes

1 lb pollock fillet
4 large tomatoes, peeled
4 garlic cloves, crushed
1 onion, chopped
2 cups fish stock
2 bay leaves, whole
½ cup olive oil
salt and black pepper

Press Sauté and heat 2 tbsp. of olive oil. Add onion and stir-fry until translucent. Add the tomatoes and cook until they soften. Keep adding fish stock from time to time. Once the tomatoes have softened and the liquid has evaporated, add the remaining ingredients. Secure the lid and set the steam handle. Press Pressure Cook and cook for 16 minutes. When done, do a quick pressure release and serve.

626. Citrusy Catfish

Servings: 4 | Ready in about: 75 minutes

1 lb of flathead catfish
3 oranges, sliced
3 cups fish stock
1 cup orange juice
½ cup lemon juice
½ cup olive oil
1 tbsp dried rosemary
1 tsp chili flakes
Salt and black pepper to taste

Line the orange slices in your Instant Pot. In a large bowl, combine the orange juice, lemon juice, olive oil, rosemary, chili flakes, black pepper and salt. Brush the fish with this mixture and cool for 45 minutes. Set the steamer insert of your Instant Pot. Drain the fish and pour in the fish stock and the marinade, then place the fish onto the insert. Secure the lid, press Pressure Cook and cook for 20 minutes on High. When ready, perform a quick pressure release and serve immediately.

627. Spicy Caramelized Tilapia

Servings: 4 | Ready in about: 50 minutes

1 lb tilapia fillets
1 scallion, minced
1 cup coconut water
3 garlic cloves, minced
⅓ cup water
3 tbsp fish sauce
¼ cup brown sugar
1 red chili, minced
Salt and black pepper to taste

Marinate the tilapia in fish sauce, salt, pepper, and garlic for 30 minutes on the counter. Combine the water and sugar in your Instant Pot. Cook on Sauté until caramelized. Add the fish and coconut water in the Instant Pot. Secure the lid, and select Pressure Cook. Cook on high for 10 minutes. Perform a quick pressure release, open the lid and top with scallion and red chili.

628. Collard Green & Seafood Casserole

Servings: 4 | Ready in about: 40 minutes

1 lb shrimp
6 oz octopus, chopped into pieces
½ lb collard greens, chopped
1 tomato, peeled and diced
2 cups fish stock
3 tbsp olive oil
2 garlic cloves
2 tbsp fresh parsley, chopped

Place the shrimp, octopus, tomato and fish stock in the Instant Pot. Secure the lid and adjust the steam release handle. Press Pressure Cook and the timer to 15 minutes. Once ready, do a quick pressure release, open the lid and remove the shrimp and the octopus, and drain the liquid. Grease the bottom of the Pot with olive oil and press Sauté. Stir-fry garlic, parsley, and collard greens. Let simmer for 12 minutes. Serve with shrimp and octopus.

629. Cheddar Haddock Stew

Servings: 4 | Ready in about: 30 minutes

12 oz haddock fillets	1 tsp ground ginger	Salt and black pepper to taste
½ cup yogurt	5 oz cheddar cheese, grated	1 tbsp butter

Combine the ginger, salt, and pepper, in a small bowl. Rub the haddock with the spice mixture. Melt the butter in the Instant Pot on Sauté. Add haddock, and cook on Sauté for 2 minutes per side. Pour the yogurt and cheese over the fillets. Secure the lid, select Pressure Cook, and cook on Pressure Cook for 10 minutes. When ready, release the pressure naturally for 5 minutes.

630. Garlicky Catfish with Dilly Oil Dressing

Servings: 4 | Ready in about: 15 minutes

½ cup olive oil	4 catfish fillets	Salt and black pepper to taste
2 tsp chopped dill	3 garlic cloves, minced	

Heat the oil in your Instant Pot on Sauté. Add 2 garlic cloves and stir-fry for 1 minute. Add the catfish and season with salt and pepper. Cook for about 2 minutes per side. In the meantime, prepare the dill sauce by adding the dill, 1 garlic clove and ⅓ cup olive oil in a food processor. Pulse until smooth. Pour the sauce over the fish. Serve.

631. Maryland´s Crab Legs

Servings: 4 | Ready in about: 15 minutes

⅓ cup organic butter	3 lb crab legs
2 garlic cloves, minced	1 tsp olive oil

Pour 2 cups of water into your Instant Pot. Place the crab legs in the steaming basket. Secure the lid, and select the Pressure Cook. Cook for 4 minutes. Once if goes off, perform a quick release. Transfer to a plate. Set the Instant Pot to Sauté. Pour the oil and add the butter, and heat until butter is melted. Add garlic, and cook for 1 minute. Pour garlic butter sauce over the crab legs and serve immediately.

632. Creole Scallops Wrapped in Bacon

Serves: 4 | Total Time: 20 minutes

8 bacon slices	1 tsp Creole seasoning
8 sea scallops	2 tbsp coconut oil, melted

Preheat your Instant Pot Duo Crisp to 375°F. Cook bacon in the air fryer for 3 minutes. Remove bacon and wrap one slice around each scallop. Secure with a toothpick and season with Cajun seasoning. Lightly spray with cooking oil and arrange the scallops in a single layer in the air fry basket. Air Fry for 5 minutes, then turn the scallops. Cook for another 5 minutes until the scallops are firm and opaque. Serve drizzled with coconut oil.

633. Old Bay Salmon Cakes

Serves: 4 | Total Time: 20 minutes

1 (10-oz) pouch cooked salmon	½ cup mayonnaise	3 tsp Old Bay seasoning
6 tbsp panko bread crumbs	1 tbsp Dijon mustard	1 tbsp dried dill

Preheat your Instant Pot Duo Crisp to 350°F. Combine all of the ingredients in a large bowl. Divide into four portions and shape into patties. Lightly spray with cooking oil and transfer to the air fry basket. Close the fry lid and Air Fry for 6 minutes, then flip the patties. Cook for another 6 minutes or until patties is firm and brown.

634. Dilly Salmon Fillets

Serves: 4 | Total Time: 15 minutes

INGREDIENTS

4 salmon fillets
Salt and black pepper to taste
3 tbsp dry white wine
1 lemon, halved
½ tsp Worcestershire sauce
3 tbsp butter, melted
1 tsp dried dill
2 tbsp chopped basil

DIRECTIONS

Preheat your Instant Pot Duo Crisp to 375°F. Season salmon with salt and pepper. Squeeze half of the lemon in a small bowl and mix with butter and Worcestershire sauce. Slice the other half of the lemon into ¼-inch thick slices. Brush the lemon butter over the salmon, sprinkle with dill, wine, and top with lemon slices. Place salmon in the air fry basket and close the fry lid. Air Fry for 10 minutes. Salmon will be flaky. Remove lemon slices. Serve warm sprinkled with basil.

635. Oregano Salmon

Servings: 4 | Ready in about: 60 minutes

1 lb fresh salmon fillets
2 cups fish stock
2 garlic cloves, crushed
¼ cup olive oil
Juice of 1 lemon
1 tbsp oregano leaves, chopped
¼ tbsp red pepper flakes
Salt to taste

In a bowl, combine the olive oil, lemon juice, oregano, garlic, red pepper and a pinch of salt. Brush the mixture over the fillets and cool for 30 minutes. Pour in the fish stock in the Instant Pot. Separate the fillets from the marinade and pat dry with paper towel. Place the fillets on the steamer insert. Secure the lid, set the steam release handle and press Pressure Cook. Cook for 20 minutes. Once ready, perform a quick release.

636. Perfect Tilapia Fillets

Serves: 4 | Total Time: 20 minutes

1 large egg
⅓ cup flour
¼ cup grated Parmesan cheese
½ tbsp lemon pepper seasoning
1 tsp cumin seeds, lightly crushed
1 tsp coriander seeds, lightly crushed
4 tilapia fillets

Preheat your Instant Pot Duo Crisp to 375°F. Whisk egg in a bowl. Mix the flour, Parmesan, cumin seeds, coriander seeds, and lemon pepper seasoning on a large plate. Dry tilapia with a paper towel, then dip in egg. Shake off drips. Then, coat both sides with the flour mixture. Lightly spray with cooking oil. Place the tilapia in the air fry basket and close the fry lid. Air Fry for 5 minutes. Flip the fillets, then cook for another 5 minutes or until the tilapia is crispy and golden. Serve warm and enjoy!

637. Yummy Snow Crab Legs

Serves: 6 | Total Time: 20 minutes

8 lb shell-on snow crab legs
2 tbsp olive oil
1 tsp garlic powder
2 tsp Old Bay Seasoning
4 tbsp butter, melted
2 tsp lemon juice
½ red chili, minced

Preheat your Instant Pot Duo Crisp to 400°F. Prepare crab legs by drizzling with oil, and season with garlic powder and Old Bay seasoning. Transfer the legs to the air fry basket and close the fry lid. Air Fry for 8 minutes. Turn the crab legs and cook for another 7 minutes or until the crab is bright red-orange. While the crab legs are cooking, prepare the dipping sauce. Whisk together butter, red chili, and lemon juice in a small bowl. When the crab legs are done, serve the crab legs and dipping sauce together and enjoy!

638. Basic Shrimp Creole

Servings: 4 | Ready in about: 25 minutes

1 lb jumbo shrimp, peeled, deveined
2 celery stalks, diced
2 garlic cloves, minced
2 tsp olive oil
1 tsp thyme
1 onion, diced
28 oz can tomatoes, diced
1 bell pepper, diced

Set the Instant Pot to Sauté and heat the oil. Stir in the onions, garlic, and celery, and cook for 3 minutes. Add the remaining ingredients. Stir to combine. Secure the lid and select Pressure Cook. Cook on High for 1 minute. When ready, release the pressure quickly. Set it to Sauté again and cook until the liquid is reduced, 10 minutes.

639. South Asparagus & Shrimp

Servings: 4 | Ready in about: 15 minutes

1 tbsp Cajun seasoning
1 lb shrimp, peeled and deveined
1 tsp olive oil
1 asparagus bunch, 12, trimmed
1 ½ cups water

Pour the water into your Instant Pot. Arrange the asparagus on the rack, in a single layer. Place the shrimp on top. Drizzle with olive oil, and season with Cajun seasoning. Secure the lid, and select Pressure Cook. Cook on low pressure for 2 minutes. When ready, release the pressure quickly, and serve.

640. Salmon al Orange

Servings: 4 | Ready in about: 35 minutes

1 lb salmon fillets
2 tbsp cornstarch
1 cup squeeze orange juice
1 tsp orange zest
1 tsp Himalayan salt
½ tsp black pepper, freshly ground
½ tsp garlic, minced

Add all the ingredients to your Instant Pot and seal the lid. Press Pressure Cook and cook on High for 15 minutes. Release the steam naturally for 10 minutes and serve.

641. Glazed Salmon Fillets

Serves: 4 | Total Time: 35 minutes

3 tbsp soy sauce
1 tsp sriracha
½ tsp minced garlic
4 salmon fillets
1 tsp red pepper flakes
2 tbsp lemon juice
2 tsp honey

Combine soy sauce, lemon juice, sriracha, pepper flakes, and garlic in a large bowl. Place salmon in the bowl, then cover and refrigerate for at least 20 minutes. Preheat your Instant Pot Duo Crisp to 375°F. Place the salmon in the air fry basket and close the fry lid. Air Fry for 8 minutes. Brush honey on the salmon and cook for another 2 minutes. Honey will be warm, and fish will be flaky. Serve and enjoy!

642. Maryland Lobster Tails

Serves: 4 | Total Time: 15 minutes

4 lobster tails
3 tbsp butter, melted
1 tbsp minced garlic
1 tbsp minced shallot
Salt and black pepper to taste
2 tbsp lemon juice
1 tbsp dill paste

Preheat your Instant Pot Duo Crisp to 400°F. Prepare the lobster tails by cutting the tails with kitchen scissors and pulling back the shell to expose the meat. Drizzle with butter and season with garlic, shallot, salt, dill, and pepper. Transfer the lobster tails to the air fry basket and close the fry lid. Air Fry for 10 minutes. The meat will be opaque and firm. Drizzle with lemon juice and serve immediately.

643. Louisiana-Style Lobster Tails

Serves: 4 | Total Time: 15 minutes

4 lobster tails
2 tbsp butter, melted
3 tsp lemon juice
2 tbsp white wine
1 tbsp Cajun seasoning
½ tsp paprika
2 tbsp chopped parsley

Preheat your Instant Pot Duo Crisp to 400°F. Prepare the lobster tails by cutting the tails with kitchen scissors and pulling back the shell to expose the meat. Drizzle with butter, wine, and lemon juice, then season with Cajun seasoning and paprika.

Transfer the lobster tails to the air fry basket and close the fry lid. Air Fry for 10 minutes. The meat will be opaque and firm, and the shells will be bright red. Serve immediately sprinkled with parsley.

644. Crispy Fried Crab Rangoon

Serves: 4 | Total Time: 15 minutes

½ cup crabmeat
4 oz cream cheese, softened
¼ tsp Worcestershire sauce
¼ tsp soy sauce
8 wonton wrappers
2 tbsp chopped green onions

Preheat your Instant Pot Duo Crisp to 400°F. Combine crabmeat, cream cheese, green onions, soy sauce, and Worcestershire in a bowl. Set up wonton wrappers on a flat surface. Add ½ tablespoon crab mixture in the middle of the wrapper. Fold opposing edges over the mixture toward the center and pinch to close. Repeat until all wonton wrappers and mixture are used up. Lightly spray with cooking oil and transfer to the air fry basket. Close the fry lid and Air Fry for 5 minutes or until the outside is brown. Serve warm.

645. Crunchy Fish Fillet Sandwich

Serves: 4 | Total Time: 30 minutes

4 cod fillets
Salt and black pepper to taste
1 tsp garlic powder
3 cups cornflakes, crushed
1 cup Italian bread crumbs
1 cup shredded iceberg lettuce
2 large eggs
4 sandwich buns

Preheat your Instant Pot Duo Crisp to 375°F. Season fish with salt and pepper on both sides. Combine cornflakes, garlic, and bread crumbs in a large bowl. Whisk eggs in a bowl. Dip cod in the egg and shake off dips, then dredge in cornflake mixture on both sides. Lightly spray with cooking oil and transfer to the air fry basket.

Close the fry lid and Air Fry for 8-10 minutes, then flips the fish. Cook for another 8-10 minutes or until the cod is brown. Serve on sandwich buns with iceberg lettuce.

646. Sesame Teriyaki Salmon

Serves: 4 | Total Time: 35 minutes

½ cup teriyaki sauce
¼ tsp salt
1 tbsp honey
1 tsp ground ginger
½ tsp garlic powder
1 tbsp dried dill
4 salmon fillets
2 tbsp toasted sesame seeds

Mix teriyaki sauce, honey, salt, dill, ginger, and garlic powder in a large bowl. Coat both sides of the salmon in the sauce, then cover the bowl and refrigerate for at least 15 minutes. Preheat your Instant Pot Duo Crisp to 375°F.

Lightly spray the salmon with cooking oil and place it in the air fryer. Close the fry lid and Air Fry for 6 minutes. Then flip the salmon. Cook for another 6 minutes or until the glaze has caramelized and the fish is flaky. Top with sesame seeds and serve warm.

LUNCH RECIPES

647. Chicken Noodle Soup

Servings: 6 | Ready in about: 40 minutes

1 tbsp olive oil	1 cup celery rib, chopped	1 lb chicken breasts, bone-in, skin-on
1 onion, minced	1 tbsp dry basil	8 oz extra-wide dry egg noodles
3 cloves garlic, minced	1 bay leaf	Salt and ground black pepper to taste
1 turnip, chopped	6 cups chicken broth	

Set your Instant Pot to Sauté. Warm olive oil stir in garlic and onion, and cook for 3 minutes until soft. Mix in celery, bay leaf, basil, and turnip. Add 3 cups chicken broth to the pot and deglaze. Scrape any brown bits from the pan's bottom and add chicken. Seal the pressure lid, choose Pressure Cook, and set the timer to 10 minutes.

When ready, naturally release the pressure for 10 minutes. Transfer chicken breasts to another bowl. Do away with the skin and bones. Shred the meat. Set the pot to Sauté. Add the chicken back to the pot. Add the noodles and the remaining stock. Simmer the stock for 10 minutes until noodles are done. Add pepper and salt for seasoning.

648. Pickle and Potato Salad with Feta

Serves: 12 | Ready in about about: 30 minutes

3 lb potatoes, peeled and chopped	1 cup mayonnaise	¼ cup diced white onion, chopped
3 cups water	¼ cup mustard	1 cup feta cheese, crumbled
1 tsp salt	¼ cup pickle	Salt to taste

In your Instant Pot, mix salt, water, and potatoes. Seal the pressure lid, select Pressure Cookand cook for 6 minutes on High. Once ready, do a natural release for 10 minutes. Drain the potatoes and chop into small pieces. In a bowl, mix salt, pickles, mayonnaise, potatoes, mustard, and onion to get the desired consistency. Chill for one hour while covered. Top with feta cheese to serve.

649. Classic French Onion Soup

Servings: 8 | Ready in about: 45 minutes

2 tbsp butter	1 tsp salt	2 sprigs fresh thyme
8 cups thinly sliced onions	½ tsp ground black pepper	2 bay leaves
½ cup water	½ cup dry white wine	4 baguette slices
2 tsp sugar	4 cups beef stock	1 cup Swiss cheese, shredded

Melt butter on Sauté in your Instant Pot. Add in onions and cook for 3 to 5 minutes until soft. To the onions, add water, pepper, sugar, and salt, and pepper as you stir. Seal the pressure lid, press Pressure Cook on High, and set the timer to 15 minutes. Once ready, do a quick release. Add beef stock, bay leaves and thyme sprigs into the pot.Seal the pressure lid again, choose Pressure Cook, and set the timer to 4 minutes. Quick-release pressure. Remove the bay leaves and thyme and discard. Divide into bowls. Top with ¼ cup swiss cheese and 1 baguette slice. Transfer the bowls to the air fryer basket and cook for 2 to 4 minutes on Roast at 400°F.

650. Minestrone Soup

Servings: 6 | Ready in about: 25 minutes

2 tbsp olive oil	3 cups chicken broth	1 (28 oz) can diced tomatoes
1 yellow onion, diced	½ tsp dried parsley	1 (6 oz) can tomato paste
1 cup celery, chopped	½ tsp dried thyme	2 cups kale
1 carrot, peeled and diced	½ tsp dried oregano	1 (14 oz) can Navy beans, rinsed
1 green bell pepper, chopped	Salt and ground black pepper to taste	½ cup white rice
2 cloves garlic, minced	2 bay leaves	¼ cup Parmesan cheese

Warm olive oil on Sauté in your Instant Pot. Stir-fry carrot, celery, and onion for 5-6 minutes until soft. Add garlic and bell pepper and cook for 2 minutes as you stir until aromatic. Stir in pepper, thyme, stock, salt, parsley, oregano, tomatoes, bay leaves, and tomato paste to dissolve. Mix in rice. Seal the pressure lid. Choose Pressure Cook and set the timer to 15 minutes. Once ready, do a quick pressure release. Add kale to the liquid and stir. Use residual heat in slightly wilting the greens. Get rid of bay leaves. Stir in navy beans. Top with Parmesan cheese.

651. Homemade Chicken Soup

Servings: 6 | Ready in about: 1 hour 10 minutes

1 ½ lb chicken drumsticks, boneless	2 carrots, diced	½ cup matzo meal
4 celery stalks	2 garlic cloves	2 eggs, beaten
1 cup fennel bulb, chopped	3 parsley, chopped	2 tbsp canola oil
2 onions, diced	2 bay leaves	1 tsp baking powder

In your pressure cooker, add chicken drumsticks, bay leaves, onion, carrots, pepper, garlic, parsley, salt, and fennel. Add enough water such that ingredients are covered by 2 inches. Seal the pressure lid, choose Pressure Cook on High, and set the timer to 30 minutes. Release natural pressure for 10 minutes. Mix baking powder, eggs, oil, pepper, salt and matzo meal in a small bowl. Use a plastic wrap to close the bowl and place in a refrigerator for 10 minutes. Get rid of celery stalks from the pressure cooker. Transfer chicken to a cutting board and strip and shred it from the bones. Take back to the pot. Select Sauté and boil the soup. Roll matzo mixture into 1-inch balls and place in the boiling soup. Cook for 3 mins to heat through as you gently stir.

652. Cream of Mushroom & Spinach Soup

Servings: 4 | Ready in about: 25 minutes

1 tbsp olive oil	4 cups vegetable stock	½ tsp sea salt
8 Button Mushrooms, sliced	2 sweet potatoes, peeled and chopped	1 cup creme fraiche
1 cup spinach, chopped	2 tbsp white wine	½ tsp black pepper
1 red onion, chopped	1 tbsp dry Porcini mushrooms, soaked	

Set your Instant Pot to Sauté. Add in olive oil and sliced mushrooms and cook for 3 to 5 minutes until browning on both sides; reserve. Add onion and spinach, and cook for 3 to 5 minutes until onion is translucent. Stir in chopped mushrooms, and cook for a further 5 minutes as you stir occasionally until golden brown. Pour in wine to deglaze the bottom of the pot. Cook for 5 minutes until all the wine evaporates. Mix in the remaining chopped fresh mushrooms, potatoes, soaked mushrooms, wine, vegetable stock, and salt. Seal the pressure lid, choose Pressure Cook on High, and set the timer to 5 minutes. Once cooking is complete, do a quick release. Add in pepper and creme fraiche to mix. Using an immersion blender, whizz the mixture until smooth. Stir in the sautéed mushrooms. Add reserved mushrooms for garnish before serving.

653. Vegetable Soup

Servings: 8 | Ready in about: 42 minutes

2 tbsp olive oil	1 celery stalk, diced	½ cup green beans
1 cup leeks, chopped	1 cup sliced mushrooms	2 tbsp nutritional yeast
2 garlic cloves, minced	1 cup broccoli florets	½ tsp dried thyme
4 cups vegetable stock	1 cup cauliflower florets	½ salt, or more to taste
1 carrot, diced	½ red bell pepper, diced	½ tsp ground black pepper
1 parsnip, diced	¼ head green cabbage, chopped	½ cup fresh parsley, chopped

Heat oil on Sauté in your Instant Pot. Add in garlic and onion and cook for 6 minutes until slightly browned. Add in vegetable stock, carrot, celery, broccoli, bell pepper, green beans, salt, nutritional yeast, cabbage, cauliflower, mushrooms, potato, thyme, and pepper. Seal the pressure lid, choose Pressure Cook on High, and set the timer to 25 minutes. When ready, release natural pressure 10 minutes. Stir in parsley and serve.

654. Broccoli & Potato Soup

Servings: 4 | Ready in about: 35 minutes

⅓ cup butter
1 head broccoli, cut into florets
2 cloves garlic, minced

1 onion, chopped
2 ½ lb potatoes, peeled and chopped
4 cups vegetable broth

½ cup heavy cream
Cheddar cheese, grated for garnish
½ cup fresh chopped scallions

Melt the butter on Sauté in your Instant Pot. Add onion and garlic and cook for 5 minutes. Add in broth, potatoes, and broccoli, and mix well. Seal the pressure lid, choose Pressure Cook on High, and set the timer to 5 minutes. When ready, allow the pressure to release naturally for 10 minutes. Transfer the mixture in an immersion blender and puree until smooth. Add in heavy cream and season with pepper and salt. Top with cheese and scallions.

655. Mexican-Style Chicken Soup

Servings: 5 | Ready in about: 35 minutes

5 boneless, skinless chicken thighs
5 cups chicken broth
14 oz canned whole tomatoes, chopped
2 jalapeno peppers, chopped
2 tbsp tomato puree

3 cloves garlic, minced
1 tbsp chili powder
1 tbsp ground cumin
½ tsp dried oregano
1 (14.5 oz) can black beans, rinsed

2 cups frozen corn kernels, thawed
Crushed tortilla chips for garnish
¼ cup Cheddar cheese, shredded
Fresh cilantro, chopped for garnish

Place the chicken in your pressure cooker. Add oregano, garlic, tomato puree, chicken stock, cumin, tomatoes, chili powder, and jalapeno peppers. Seal the pressure lid, choose Pressure Cook on High, and set the timer to 10 minutes. When ready, release pressure quickly. Transfer the chicken to a large plate. On Sauté cook corn and black beans. Shred the chicken with a pair of forks, and return to the pot, stirring well. Simmer the soup for 5 minutes until heated through. Divide in serving plates. Add a topping of cilantro, cheese, and crushed tortilla chips.

656. Spicy Acorn Squash Soup

Servings: 4 | Ready in about: 25 minutes

4 cups vegetable broth
2 tbsp butter
1 onion, diced

1 (2 lb) acorn squash, chopped
2 carrots, peeled and diced
½ tsp ground cinnamon

¼ tsp chili pepper
½ cup coconut milk
1/3 cup sour cream

Set your Instant Pot to Sauté. Melt butter. Add onion and cook for 3 minutes until soft. Add in carrots, cinnamon, squash, salt, and chili pepper and stir-fry for 2 minutes until fragrant. Add the stock to the vegetable mixture. Seal the pressure lid, choose Pressure Cook on High, and set the timer to 12 minutes. Quick-release the pressure. Add soup to a food processor and puree to obtain a smooth consistency. Take the soup back to the pot, stir in coconut milk until you get a consistent color. Divide into serving bowls. Serve hot with a dollop of sour cream.

657. Chicken & Farro Soup

Servings: 6 | Ready in about: 1 hour

1 tbsp olive oil
4 boneless, skinless chicken thighs
¼ cup white wine
1 cup farro

1 large onion, sliced
2 celery stalks, cut into squares
3 large carrots, sliced
1 tsp garlic powder

1 tsp ground cumin
1 bay leaf
6 cups chicken broth
2 tsp fresh parsley leaves to garnish

Warm oil on Sauté in your Instant Pot. Brown the chicken on all sides, approximately 6 minutes. Transfer the chicken to a bowl. To your Instant Pot, add wine to deglaze, scraping any brown bits present at the bottom of the cooker. Mix the wine with farro, cumin, stock, onion, carrots, celery, garlic powder, and bay leaf. Close the lid and turn steam vent to sealing. Seal the pressure lid, choose Pressure Cook on High, and set the timer to 20 minutes. When cooking is done, naturally release the pressure for about 10 minutes. Add parsley for garnish. Serve.

658. Cream of Pumpkin Chipotle Soup

Servings: 4 | Ready in about: 25 minutes

1 tbsp olive oil	¼ tsp grated nutmeg	1 butternut pumpkin, cut into pieces
1 onion, chopped	¼ tsp ground cloves	4 cups vegetable broth
2 chipotle peppers, finely minced	1 pinch ground cinnamon	1 cup half-and-half

Warm oil on Sauté in your Instant Pot and sauté nutmeg, pepper, clove, cinnamon, and onion for 3 minutes. Add pumpkin and cook for 5 minutes as you stir infrequently. Pour in broth. Add chipotle peppers and remaining pumpkin. Seal the pressure lid, choose Pressure Cook, and set the timer to 10 minutes. When ready, release pressure quickly. Stir in half-and-half and transfer to a blender to purée until you obtain a smooth consistency.

659. Tomato Soup with Cheese Croutons

Servings: 6 | Ready in about: 1 hour

2 tbsp olive oil	1 cup vegetable stock	4 slices of bread
1 onion, chopped	28 oz canned tomatoes	2 Gouda cheese, sliced
1 carrot, peeled and chopped	1 cup heavy cream	4 tbsp butter, at room temperature
1 garlic clove, minced	4 Monterey Jack cheese, sliced	2 tbsp parsley, finely chopped

Warm oil on Sauté in your Instant Pot. Add in garlic, onion, carrot, pepper and salt and sauté for 6 minutes until soft. To your Instant Pot, add vegetable stock to deglaze. Scrape any brown bits from the pot. Mix the stock with tomatoes. Seal the pressure lid, choose Pressure Cook on High, and set the timer to 30 minutes.

When the cooking is over, let naturally release pressure, for about 10 minutes. Transfer soup to a blender and process to get a smooth consistency. Add in heavy cream and stir. Add pepper and salt for seasoning. Place 2 slices Monterey Jack cheese onto 1 bread slice and cover with 1 Gouda cheese slice, and the second slice of bread. Spread a tbsp of butter and parsley over the top. Do the same with the rest of the cheese, bread, parsley, and butter.

Place the sandwiches on the air fry basket. Spread 1 tbsp butter on top of each sandwich. Close the air fry lid, choose Air Fry, set the temperature to 390°F, and set the time to 5 minutes. After 3 minutes, flip the sandwiches and cook for 2 minutes. Transfer sandwiches to a cutting board and chop into bite-sized cubes. Divide the soup into serving plates and apply a topping of parsley cheese croutons before serving.

660. Quick Chicken Noodle Soup

Servings: 6 | Ready in about: 15 minutes

1 tbsp canola oil	1 carrot, chopped	6 cups chicken broth
6 spring onions, chopped	2 celery stalks, chopped finely	8 oz dry egg noodles
2 garlic cloves, finely diced	2 chicken breasts, cut into chunks	2 tbsp chopped fresh parsley leaves

Heat oil on Sauté in your Instant Pot. Add in celery, spring onion, garlic, and carrots. Cook for 5 minutes until tender. Add in chicken, egg noodles, and broth. Seal the pressure lid, choose Pressure Cook, and set the timer to 15 minutes. When ready, do a quick release. Add in parsley. Taste and adjust the seasoning before serving.

661. Vegetarian Black Bean Soup

Servings: 6 | Ready in about: 30 minutes

1 tsp olive oil	3 carrots, chopped	30 oz canned diced tomatoes
1 onion, chopped	2 serrano peppers, chopped	1 (14 oz) can black beans, rinsed
2 celery stalks, chopped	5 cups vegetable broth	¼ cup chopped fresh cilantro

Set your Instant Pot to Sauté. Warm oil. Add in carrots, onion, jalapeño peppers and celery and cook for 6 to 7 minutes until soft. Mix in broth, sea salt, black beans, tomatoes, and cilantro. Seal the pressure lid, press Pressure Cook on High, and set the timer to 8 minutes. Once ready, release pressure naturally for 10 minutes.

LUNCH RECIPES

662. Acorn Squash Soup with Coconut Milk

Servings: 6 | Ready in about: 1 hour PREP TIME: 25 minutes COOK TIME: 25 minutes

1 tbsp olive oil	2 garlic cloves, minced	1 cup coconut milk
1 onion, diced	1 lb acorn squash, peeled diced	Salt and freshly ground black pepper
1 stalk celery, diced	6 cups chicken stock	2 tbsp cilantro leaves, chopped
1 large carrot, diced	Juice from 1 lemon	

Heat oil on Sauté in your Instant Pot and stir-fry carrot, celery, garlic, salt and onion, for 4 to 5 minutes until soft. Mix acorn squash with the vegetables and cook for 1 more minute until tender. Pour in chicken broth. Seal the pressure lid, press Pressure Cook on High, and set the timer to 20 minutes. Release pressure naturally for 10 minutes. Add in lemon juice and coconut milk and stir. Transfer the soup to an a blender and process to obtain a smooth consistency. You may add pepper and salt if desired. Garnish with cilantro and black pepper to serve.

663. Hearty Winter Vegetable Soup

Servings: 5 | Ready in about: 30 minutes

2 tbsp olive oil	5 cups chicken broth	2 bay leaves
1 onion, chopped	2 turnips, peeled and chopped	1 sprig fresh sage
2 carrots, peeled and chopped	28 oz canned tomatoes	Salt and ground black pepper to taste
1 cup celery, chopped	15 oz canned garbanzo beans, rinsed	¼ cup parmesan cheese, grated
2 cloves garlic, minced	1 cup frozen green peas	

Set your Instant Pot to Sauté. Warm oil, stir in celery, carrots, and onion, and cook for 4 minutes until soft. Add in garlic and cook for 30 seconds until crispy. To the pot, add vegetable broth, parsnip, garbanzo beans, bay leaves, tomatoes, pepper, salt, peas, and sage. Seal the pressure lid, press Pressure Cook on High, and set the timer to 12 minutes. Once done, release remaining pressure quickly. Serve topped with parmesan cheese.

664. Cauliflower Cheese Soup

Servings: 5 | Ready in about: 20 minutes

2 tbsp butter	1 large head cauliflower, cut into florets	2 cups milk
½ tbsp olive oil		4 oz blue cheese
1 onion, chopped	1 potato, peeled and finely diced	
2 stalks celery, chopped	3 cups vegetable broth	

Set your Instant Pot to Sauté. Warm oil and butter. Add celery and onion and sauté for 3 to 5 minutes until onion becomes fragrant. Stir in half the cauliflower and cook for 5 minutes. Add in stock, bay leaf and the remaining cauliflower. Seal the pressure lid, choose Pressure Cook on High, and set the timer to 5 minutes. When ready, release the pressure quickly. Remove the bay leaf and discard. Place the soup in an immersion blender, add in the milk and puree until smooth. Spoon the soup into bowls and top with blue cheese before.

665. Ramen Spicy Soup with Collard Greens

Servings: 4 | Ready in about: 20 minutes

1 tbsp olive oil	2 tbsp soy sauce	1 lb fresh collard greens, trimmed
½ tsp ground ginger	1 tbsp chili powder	A bunch of fresh cilantro, chopped
2 tbsp garlic, minced	1 cup mushrooms, sliced	1 red chilli, sliced to serve
6 cups chicken broth stock	10 oz ramen noodles	

Set your Instant Pot to Sauté. Warm oil, stir in garlic and ginger, and cook for 2 minutes until soft. Add vegetable stock to the pot. Mix in chili powder, ramen noodles and soy sauce. Seal the pressure lid, press Pressure Cook on High, and set the timer to 10 minutes. When ready, release pressure quickly. Stir in collard greens until wilted. Ladle the soup into serving bowls and add red chili and cilantro to serve.

666. Sweet Potato & Egg Salad

Servings: 8 | Ready in about: 20 minutes

1 ½ cups water
6 sweet potatoes, peeled and diced
4 large eggs
2 ½ cups mayonnaise
¼ cup dill, chopped
⅓ cup Greek yogurt
Salt and ground black pepper to taste
½ cup Arugula

To your Instant Pot, add water. Place eggs and potatoes into a steamer basket, transfer to the pot, and seal the pressure lid. Choose Pressure Cook and set timer to 4 minutes. After cooking has completed, release pressure quickly. Open the lid. Take out the eggs and place in a bowl of ice-cold water for purposes of cooling. In a large bowl, combine yogurt, mayonnaise, and dill. In a separate bowl, mash potatoes using a potato masher. Mix with mayonnaise mixture to coat. Skin and dice the eggs and transfer to the potato salad and mix. Add pepper and salt to the salad before serving.

667. Ragu Bolognese

Servings: 10 | Ready in about: 45 minutes

4 oz bacon, chopped
1 tbsp butter
1 large onion, minced
2 celery stalks, minced
2 large carrots, minced
2 lb ground beef
3 tbsp dry white wine
2 (28 oz) cans crushed tomatoes
3 bay leaves
Sea salt and black pepper to taste
½ cup yogurt
¼ cup chopped fresh basil

Set your Instant Pot to Sauté. Place in bacon and cook until crispy for 4 to 5 minutes. Mix in celery, butter, carrots, and onion, and continue cooking for about 5 minutes until vegetables are softened. Mix in ¼ tsp pepper, ½ tsp salt, and beef, and cook for 4 minutes until golden brown. Stir in the wine and allow to soak, approximately 4 more minutes. Add in bay leaves, tomatoes, and remaining pepper and salt. Seal the pressure lid, choose Pressure Cook on High, and set the timer to 15 minutes. Once ready, release pressure naturally for 10 minutes. Add yogurt and stir. Serve alongside noodles and use basil to garnish.

668. Butternut Squash Curry

Servings: 5 | Ready in about: 30 minutes

1½ lb butternut squash, chopped
4 cups chicken stock
½ cup buttermilk
4 spring onions, chopped into lengths
2 tbsp curry powder
1½ tsp ground turmeric
1½ tsp ground cumin
¼ tsp cayenne pepper, or more to taste
2 bay leaves
Salt and black pepper to taste
A bunch of cilantro leaves, chopped

In your pressure cooker's pot, stir in squash, buttermilk, curry powder, turmeric, spring onions, stock, cumin, and cayenne pepper. Apply pepper and salt for seasoning. Add bay leaves to the liquid and ensure they are submerged. Seal the pressure lid, choose Pressure Cook on High, and set the timer to 10 minutes. When ready, naturally release the pressure for 10 minutes. Discard bay leaves. Transfer the soup to a blender and process until smooth. Use a fine-mesh strainer to strain the soup. Garnish with cilantro before serving.

669. Ham & Mozzarella Eggplant Boats

Servings: 2 | Ready in about: 17 minutes

2 eggplants
6 ham slices, chopped
1 cup mozzarella cheese, shredded
1 tsp dried parsley
Salt and black pepper to taste
Cooking spray

Grease the air fry basket with cooking spray. Cut the eggplants lengthwise in half and scoop some of the flesh out, leaving the skin intact. Season with salt and pepper. Chop the scooped flesh and mix with mozzarella, salt, and pepper. Divide the cheese mixture between the eggplant halves. Cover with ham slices, and sprinkle with parsley. Put the eggplant in the greased basket, close the air fry lid and cook for 12 minutes on Air Fry mode at 350°F.

670. Spicy Borscht Soup

Servings: 4 | Ready in about: 30 minutes

2 tbsp olive oil
1 cup leeks, chopped
1 tsp garlic, smashed
2 beets, peeled and diced
1 tbsp cayenne pepper, finely minced
1 dried habanero pepper, crushed
4 cups beef stock
3 cups white cabbage, shredded
Salt and black pepper to taste
2 tsp red wine apple cider vinegar
¼ tsp paprika
Greek yogurt for garnish

Set your Instant Pot to Sauté. Warm the oil, stir in garlic and leeks, and cook for 5 minutes until soft. Mix in the remaining ingredients. Seal the lid, choose Pressure Cook on High, and set the timer to 20 minutes. When ready, do a quick pressure release. Place in serving bowls and apply a topping of Greek yogurt before serving.

671. Chicken Broth

Servings: 16 | Ready in about: 50 minutes

2 lb chicken carcasses
4 carrots, cut into chunks
1 cup leeks, chopped
1 onion, quartered
1 cup celery, chopped
2 large garlic cloves
1 sprig fresh thyme
1 bunch fresh parsley
Salt to taste
10 peppercorns
2 bay leaves

To your Instant Pot, add chicken carcasses, onion, pepper, thyme, celery, carrots, garlic, parsley, and bay leaves. Top with enough water. Seal the pressure lid, press Pressure Cook, and set the timer to 30 minutes. When ready, release the pressure quickly. Use a colander to drain the broth and do away with solids. Allow the broth to cool.

672. Red Lentil Soup with Tortilla Topping

Servings: 6 | Ready in about: 50 minutes

2 ½ cups vegetable broth
1 ½ cups tomato sauce
1 onion, chopped
1 cup dry red lentils
½ cup prepared salsa verde
2 garlic cloves, minced
1 tbsp smoked paprika
2 tsp ground cumin
1 tsp chili powder
¼ tsp cayenne pepper
Salt and ground black pepper to taste
Crushed tortilla chips for garnish

To your Instant Pot, add in tomato sauce and vegetable broth. Stir in onion, salsa verde, cumin, cayenne pepper, chili powder, garlic, red lentils, and paprika. Season with salt and pepper. Seal the pressure lid, press Pressure Cook on High, and set the timer to 20 minutes. Release pressure quicky. Add crushed tortilla topping.

673. Beef Neck Bone Stock

Servings: 8 | Ready in about: 2 hour 10 minutes

1 carrot, chopped
2 onions, chopped
2 cups celery, chopped
2 lb Beef Neck Bones
12 cups water, or more
1 tsp cider vinegar
2 bay leaves
10 peppercorns
Salt to taste

To your Instant Pot, add carrot, ginger, vinegar, onion, and beef bones. Add enough water to cover ingredients. Seal the pressure lid, press Pressure Cook on High, and set the timer to 120 minutes. Release pressure naturally for about 20 minutes. Remove the bones and bay leaves, and discard. Use a fine-mesh strainer to strain the liquid. Allow the broth to cool. From the surface, skim fat and throw away. Refrigerate for a maximum of 7 days.

674. Leek and Potato Soup with Sour Cream

Servings: 5 | Ready in about: 30 minutes

2 tbsp butter
3 leeks, white part only, thinly sliced
2 cloves garlic, minced
4 cups vegetable broth
3 potatoes, peeled and cubed
½ cup sour cream
2 tbsp rosemary
2 bay leaves
2 tbsp fresh chives, to garnish

LUNCH RECIPES

Melt butter on Sauté in your Instant Pot. Stir in garlic and leeks and cook for 3 to 4 minutes until soft. Stir in bay leaves, potatoes, and broth. Seal the pressure lid, press Pressure Cook on High, and set the timer to 15 minutes. When ready, release pressure quickly. Remove the bay leaves and cobs and discard. Transfer soup to a blender and puree soup to obtain a smooth consistency. Season. Top with chives. Serve with sour cream.

675. Egg Rolls

Servings: 3 | Ready in about: 18 minutes

12 egg roll wrappers	½ onion, chopped	2 tsp olive oil
1 cup ground beef	1 large grated carrot	¼ tsp salt
2 garlic cloves, minced	1 cup grated mozzarella cheese	¼ tsp pepper

Place the onion, garlic, carrot, and beef in a saucepan over medium heat, and cook for 6-7 minutes. Take the pan off the heat. Leave to cool for a few minutes, then mix in the mozzarella. Season to taste with salt, and pepper. Grease your Instant Pot cooking basket with 1 tsp of the olive oil and set aside. Lay the egg roll sheets onto a dry and clean surface. Divide the mixture between them. Roll the egg rolls and tuck the corners and edges in to create secure rolls. Lower the rolls into the cooking basket and brush them with the remaining olive oil. Close the air fry lid and cook for 13 minutes on Air Fry mode at 390°F. Once ready, check if the rolls are golden and crispy. Serve.

676. Italian Sausage Patties

Servings: 4 | Ready in about: 20 minutes

1 lb ground Italian sausage	1 tsp dried parsley	¼ tsp garlic powder
¼ cup breadcrumbs	1 tsp red pepper Flakes	1 egg, beaten

Line the basket with parchment paper. Combine all ingredients in a large bowl. Use your hands (clean!) to combine the mixture thoroughly. Make patties out of the sausage mixture and arrange them on the basket. Close the air fry lid and cook for 14 minutes on Air Fry at 350°F. After 7 minutes, flip each patty. Serve with tzatziki sauce.

677. Perfect Chicken Wings Broth

Servings: 8 | Ready in about: 1 hour 30 minutes

2 lb chicken wings	2 large carrots, diced	1 small handful fresh parsley
4 spring onions, diced	4 cloves garlic	1 bay leaf

To your Instant Pot, add chicken, carrots, parsley, onions, garlic, and bay leaf. Pour in 6 cups water. Seal the pressure lid, choose Pressure Cook on High, and set the timer to 45 minutes. Release pressure naturally for about 10 minutes. Use a fine-mesh strainer to strain the broth and Allow cooling to room temperature. Transfer the broth to containers and seal. Place in the refrigerator for a maximum of one week.

678. Fire-Roasted Tomato and Chorizo Soup

Servings: 6 | Ready in about: 30 minutes

1 tbsp olive oil	4 cups beef broth	1 tbsp red wine vinegar
2 shallots, sliced	28 oz fire-roasted diced tomatoes	3 chorizo sausage, chopped
3 cloves garlic, minced	½ cup fresh ripe tomatoes	½ tsp ground black pepper
1 tsp salt	½ cup raw cashews	½ cup thinly sliced fresh basil

Warn oil on Sauté in your Instant Pot and cook chorizo until crispy. Remove to a to a plate lined with paper towel. To the pot, add in garlic and onion and cook for 5 minutes until soft. Season with salt. Stir in red wine vinegar, broth, diced tomatoes, cashews, tomatoes, and black pepper. Seal the pressure lid, choose Pressure Cook on High. Set the timer to 8 minutes. When ready, release pressure quickly. Pour the soup into an immersion blender and process to obtain a smooth consistency. Divide into deep bowls, top with crispy chorizo and decorate with basil.

LUNCH RECIPES

679. Spicy Beef Broth

Servings: 8 | Ready in about: 1 hour 10 minutes

2 lb beef stew meat
2 leeks, chopped
1 onion, chopped
2 cups celery, chopped
2 red chilies, deseeded and chopped
2 carrots, chopped
1 tsp fresh ginger, grated
4 garlic cloves
8 cups water
1 tsp cider vinegar
Salt to taste

In your Instant Pot, mix meat, celery, garlic carrots, leeks, onion, red chilies, and ginger. Top with vinegar and water. Seal the pressure lid, choose Pressure Cook, and set the timer to 45 minutes. Release pressure naturally for 10 minutes. Strain the broth into a bowl. Add salt for seasoning. Serve or refrigerate using sealable containers.

680. Two-Bean Zucchini Soup

Servings: 5 | Ready in about: 35 minutes

1 tbsp olive oil
1 onion, chopped
2 cloves garlic, minced
5 cups vegetable broth
1 cup dried chickpeas
½ cup pinto beans, soaked overnight
½ cup navy beans, soaked overnight
3 carrots, chopped
1 large celery stalk, chopped
1 tsp dried thyme
16 oz zucchini noodles
Sea salt and black pepper to taste

Set your Instant Pot to Sauté. Warm oil, stir in garlic and onion and cook for 5 minutes until golden brown. Mix in pepper, vegetable broth, carrots, salt, celery, beans, and thyme. Seal the pressure lid, choose Pressure Cook on High, and set the timer to 15 minutes. Once ready, naturally pressure release for about 10 minutes. Mix zucchini noodles into the soup and stir until wilted. Adjust the seasoning.

681. Cheat Hawaiian Pizza

Servings: 2 | Ready in about: 15 minutes

2 tortillas
8 ham slices
8 mozzarella slices
8 thin pineapple slices
2 tbsp tomato sauce
Fresh basil leaves, chopped

Spread each tortilla with tomato sauce. Scatter over the ham, pineapple, and mozzarella. Place the pizza into the air fry basket, close the air fry lid and cook for 10 minutes on Air Fry mode. When the timer beeps, remove and allow to sit for 2 minutes before slicing. Sprinkle the basil over and serve with napkins.

682. Flavorful Vegetable Stock

Servings: 10 | Ready in about: 55 minutes

2 onions, chopped
2 cups celery, chopped
2 carrots, chopped
4 garlic cloves
1 cup kale
1 cup bell pepper, chopped
A handful of rosemary
A handful of parsley
10 peppercorns
2 bay leaves
Salt to taste
8 cups cold water, filtered

To your Instant Pot, add onions, carrots, parsley, bay leaves, garlic, kale, celery, rosemary, and peppercorns. Top with cold water. Seal the pressure lid, press Pressure Cook, and set the timer to 15 minutes. Release pressure naturally for 15 minutes. Use a wide and shallow bowl to hold the stock you strain through a fine-mesh strainer. Allow cool to room temperature. Seal into jars and place in the refrigerator.

683. Warm Bacon & Potato Salad

Servings: 6 | Ready in about: 19 minutes

6 slices smoked bacon, chopped
½ cup apple cider vinegar
½ cup water
3 tbsp honey
2 tsp mustard
1 tsp fresh flat-leaf parsley, chopped
Salt and black pepper to taste
6 red potatoes, peeled and quartered
2 red onions, sliced

Set to Sauté your Instant Pot and brown the bacon for 2 minutes per side. Set aside. In a bowl, mix honey, salt, mustard, vinegar, water, and black pepper. In the inner pot, add potatoes, chopped bacon, and onions and top with vinegar mixture. Seal the pressure lid, choose Pressure Cook on High, and set the timer to 6 minutes. When ready, allow the pressure to release naturally for 10 minutes. Sprinkle with parsley and serve.

684. Homemade Vegetables Soup

Servings: 5 | Ready in about: 40 minutes

2 tbsp olive oil
1 leek, sliced
2 cloves garlic, minced
2 carrots, diced

1 celery stalk, chopped
4 potatoes, quartered
1 red bell pepper, diced
¼ tsp red pepper flakes

Salt and black pepper to taste
1 ½ cups vegetable stock
2 tbsp parsley

Heat olive oil on Sauté in your Instant Pot. Add garlic and leek and cook for 5 minutes. Add in red bell pepper, carrots, salt, potatoes, red pepper flakes, and pepper. Mix in vegetable stock. Seal the pressure lid, choose Pressure Cook on High, and set the timer to 15 minutes. When ready, allow the pressure to release naturally for 10 minutes. Add cilantro and coconut milk to the soup. Use an immersion blender to blend the soup until smooth.

685. Garlicky Chicken on Green Bed

Servings: 1 | Ready in about: 20 minutes

½ cup baby spinach leaves
½ cup shredded romaine lettuce
3 large kale leaves, chopped

4 oz chicken breasts, cubed
3 tbsp olive oil, divided
1 tsp balsamic vinegar

1 garlic clove, minced
Salt and black pepper to taste

Place the chicken in a bowl along with 1 tbsp olive oil and garlic. Season with salt and pepper; toss to combine. Place on a lined baking dish and cook for 14 minutes on Roast mode in your Instant Pot at 390°F. Add the greens in a large bowl. Pour the remaining olive oil, balsamic vinegar, salt, and pepper, and toss to combine. When the timer rings out, remove the chicken. Arrange the greens on a serving platter and top with the chicken to serve.

686. Curry Egg Salad

Servings: 6 | Ready in about: 10 minutes

2 cups water
Cooking spray
6 eggs

¼ cup crème fraîche
2 spring onions, minced
1 tbsp dill, minced

1 tbsp curry paste
2 tsp mustard
Salt and black pepper to taste

Grease a cake pan with cooking spray. Carefully crack in the eggs. To the inner pot, add water. Set the pan with the eggs on the trivet. Seal the pressure lid, choose Pressure Cook on High, and the timer to 5 minutes. Once ready, do a quick release. Drain any water from the eggs in the pan. Loosen the eggs on the edges with a knife. Transfer to a cutting board and chop into smaller sizes. Transfer the chopped eggs to a bowl. Add in onion, mustard, salt, dill, crème fraîche, curry powder, and black pepper.

687. Mushroom & Chicken Egg Soup

Servings: 6 | Ready in about: 40 minutes

1 lb chicken breasts, chopped
2 carrots, peeled and sliced
2 onions, chopped

6 cups water
3 tbsp quinoa flour
3 sweet potatoes, peeled and chopped

1 cup sliced mushrooms
4 tbsp olive oil

Warm the olive oil on Sauté in your Instant Pot. Stir-fry the onions for 2-3 minutes or until translucent. Add the remaining ingredients and seal the lid. Press Pressure Cook and cook for 15 minutes on High. Once it goes off, release the pressure naturally, for 15 minutes. Carefully open the lid and serve immediately.

688. Creamy Quinoa & Mushroom Pilaf

Servings: 4 | Ready in about: 20 minutes

4 cups vegetable broth
1 carrot, peeled and chopped
1 stalk celery, diced
2 cups quinoa, rinsed

1 cup mushrooms, sliced
1 onion, chopped
2 garlic cloves, smashed
1 tsp salt

½ tsp dried thyme
3 tbsp butter
½ cup heavy cream

Melt the butter on Sauté in your Instant Pot. Add onion, garlic, celery, and carrot, and cook for 8 minutes. Mix in broth, thyme, quinoa, mushrooms, and salt. Seal the pressure lid, choose Pressure Cook, and set the timer to 10 minutes. Release pressure quickly. Stir in heavy cream. Cook for 2 minutes to obtain a creamy consistency. Serve.

689. Basic Applesauce with Cinnamon

Servings: 4 | Ready in about: 45 minutes

4 apples, cored, sliced
1 tsp ground cinnamon
1 tsp honey

Add apples, cinnamon, ½ cup water, and honey to your Instant Pot. Seal the pressure lid, choose Pressure Cook on High, and set the timer to 4 minutes. Once ready, release pressure naturally for 10 minutes. For smooth applesauce, puree the mixture in a blender. Allow cooling before transferring in containers for storage.

690. Sweet Potato & Chicken Soup

Servings: 4 | Ready in about: 30 minutes

½ onion, diced
2 chicken breasts, cubed

16 oz chicken stock
16 oz water

3 carrots, peeled and chopped
4 sweet potatoes, cubed

Place the ingredients in your Instant Pot. Secure the lid, select Pressure Cook, and cook on High for 15 minutes. When ready, wait 10 minutes before releasing the pressure. Carefully open the lid and shred the chicken with 2 forks inside the pot. Serve hot.

691. Spicy Bean Soup

Servings: 4 | Ready in about: 45 minutes

15 oz can red kidney beans, rinsed
14.5 oz can tomatoes
2 fresh red chilies, finely chopped

2 ½ tbsp oil
½ onion, chopped
⅓ cup tomato pasta sauce

1 cloves garlic, crushed
1 green bell pepper, diced
1 tsp sugar

Warm the olive oil on Sauté in your Instant Pot. Add garlic, chili, and onions. Stir-fry for 2 minutes, or until translucent. Add the remaining ingredients, and securely lock the lid. Press Pressure Cook and cook on High for 25 minutes. When ready, allow for a natural release, for 10 minutes. Serve warm.

692. Vegetarian Cream Soup

Servings: 4 | Ready in about: 40 minutes

6 oz broccoli, chopped
2 cups vegetable broth
1 garlic clove

2 tbsp sesame oil
1 carrot, sliced
1 onion, chopped

1 cup soy milk
½ cup quinoa flour
¼ cup tofu, seasoned and crumbled

Warm the olive oil on Sauté in your Instant Pot. Add onion and garlic, and stir-fry for 2 minutes. Add vegetable broth, 1 cup of water, carrot, and broccoli. Seal the lid and press Pressure Cook for 5 minutes on High. Perform a quick release, and open the lid. Let cool, then transfer to a food processor. Blend until creamy. Transfer the mixture back into the cooker, and add the remaining ingredients. Secure the lid, press Pressure Cook and set to 13 minutes on High. Once ready, release the pressure naturally, for 10 minutes and serve.

693. Creamy Bean Soup

Servings: 4 | Ready in about: 35 minutes

4 cups chicken broth	1 sweet potato, chopped	1 tsp ground black pepper
1 cup canned black beans, cooked	1 tsp garlic powder	

Add all ingredients in your pressure cooker and secure the lid. Select Pressure Cook and cook for 10 minutes on High. Once the timer goes off, release the pressure naturally for 10 minutes. Then carefully open the lid and transfer everything to a food processor. Blend until smooth. Return the Pressure Cook to the clean stainless steel insert and add half cup of water. Cook on Sauté for 5 more minutes, with the lid off. Serve immediately.

694. Autumn Soup

Servings: 4 | Ready in about: 35 minutes

3 carrots, sliced	1 tsp turmeric	1 tbsp oil
2 sweet potatoes, chopped	2 garlic cloves, minced	1 onion, diced
3 cups veggie broth	½ tsp paprika	

Set your Instant Pot to Sauté. Heat the oil and sauté the onions, carrots, and garlic for 3 minutes. Stir in the remaining ingredients. Secure the lid, select Pressure Cook, and cook on High for 20 minutes. When completed, do a quick pressure release. Transfer the Pressure Cook to deep bowl and blend with a hand blender. Serve hot.

695. Mixed Vegetable & Herb Soup

Servings: 6 | Ready in about: 30 minutes

¼ cup chopped parsley	12 oz green beans	½ tsp oregano
1 can tomatoes, diced	2 ¾ cups veggie broth	½ cup of chopped onions
12 oz frozen mixed veggies	2 tsp olive oil	2 garlic cloves, minced
1 onion, chopped	1 tsp thyme	

Warm the olive oil on Sauté in your Instant Pot. Add the onions and stir-frying for 3 minutes. Add garlic, thyme, oregano, and cook for 1 more minute. Then, stir in the remaining ingredients. Secure the lid, press Pressure Cook, and cook on High for 5 minutes. Allow pressure to release naturally, for 10 minutes. Serve and enjoy!

696. Tasty Chicken Soup with Noodles

Servings: 4 | Ready in about: 55 minutes

1 lb chicken meat, cut in pieces	½ cup soup whole-wheat noodles	2 tbsp parsley, chopped
4 cups chicken broth	Salt and black pepper to taste	

Sprinkle the chicken bites with salt and place them in the Instant Pot. Pour in the chicken broth and seal the lid. Press Pressure Cook and cook for 15 minutes. Once the cooking is complete, release the pressure naturally, for 10 minutes. Open the lid carefully and add the Pressure Cook noodles. Secure the lid and cook for 5 more minutes on Sauté. Release the pressure naturally for 10 minutes. Sprinkle with black pepper and parsley and serve hot.

697. Spinach-Chicken Soup

Servings: 6 | Ready in about: 50 minutes

½ onion, chopped	2 cups chicken broth	1 cup spinach
4 scallions, chopped	1 pound chicken, cut into chunks	3 garlic cloves, minced

Place all of the ingredients into your Instant Pot. Secure the lid, select Pressure Cook, and cook for 30 minutes on High. Allow pressure to release naturally, for 10 minutes. Serve and enjoy!

698. Spanish-Style Lentil Soup

Servings: 4 | Ready in about: 30 minutes

4 cups vegetable broth	2 tomatoes, wedged	½ tsp thyme, dried, ground
3 tbsp tomato paste	1 carrot, thinly sliced	1 medium-sized onion, diced
3 garlic cloves, peeled, crushed	1 tbsp parsley, chopped	½ tsp cumin, ground
2 cups lentils, soaked, drained	½ small onion, chopped	

Combine all ingredients in the Instant Pot and give it a good stir. Secure the lid, press Pressure Cook, and cook for 8 minutes on High. When ready, Rrlease the steam naturally, for 10 minutes. Carefully open the lid and serve.

699. Pinto Bean & Turkey Soup

Servings: 4 | Ready in about: 1 hour 10 minutes

6 oz smoked turkey, chopped	1 garlic clove, minced	½ tbsp olive oil
1 cup dried pinto beans	3 cups water	Salt and black pepper to taste
1 onion, chopped	1 carrot, chopped	

Warm olive oil on Sauté in your Instant Pot. Cook the onions and carrots for 5 minutes. Add garlic and cook for 1 more minute. Stir in the remaining ingredients, except the salt and pepper. Secure the lid, select Pressure Cook, and cook on High for 45 minutes. Allow pressure to release naturally for 10 minutes. Season with salt and pepper.

700. Chili Parsnip Soup

Servings: 4 | Ready in about: 20 minutes

4 cups vegetable stock	2 tbsp vegetable oil	juice from 1 lemon
1 red onion, finely chopped	2 garlic cloves, crushed	
4 parsnip, chopped	½ tsp chili powder	

Heat the olive oil on Sauté in your Instant Pot. Add the onions, parsnips, garlic and cook for 5 minutes, or until softened. Add the chili powder and stir constantly for 25 seconds. Stir in the stock and the lemon juice, and securely lock the lid. Select Pressure Cook and cook on High for 5 minutes. Once it goes off, perform a quick release. Transfer to a food processor and blend for 1 minute to a smooth puree. Return the Pressure Cook to the pot and press Keep Warm for 2 minutes until piping hot. Serve immediately.

701. Veggie & Lentil Chili

Servings: 6 | Ready in about: 35 minutes

1 onion, chopped	2 bell peppers, chopped	¼ tsp pepper
28 oz tomatoes, diced	2 tsp minced garlic	2 tsp cumin
1 cup lentils	1 tsp salt	7 cups veggie stock
1 ⅔ cups lentils	2 tbsp olive oil	1 tbsp chili powder

Set your Instant Pot to Sauté. Heat the oil and sauté the onions and peppers for 4 minutes. Add garlic and cook for another minute. Stir in the remaining ingredients and secure the lid. Select Pressure Cook and cook on High for 15 minutes. When ready, release the pressure naturally for 10 minutes. Serve and enjoy!

702. Cheesy Turkey Chili

Servings: 4 | Ready in about: 60 minutes

1 tbsp olive oil	4 garlic cloves, minced	1 lb ground turkey
½ tsp oregano	1 cup grated cheddar cheese	2 bell peppers, chopped
1 onion, chopped	1 can beans, drained	
¼ cup hot sauce	1 can crushed tomatoes, undrained	

Set your Instant Pot to Sauté and heat the olive oil. Stir in the onions and peppers, and stir-fry for 5 minutes. Add garlic and sauté for 2 more minutes. Add in the spices and turkey and cook for 6 - 7 minutes. Stir in the remaining ingredients, except for the cheese. Secure the lid and select Pressure Cook. Cook on the default setting. Once the cooking is completed, release the pressure naturally for 10 minutes. Top with the cheese and serve.

703. Tomato Shrimp Stew

Servings: 6 | Ready in about: 35 minutes + marinating time

1 lb shrimp, cleaned	2 cups chicken broth	½ cup balsamic vinegar
4 oz Brussels sprouts, trimmed	2 tomatoes, diced	½ tbsp chili powder
4 oz whole okra	2 tbsp tomato paste	1 tbsp fresh rosemary, chopped
2 carrots, sliced	1 cup olive oil	Sea salt and black pepper to taste

In a large bowl, combine olive oil, rosemary, balsamic vinegar, salt and black pepper. Stir well and add the shrimp to the bowl. Toss well to coat and cool in the fridge for 25 minutes. Place the diced tomatoes in the Instant Pot and add tomato paste, 2 tbsp. olive oil and chili powder. Press Sauté and cook for 6 minutes, stirring continuously. Transfer the sauce to a bowl and cover. Pour the chicken broth into your Pot and add Brussels sprouts, carrots, okra, salt, pepper and secure the lid. Set the steam release handle and cook on Pressure Cook for 15 minutes. Perform a quick release, and then remove the vegetables.

Place the shrimp in the remaining broth. Seal the lid, select Pressure Cook and cook for 3 minutes. Perform a quick release and set aside. Heat the remaining oil in the Instant Pot on Sauté. Add the cooked vegetables, stir well and cook for 3 minutes. Transfer to a serving bowl. Add the shrimp and the tomato sauce. Drizzle with marinade.

704. Plantain Bean Stew

Servings: 4 | Ready in about: 75 minutes

2 carrots, chopped	½ lb dry red beans	1 green onion, sliced
1 plantain, chopped	½ onion, chopped	Water, as needed
1 tomato, chopped	1 ½ tbsp oil	

Set your Instant Pot on Sauté. Heat the oil, then sauté the onions for about 3 minutes. Add beans and pour enough water to cover. Secure the lid, select Pressure Cook, and cook on High for 30 minutes. When ready, release the pressure naturally, for about 10 minutes. Carefully opne the lid and stir in the remaining ingredients. Seal the lid, and cook on High for another 10 minutes. Do a natural pressure release for 10 minutes and serve.

705. The Best Turkey Soup

Servings: 3 | Ready in about: 55 minutes

5 oz turkey breast, chopped into pieces	2 carrots, sliced	½ tsp freshly ground white pepper
3 cups chicken broth	2 tbsp cilantro, chopped	

Add all the ingredients and seal the lid, setting the steam release handle. Press Pressure Cook and set the cooking time to 35 minutes on High. When ready, release the pressure naturally for 10 minutes. Serve warm.

706. Parsley Chickpea Stew

Servings: 4 | Ready in about: 45 minutes

1 lb chickpeas, soaked	2 cups vegetable broth	2 tbsp organic butter
2 tomatoes, diced	2 onions, sliced	1 tbsp olive oil
2 oz parsley, chopped	¼ tbsp cayenne pepper	½ tsp salt and black pepper

Heat oil on Sauté and add onions. Stir fry for 3-4 minutes. Add all ingredients, secure the lid and set the steam release handle. Press Pressure Cook and cook for 30 minutes. When ready, perform a quick pressure release. Serve.

LUNCH RECIPES

707. Chili Cheese Dip

Servings: 5 | Ready in about: 15 minutes

1 cup tomato sauce
1 cup cream cheese
1 tsp dried oregano
1 tsp ground cayenne pepper
1 tsp ground chili pepper

Combine all ingredients in a large bowl and stir well. Pour the mixture into the Instant Pot. Select Pressure Cook and cook on High for 8 minutes. Perform a quick pressure release.

708. Sunset Vegetable Stew

Servings: 3 | Ready in about: 50 minutes

1 lb sweet potatoes, cubed
2 carrots, sliced
3 celery stalks, chopped
2 cups vegetable broth
2 tbsp olive oil
2 onions, chopped
1 zucchini, half-inch thick slices
¼ tbsp cayenne pepper

Select Sauté, heat the oil and add the onions. Stir-fry until translucent. Add carrots, zucchini, celery stalks, and half cup of vegetable broth. Cook for 10 minutes, stirring constantly. Add potatoes and cayenne pepper. Seal the lid and press Pressure Cook. Set the pressure release handle and cook for 30 minutes. Do a quick release. Serve.

709. Juicy Chicken Stew

Servings: 3 | Ready in about: 55 minutes

1 lb chicken breasts
1 cup fire roasted tomatoes, diced
Salt and black pepper to taste
1 tbsp chili powder
2 cups chicken broth
Juice from 1 orange

Sprinkle the chicken with salt and pepper, and place it in the Instant Pot. Add the remaining ingredients, except the orange juice and the chicken broth. Press Sauté and cook for 10 minutes, stirring occasionally. Open the lid. Pour in the chicken broth and orange juice. Then seal the lid, and set the steam release handle. Press Pressure Cook and cook for 25 minutes. When ready, allow for a natural pressure release for 10 minutes and serve.

710. Hot Cheddar Chicken Stew

Servings: 4 | Ready in about: 30 minutes

¼ cup diced onion
2 tbsp organic butter
1 garlic clove, minced
½ cup diced celery
2 cups grated cheddar cheese
2 chicken breasts
2 ½ cups chicken broth
⅓ cup hot sauce

Place everything except the cheddar into the Instant Pot. Secure the lid and select Pressure Cook. Cook on High for 15 minutes. Release the pressure naturally for 5 minutes then release any remaining pressure. Shred the chicken inside the Instant Pot. Stir in the cheese and serve.

711. Salmon Broth

Servings: 4 | Ready in about: 75 minutes

2 lemongrass stalks, chopped
1 cup chopped celery
1 cup chopped carrots
2 garlic cloves, minced
2 salmon heads, cut into quarters
1 tbsp olive oil
Water
A handful of thyme

Set the Instant Pot to Sauté. Heat the oil, and sauté the salmon heads, for a couple of minutes. Add the veggies and thyme. Pour water until it reaches 3 quarts. Secure the lid, select Pressure Cook, and cook on High for 45 minutes. When ready, release the pressure naturally for 15 minutes. Carefully open the lid and strain the broth.

712. Seafood Stew

Servings: 6 | Ready in about: 20 minutes

2 lb fish and seafood, any kind
¼ cup olive oil, divided
2 onions, peeled and chopped
2 carrots, grated
fresh parsley
2 garlic cloves, crushed

Grease the bottom of the Instant Pot with 3 tbsp. olive oil. Press Sauté and add onion and garlic. Stir-fry for 3 minutes, or until translucent. Add the remaining ingredients and secure the lid. Set the steam release handle and press Pressure Cook. Cook for 12 minutes. Once it goes off, perform a quick release and serve warm.

713. Winter Veggie Stew

Servings: 4 | Ready in about: 35 minutes

1 onion, diced
2 cups chopped parsnips
4 carrots, peeled and chopped
4 tomatoes, chopped
1 tbsp chopped tarragon
2 tbsp olive oil
3 garlic cloves, minced
4 cups veggie stock
2 cups cubed sweet potatoes
1 cup chopped red bell peppers
Salt and black pepper to taste

Set your Instant Pot on Sauté. Heat the olive oil, add garlic and onion, and cook for 3 minutes. Add the other veggies and cook for 3 minutes. Pour the broth in, and season with salt and pepper. Secure the lid and select the Pressure Cook. Cook on high for 7 minutes. When ready, release the pressure naturally for 10 minutes and serve.

714. Green Pea Stew

Servings: 4 | Ready in about: 30 minutes

2 cups green peas
3 gloves garlic, chopped
2 tbsp olive oil
1 onion, chopped
1 tbsp ginger powder
1 tbsp turmeric
3 cups chicken stock

Heat oil on Sauté. Stir-fry the onions and garlic for 3 minutes, stirring constantly. Add the remaining ingredients and seal the lid. Set the steam handle and press Pressure Cook button on default time. Once completed, perform a quick release and serve.

715. Vegetable Broth

Servings: 4 | Ready in about: 50 minutes

1 green onion, sliced
1 bay leaf
1 tsp minced garlic
2 carrots, chopped
2 celery stalks, copped
3 parsley sprigs, chopped
2 thyme sprigs
3 black peppercorns
Salt and black pepper to taste
water, as needed

Place first 8 ingredients into your Instant Pot. Pour water to just below the max line. Secure the lid, select Pressure Cook, and cook for 30 minutes. When ready, allow pressure to release naturally for 10 minutes. Strain the broth and season with salt and pepper.

716. Peppery Chicken Broth

Servings: 4 | Ready in about: 140 minutes

½ onion, chopped
1 tbsp apple cider vinegar
1 chicken carcass
1 bay leaf
8 peppercorns
Salt and black pepper to taste

Place first 6 ingredients into your Instant Pot. Add enough water to cover the pot below the max line. Secure the lid, select Pressure Cook, and cook for 120 minutes. When ready, allow pressure to release naturally for 10 minutes. Strain the stock.

717. Filled Portobello Mushrooms

Serves: 4 | Total Time: 15 minutes

1 tbsp olive oil
4 large portobello mushroom caps
2 cups grated mozzarella cheese
½ cup ricotta cheese
1 cup baby spinach
1 tbsp chopped yellow onions
Salt and black pepper to taste
1 tsp Italian seasoning
1 cup pizza sauce
2 tbsp chopped fresh basil

Preheat your Instant Pot Duo Crisp to 350°F. Lightly drizzle the mushrooms with olive oil. Add ¼ cup mozzarella to each cap. Combine ricotta, onion, spinach, salt, pepper, and Italian seasoning in a small bowl. Divide into 4 portions and spoon into the mushroom caps. Top the ricotta mixture with ¼ cup pizza sauce, then ¼ cup mozzarella. Season with salt. Transfer mushroom caps to the air fryer basket and close the fry lid. Bake for 10 minutes. The cheese will be melted and bubbling. Serve warm sprinkled with basil and enjoy!

718. Vegetarian Skewers with Pesto

Serves: 4 | Total Time: 20 minutes

INGREDIENTS

12 oz button mushrooms
12 oz cherry tomatoes
2 zucchini, sliced
1 red onion, cubed
1 cup pesto
1 yellow pepper, cut into chunks
2 tbsp fresh lemon juice
2 tsp lemon zest
Salt and black pepper to taste

Preheat your Instant Pot Duo Crisp to 350°F. Prepare the kebabs. Spear a mushroom with a skewer, then a tomato followed by a zucchini slice, pepper chunk, and finally a red onion. Repeat the pattern to fill the skewer. Continue with the rest of the skewers until all of the vegetables are used. Brush the skewer with ½ cup pesto mixed with lemon juice and lemon zest and season with salt and pepper.

Place the skewers in the air fry basket and close the fry lid. Air Fry for 5 minutes. Turn the kebabs and cook for another 5 minutes or until the vegetables are tender. Brush with the remaining pesto. Serve immediately.

719. Pasta Primavera

Servings: 4 | Ready in about: 25 minutes

4 cups pasta
2 garlic cloves, minced
½ onion, chopped
1 bell pepper, chopped
1 zucchini, chopped
⅓ cups grated Parmesan cheese
3 cups chicken broth
Salt and black pepper
1 tbsp olive oil

Set your Instant Pot to Sauté. Heat the oil, and cook the onion and bell pepper for 3 minutes. Add garlic, and cook for 1 minute. Add zucchini and cook for 1 minute. Stir in pasta, broth, and season with salt and pepper. Secure the lid, select Pressure Cook, and cook on high for 5 minutes. When ready, release the pressure naturally for 5 minutes. Stir in the Parmesan cheese and serve.

720. Original Pomodoro Sauce

Servings: 4 | Ready in about: 30 minutes

½ cup chopped basil
1 tbsp olive oil
2 ½ lb roma tomatoes, diced
½ onion, diced
1 tbsp Italian seasoning
3 garlic cloves, minced

Set your Instant Pot to Sauté. Heat the olive oil and sauté the onions and garlic for about 4 - 5 minutes. Stir in the remaining ingredients. Secure the Instant Pot, select Pressure Cook, and cook on high for 10 minutes. When ready, release the pressure quickly. Carefully open the lid and select Sauté. Sauté for 5 minutes.

721. Turkey Meatballs with Goat Cheese

Serves: 5 | Total Time: 30 minutes

1 lb ground turkey
1 cup chopped spinach
½ cup diced red onion
½ cup crumbled goat cheese
½ cup bread crumbs
1 tbsp chopped parsley
Salt and black pepper to taste

Preheat your Instant Pot Duo Crisp to 350°F. Combine all of the ingredients in a large bowl. Measure about 1 heaping tablespoon of the meat and roll it into a ball. Make about 20 meatballs. Lightly spray the meatballs with cooking oil and place in the air fry basket and close the fry lid. Air Fry for 15-18 minutes, shaking twice the basket until the meatballs are golden. Serve warm.

722. Tomato-Lentil Sauce

Servings: 4 | Ready in about: 35 minutes

⅓ cup lentils
14 oz can crushed tomatoes
½ tsp salt
1 ½ tsp minced garlic
1 cup water
1 sweet potato, diced

Set your Instant Pot to Sauté. Add lentils, sweet potato, garlic, and salt. Sauté for 2 minutes. Add tomatoes and water and stir to combine. Secure the lid, select Pressure Cook, and cook on high for 13 minutes. Once it goes off, allow pressure to release naturally for 10 minutes. Blend with a hand blender, and serve.

723. Honey-Apple Sauce

Servings: 4 | Ready in about: 25 minutes

Juice from ½ lemon
12 apples, quartered
¼ tsp sea salt
2 tbsp ghee
1 tbsp honey
1 tbsp cinnamon
1 cup water

Place all of the ingredients in your Instant Pot. Secure the lid, select Pressure Cook, and cook on high for 3 minutes. When ready, release the pressure naturally for 10 minutes. Transfer all of the solids and half of the cooking liquid to your blender. Blend until smooth.

724. Feta Pizza Dip

Servings: 6 | Ready in about: 10 minutes

1 ½ cups tomato sauce
1 ½ cups feta cheese
2 eggs, beaten
2 ½ cups mozzarella cheese
1 tsp thyme, dried
2 tbsp parsley, dried
Black pepper to taste

In a bowl, mix the eggs, feta cheese, thyme, parsley, and pepper. Pour the mixture into the stainless steel insert. Add tomato sauce and mozzarella. Select Pressure Cook and cook on High for 5 minutes. Do a quick release.

725. Cashew Veggie Sauce

Servings: 4 | Ready in about: 15 minutes

2 sweet potatoes, peeled and chopped
2 carrots, sliced
3 cups water
1 onion, chopped
1 tbsp turmeric, ground
1 garlic cloves, chopped
½ cup cashews, chopped
1 cup yeast

Place all ingredients in the Pot. Secure the lid and set the steam release handle. Press Pressure Cook and cook on High for 6 minutes. Perform a quick steam release. Open the lid, let cool and transfer to a blender, and blend until creamy. Can be stored in airtight container, and refrigerated up to 8 days.

726. Meatless Nuggets

Serves: 6 | Total Time: 20 minutes

1 cup grated carrots
2 tbsp chopped onions
1 tbsp lemon juice
3 cups broccoli florets
2 large eggs
1 cup grated cheddar cheese
1 cup Italian bread crumbs
Salt and black pepper to taste

Preheat your Instant Pot Duo Crisp to 400°F. Add carrots, onions, lemon juice, and broccoli in the food processor and pulse 5 times. Next, add eggs, cheddar cheese, bread crumbs, salt, and pepper, then pulse 10 times.

Divide the mixture into 24 balls and lightly spray with cooking oil. Transfer the balls to the air fry basket and close the fry lid. Air Fry for 3 minutes. Shake the basket and cook for another 3 minutes. Shake the basket again and cook for 4 minutes. Nuggets will be browned. Serve warm and enjoy!

727. The Ultimate BBQ Sauce

Servings: 4 | Ready in about: 25 minutes

1 ½ cups tomatoes, diced
3 tsp brown sugar
1 cup organic ketchup
2 tsp lemon juice, juiced
2 tbsp onion powder
½ cup apple cider vinegar
1 tbsp garlic powder
1 tbsp dried oregano

Place all ingredients in the stainless steel insert. Secure the lid and adjust the handle. Press Pressure Cook and cook on high for 6 minutes. When ready, allow for a natural release, for 10 minutes.

728. Casserole di Pollo

Serves: 4 | Total Time: 30 minutes

2 cups cubed cooked chicken breasts
Salt and black pepper to taste
¾ cup marinara sauce
3 tsp Italian seasoning
1 cup grated Fontina cheese
½ cup grated Parmesan cheese
2 tbsp chopped parsley

Preheat your Instant Pot Duo Crisp to 320°F. Combine chicken salt, pepper, marinara, and 2 teaspoons of Italian seasoning in a large bowl. Toss to coat. Transfer the chicken to a baking pan, then top with the remaining Italian seasoning and cheeses. Place the pan in the air fry basket and close the fry lid. Bake for 20 minutes. The sauce will be bubbling, and cheese will be melted and browning. Serve warm sprinkled with parsley and enjoy!

729. Party Broccoli Cheese Sauce

Servings: 6 | Ready in about: 20 minutes

1 ½ cups broccoli, chopped
1 ½ cups cheddar cheese, shredded
1 ½ cups cheese
1 tsp garlic powder
2 tsp parsley, dried
1 ½ cups chicken broth

Mix all ingredients in a large bowl and stir well. Transfer the mixture into the Instant Pot. Select Pressure Cook and seal the lid. Cook on High for 8 minutes. When done, allow for a natural release for 5 minutes.

730. Luxury White Sauce

Servings: 4 | Ready in about: 20 minutes

½ cup water
12 oz cauliflower florets
Salt and black pepper to taste
2 tbsp almond milk

Combine the water, cauliflower, salt, and black pepper, in your Instant Pot. Secure the lid, select Pressure Cook, and cook for 3 minutes. When ready, allow pressure to release naturally for 10 minutes. Carefully open the lid and blend with a hand blender. Stir in the almond milk and serve.

731. Salsa Picante

Servings: 4 | Ready in about: 20 minutes

6 oz hot peppers, stems removed, chopped
½ cup apple cider vinegar

Set the Instant Pot to Sauté. Place the peppers in your Instant Pot. Add a splash of vinegar and sauté for 2-3 minutes. Secure the lid, select Pressure Cook, and cook on high for 1 minute. When ready, allow pressure to release naturally for 10 minutes. Open the lid and blend the sauce with a hand blender.

732. Taco Meatballs

Serves: 6 | Total Time: 40 minutes

| 4 oz shredded cheddar cheese | 1 cup chopped onions | ½ cup bread crumbs |
| 1 lb ground beef | 1 tbsp taco seasoning | |

Preheat your Instant Pot Duo Crisp to 350°F. Freeze shredded cheddar cheese for 15 minutes. Combine beef, onions, taco seasoning, and bread crumbs in a large bowl. Shape into balls. Take cheese from the freezer. Press one cube into each meatball gently and shape the meat around it until you form a ball. Lightly spray with cooking oil and place in the air fry basket. Close the fry lid and Air Fry for 14-16 minutes, shaking twice the basket until the meatballs are brown. Serve warm.

733. Bagel-Seasoned Tuna Steaks

Serves: 2 | Total Time: 20 minutes

| 2 ahi tuna steaks | ½ tsp cayenne pepper | 2 tbsp chopped cilantro |
| 2 tbsp canola oil | 3 tbsp bagel seasoning | |

Preheat your Instant Pot Duo Crisp to 400°F. Drizzle both sides of the tuna with canola oil, then coat with bagel seasoning and cayenne pepper on a medium plate. Transfer the tuna steaks to the air fry basket and close the fry lid. Air Fry for 7 minutes. Turn the steaks and cook for another 7 minutes. Serve warm decorated with cilantro.

734. Sweet Pretzel Bites

Serves: 4 | Total Time: 1 haur 15 minutes

1 cup flour	¼ tsp maple extract	1 tbsp olive oil
1 tsp quick-rise yeast	1 tsp lemon zest	⅓ cup warm water
2 tbsp granulated sugar	¼ tsp salt	1 tsp ground cinnamon

Combine flour, yeast, sugar, maple extract, lemon zest, and salt in a bowl. Stir in oil and water until the dough comes together and pulls away from the bowl. Transfer the dough out of the bowl onto a floured work surface and knead for 10 minutes. When the dough is smooth, transfer to a large, clean bowl and lightly spray with cooking oil. Cover with plastic and let rise for 1 hour. Stretch the dough into a rectangle and cut it into 24 pieces.

Set your Instant Pot to Sauté. Pour in 4 cups of water and bring to a boil. Add baking soda and let boil for 1 minute. Add the dough into the water and cook for 45 seconds. Remove and drain. The pretzel bites will puff up, but they will keep most of their shape. Preheat your Instant Pot Duo Crisp to 400°F. Lightly spray with cooking oil and transfer to the air fry basket. Close the fry lid and Air Fry for 5 minutes or until the bites have turned golden.

While the pretzel bites are cooking, prepare the cinnamon-sugar mixture by mixing the rest of the cinnamon and sugar in a small bowl. Place the pretzel bites into the cinnamon sugar bowl and serve immediately. Enjoy!

LUNCH RECIPES

DESSERTS

735. Wheat Flour Cinnamon Balls

Servings: 4 | Ready in about: 20 minutes

⅓ cup whole-wheat flour
⅓ cup all-purpose flour
½ tsp baking powder
3 tbsp sugar, divided
¼ tsp ground cinnamon, plus ½ tbsp
¼ tsp sea salt
2 tbsp cold butter, cut into small pieces
¼ cup plus 1½ tbsp whole milk

Mix the whole-wheat flour, all-purpose flour, baking powder, 1 tablespoon of sugar, ¼ teaspoon of cinnamon, and the salt in a medium bowl. Add the butter and use a pastry cutter to cut into the butter to be broken into little pieces until resembling cornmeal. Pour in the milk and mix until the dough forms into a ball.

Knead the dough on a flat surface until a smooth both is achieved. Divide the dough into 8 pieces and roll each piece into a ball. Put the balls in the air fry basket with space in between each ball and oil the balls with cooking spray. Close the air fry lid. Choose Air Fry, set the temperature to 350°F, and cook for 10 minutes. In a bowl, combine the remaining sugar and cinnamon. When done, toss the balls in the cinnamon and sugar mixture.

736. Apple Vanilla Hand Pies

Servings: 8 | Ready in about: 40 minutes

1 (2-crust) package refrigerated pie crusts, softened
2 apples, peeled, cored, and diced
3 tbsp sugar
1 lemon, juiced
¼ tsp salt
1 tsp vanilla extract
1 tsp corn-starch

In a bowl, combine the apples, sugar, lemon juice, salt, and vanilla. Allow the mixture to stand for 10 minutes, then drain, and reserve 1 tablespoon of the liquid. In a small bowl, whisk the corn-starch into the reserved liquid and then, mix with the apple mixture. Put the piecrusts on a lightly floured surface and cut into 8 (4-inch- diameter) circles. Spoon a tablespoon of apple mixture in the center of the circle, with ½ an inch's border around the dough.

Brush the edges with water and fold the dough over the filling. Press the edges with a fork to seal. Cut 3 small slits on top of each pie and oil with cooking spray. Arrange the pies in a single layer in the air fry basket. Close the air fry lid. Choose Air Fry, set the temperature to 350°F, and set the time to 12 minutes. Once done baking, remove, and place the pies on a wire rack to cool. Repeat with the remaining hand pies.

737. White Filling Coconut and Oat Cookies

Servings: 4 | Ready in about: 30 minutes

5 ½ oz flour
1 tsp vanilla extract
Filling
1 oz white chocolate, melted
2 oz butter
3 oz sugar
½ cup oats

4 oz powdered sugar
1 tsp vanilla extract
1 small egg, beaten
¼ cup coconut flakes

Beat all cookie ingredients, with an electric mixer, except the flour. When smooth, fold in the flour. Drop spoonfuls of the batter onto a prepared cookie sheet. Close the air fry lid and cook in your Instant Pot at 350°F for about 18 minutes on Air Fry mode. Let cool. Prepare the filling by beating all ingredients together. Spread the mixture on half of the cookies. Top with the other halves to make cookie sandwiches.

738. Tasty Créme Brulee

Servings: 4 | Ready in about: 30 minutes + 6 hours of cooling

3 cups heavy whipping cream
6 tbsp sugar
7 large egg yolks
2 tbsp vanilla extract
2 cups water

In a mixing bowl, add the yolks, vanilla, whipping cream, and half of the swerve sugar. Use a whisk to mix them until they are well combined. Pour the mixture into the ramekins and cover them with aluminium foil. Open your Instant Pot, fit in a trivet, and pour in the water. Place 3 ramekins on the trivet and place the remaining ramekins to sit on the edges of th e ramekins below. Seal the lid and select Pressure Cook on High for 8 minutes.

Once the timer has stopped, do a natural pressure release for 10 minutes, then a quick pressure release to let out the remaining pressure. With a napkin in hand, remove the ramekins onto a flat surface and then into a refrigerator to chill for at least 6 hours. After refrigeration, remove the ramekins and remove the aluminium foil. Equally, sprinkle the remaining sugar on it and return to the pot. Close the crisping lid, select Bake mode, set the timer to 4 minutes on 380°F. Serve the crème brulee chilled with whipped cream.

739. Raspberry Cream Tart

Servings: 4 | Ready in about: 55 minutes+ Chilling time

1 refrigerated piecrust
2 ½ cups fresh raspberries, divided
1 tbsp arrowroot starch
For The Filling
1 tsp vanilla extract
8 oz cream cheese, softened

2 tbsp water
¼ cup sugar
¼ tsp grated lemon zest

½ cup confectioners' sugar
¼ cup heavy cream

1 tsp lemon juice
Pinch salt

Roll out the pie crust and fit into a tart pan. Do not stretch the dough to prevent shrinking when cooking. Use a fork to prick all over the bottom of the dough. Place a trivet in your Instant Pot in the lower position of the pot and put the tart pan on top. Close the air fry lid, choose Bake. Adjust the temperature to 250°F, and the cook time to 15 minutes. When done baking, open the lid and check the crust. It should be lightly brown around the edges. Close the air fry lid again. Adjust the temperature to 375°F and the cook time to 4 minutes. Press Start to begin baking. After 3 minutes, check the crust, which should be a deep golden brown color by now. If not, cook for the remaining 1 minute. Remove the trivet and set the crust aside to cool.

Fetch out 1 cup of berries into the inner pot. In a small bowl, whisk the arrowroot starch and water until smoothly mixed. Pour the slurry on the raspberries along with the sugar, lemon zest, lemon juice, and salt. Mix to distribute the slurry among the raspberries. Seal the pressure lid, choose Pressure Cook and the cook time to 2 minutes. Once done cooking, perform a quick pressure release and carefully open the lid. The raspberries will have softened. Add the remaining 1 ½ cups of raspberries, stirring to coat with the cooked mixture. Then, allow cooling.

In a bowl and with a hand mixer, whisk the vanilla extract and cream cheese until evenly combined and smooth. Mix in the confectioners' sugar and whisk again until the sugar has fully incorporated and the mixture is light and smooth. With clean whisks and in another bowl, beat the heavy cream until soft peaks form. Fold the heavy cream into the vanilla mixture until both are evenly combined. To assemble, spoon the cream filling into the piecrust and scatter the remaining raspberries on the cream. Chill for 30 minutes before cutting.

740. Dark Chocolate Brownies

Servings: 6 | Ready in about: 40 minutes

1 cup water
2 eggs
⅓ cup granulated sugar
¼ cup olive oil

⅓ cup flour
⅓ cup cocoa powder
⅓ cup dark chocolate chips
⅓ cup chopped Walnuts

1 tbsp milk
½ tsp baking powder
1 tbsp vanilla extract
A pinch salt

To your Instant Pot, add water and set in a trivet. In a bowl, beat eggs and sugar to mix until smooth. Stir in olive oil, cocoa powder, milk, salt baking powder, chocolate chips, flour, walnuts, vanilla, and sea salt. Transfer the batter to a greased springform pan and place the pan on the trivet. Close the air fry lid and select Bake. Adjust the temperature to 250°F and the cook time to 20 minutes. When the time is up, open the lid. Allow the brownie to cool for 10 minutes before cutting. Use powdered sugar to dust the brownies before serving lightly.

741. Raspberry Crumble

Servings: 6 | Ready in about: 40 minutes

1 (16-oz) package frozen raspberries	5 tbsp sugar, divided	½ cup rolled oats
2 tbsp arrowroot starch	½ cup all-purpose flour	⅓ cup cold butter, cut into pieces
1 tsp freshly squeezed lemon juice	⅔ cup brown sugar	1 tsp cinnamon powder

Place the raspberries in the baking pan. In a small mixing bowl, combine the arrowroot starch, 1 tablespoon of water, lemon juice, and 3 tablespoons of sugar. Pour the mixture all over the raspberries. Put a trivet in the lower position of the pot. Cover the pan with foil and pour 1 cup water into your Instant Pot. Put the pan on the trivet. Put the pressure lid together, and lock in the Seal position. Choose Pressure Cook for 10 minutes.

In a bowl, mix the flour, brown sugar, oats, butter, cinnamon, and remaining sugar until crumble forms. When done pressure-cooking, do a quick release and carefully open the lid. Remove the foil and stir the fruit mixture. After, spread the crumble evenly on the berries. Close the air fry lid, choose Air Fry, set the temperature to 400°F, and the time to 10 minutes. Cook until the top has browned and the fruit is bubbling. Serve.

742. Almond Banana Dessert

Servings: 1 | Ready in about about: 8 minutes

1 Banana, sliced	2 tbsp Almond Butter
1 tbsp Coconut oil	½ tsp Cinnamon

Melt oil on Sauté in your Instant Pot. Add banana slices and fry them for a couple of minutes, or until golden on both sides. Top the fried bananas with almond butter and sprinkle with cinnamon.

743. Vanilla Hot Lava Cake

Servings: 8 | Ready in about: 40 minutes

1 cup butter	1 ½ cups chocolate chips	7 tbsp flour
4 tbsp milk	1 ½ cups sugar	5 eggs
4 tsp vanilla extract	Powdered sugar to garnish	1 cup water

Grease the cake pan with cooking spray. Open your Instant Pot, fit in a trivet and pour in the water. In a heatproof bowl, add the butter and chocolate and melt them in the microwave for about 2 minutes. Remove it from the microwave. Add sugar and stir it well. Add the eggs, milk, and vanilla extract and stir again. Finally, add the flour and stir it until even and smooth. Pour the batter into the greased cake pan and use the spatula to level it.

Place the pan on the trivet in the pot, close the lid, secure the pressure valve, and select Pressure on High for 15 minutes. Once the timer has gone off, do a natural pressure release for 10 minutes. Place the pan on a flat surface. Put a plate over the pan and flip the cake over into the plate. Pour the powdered sugar in a fine sieve and sift it over the cake. Use a knife to cut the cake into 8 slices and serve immediately (while warm).

744. Mixed Berry Cobbler

Servings: 4 | Ready in about: 40 minutes

2 bags frozen mixed berries	3 tbsp arrowroot starch	1 cup sugar
For the topping		
1 cup self-rising flour	5 tbsp powdered sugar, divided	1 tbsp melted unsalted butter
¼ tsp cinnamon powder	⅔ cup crème fraiche	1 tbsp whipping cream

Pour the blackberries into your Instant Pot along with the arrowroot starch and sugar. Mix to combine. Seal the pressure lid, choose Pressure Cook and the time to 3 minutes. After cooking, perform a quick pressure release. In a small bowl, whisk the flour, cinnamon powder, and 3 tablespoons of sugar. In a separate small bowl, whisk the crème fraiche with the melted butter. Pour the cream mixture on the dry ingredients and combine evenly.

Spoon 2 to 3 tablespoons of dough on top over the peaches and spread out slightly on top. Brush the topping with the whipping cream and sprinkle with the remaining sugar. Close the air fry lid and choose Bake. Adjust the temperature to 325°F and the cook time to 12 minutes. Check after 8 minutes. When ready, the topping should be cooked through and lightly browned. Allow cooling before slicing. Serve warm.

745. White Chocolate Chip Cookies

Servings: 8 | Ready in about: 30 minutes

| 6 oz self-rising flour | 2 oz white chocolate chips | 1 ½ tbsp milk |
| 3 oz brown sugar | 1 tbsp honey | 4 oz butter |

Beat the butter and sugar until fluffy. Then, beat in the honey, milk, and flour. Gently fold in the chocolate chips. Drop spoonfuls of the mixture onto a prepared cookie sheet. Close the air fry lid and cook for 18 minutes on Air Fry mode at 350°F. Once the timer beeps, make sure the cookies are just set.

746. New York Cheesecake

Servings: 12 | Ready in about: 1 hour

For the Crust:
| 1 cup graham crackers crumbs | 2 tbsp butter, melted | 1 tsp sugar |

For the Filling:
| 2 cups cream cheese, softened | 1 tsp vanilla extract | 1 pinch salt |
| ½ cup sugar | Zest from 1 orange | 2 eggs, softened |

Fold a 20-inch piece of aluminum foil in half lengthwise twice and set on the pressure cooker. Spray a parchment paper with cooking spray and line to the base of a 7-inch springform pan. In a bowl, combine melted butter, salt, sugar and graham crackers crumbs. Press into the bottom and about ⅓ up the sides of the pan.

Transfer the pan to the freezer as you prepare the filling. In a separate bowl, beat sugar, cream cheese, salt, orange zest, and vanilla until smooth. Beat eggs into the filling, one at a time. Stir until combined. Add the filling over the chilled crust in the pan. To your Instant Pot, add 1 cup water and set a trivet into the pot. Carefully center the springform pan on the prepared foil sling. Lower pan into the inner pot using sling and place on steam trivet.

Close the air fry lid and select Bake. Adjust the temperature to 250°F and the cook time to 40 minutes. Let cool the cheesecake before transferring to a refrigerator for 2 hours or overnight. Use a paring knife to run along the edges between the pan and cheesecake to remove the cheesecake and set to the plate.

747. Simple Vanilla Cheesecake

Servings: 6 | Ready in about: 60 minutes

1 ½ cups crushed graham crackers	16 oz cream cheese, softened	1 tbsp all-purpose flour
2 tbsp sugar	½ cup brown sugar	1½ tsp vanilla extract
4 tbsp unsalted butter, melted	¼ cup sour cream	2 eggs

Grease a spring form pan with cooking spray, then line the pan with parchment paper, grease with cooking spray again, and line with aluminium foil. This is to ensure that there are no air gaps in the pan. In a mixing bowl, mix the graham cracker crumbs, sugar, and butter. Spoon the mixture into the pan and press firmly into with a spoon.

In a deep bowl and with a hand mixer, beat the beat the cream cheese and brown sugar until well-mixed. Whisk in the sour cream to be smooth and stir in the flour, vanilla, and salt. Crack the eggs in and beat but not to be overly smooth. Pour the mixture into the pan over the crumbs. Pour 1 cup water into your Instant Pot. Put the spring form pan on the trivet and put the trivet in the pot. Seal the pressure lid, choose Pressure Cook on High, and set the time to 35 minutes. Once done baking, perform a natural pressure release for 10 minutes, then a quick pressure release to let out any remaining pressure. Carefully open the lid. Remove the pan from the trivet and allow the cheesecake to cool for 1 hour. Cover the cheesecake with foil and chill in the refrigerator.

748. Holiday Cranberry Cheesecake

Servings: 8 | Ready in about: 1 hour

1 cup coarsely crumbled cookies	½ cup sugar	2 eggs, room temperature
2 tbsp butter, melted	2 tbsp sour cream	1/3 cup dried cranberries
1 cup mascarpone cheese, softened	½ tsp vanilla extract	1 cup water

Fold a 20-inch piece of aluminum foil in half lengthwise twice and set on the pressure cooker. In a bowl, combine melted butter and crushed cookies. Press firmly to the bottom and about 1/3 of the way up the sides of a 7-inch springform pan. Freeze the crust while the filling is being prepared.

In a separate bowl, beat together mascarpone cheese and sugar to obtain a smooth consistency. Stir in vanilla extract and sour cream. Beat one egg and add into the cheese mixture to combine well. Do the same with the second egg. Stir cranberries into the filling. Transfer the filling into the crust. Into your Instant Pot, add water and set a trivet at the bottom. Center the springform pan onto the prepared foil sling. Lower the pan onto the trivet.

Fold foil strips out of the way of the lid. Close the air fry lid and select Bake. Adjust the temperature to 250°F and the cook time to 40 minutes. When the time is up, open the lid and let to cool the cheesecake. When, transfer the cheesecake to a refrigerator for 2 hours or overnight. Use a paring knife to run along the edges between the pan and cheesecake to remove the cheesecake and set to the plate.

749. Strawberry & Lemon Ricotta Cheesecake

Servings: 6 | Ready in about: 35 minutes

10 oz cream cheese	One lemon, zested and juiced	3 tbsp sour cream
¼ cup sugar	2 eggs, cracked into a bowl	1 ½ cups water
½ cup Ricotta cheese	1 tsp lemon extract	10 strawberries, halved to decorate

In the electric mixer, add the cream cheese, quarter cup of sugar, ricotta cheese, lemon zest, lemon juice, and lemon extract. Turn on the mixer and mix the ingredients until a smooth consistency is formed. Reduce the speed of the mixer and add the eggs. Fold it in at low speed until it is fully incorporated.

Make sure not to fold the eggs in high speed to prevent a cracker crust. Grease the spring form pan with cooking spray and use a spatula to spoon the mixture into the pan. Level the top with the spatula and cover it with foil. Open your Instant Pot, fit in a trivet, and pour in the water. Place the cake pan on the trivet. Seal the lid and select Pressure Cook on High for 15 minutes. Mix the sour cream and one tablespoon of sugar. Set aside.

Once the timer has gone off, do a natural pressure release for 10 minutes, then a quick pressure release to let out any extra steam, and open the lid. Remove the trivet with pan, place the spring form pan on a flat surface, and open it. Use a spatula to spread the sour cream mixture on the warm cake. Refrigerate the cake for 8 hours. Top with strawberries. Slice it into 6 pieces and serve while firming.

750. Chocolate Vanilla Swirl Cheesecake

Servings: 6 | Ready in about: 60 minutes + Chilling time

4 oz chocolate wafer cookies, crushed into crumbs

2 tbsp unsalted butter, melted	2 tbsp heavy cream	2 large eggs
16 oz cream cheese, softened	2 tsp vanilla extract	3 oz sweet chocolate chips, melted
½ cup sugar	2 tbsp sour cream	

In a bowl, mix the cookie crumbs and butter. Spoon the crumbs into a spring form pan and press all around with a spoon. Place a trivet in your Instant Pot and put the spring form pan on top. Close the air fry lid and choose Air Fry. Adjust the temperature to 350°F and the time to 6 minutes. Bake until fragrant. Remove the pan and let cool. In a medium bowl and using a hand mixer, beat the cream cheese until smooth. Add the sugar and beat until smooth. Pour in the heavy cream, vanilla extract, and sour cream. Whisk again and crack the eggs into the bowl one after the other while whisking. Spoon ½ cup of the cream mixture into a bowl and mix in chocolate chips.

Pour the remaining cream mixture into the spring form pan, drop spoonfuls of the chocolate mixture with even distance on the filling and run the tip of a skewer through each chocolate drop to marbleize the top of the filling. Cover the filling with aluminium foil. Pour 1 cup of water into the inner pot. Fix in a trivet the pot and put the spring form pan on top. Seal the pressure lid, choose Pressure Cook on High and the cook time to 25 minutes. After cooking, do a natural pressure release for 10 minutes, and then a quick pressure release to let out any remaining pressure. Carefully open the lid and remove the cheesecake from the pot. Take off the foil. Let the cheesecake rest for 15 to 20 minutes and then refrigerate the cooled cake for 3 to 4 hours to chill through.

751. Classic Caramel-Walnut Brownies

Servings: 4 | Ready in about: 60 minutes+ cooling time

8 oz white chocolate	2 tsp almond extract	¾ cup all-purpose flour
8 tbsp unsalted butter	A pinch of salt	½ cup caramel sauce
1 cup sugar	2 large eggs, softened	½ cup toasted walnuts

Put the white chocolate and butter in a small bowl and pour 1 cup of water into the inner pot. Place a trivet in the lower position of the pot and put the bowl on top. Close the air fry lid. Choose Bake. Adjust the temperature to 375°F and the cook time to 10 minutes to melt the white chocolate and butter. Check after 5 minutes and stir. As soon as the chocolate has melted, remove the bowl from the pot.

Use a small spatula to transfer the chocolate mixture into a medium and stir in the almond extract, sugar, and salt. One after another, crack each egg into the bowl and whisk after each addition. Mix in the flour until smooth, about 1 minute. Grease a round cake pan with cooking spray or line the pan with parchment paper. Pour the batter into the prepared pan and place on the trivet.

Close the air fry lid and choose Bake. Adjust the temperature to 250°F and the time to 25 minutes. Once the time is up, open the lid and check the brownies. The top should be just set. Blot out the butter that may pool to the top using a paper towel. Close the air fry lid again and adjust the temperature to 300°F for 15 minutes.

Once the time is up, open the lid and check the brownies. A toothpick inserted into the center should come out with crumbs sticking to it but no raw batter. Drizzle the caramel sauce on top of the brownies and scatter with the walnuts. Close the air fry lid again and adjust the temperature to 325°F for 8 minutes. When the nuts are brown and the caramel is bubbling, take out the brownies, and allow cooling for at least 30 minutes and cut into squares.

752. Blueberry Muffins

Servings: 10 | Ready in about: 30 minutes

1 ½ cup flour	¼ cup vegetable oil	1 egg
½ tsp salt	2 tsp vanilla extract	2 tsp baking powder
½ cup sugar	1 cup blueberries	Yogurt, as needed

Combine all the flour, salt and baking powder in a bowl. In a bowl, place the oil, vanilla extract, and egg. Fill the rest of the bowl with yogurt. Whisk the mixture until fully incorporated. Combine the wet and dry ingredients. Gently fold in the blueberries. Divide the mixture between 10 muffin cups. Close the air fry lid and cook for 10 minutes on Air Fry mode at 350°F, until nice and crispy.

753. Molten Lava Cake

Servings: 4 | Ready in about: 20 minutes

3 ½ oz butter, melted	1 ½ tbsp self-rising flour	2 eggs
3 ½ tbsp sugar	3 ½ oz dark chocolate, melted	

Grease 4 ramekins with butter. Beat the eggs and sugar until frothy. Stir in the butter and chocolate. Gently fold in the flour. Divide the mixture between the ramekins and bake in your Instant Pot for 10 minutes on Air Fry mode at 390°F. Let cool for 2 minutes before turning the lava cakes upside down onto serving plates.

754. Lemon Cheesecake with Strawberries

Servings: 8 | Ready in about: 3 hour

Crust:
- 4 oz graham crackers
- 1 tsp ground cinnamon
- 3 tbsp butter, melted

Filling:
- 1 lb mascarpone cheese, softened
- 2 eggs, softened
- 1 tbsp lemon juice
- ¾ cup sugar
- 1 tsp vanilla extract
- 1 pinch salt
- ¼ cup sour cream, softened
- 1 tsp lemon zest
- 1 cup strawberries, halved

In a food processor, beat cinnamon and graham crackers to attain a texture almost same as sand. Mix in melted butter. Press the crumbs into the bottom of a 7-inch springform pan in an even layer. In a stand mixer, beat sugar, mascarpone cheese, and sour cream for 3 minutes to combine well and have a fluffy and smooth mixture. Scrape the bowl's sides and add eggs, lemon zest, salt, lemon juice, and vanilla extract. Carry on to beat the mixture until you obtain a consistent color and all ingredients are completely combined. Pour filling over crust.Into the inner pot of your Instant Pot, add 1 cup water and set in a trivet. Insert the springform pan on the trivet.

Close the air fry lid and select Bake. Adjust the temperature to 250°F and the cook time to 40 minutes. Remove cheesecake and let cool for 1 hour. Transfer to a serving plate and garnish with strawberry halves on top. Use a paring knife to run along the edges between the pan and cheesecake to remove the cheesecake and set to the plate.

755. Berry Vanilla Pudding

Servings: 4 | Ready in about: 35 minutes + 6h for refrigeration

- 1 cup heavy cream
- ½ cup milk
- 4 raspberries
- 4 egg yolks
- 1 tsp vanilla extract
- 4 blueberries
- 4 tbsp water + 1 ½ cups water
- ½ cup sugar

Turn on your Instant Pot and select Sauté. Add four tablespoons for water and the sugar. Stir it constantly until it dissolves. Press Stop. Add milk, heavy cream, and vanilla. Stir it with a whisk until evenly combined. Crack the eggs into a bowl and add a tablespoon of the cream mixture. Whisk it and then very slowly add the remaining cream mixture while whisking. Fit a trivet at the bottom of the pot, and pour one and a half cup of water in it.

Pour the mixture into four ramekins and place them on the trivet. Close the lid of the pot, secure the pressure valve, and select Pressure Cook on High for 4 minutes. Once done, do a quick pressure release. With a napkin in hand, remove the ramekins onto a flat surface. Let cool for about 15 minutes and then refrigerate them for 6 hours. Garnish with the raspberries and blueberries. Enjoy immediately or refrigerate.

756. Air Fried Doughnuts

Servings: 4 | Ready in about: 25 minutes

- 8 oz self-rising flour
- ½ cup milk
- 1 egg
- 1 tsp baking powder
- 2 ½ tbsp butter
- 2 oz brown sugar

Beat the butter with the sugar, until smooth. Beat in eggs, and milk. In a bowl, combine the flour with the baking powder. Gently fold the flour into the butter mixture. Form donut shapes and cut off the center with cookie cutters. Arrange on a lined baking sheet and cook in your Instant Pot for 15 minutes on Air Fry mode at 350°F. Serve with whipped cream.

757. Homemade Apple Cider

Servings: 6 | Ready in about: 45 minutes

- 6 green apples, cored and chopped
- ¼ cup orange juice
- 3 cups water
- 2 cinnamon sticks

In a blender, add orange juice, apples, and water and blend until smooth. Use a fine-mesh strainer to strain and press using a spoon. Get rid of the pulp. In the cooker, mix the strained apple puree, and cinnamon sticks. Seal the pressure lid, choose Pressure Cook on High, and set the timer to 10 minutes. Release the pressure naturally for 15 minutes, then quick release the remaining pressure. Strain again and do away with the solids.

758. Pumpkin Cake

Servings: 6 | Ready in about: 1 hour 30 minutes

3 eggs	¼ cup olive oil	½ tsp ground nutmeg
⅔ cup sugar	1 tsp baking powder	1 cup shredded pumpkin + for topping
1 cup flour	1 tsp vanilla extract	½ cup chopped walnuts
½ cup half-and-half	1 tsp ground cinnamon	2 cups water

Frosting:
4 oz cream cheese, room temperature	½ cup confectioners sugar	⅛ tsp salt
8 tbsp butter	½ tsp vanilla extract	

In a bowl, beat eggs and sugar to get a smooth mixture. Mix in oil, flour, vanilla extract, cinnamon, half-and-half, baking powder, and nutmeg. Stir well to obtain a fluffy batter. Fold walnuts and pumpkin through the batter. Add batter into a 6-inch cake pan and cover with aluminum foil. Into your Instant Pot, add water and set a trivet. Lay cake pan gently onto the trivet. Close the air fry lid and select Bake. Adjust the temperature to 250°F and the cook time to 40 minutes. Beat cream cheese, confectioners' sugar, salt, vanilla extract, and butter in a mixing bowl until smooth. Place in the refrigerator until needed for use. Remove cake from the pan and transfer to the cooking wire rack to cool. Over the cake, spread frosting and apply a topping of shredded carrots, as desired.

759. Cinnamon Apple Crisp

Servings: 5 | Ready in about: 30 minutes

Topping:
½ cup oat flour	½ cup granulated sugar
½ cup old-fashioned rolled oats	¼ cup olive oil

Filling:
5 apples, peeled, cored, and halved	½ cup water	¼ tsp ground nutmeg
2 tbsp arrowroot powder	1 tsp ground cinnamon	½ tsp vanilla paste

In a bowl, combine sugar, oat flour, rolled oats, and olive oil to form coarse crumbs. Ladle the apples into your Instant Pot. Mix water with arrowroot powder in a bowl. Stir in salt, nutmeg, cinnamon, and vanilla and toss in the apples to coat. Apply oat topping to the apples. Seal the pressure lid, choose Pressure Cook on High, and set the timer to 10 minutes. Release pressure naturally for 5 minutes, then release the remaining pressure quickly.

760. Tiramisu Cheesecake

Servings: 12 | Ready in about: 1 hour + chilling time | Serves: 12

1 tbsp Kahlua Liquor	16 oz Cream Cheese, softened	½ cup White Sugar
1 ½ cups Ladyfingers, crushed	8 oz Mascarpone Cheese, softened	1 tbsp Cocoa Powder
1 tbsp Granulated Espresso	2 Eggs	1 tsp Vanilla Extract
1 tbsp Butter, melted	2 tbsp Powdered Sugar	

In a bowl, beat the cream cheese, mascarpone, and white sugar. Gradually beat in the eggs, powdered sugar, and vanilla. Combine the Kahlua Liquor, Ladyfingers, Espresso, and melted butter f in another bowl. Spray a springform pan with cooking spray. Press the ladyfinger crust at the bottom. Pour the filling over. Cover the pan with a paper towel and then close it with aluminum foil. Pour 1 cup of water in your Instant Pot and lower a trivet. Place the pan inside and seal the pressure lid. Select Pressure Cook and set time to 35 minutes. Do a quick pressure release. Allow to cool completely before refrigerating the cheesecake for 4 hours.

761. Cheat Apple Pie

Servings: 9 | Ready in about: 30 minutes

4 apples, diced
2 oz butter, melted
2 oz sugar
1 oz brown sugar
2 tsp cinnamon
1 egg, beaten
3 large puff pastry sheets
¼ tsp salt

Whisk the white sugar, brown sugar, cinnamon, salt, and butter together. Place the apples in a baking dish and coat them with the mixture. Slide the dish into your Instant Pot and cook for 10 minutes on Roast at 350°F. Roll out the pastry on a floured flat surface, and cut each sheet into 6 equal pieces. Divide the apple filling between the parts. Brush the edges of the pastry squares with the egg. Fold and seal the edges with a fork. Place on a lined baking sheet and cook in the fryer at 350°F for 8 minutes on Roast. Flip over, increase the temperature to 390°F, and cook for 2 more minutes.

762. The Most Chocolaty Fudge

Servings: 8 | Ready in about: 55 minutes

1 cup sugar
7 oz flour, sifted
1 tbsp honey
¼ cup milk
1 tsp vanilla extract
1 oz cocoa powder
2 eggs
4 oz butter
1 orange, juice and zest

Icing:
1 oz butter, melted
4 oz powdered sugar
1 tbsp brown sugar
1 tbsp milk
2 tsp honey

In a bowl, mix the dry ingredients for the fudge. Mix the wet ingredients separately. Combine the two mixtures gently. Transfer the batter to a prepared The air fry basket. Close the air fry lid and cook for about 35 minutes on Roast mode at 350°F. Once the timer beeps, check to ensure the cake is cooked. For the Topping: whisk together all of the icing ingredients. When the cake is cooled, coat it with the icing. Let set before slicing the fudge.

763. Milk Dumplings in Sweet Sauce

Servings: 20 | Ready in about about: 30 minutes

6 cups Water
2 ½ cups Sugar
3 tbsp Lime Juice
6 cups Milk
1 tsp ground Cardamom

Bring to a boil the milk on Sauté your Instant Pot and stir in the lime juice. The solids should start to separate. Pour milk through a cheesecloth-lined colander. Drain as much liquid as you can. Place the paneer on a smooth surface. Form a ball and divide into 20 equal pieces. Pour water in the Foofi and bring to a boil on Sauté in the pot. Add in sugar and cardamom and cook until dissolved. Shape the dumplings into balls, and place them in the syrup. Seal the pressure lid and choose Pressure Cook on High, and set the time to 5 minutes. Once done, do a quick pressure release. Let cool and serve.

764. Pineapple Cake

Servings: 4 | Ready in about: 50 minutes

2 oz dark chocolate, grated
8 oz self-rising flour
4 oz butter
7 oz pineapple chunks
½ cup pineapple juice
1 egg
2 tbsp milk
½ cup sugar

Preheat your Instant Pot to 390°F. Place the butter and flour into a bowl and rub the mixture with your fingers until crumbed. Stir in the pineapple, sugar, chocolate, and juice. Beat the eggs and milk separately, and then add them to the batter. Transfer the batter to a previously prepared (greased or lined) cake pan, and cook for 40 minutes on Roast mode. Let cool for at least 10 minutes before serving.

765. Raspberry Cheesecake

Servings: 6 | Ready in about about: 30 minutes

1 ½ cups Graham Cracker Crust
1 cup Raspberries
3 cups Cream Cheese

1 tbsp fresh Orange Juice
3 Eggs
½ stick Butter, melted

¾ cup Sugar
1 tsp Vanilla Paste
1 tsp finely grated Orange Zest

Insert a trivet into your Instant Pot and add 1 ½ cups of water. Grease a spring form. Mix in graham cracker crust with sugar and butter in a bowl. Press the mixture to form a crust at the bottom. Blend the raspberries and cream cheese with an electric mixer. Crack in the eggs and keep mixing until well combined. Mix in the remaining ingredients, and give it a good stir. Pour this mixture into the pan, and cover the pan with aluminium foil. Lay the spring form on the tray. Select Pressure Cook and set the time to 20 minutes at High pressure. Once the cooking is complete, do a quick pressure release. Refrigerate the cheesecake for at least 2 hours.

766. Chocolate and Banana Squares

Servings: 6 | Ready in about about: 25 minutes

½ cup Butter

3 Bananas

2 tbsp Cocoa Powder

Place bananas and butter in a bowl and mash finely with a fork. Add the cocoa powder and stir until well combined. Pour the banana and almond batter into a greased baking dish. Pour 1 cup water in the pot and lower a trivet. Place the baking dish on top of the trivet and seal the pressure lid. Select Pressure, set the timer to 15 minutes at High pressure. When it goes off, do a quick release. Let cool for a few minutes before cutting into squares

767. No Flour Lime Muffins

Servings: 6 | Ready in about: 30 minutes

2 eggs plus 1 yolk
Juice and zest of 2 limes

1 cup yogurt
¼ cup superfine sugar

8 oz cream cheese
1 tsp vanilla extract

With a spatula, gently combine the yogurt and cheese. In another bowl, beat together the rest of the ingredients. Gently fold the lime with the cheese mixture. Divide the batter between 6 lined muffin tins. Close the air fry lid and cook in your Instant Pot for 10 minutes on Air Fry mode at 330°F.

768. Air Fried Snickerdoodle Poppers

Servings: 6 | Ready in about: 30 minutes

1 can of Pillsbury Grands Flaky Layers Biscuits
1 box instant vanilla Jell-O

1 ½ cups cinnamon sugar

Melted butter, for brushing

Unroll the flaky biscuits and cut them into fourths. Roll each ¼ into a ball. Arrange the balls on a lined baking sheet, and cook in your Instant Pot for 7 minutes, or until golden, on Air Fry mode at 350°F. Prepare the Jell-O following the package's instructions. Using an injector, inject some of the vanilla pudding into each ball. Brush the balls with melted butter and then coat them with cinnamon sugar.

769. Almond and Apple Delight

Servings: 4 | Ready in about about: 14 minutes

3 Apples, peeled and diced
½ cup Almonds, chopped or slivered

½ cup Milk
¼ tsp Cinnamon

Place all ingredients in your Instant Pot. Stir well to combine and seal the pressure lid. Cook on Pressure for 4 minutes at High. Release the pressure quickly. Divide the mixture among 4 serving bowls.

770. Cinnamon Mulled Red Wine

Servings: 6 | Ready in about: 30 minutes

3 cups red wine
2 tangerines, sliced
¼ cup honey

6 whole cloves
6 whole black peppercorns
2 cardamom pods

8 cinnamon sticks
1 tsp fresh ginger, sliced
6 tangerine wedges

In the pot, combine red wine, honey, cardamom pods, 2 cinnamon sticks, cloves, tangerines slices, ginger, and peppercorns. Seal the pressure lid, choose Pressure Cook on High, and set the timer to 5 minutes. Release pressure naturally for 20 minutes. Using a fine mesh strainer, strain your wine. Discard spices. Divide the warm wine into glasses and add tangerine wedges and a cinnamon stick for garnishing before serving.

771. Moon Milk

Servings: 2 | Ready in about: 10 minutes

1 cup milk
1 tsp coconut oil
1/2 tsp cinnamon, + more for garnish
1/2 tsp ground turmeric

¼ cup hemp hearts
1/2 tsp maca powder
1/8 tsp ground cardamom
1 pinch ground nutmeg

1 pinch ground ginger
1 pinch freshly ground black pepper
1 tsp honey

To your Instant Pot, add milk. Press Sauté and heat the milk for 4 minutes until the point of starting to bubble. Stir in coconut oil, turmeric, nutmeg, pepper, ginger, hemp hearts, maca powder, cinnamon, and cardamom. Press Cancel and allow mixture to cool for about a minute. Whisk in honey. Transfer the mixture into a mug to serve.

772. Chocolate Soufflé

Servings: 2 | Ready in about: 25 minutes

2 eggs, whites and yolks separated
¼ cup butter, melted

2 tbsp flour
3 tbsp sugar

3 oz chocolate, melted
½ tsp vanilla extract

Beat the yolks along with the sugar and vanilla extract. Stir in butter, chocolate, and flour. Whisk the whites until a stiff peak forms. Working in batches, gently combine the egg whites with the chocolate mixture. Divide the batter between two greased ramekins. Close the air fry lid and cook for 14 minutes on Roast at 330°F.

773. Pear Wedges

Servings: 3 | Ready in about about: 15 minutes

2 Pears, peeled and cut into wedges   3 tbsp Almond Butter   2 tbsp Olive Oil

Pour 1 cup of water in the pot. Place the pear wedges in a steamer basket and then lower the basket at the bottom. Seal the pressure lid, and cook for 2 minutes on High pressure. When the timer goes off, do a quick pressure release. Remove the basket, discard the water and wipe clean the cooker. Press the Sauté and heat the oil. Add the pears and cook until browned. Top them with almond butter, to serve.

774. Delicious Pecan Stuffed Apples

Servings: 6 | Ready in about about: 20 minutes

3 ½ lb Apples, cored
½ cup dried Apricots, chopped
¼ cup Sugar

¼ cup Pecans, chopped
¼ cup Graham Cracker Crumbs
¼ tsp Cardamom

½ tsp grated Nutmeg
½ tsp ground Cinnamon
1 ¼ cups Red Wine

Lay the apples at the bottom of your Instant Pot and pour in the red wine. Combine the other ingredients, except the crumbs. Seal the pressure lid, and cook on Pressure Cook for 15 minutes. Once ready, do a quick pressure release. Top with graham cracker crumbs and serve!

775. The Best Molten Lava Cakes

Serves: 3 | Total Time: 20 minutes

2 large eggs	¼ tsp salt	¼ cup flour
1 tsp vanilla extract	3 tbsp butter	2 tbsp powdered sugar
1 tsp orange zest	¾ cup chocolate chips	

Preheat your Instant Pot Duo Crisp to 350°F. Whisk together eggs, vanilla, orange zest, and salt in a bowl. Microwave butter and chocolate chips in a large bowl for 20-second intervals and stir between intervals until chocolate is smooth and melted. Whisk the chocolate and slowly add the egg mixture so that the eggs are not cooked. Slowly stir in flour. Grease 3 ramekins and portion the batter evenly between the ramekins. Transfer the ramekins to the air fryer basket and close the fry lid. Bake for 5 minutes. The edges and tops will be just set. Allow the cakes to cool for 5 minutes. Loosen the edges with a butter knife and flip the cake out onto a small dessert plate. Let cool another 5 minutes. Serve sprinkled with powdered sugar and enjoy!

776. Glam Donut Bites

Serves: 5 | Total Time: 35 minutes

1 cup self-rising flour	½ cup granulated sugar	¼ cup heavy cream
¼ cups Greek yogurt	1 cup confectioners' sugar	1 tsp almond extract
¼ cup cocoa powder	1 tbsp raspberry jam	

Preheat your Instant Pot Duo Crisp to 350°F. Lightly spray the basket with cooking oil. Combine flour, yogurt, cocoa powder, and granulated sugar in a large bowl. Transfer to a floured work surface and knead for 5 minutes or until a large yet sticky ball of dough is formed. Divide the dough into 20 balls, about 2 tablespoons of dough per ball. Transfer the doughnut holes to the air fry basket and close the fry lid. Air Fry for 12 minutes. Let the holes cool for 5 minutes. Combine confectioners' sugar, heavy cream, raspberry jam, and almond extract in a bowl. When the holes are cooled, roll each doughnut hole in the glaze. Refrigerate for 5 minutes to set the glaze.

777. Brown Sugar & Butter Bars

Servings: 6 | Ready in about about: 55 minutes

1 cup Flour	½ cup Peanut Butter, softened	½ cup Sugar
1 ½ cups Water	½ cup Butter, softened	½ tsp Baking Soda
1 Egg	1 cup Oats	½ cup Brown Sugar

Grease a springform pan and line it with parchment paper. Set aside. Beat together the eggs, peanut butter, butter, white sugar, and brown sugar. Fold in the oats, flour, and baking soda. Press the batter into the pan. Cover the pan with a paper towel and with a piece of foil. Pour the water into the pot and add a trivet. Lower the springform pan onto the trivet. Seal the pressure lid, choose Pressure Cook, and set the time to 35 minutes. When ready, do a quick release. Wait for 15 minutes before inverting onto a plate and cutting into bars.

778. Cherry Pie

Servings: 6 | Ready in about about: 45 minutes

1 9-inch double Pie Crust	4 cups Cherries, pitted	1 cup Sugar
2 cups Water	¼ tsp Almond Extract	A pinch of Salt
½ tsp Vanilla Extract	4 tbsp Quick Tapioca	

Pour water your Instant Pot and add a trivet. Combine the cherries with tapioca, sugar, extracts, and salt in a bowl. Place one pie crust at the bottom of a lined springform pan. Spread the cherries mixture and top with the other crust. Lower the pan onto the trivet. Seal the pressure lid, choose Pressure Cook on High, and set the time to 18 minutes. Once ready, do a quick pressure release. Let cool the pie on a cooling rack. Slice to serve.

779. Gingery Chocolate Pudding

Servings: 4 | Ready in about about: 20 minutes

Zest and Juice from ½ Lime	3 Eggs, separated into whites and yolks	½ tsp Ginger, caramelized
2 oz chocolate, coarsely chopped	¼ cup Cornstarch	1 ½ cups of Water
¼ cup Sugar	1 cup Almond Milk	
2 tbsp Butter, softened	A pinch of Salt	

Combine together the sugar, cornstarch, salt, and softened butter in a bowl. Mix in lime juice and grated lime zest. Add in the egg yolks, ginger, almond milk, and whisk to mix well. Mix in egg whites. Pour this mixture into custard cups and cover with aluminium foil. Add 1 ½ cups of water to your Instant Pot. Place a trivet into the pot, and lower the cups onto the trivet. Seal the pressure lid, choose Pressure Cook on High, and set the time to 25 minutes. Do a quick pressure release. Carefully open the pressure lid, and stir in the chocolate. Serve chilled.

780. Homemade Brownies

Serves: 8 | Total Time: 25 minutes

½ cup flour	½ tsp baking powder	¼ tsp peppermint extract
1 cup granulated sugar	5 tbsp butter, melted	1 large egg
¼ cup cocoa powder	1 tsp lemon juice	½ cup chocolate chips

Preheat your Instant Pot Duo Crisp to 350°F. Combine flour, peppermint extract, sugar, cocoa powder, and baking powder in a large bowl. Stir in butter, lemon juice, egg, and chocolate chips until completely combined. Pour the dough into a greased cake pan. Transfer the pan to the air fryer basket and close the fry lid. Bake for 20 minutes or until a toothpick in the middle comes out clean. Allow cooling for 5 minutes. Serve and enjoy!

781. Amazing Lemon Bars

Serves: 6 | Total Time: 30 minutes

6 tbsp butter, softened	1 ¼ cups flour	1 tsp lemon zest
¾ cup granulated sugar	¼ cup lemon juice	1 tbsp coconut flakes
1 tsp vanilla extract	2 large eggs	2 tbsp powdered sugar

Preheat your Instant Pot Duo Crisp to 350°F. Lightly spray a cake pan with cooking oil. Cream butter and ¼ cup sugar in a large bowl, then stir in vanilla and 1 cup flour. Transfer to the cake pan and spread to cover the bottom. Place in the air fry basket and close the fry lid. Bake for 5 minutes or until golden. Combine the remaining sugar, lemon juice, coconut flakes, eggs, remaining flour, and lemon zest in a bowl. Pour the batter over the crust and Bake in the air fryer for 15 minutes. Cool completely before cutting. Serve sprinkled with powdered sugar.

782. Mini Apple Pies

Serves: 6 | Total Time: 30 minutes

1 cup flour	1 tbsp lemon juice	3 cups apple pie filling
½ cup cold butter, grated	1 tsp cinnamon powder	1 large egg, whisked
5 tbsp ice water	2 tbsp granulated sugar	2 tbsp powdered sugar

Preheat your Instant Pot Duo Crisp to 320°F. Line the air fry basket with parchment paper. Combine flour, cinnamon, butter, lemon juice, ice water, and sugar in a large bowl. Turn out the dough on a lightly floured flat surface. Roll the dough into a rectangle. Cut the rectangle into 6 smaller rectangles: cut across the center, then cut 3 lines vertically. Add ½ cup of apple pie filling on the lower part of each rectangle. Fold the top over the filling and seal all of the edges with a fork. Brush the tops of each pie with the beaten egg. Transfer the pies to the air fryer basket and close the fry lid. Bake for 10 minutes. Flip the pies and Bake for another 5 minutes or until the crust is flaky and golden. Cool for 10 minutes. Serve warm sprinkled with powdered sugar and enjoy!

783. Cinnamon Monkey Bread

Serves: 6 | Total Time: 25 minutes

1 (16.3-oz) can refrigerated biscuit dough
½ cup granulated sugar
1 tbsp ground cinnamon
¼ cup butter, melted
1 tsp vanilla extract
2 tbsp chopped walnuts
¼ cup brown sugar

Preheat your Instant Pot Duo Crisp to 325°F. Lightly spray a cake pan with cooking oil. Separate the biscuit dough into 4 pieces. Combine granulated sugar and cinnamon in a large bowl. Coat the biscuits in cinnamon sugar and place them in the cake pan. Mix butter, vanilla extract, and brown sugar in a bowl, then pour it evenly over the coated biscuits. Sprinkle with walnuts. Place the pan in the air fry basket and close the fry lid. Bake for 20 minutes. The bread will be brown. Cool for 10 minutes in the pan before flipping out on a serving plate. Serve and enjoy!

784. Vanilla-Almond Shortbread Cookies

Serves: 6 | Total Time: 15 minutes + chilling time

½ cup butter, softened
¼ cup granulated sugar
1 tsp almond extract
1 tsp vanilla extract
8 blanched almonds
1 cup flour
1 cup almond flour

Cream together the butter, sugar, almond extract, and vanilla extract. Slowly add flour and almond flour and mix until combined. Transfer the dough to a work surface and roll it into a log. Wrap the dough in plastic and refrigerate for at least an hour. Preheat your Instant Pot Duo Crisp to 300°F. Line air fryer basket with parchment paper. Slice the dough into ¼-inch pieces. Place in the middle of the pieces 1 almond and slightly press. Place the dough in the air fry basket 2-inch apart. Close the fry lid and Bake for 10 minutes or until the edges are just browning. Cool completely. Serve and enjoy!

785. Irresistible Almond Butter Cookies

Serves: 9 | Total Time: 20 minutes

1 cup almond butter
1 cup brown sugar
½ cup butter, melted
2 large eggs
½ tbsp honey
2 cups flour
1 ½ tsp baking powder

Preheat your Instant Pot Duo Crisp to 325°F. Line the air fry basket with parchment paper. Combine almond butter and brown sugar in a large bowl. Next, add melted butter, honey, and eggs and stir until well mixed. Mix flour and baking powder in a bowl, then slowly add the flour to the almond butter mixture. Roll into 9 balls and place them 2-inch apart in the air fry basket and close the fry lid. Bake for 10 minutes or until the bottoms are golden. Cool for 5 minutes. Serve and enjoy!

786. Festive Snickerdoodles

Serves: 6 | Total Time: 20 minutes

½ cup butter, melted
3 tbsp sugar
½ tsp salt
1 tsp vanilla powder
1 cup flour
½ tsp baking powder
½ tsp cream of tartar
1 tsp ground cinnamon

Preheat your Instant Pot Duo Crisp to 325°F. Line the air fry basket with parchment paper and prepare 3 more pieces for each batch. Combine butter and 2 tablespoons of sugar in a bowl. Mix the flour, salt, vanilla powder, baking powder, and cream of tartar in a large bowl. Slowly add butter mixture to the flour bowl and stir until the dough is formed. Divide the dough into 18 balls. Roll each ball in a small bowl of sugar and cinnamon. Place in the lined air fryer basket 2-inch apart. Close the fry lid and Air Fry for 10 minutes or until the edges are brown and a toothpick comes out clean. Let cool for 5 minutes and continue with the next three batches. Serve.

DESSERTS

787. Chocolate Cheesecake

Serves: 8 | Total Time: 30 minutes + chilling time

12 oz mascarpone cheese	2 tbsp sour cream	½ cup chocolate chips, melted
½ cup sugar	¼ tbsp instant coffee powder	1 tsp vanilla extract
1 pinch of salt	2 tbsp cocoa powder	1 large egg

Preheat your Instant Pot Duo Crisp to 300°F. Mix mascarpone cheese, salt and sugar until smooth. Stir in sour cream, cocoa powder, chocolate chips, coffee powder, and vanilla until well blended. Next, stir in the egg. Pour the batter into the greased pan and place the pan in the air fry basket and close the fry lid. Bake for 20 minutes or until the top of the cheesecake is firm. Refrigerate completely. Serve and enjoy!

788. Vanilla-Chocolate Chip Cookies

Serves: 6 | Total Time: 25 minutes

½ cup butter, melted	½ tsp cocoa powder	1 tsp lemon juice
½ cup brown sugar	1 large egg	1 tsp vanilla extract
1 cup flour	1 tsp baking powder	⅓ cup chocolate chips

Mix butter, brown sugar, flour, lemon juice, cocoa powder, egg, baking powder, and vanilla. Fold in chocolate chips, then refrigerate the dough for 10 minutes. Preheat your Instant Pot Duo Crisp to 350°F. Line the air fry basket with parchment paper. Divide the dough into 12 balls. Space out the dough 2-inch apart. Close the fry lid and Bake for 10 minutes or until the bottom of the cookies is golden. Serve warm and enjoy!

789. Cinnamon Apple Fritters

Serves: 6 | Total Time: 25 minutes

1 cup self-rising flour	½ tsp pumpkin pie spice	1 large egg
½ cup granulated sugar	1 tsp lemon juice	1 diced Granny Smith apple
1 ½ tsp ground cinnamon	¼ cup milk	

Preheat your Instant Pot Duo Crisp to 375°F. Mix together flour, pumpkin pie spice, lemon juice, sugar, cinnamon, and milk in a large bowl. Stir in egg. Fold the apples into the batter. Place ¼-cup portions on parchment paper, then place the paper in the air fry basket and close the fry lid. Air Fry for 8 minutes. Flip the fritters and cook for another 7 minutes or until the fritters are golden and a toothpick in the middle comes out clean. Let cool. Serve .

790. Winter Cookies

Serves: 6 | Total Time: 25 minutes

½ cup butter, melted	1 cup flour	2 tbsp orange juice
¼ cup sugar	1 cup peanuts, chopped	1 tsp black sesame seeds
1 tsp vanilla extract	½ tsp grated nutmeg	2 cups confectioners' sugar

Preheat your Instant Pot Duo Crisp to 300°F. Combine butter, orange juice, sugar, nutmeg, and vanilla in a large bowl. Slowly stir in flour, black sesame seeds and peanuts until completely combined. Divide the dough into 16 balls. Place in the air fry basket and close the fry lid. Air Fry for 15 minutes. Let cool for 5 minutes. Add sugar to a bowl. Roll the slightly cool cookies in the sugar, then cool completely. Serve and enjoy!

791. Tasty Coconut Cake

Servings: 4 | Ready in about about: 55 minutes

3 Eggs, Yolks and Whites separated	½ tsp Coconut Extract	½ cup Coconut Sugar
¾ cup Coconut Flour	1 ½ cups warm Coconut Milk	2 tbsp Coconut Oil, melted

In a bowl, beat in the egg yolks along with the coconut sugar. In a separate bowl, beat the whites until soft form peaks. Stir in coconut extract and coconut oil. Fold in the coconut flour. Line a baking dish and pour the batter inside. Cover with aluminum foil. Pour 1 cup water in your Instant Pot and add a trivet. Lower the dish onto the trivet. Seal the pressure lid, choose Pressure Cook, and set the time to 35 minutes. Do a quick pressure release.

792. Pink Lady Baked Apples

Serves: 4 | Total Time: 30 minutes

4 Pink Lady apples
½ cup butter
8 soft caramel chews
½ cup rolled oats
½ tsp grated nutmeg
¼ cup granulated sugar
1 tsp ground cinnamon
1 tsp vanilla extract

Preheat your Instant Pot Duo Crisp to 350°F. Carefully core each apple and remove seeds. Microwave butter in a bowl for 30 seconds. Add caramels to the bowl and microwave for 15 seconds. Stir to combine the caramel, vanilla extract, and butter completely. Next, stir in oats, sugar, nutmeg, and cinnamon until crumbly. Divide the caramel mixture and spoon into each cored apple. Transfer the apples to the air fryer basket and close the fry lid. Bake for 15 minutes. Apple will soften and appear wrinkled. Serve warm and enjoy!

793. Coconut Muffins

Serves: 6 | Total Time: 25 minutes

1 cup flour
½ cup sugar
1 tsp baking powder
¼ cup butter, melted
1 tbsp orange juice
1 tsp orange extract
1 large egg
½ cup canned coconut milk
½ cup grated coconut

Preheat your Instant Pot Duo Crisp to 300°F. Whisk flour, sugar, and baking powder in a large bowl. Stir in butter, egg, orange juice, orange extract, and coconut milk until well mixed. Fold in coconut. Fill 12 silicone or aluminum muffin cups about halfway full. Place the cups in the air fry basket and close the fry lid. Bake for 15 minutes. The edges will be brown, and the toothpick in the middle comes out clean. Cool for 5 minutes. Serve.

794. Orange Banana Bread

Servings: 12 | Ready in about about: 45 minutes

3 ripe Bananas, mashed
1 ¼ cups Sugar
1 cup Milk
2 cups all-purpose Flour
1 tsp Baking Soda
1 tsp Baking Powder
1 tbsp Orange Juice
1 stick Butter, room temperature
A pinch of Salt
¼ tsp Cinnamon
½ tsp Vanilla Extract

In a bowl, mix flour, baking powder, baking soda, sugar, vanilla, and salt. Add in the bananas, cinnamon, and orange juice. Slowly stir in the butter and milk. Stir until everything is well combined. Pour the batter into a round pan. Place a trivet in your Instant Pot and fill with 2 cups of water. Place the pan on the trivet. Seal the pressure lid, select Pressure Cook and and set the time to 40 minutes at High. Do a quick pressure release.

795. Savory Peaches with Chocolate Biscuits

Servings: 4 | Ready in about about: 20 minutes

4 small Peaches, halved lengthwise and pitted
8 dried Dates, chopped
4 tbsp Walnuts, chopped
1 cup Coarsely Crumbled Cookies
1 tsp Cinnamon Powder
¼ tsp grated nutmeg
¼ tsp ground Cloves

Pour 1 cup water into your Instant Pot and add a trivet. Arrange the peaches on a greased baking dish cut-side-up. To prepare the filling, mix all of the remaining ingredients. Stuff the peaches with the mixture. Cover with aluminium foil and lower it onto the trivet. Seal the lid, choose Pressure Cook on High, and set the time to 15 minutes. Do a quick pressure release. Let cool completely and serve.

796. Apricots with Honey Sauce

Servings: 4 | Ready in about about: 15 minutes

8 Apricots, pitted and halved	1 ½ tbsp Cornstarch	½ Cinnamon stick
2 cups Blueberries	½ Vanilla Bean, sliced lengthwise	1 ¼ cups Water
¼ cup Honey	¼ tsp ground Cardamom	

Add all ingredients, except for the honey and the cornstarch to your Instant Pot. Seal the pressure lid and cook on Pressure Cook for 8 minutes. Do a quick pressure release. Remove the apricots. Hit Sauté, add the honey and cornstarch, then let simmer until the sauce thickens, 5 minutes. Serve the apricots topped with blueberry sauce

797. Coconut Milk Crème Caramel

Servings: 4 | Ready in about about: 20 minutes

2 Eggs	½ cup Coconut Milk	½ tsp Vanilla
7 oz Condensed Coconut Milk	1 ½ cups Water	4 tbsp Caramel Syrup

Divide the caramel syrup between 4 small ramekins. Pour water in your Instant Pot and add a trivet. In a bowl, beat the rest of the ingredients. Divide them between the ramekins. Lower them onto the trivet. Seal the pressure lid and choose Pressure Cook for 15 minutes. Once cooking is completed, do a quick pressure release. Let cool completely. To unmold the flan, insert a spatula along the ramekin' sides and flip onto a dish.

798. Homemade Egg Custard

Servings: 4 | Ready in about about: 20 minutes

1 Egg plus 2 Egg yolks	½ cups Milk	½ tsp pure rum extract
½ cup Sugar	2 cups Heavy Cream	1 cup water

Beat the egg and the egg yolks in a bowl. Gently add rum extract. Mix in the milk and heavy cream. Stir in the sugar. Divide the mixture between 4 ramekins. Add the water in your Instant Pot, insert a trivet, and lay the ramekins on the trivet. Cook on Pressure Cook for 10 minutes. Do a quick pressure release. Serve.

799. Cheesy Pound Cake

Serves: 6 | Total Time: 35 minutes

1 ½ cups flour	4 oz cream cheese, softened	2 tsp vanilla extract
1 tsp baking powder	1 cup sugar	1 tsp lemon extract
½ cup butter, melted	1 tbsp lemon juice	3 large eggs

Preheat your Instant Pot Duo Crisp to 300°F. Mix flour and baking powder in a bowl. combine butter, cream cheese, sugar, lemon juice, lemon extract, and vanilla in another bowl. Stir the cream cheese mixture into the flour mixture. Stir in the eggs. Pour the batter into a greased cake pan. Transfer the pan to the air fry basket. Close the fry lid and Bake for 25 minutes or until a toothpick in the middle comes out clean. Cool completely. Serve.

800. Poached Peaches

Servings: 4 | Ready in about about: 20 minutes

½ cup Black Currants	1 cup Freshly Squeezed Orange Juice
4 Peaches, peeled, pits removed	1 Cinnamon Stick

Place black currants and orange juice in a blender. Blend until the mixture becomes smooth. Pour the mixture in your Instant Pot, and add the cinnamon stick. Add the peaches to the steamer basket and then insert the basket into the pot. Seal the pressure lid, select Pressure, and set to 5 minutes at High pressure. When done, do a quick pressure release. Serve the peaches drizzled with sauce, to enjoy!

Made in the USA
Coppell, TX
25 November 2021